GEORGIA

A SHORT HISTORY

The Board of Trustees Receiving
the Indian Delegation in 1734

From a copy of the original painting by William Verelst.

GEORGIA
A SHORT HISTORY

By E. MERTON COULTER

REVISED AND ENLARGED EDITION OF
A Short History of Georgia

CHAPEL HILL
THE UNIVERSITY OF NORTH CAROLINA PRESS

TO THE MEMORY OF

Mrs. B. F. Bullard

WHO MADE GEORGIA'S COLONIAL MOTTO
THE PHILOSOPHY OF HER LIFE

Non Sibi, Sed Aliis

PREFACE TO FIRST EDITION

THE NEED for a short history of Georgia brought down to the present has led me to write this book. I hope it will be of value both to the general reader and to the student. Though it has been written from a wide examination of the sources, I have felt it unnecessary to encumber the pages with footnotes. References to additional readings, largely to the more accessible secondary works, I have grouped at the end of the book and arranged according to chapters.

My long-felt desire to do this work was translated into action by the enthusiasm and generosity of Mrs. B. F. Bullard, of Savannah. She has made possible the publication of this book, though she bears none of the responsibility for what is in it. Dr. S. V. Sanford, President of the University of Georgia and Dr. J. H. T. McPherson, the head of the History Department, kindly hastened its appearance by reducing the time I should have otherwise devoted to teaching.

E. M. C.

PREFACE TO REVISED AND ENLARGED EDITION

THE EXHAUSTION of the first edition of this work and the necessity for resetting the type anew throughout has made possible a thorough revision. I have added a great many short bits of information, and here and there longer passages, in addition to remaking the last chapter entirely, to bring the narrative up to the present. And needless to say I have taken advantage of suggestions on clarification as well as corrections made by various reviewers and critics, to whom I wish here to express my thanks. I still hold to my original position against peppering my pages with footnotes; but I have thought it desirable to add a list of some of the chief sources of Georgia's history as well as to bring up to date the secondary works suggested for further reading in connection with each chapter.

E. M. C.

November, 1945.

PREFACE TO THIRD EDITION

THE CONTINUED demand for this work has made necessary a new edition. No changes have been made up to Chapter XXXI, but this chapter in part has been re-written. Another chapter has been added, bringing the book down to 1959, and some of the works dealing directly with Georgia appearing in most recent years have been added to the Select Bibliography.

E. M. C.

January, 1960

TABLE OF CONTENTS

ILLUSTRATIONS

GEORGIA

A SHORT HISTORY

CHAPTER I

IN THE BEGINNING

A MILLION YEARS ago, only the northern part of what is now Georgia was above the ocean. Then, through vast natural forces the land arose, the waters receded, and the mouths of unnamed streams which today are called Savannah, Ocmulgee, and Chattahoochee worked their way to the southward, cutting themselves channels to keep contact with the retreating ocean waters. The land took on its present shape and proportions; vegetation and animal life crept out of the unknown to spread over the country; and after the ice ages had come and gone, the climate became fixed, and the plants and animals of historic times grew up.

Nature abhors monotony; in Georgia she worked a wondrous variety. Instead of receiving all mountains like West Virginia, or all plains like Kansas, Georgia was given both plains and mountains, and a great intervening space between the two, which is neither, but which people call Piedmont. Being merely a slice out of a great belt of these three kinds of land extending from New Jersey to Mississippi, the state is, therefore, not unique in its formation. From the seacoast inward for 150 miles, and covering more than half the state, is the Coastal Plain, so low that if it should sink 500 feet, it would disappear beneath the ocean, with only a few peninsulas and small islands left. Where the Coastal Plain ends is the old shoreline where once the waves beat against the land and left marks which geologists can readily recognize; and where this old shoreline crosses the streams the marks are so plain that anyone may see them, for here the waters take their last swift descent from

the Piedmont highlands. For this reason, this old shoreline is
called the fall line.

Beyond and embracing about a third of the state is this rolling
Piedmont country which rises to the height of 1,500 feet before
it swings up into a mountainous region to round out the area of
the state. Though the great Appalachian system comes nearest
the clouds in the Great Smokies of western North Carolina, it
reaches heights of more than 4,700 feet in Georgia. In the extreme northwestern part of the state the mountains take on the
characteristic formation of this system, the great ridges and
intervening valleys running northeast and southwest; but elsewhere they are jumbled about as if some vast drunken giant
had wantonly scattered them around.

Diversity in land formations makes diversity in climate, in
soil, in vegetation, and in animal life. The sub-tropical heat of
the coast gives way to the cooling breezes of the mountains;
there are the sand-clay lands of the plains, the Piedmont red
hills, and the rocky soil of the mountains; the marsh grass and
the cypress, the wire grass and the pines, and the hardwoods
and the spruce mark the northward march of vegetation across
the state; and the animal kingdom progresses from the alli-
gator wallowing in the mud flats of the coast to the grinning
opossum in the persimmon tree of the Piedmont to the red
fox in the mountain cave. In prehistoric and early historic
times, the ponderous buffalo, the nimble deer, and the industrious beaver held principal sway over the land; great stretches
of the coastal plain were covered with the trim tall pines,
thickly grown up; but when civilization came to the land these
conditions were to be greatly changed.

Georgia was awaiting occupation ages before anyone came
to lay claim. When the first people arrived, or how or why, no
one knows; likely not even they, themselves, knew. When
Columbus discovered America he also discovered people here,
and for want of a name he mistakenly called them Indians.
No one has ever succeeded in correcting this mistake. Just be-

cause some large mounds of earth were found in northern Georgia as well as in other parts of America, it was formerly the custom to refer to the earliest settlers as Mound-Builders to indicate a different race of people. Today it is a generally accepted supposition that the Mound-Builders and the Indians were the same people, and that they left off building mounds from a change in customs and a dawning intelligence of the futility of piling up earth.

The Indians who lived in Georgia belonged to the two great tribes known as Cherokees and Creeks, the former occupying the mountainous section, and the latter living to the southward. To the westward in regions at one time belonging to Georgia, but later to become the states of Alabama and Mississippi, were the Upper Creeks, the Choctaws, and Chickasaws. All the Creeks were banded together in a loose confederation; but it restrained the actions of individual tribes very little. These southeastern Indians were much like the Indians elsewhere, except that they were somewhat more attached to the land through their agricultural activities than were the Plains Indians of the West, and thereby they had approached nearer civilization than most other Indians in the United States but not so close as the Aztecs in Mexico.

The occupation of America by the Indians was an inducement rather than a repulsion to Europeans to seize the country; here were souls to be saved and money to be made. In this struggle, southeastern North America became a sort of cockpit for the grasping Europeans.

The Spaniards, spurred on by the excitement of their discovery of the New World, were the first to appear on the Georgia scene. There is no proof that Ponce de Leon, who discovered Florida for the Spaniards in 1512, came as far north as Georgia, but as boundary lines had not yet been brought to America, there was nothing to prevent the Spaniards from writing *Florida* across this whole southeastern region. What De Leon had left undone, twenty-eight years later Hernando de

Soto was to fill in. Landing with a large expedition near the future site of Tampa, or possibly in the Fort Myers region to the southward, he marched northward impelled by the insatiate desire for gold, which he had acquired on a previous expedition with Pizarro in Peru. The route he took has long afforded an engaging guessing contest, made more interesting by landmarks mentioned by a Gentleman of Elvas, the scribe of the expedition. De Soto crossed the Ocmulgee River somewhere, perhaps near where Macon is today, and also the Savannah, and came to an Indian village which was called Cofitachequi, ruled over by a princess. Georgians have delighted to locate it near Augusta, but others have placed it as far eastward as Columbia, in South Carolina. Thence he marched northwestward and either entered North Carolina before he turned to the southwest, or he took a shorter cut through the Nacoochee Valley of northern Georgia. It seems rather certain that he departed down the Coosa River, passing by the future location of Rome.

A dozen years after De Soto had left to find a grave in the Mississippi, a note of barbarism and blood was written on the fringes of Georgia. The French, who had up to this time been paying little attention to the New World, except to send an expedition or two to Canada, now decided to seek a location farther southward. A group of Huguenots led by Jean Ribault set out from Havre in 1562 and touched the coast of Florida not far from where St. Augustine was soon to rise. Hugging the coast they sailed northward along the island-fringed edge of Georgia, and each important river mouth or inlet they saw they gave a good French name. The St. Marys was the Seine, and as they proceeded they tolled out the Somme, the Loire, the Garonne, the Gironde, and the Savannah they called the Grande. Beyond naming these Georgia rivers and inlets, they had no further connection with the region. The settlement they made at Port Royal, South Carolina, soon broke up. Two years later, another expedition, this time under René de Laudonnière, landed at the mouth of the St. Johns River and built Fort Caroline.

This impertinence of the French, and of all the French, the Huguenots, was too much for Philip the Great of Spain to endure. He sent Menéndez with 1,500 men in 19 vessels to root out these heretics. This conqueror founded St. Augustine in 1565, and then set out against the French, most of whom he put to the sword. Two years later Dominique de Gourgues, at his own expense, sailed for Florida to have his vengeance out on the wicked Spaniards, and he hacked to pieces all of them he could find outside St. Augustine.

This intrusion of the French convinced the Spaniards that they must occupy with strength this whole southeastern country, and so sure were they that this unlimited country was theirs that years later they disputed the right of Sir Walter Raleigh to send out his Roanoke Island Colony and of John Smith to settle on the James. But, immediately, Menéndez began to work up the coastline with the characteristically Spanish twin-method, the presidio and the mission. In 1566 he set out up the Georgia coast and came to St. Catherines Island where he met the Indian ruler, Guale, which name the Spaniards applied to the island as well as to the whole mainland. Thus, the first name the Spaniards gave specifically to the Georgia country was Guale. Here he left a garrison of 30 men, which became the first Spanish outpost in Georgia. This same year the Spanish occupied Port Royal, which they called Santa Elena, and at once detailed Juan Pardo and Boyano to march westward to discover and conquer all the country from there to Mexico. They reached western Georgia before they were turned back by the Indians. As presidios were not complete without missions, Menéndez sent Jesuit priests up the coast, who founded a mission, Santa Catalina, on St. Catherines Island and San Pedro on Cumberland Island. This strange religion which the Jesuits displayed with so much zeal, at first charmed the Indians, but after two years, it began to frighten them, and rather than suffer it longer, they rose up and drove out the missionaries.

So intent were the Spaniards on saving the souls of the Indians, that only three years elapsed before a new order of missionaries came in, the Franciscans, and they for the next hundred years and more built and labored in Guale land. They made Cumberland Island the center of their hierarchy and many missions did they establish up and down the coast, confining them mostly to the islands. By the middle of the seventeenth century, in addition to lesser missions they were maintaining five outstanding ones: San Pedro on Cumberland Island, San Buenaventura on St. Simons, Santo Domingo on the mainland near the mouth of the Altamaha River, San José on Sapelo Island, and Santa Catalina on St. Catherines Island.

The friars did not hold indisputed sway. From various sources trouble came. French corsairs and Elizabethan sea-dogs, from motives of plunder and national vengeance, harried the coast now and then; and the Indians, themselves, rose in revolt. In 1587 the Spaniards retreated before these dangers, withdrawing from Santa Elena and concentrating their strength in their most northern outpost at Santa Catalina. Ten years later, almost all the missions fell before the onslaught of an Indian uprising under a young chief named Juan. But soon the missions were so effectively restored, that in 1606, the year before the settlement at Jamestown, the Bishop of Cuba visited the Georgia missions and confirmed more than a thousand Indians.

Successfully maintaining themselves on the coast against French and English pirates and revolting Indians, the Spaniards began in the latter part of the seventeenth century to send out their tentacles tipped with missions and presidios into the Apalache region, the northern Florida and southwestern Georgia country. Far up the Chattahoochee they built the mission Savacola in 1680, and the next year they set up Santa

Cruz de Savacola at the forks of the Chattahoochee and the Flint rivers.

For years after the discovery of America, England seemed to have been content with sending out a few expeditions for exploration, and when the Spanish gold galleons began to ply the ocean, to turn loose her sea-dogs against them. It was twenty years after St. Augustine had been founded, before she made her first serious effort, in Raleigh's Roanoke Island venture, to settle any part of the New World. With the settlement at Jamestown in 1607, permanent English colonies began, but none sprang up to the southward for more than a half century. In 1629 Charles I, like most kings of his time, liberal with property whose ownership was uncertain, gave to Sir Robert Heath a grant of land, beginning south of Virginia at 36° and extending to 31°, at the north tip of Cumberland Island. King Charles had either wittingly or unwittingly included in this generosity most of the Georgia coastland with its string of Spanish missions and presidios. As Sir Robert was not interested in planting colonies he parted with his land to another and soon the grant reverted to the crown.

English interest in southeastern North America was not kindled again until Charles II in 1663 gave the identical Heath grant to eight of his friends, known to history as the Eight Lords Proprietors. The English had named this extensive region Carolina in honor of Charles I; and thus did Spanish Guale (which to the Spaniards was only a part of Florida) become part of English Carolina. As if giving away a half dozen and more Spanish missions in Georgia were not enough, King Charles two years later extended the grant 30 seconds to the northward and two whole degrees to the southward, so that it might include the remainder of the Georgia missions and even St. Augustine, which this very year could have celebrated its centennial. Either this was astounding liberality to the Eight Lords or it was a gross insult to the Spaniards, or both. Spain took offence, and five years later in a treaty brought the English to agree that actual possession should determine ownership. This restored Georgia to the Spaniards; but the English having founded Charleston this very year (1670), confirmed their rights as far south as the Ashley River.

Now began a contest between England and Spain to determine the proper division of the territory lying between Charleston and St. Augustine, which was to continue for almost a century and was not to be settled until the Treaty of Paris in 1763, ending the French and Indian War; and before the settlement came, the French from the southwest were to intrude their ambitions into this southeastern region and add the complications of a three-cornered struggle.

The English now began a steady push down the coast and across the interior toward the Mississippi, and Georgia became the stronghold which English, Spanish, and French were trying to storm or maintain. The mere possession of the land was not the object sought; this region was rich in beavers and deer, and the Indians, who secured them, had a wealth of fur trade for any nation which could control it. The Carolinians, who became the point of the English spear, in 1680 pushed southward at the head of 300 Yamassee Indians, attacked the presidio and mission at Santa Catalina, and forced the Spaniards to give up forever this outpost and to retreat to Zapala (San José) on Sapelo Island. The pirate Abraham and others plundered the Georgia missions for the next few years, until in 1686 the Spaniards retreated to the St. Marys River. Though no war had been declared between England and Spain, the Georgia coast was now cleared of the Spanish missions, and only rubble and charred remains were left to dispute with the encroaching jungles. Though the Spaniards never succeeded in reoccupying their Guale land, the year they were forced out they sailed up to Port Royal, destroyed it, and only an intervening storm prevented them from plundering Charleston.

It was convenient to be rid of the Spaniards on the Georgia coast; but the problem of the Spaniards, and the French, too, in the interior, where the greatest prize was to be had, continued to engage the particular attention of the Carolinians. The Spaniards had further strengthened themselves in this region by establishing Pensacola in 1698, and the French had made themselves a major menace by setting themselves up at Biloxi the next year and by moving over closer three years later and founding Mobile. Here was tinder enough to start a conflagration, even if the home governments in Europe had not concocted for themselves a war over the succession to the throne of Spain. In Europe the contest became the War of the Spanish Succession, but in America it came to be known as Queen Anne's War, because it broke out the year Anne became the English ruler.

The Carolinians sought now to rid the southeast of the Spaniards and the encroaching French, but as the former were closer at hand they bore the brunt of the fighting. Since 1674, when Dr. Henry Woodward crossed the Savannah to engage in the Indian trade, there had been a state of warfare in the western Georgia wilderness, with the Spaniards using every effort to expel the Carolina traders. The fighting in Queen Anne's War broke out first on the coast, where one Carolina force drove the Spaniards out of their St. Marys outposts to the St. Johns and another under Governor James Moore attacked and burned St. Augustine. Two years later, in 1704, Moore with 50 Carolinians and 1,000 Indian allies marched across Georgia, defeated the Spanish and their Indian warriors near Tallahassee, demolished a dozen Spanish missions with their Indian villages, and carried away 1,400 Indian prisoners, many of whom they threw into slavery. The Treaty of Utrecht in 1713, which ended the war, left the territorial problem of the southeast unsolved.

Because of the uncertainty which overspread this whole region, there was destined to be a long struggle followed by a solution which was to be the result of widely scattered and unrelated forces, ambitions, and aspirations.

CHAPTER II

THE GENESIS OF GEORGIA

THE CAROLINIANS were vitally interested in their territorial possessions south and west of the Savannah, for there lay the valuable fur trade and the new lands for their expanding plantations. The Lords Proprietors were less interested in this expansion; in fact, they had developed a definite policy against crowding the Indians. Frontiersmen then were like frontiersmen thereafter; they could not be restrained either from seizing what land they wanted or from dealing with the Indians in their own way. So in 1715, two years after the signing of the Treaty of Utrecht, there broke upon the settlements an uprising of the heretofore friendly Yamassee Indians, who were living east of the Savannah, and who had been a bulwark against the Spaniards. Crowded by settlers and dishonest traders and possibly urged on by Spanish and French emissaries, they wrought terrible havoc before they were finally subdued and driven to the protection of the Spanish at St. Augustine.

This war gave additional proof that the greatest problem the Carolinians had lay beyond the Savannah. This region should be colonized and a ring of forts should be built to protect it. Thomas Nairne, who had been much interested in the fur trade and had spent a great deal of time in the Indian country, had in the days of Queen Anne's War advocated the planting of a colony west of the Savannah, but an end was put to his efforts by the Yamassees, who burned him at the stake in their war in 1715.

Nairne's idea of a colony had the practical background of the fur trade; but a few years later, in 1717, Sir Robert Montgomery, a Scotchman, made more progress with a colony based on nothing but speculation aided by poetry and rhetoric. Sir Robert secured from the Lords Proprietors a strip of land directly west of the Savannah and extending to the Altamaha, which he called the Margravate of Azilia. Here in this lordly domain he would build a palace for the Margrave, and there would be gentry and laborers, and the Golden Age would be restored to the earth. He got together his advertisers and promoters and attempted to stampede a people who were soon to witness the bursting of the great South Sea Bubble. Here would he rebuild the Garden of Eden. In this garden would flourish rice, coffee, tea, figs, currants, almonds, olives, silk, and cochineal. Sir Robert was very anxious to colonize St. Catherines Island, and to further the project he published a book called *A Description of the Golden Islands* (1720). In his principal account, which he published in 1717 and named *A Discourse Concerning the design'd Establishment of a New Colony To The South of Carolina In The Most delightful Country of the Universe,* he declared that "Paradise with all her virgin beauties may be modestly suppos'd at most but equal" to this land of Azilia. He made some progress in having it erected into another English colony, but failing to attract settlers he sold it to Aaron Hill, under whom it died a speedy death.

Scarcely had Azilia gone up in an outburst of rhetoric, before Jean Pierre Purry, another dreamer, was seeking from the Eight Lords the right to bring over a group of Swiss to settle them west of the Savannah in a colony which he suggested should be named Georgia or Georgiana. Though he assured the Lords it would be a perfect bulwark against the French and Spaniards, he failed to secure their permission; and so he was forced to be content with having his name preserved for posterity in Purrysburg, a little settlement on the eastern side of the Savannah.

No colonial bubble could settle the problem of Carolina's international frontier, and the Carolinians soon discovered that fact. They proposed to set up a line of forts and place in them soldiers and guns, and then in this trans-Savannah country people could settle and trade in peace. The first fort to defy the Spanish and French was constructed in 1721 near the mouth of the Altamaha in a marsh and was called Fort King George. Four years later a movement was started to build another one up the Altamaha at the forks of the Ocmulgee and Oconee rivers, but the cost of constructing and maintaining forts was too much for Carolina to meet, and England had not yet agreed to assume responsibility. The Carolinians had definitely decided that their territory extended as far southward as the Altamaha; but the Spaniards were sure that their possessions continued as far to the north as the Edisto River, if not farther. By loud protests both in Charleston and in Europe they sought to force the Carolinians to give up Fort King George, and finally in 1727 the fort was abandoned, not because of Spanish protests but because of mutinous garrisons, the destruction of much of it by fire, and the cost of maintaining it.

This southern frontier had come to be the most dangerous spot in all the English possessions in America. The friction of Carolinians and Spaniards was constantly working itself out in clashes and threats in an undeclared war. The year after Fort King George had been abandoned, a Carolina expedition marched to the gates of St. Augustine to punish the Yamassees. It was time the home government should look upon the situation as an imperial problem, not a provincial one. Forces in Carolina and in Europe were converging and conspiring to produce this viewpoint.

Conditions in England and especially in London at this time were lamentable. Great numbers of people drifted around unable to find work, and even members of the more privileged classes were falling into debt from which they found it impossible to extricate themselves. The law of the land gave the creditor the right to restrain the freedom of the debtor, even to the extent of throwing him into prison, and constantly the debtor prisons were being gorged with these unfortunate Englishmen.

English prisons made two names forever famous, James Edward Oglethorpe and John Bunyan; the former, because he was responsible for liberating many unfortunate prisoners, the latter because he wrote his well-known book in a prison, though he was not there for debt. Oglethorpe was well-born; he entered Oxford University and stayed a short while before engaging in the War of the Spanish Succession. He later served with Prince Eugene on the continent, and in 1722 he was elected to Parliament. He played no part of any consequence until 1729 when he was made chairman of a committee to investigate the debtor prisons. He had become interested among other reasons because a friend of his was so unfortunate as to be thrown into one of these prisons. The investigations this committee made were reported in 1729 and again in 1730, and resulted in the liberation of 10,000 unfortunates according to Oglethorpe.

The lot of many of these released debtors was little better out of prison than in; England was crowded and, therefore, could hold out little hope for their future. At this juncture another element entered into the situation and another name finds a place in the picture. The work and personality of Dr. Thomas Bray played no mean part indirectly in solving the difficulty. Dr. Bray had for years been a great promoter of philanthropy and moral betterment. His work had been directed principally along the lines of organizing libraries in England and America and in promoting Christianity and education among Negro slaves. He was the organizer of two societies, whose usefulness and fame had already become established by this time, the Society for the Propagation of the Gospel in Foreign Parts and the Society for the Promotion of Christian Knowledge, familiarly known respectively as the S. P. G. and the S. P. C. K. In 1723 feeling the disintegrating effects of ill health and approaching old age, and fearful of the effect this situation might have on his work, he organized a group of associates who after his death in 1730 came to be called the Associates of the Late Dr. Bray.

Here was an organization which would be interested in any plausible scheme for relieving the debtors. One of the Associates was John Lord Viscount Percival, afterwards the first Earl of Egmont, who was a friend of Oglethorpe's, and to him Oglethorpe mentioned in 1730 the scheme he had been considering of sending to America some of the released debtors "who were starving about the town for want of employment." He also mentioned to Percival that he had stumbled upon £15,000 in a charity which could easily be added to the funds of the Bray Associates and used on the debtor project.

Assured of this money, on July 30, 1730, Oglethorpe, Percival, and nineteen other prominent men, many of them members of Parliament, petitioned the King for a tract of land "on the south-west of Carolina for settling poor persons of London"; but owing to a few changes that needed to be made in the original draft of the charter and to the proverbial slowness of official action, the charter was not granted until June 9, 1732.

Although debtor distress had earliest been identified with the plan to set up a new colony, this idea by the time the charter was granted had been broadened into including all unfortunates, and probably not a dozen people who had been in jail for debt ever went to Georgia. A number of causes joined hands to bring about the founding of this new English colony, called Georgia in the charter, the first since Pennsylvania, fifty years previously; and each of the various groups interested read into the venture its own particular purpose. There were imperialistic, economic, and philanthropic factors involved. The English government was willing to grant this charter because it had come to see the Carolina point of view concerning the international situation beyond the Savannah and to recognize that it was not a provincial but an imperial problem. The difficulty of the King's making a grant of land in a region already given away to the Eight Lords had been removed in 1728 when seven of the Lords sold their rights back to the King. In 1729 the province was cut into North and South Carolina. The government would make out of this colony an instrument of British imperialism to push forward the boundaries and to defend South Carolina against the French and Spanish. With strong mercantile backing, it also felt that in this new colony there would be an effective working of the mercantilist theory of national wealth, for this colony would produce many of the raw products which England was then buying from foreign nations and it would afford a market for the manufactures of the home-land.

The government and the merchants could read into Georgia what purposes they would; but Georgia to others meant the blossoming forth of a great ecclesiastical imperialism, a refuge for those people in Europe persecuted on account of their religion, a gigantic philanthropy even wider than all Britain, a Utopia that might set the pattern for a new world organization. This new colonial venture soon came to attract more widespread attention than attended the founding of any other American colony.

A poet in the *South Carolina Gazette*, in 1733, foresaw Georgia in this light:

> THEN may the great Reward assign't by FATE
> Prove thy own Wish—to see the Work compleat;
> Till GEORGI'S Silks on ALBION'S Beauties shine,
> Or gain new Lustre from the ROYAL LINE;
> Till from the sunny Hills the Vines display
> Their various Berries to the gilded Day;
> Whence glad Vintage to the Vale may flow,
> Refreshing Labour, and dispelling Woe;
> While the fat Plains with pleasant Olives shine,
> And Zaura's Date improves the barren Pine.
> Fair in the Garden shall the Lemon grow,
> And every Grove HESPERIAN Apples show;

The Almond the delicious Fruit behold,
Whose Juice the feign't Immortals quaff'd of old,
Nor haply on the well examin'd Plain
Shall CHINA'S fragrant Leaf be sought in vain;
While the consenting Climate gladly proves
The costly Balms that weep in INDIAN Groves.
And when in time the wealthy Lands increase,
Shall bend the Curious to the Arts of Peace;
They, with small Pain, assisted by the Clime,
Shall pull the Anana and unload the Lime;
Thro' Groves of Citron breath ARABIA'S Gale,
And parch the Berry drank in MECCA'S Vale.

* * * * *

IBERIA'S motly Race a Bound shall know,
And Slave contented in the Mine below;
Nor GALLIA'S Sons of new Encroachments dream,
Glad while they taste the MISSISSIPPI Stream;
In Peace, 'till we preside, in War prevail,
And the New World allows the British Scale.

The charter with all the sonorous expressions characteristic of the day progressed through long sentences to more than 6,000 words. Out of all these words came these facts: that twenty-one persons, whose names were given, should constitute a Board of Trustees to manage the colony; that they should have definite powers therein set down; that the area of the colony should be all the land lying between the Savannah and Altamaha rivers and lines drawn from their headwaters to the South Seas, including all islands not more than twenty leagues from the eastern shore; and that this charter should expire after twenty-one years. The limits set would today include Little Rock, Phoenix, Los Angeles, and the northern part of Mexico.

The following month the Trustees organized themselves into a body to carry out their trust. Naturally the twenty-one named in the charter did not continue throughout the following twenty-one years. They moved on through death or resignation

JOHN, LORD VISCOUNT PERCIVAL
FIRST EARL OF EGMONT

The Colony of Georgia owed much to Percival, who long remained one of the most active members of the Board of Trustees. *Courtesy of the W. J. De Renne Georgia Library.*

THE GEORGIA PROSPECT IN 1732

This highly imaginative representation of Georgia is an excellent example of the promotion campaign carried on for settling the colony. Mulberry groves extended in one grand vista from the Savannah River to the Mountains, while a strong fortress protected the people from the Spaniards. *Reasons for establishing the Colony of Georgia, With Regard to the Trade of Great Britain*. London, 1733.

Britain. The propaganda moved much along these lines: Georgia could relieve England from dependence on Madeira and other foreign parts for wine; she would largely stop the importations from Russia of hemp, flax, and potash; she could produce enough silk to supply all England and have much left to export; she would relieve the over-population in England, give a new start in life to the poor and unfortunate, and make much better the lot of those left in England; and she would afford a refuge for the persecuted Protestants of Europe. And the climate had not changed since Sir Robert Montgomery had sung its praises. A booklet called *A New and Accurate Account of the Provinces of South Carolina and Georgia,* which Benjamin Martyn probably wrote and which in its title sought to reënforce some of its remarkable statements, declared that "Such an air and soil can only be fitly described by a poetical pen, because there is but little danger of exceeding the truth." Proof of the healthfulness of this part of the world was seen in the claim that one of the Florida Indian kings was already 300 years old and his father was still living at the age of 350.

Noblemen and yeoman, Gentile and Jew, clergyman and layman got commissions from the Trustees to canvass for Georgia, and each giver gave money or objects according to his interests. The Bank of England gave £252; Joseph Jekyl £500 and Lady Jekyl £100; the Earl of Abercorn £100; and so it went with the money gifts, many giving more than once. The Trustees, giving a great deal of their time, never donated in money more than £900 throughout the life of the venture. The mercantilists gave Egyptian kale, madder roots, Lucerne seeds, bamboo plants, Lippora raisins, Neapolitan chestnuts, Barilla seeds, mulberry seeds, olive plants, cotton seeds, Burgundy vines, and various other plants whose products they expected to see soon flowing from Georgia. The militarists gave cartridge boxes and belts, powder flasks, bayonets, swords, and drums. The preachers and the literati gave thousands of books, mostly of a religious or reforming nature, such as *A*

Friendly Admonition to the Drinkers of Gin, Brandy, and other Spirituous Liquors, written by Hales, one of the Trustees, *Duty of Man, Christian Monitor and Companion, Young Christians Instructed,* Bibles, Psalters, Prayer Books, and Catechisms. Others gave various farming implements, tools, articles of clothing, and food, wines, and beer for the voyage.

The next important duty of the Trustees was to select those who should first wear the name Georgian.

CHAPTER III

SAVANNAH

FOR BUILDING an ordinary colony, money and land and any people who could be induced to go, were necessary; but for carrying out the great philanthropic and social experiment in Georgia, the population element was of first and supreme importance, for that was the variable which would determine success or failure. Realizing well this requirement, the Trustees set up a sifting process more exacting and rigid than was ever used in securing settlers for any other American colony. It was announced that people would be received "of reputable families, and of liberal or, at least, easy education; some undone by guardians, some by lawsuits, some by accidents in commerce, some by stocks and bubbles, and some by suretyship. . . . These are the people that may relieve themselves and strengthen Georgia by resorting thither, and Great Britain by their departure."

For months, the Trustees were busy selecting their first expedition. Not all who applied were accepted. No one was taken without an investigation. Time and again did they insert in their records this minute, "Examined several Persons who Offered themselves to Go to Georgia, and Enter'd their Names for further Consideration." Unless a debtor could come to an agreement with his creditor, he was not accepted.

Well might the Trustees guard the gates to their experiment, for there was great expense attached to each settler. These prospective Georgians should receive free passage to the New World, be given tools, agricultural implements, and seeds, be supported until the first crop was harvested, and be allowed fifty acres of land. Moreover, they were to have all the rights of British subjects, and all people born in Georgia should "have and enjoy all liberties, franchises and immunities" held by Englishmen.

By the fall of 1732, more than a hundred people had been accepted for the first ship to Georgia, and so important was it that the first step in this undertaking be taken with great care and precision, it was determined that Oglethorpe, one of the Trustees, should accompany the expedition. Oglethorpe, scarcely less a military personage than a philanthropist, was fast becoming an imperial idealist. Although to the Trustees the Georgia venture was not a military expedition, to Oglethorpe and to others, including the British government and South Carolina, it might well soon become one. The charter had placed the duty on the Trustees of organizing the militia and training them, and of defending the colony against foreign enemies; and while the colonists were yet waiting in London for the ship to sail, an uninformed spectator might well have guessed that soldiers were being got ready for some war, for sergeants of the Royal Guard gave these prospective Georgians military training.

Before going aboard the *Anne,* a vessel of 200 tons, which was to convey them to America, the settlers, "sober, industrious, and moral persons," appeared before the Trustees, signified their final desire to go, and signed articles of agreement.[1] Though strong drink had undoubtedly helped to reduce some of these people to their sad estate, ten tuns of beer (252 gallons being a tun) were loaded on the *Anne,* and when it reached the Azores five tuns of wine were taken on. Rum and gin were dangerous, but wines and beer were considered necessities. Off to a new world and a new life started a cargo of people, whose poverty was much less a disgrace than an inconvenience.

On January 13, 1733 they arrived at Charleston and remained until the next day before departing for Beaufort, where

---

[1] There were men, women, and children, and the total number has been variously stated from 114 to 125.

they would stay until a place to settle should be found in Georgia. Well might South Carolina now rejoice that a deliverer had come; a buffer colony was about to be planted to shield her from the wrath of the Spanish, the French, and the Indians. Little was she interested in philanthropic experiments. Accompanied by William Bull, a generous-hearted South Carolinian, Oglethorpe ascended the Savannah River, looking for the bluff on which he would build his city. About eighteen miles from the mouth, they found it, occupied by an encampment of Yamacraw Indians, an outlawed tribe of the Creeks, with their old chief Tomo-Chi-Chi. Fortunately and yet strangely enough, Oglethorpe also found a half-breed Indian woman, Mary, the wife of John Musgrove, a renegade South Carolina trader. Being able to speak English, Mary Musgrove soon established an agreement between Oglethorpe and Tomo-Chi-Chi, and a friendship developed which died only with the old chieftain. Returning to Beaufort, Oglethorpe brought up his colonists in small boats and sheltered them in four large tents on the edge of a great pine wood interspersed and made more charming with live-oaks and magnolias. This was February 12, 1733, which was later to be celebrated as Georgia's birthday.

Aided by William Bull, Oglethorpe laid out a town in an orderly fashion, with its distinctive squares regularly interspersed, and soon set the people to building their houses. The town he called Savannah. South Carolina not only aided the colonists in finding a proper location, but she was so interested and overjoyed with this new buffer colony that her people gave the Georgians horses, cattle, sheep, hogs, and rice; and the assembly voted Georgia £2,000 in South Carolina currency and later increased the amount. With the value added to her property through this protection, she could well afford to display generosity; and to show its appreciation the new city named a square Johnson for the South Carolina governor, a principal street for William Bull, and it perpetuated the mem-

ory of other Carolinians in the names of streets. The founding
of Georgia was an important event in the eyes of the other
English colonies in America. Thomas Penn, the proprietor of
Pennsylvania, gave the colony £100 and the governor of
Massachusetts showered Oglethorpe with his own congratula-
tions and called down for him the blessings of God.

Though the Trustees had secured their land from the King,
they could not begin a philanthropy for one group by making
beggars and outcasts of another. Oglethorpe had secured from
the Yamacraws permission to settle Savannah, but if he were
to spread out over the land with his settlers, it were proper
that he come to terms with the Creek nation, which laid
claim to this region. Through the aid of Mary Musgrove as
interpreter at £100 a year, and especially by the help of his
new friend Tomo-Chi-Chi, Oglethorpe succeeded in gathering
together in Savannah, in May, fifty Indians chiefs and braves
representing eight of the principal Creek tribes. There under
four tall pines, after a few days of high formalities interspersed
with ornate speech-making, a treaty was signed regulating
trade and dealing with the ownership of the land. The Creeks
agreed to become the allies of the British government and to
grant to Georgia all the land between the Savannah and Altamaha rivers as far up as the tide ebbed and flowed, excepting
a small tract above Yamacraw Bluff where they might encamp
when they should come to visit Savannah, and the islands of
Ossabaw, Sapelo, and St. Catherines, which they would keep
to satisfy their desire for hunting, bathing, and fishing. To
prevent the Indians from being cheated by unprincipled traders, a schedule of prices was fixed which set such values as ten
buckskins for one gun, five for a pistol, and one for a blanket.

Georgia had not been set up for the poor and unemployed
only. The Trustees had a much broader vision; there was a
place for fortunate Englishmen as well as unfortunate Englishmen; and there was even room for foreigners, with the state
of their fortune no barrier to their entry. But naturally, in the

eyes of the philanthropists, the needy should have first attention, and so the persecuted Protestants of Europe received
consideration almost as soon as the English debtors. Far over
in the mountains of the Archbishopric of Salzburg, before people had learned to be as tolerant as they are today, the Catholic
clergy began such a fierce persecution of the Lutheran Salzburgers that, during the three years before the settlement of
Georgia, 30,000 of them had fled to various parts of Europe.
Through the efforts of the only foreign members of the Board
of Trustees, Samuel Urlsperger, Bishop of Augsburg, and
Chretien von Munch, an Augsburg banker, a group of these
Salzburgers were directed to Georgia. Much of their expense
in coming was paid by Bray's S. P. C. K. and by the German
Evangelical Lutheran Church, to which they belonged.

Under their leader John Martin Bolzius, the first party embarked exactly eleven months after Oglethorpe's vanguard had
set out. They came to Savannah, where they were cared for,
until Oglethorpe and one of their number, Georg Philipp
Friedrich, Baron von Reck, should find them a place to settle—
for, speaking a different language, they wanted to live in a
group by themselves, and having left their beloved mountains,
they wanted a region as nearly as possible like their old home.
There was little likelihood of finding in coastal Georgia a place
like Salzburg, but at least they could have a location apart
from the Savannah settlers, and so Oglethorpe selected for
them a site on a crooked sluggish little stream which chose
to run twenty-five miles to the Savannah when a straight cut
would have been six miles. Both the stream and the town
were called Ebenezer.

Thither the Salzburgers went to build their town, but so
inaccessible was the place and so marshy that they begged for
a new location. Unable to dissuade them, Oglethorpe laid out
for them another town, at Red Bluff on the Savannah River,
and here in 1736 Ebenezer took a new start. Old Ebenezer

quickly disintegrated and soon degenerated into a cow-pen—the first of Georgia's dead towns.

The Salzburgers continued to come to Georgia in small parties and by 1741 the number was estimated to be 1,200. They made Ebenezer the center of their little domain, with small groups settling in nearby places like Bethany and Goshen, and a few as far away as St. Simons Island. They were a frugal, straightforward, and industrious people, who put an undivided faith in God and a simple reliance in their ministers. They built their New Jerusalem at Ebenezer and their Zion four miles to the southward, and in these sanctuaries their political and economic life was controlled almost as much as their religion. Under such leaders as Bolzius, Israel Gronau, Herman Henry Lemke, and Christian Rabenhorst the people prospered in agriculture and silk-raising, and the organized congregation accumulated in its own name property sufficient to pay the pastor's salary and provide for the orphans and unfortunates. The Salzburgers developed the most numerous single population element in Georgia during the period of the Trustees, which, in fact, made Georgia more German than English.

Another group of persecuted Protestants, German-speaking like the Salzburgers, who found refuge in Georgia were the Moravians. Having fled Moravia for the protection of Count Zinzendorf, in Saxony, they later found it necessary to leave this refuge. The Count in 1733 petitioned the Trustees to let these people migrate to Georgia, but with the understanding that they should not be required to violate their article of faith against bearing arms. Desirous of aiding unfortunates and of promoting their Georgia experiment, but forgetful of one of the important purposes of the new colony, the Trustees unwisely agreed to the condition and the Moravians foolishly accepted. The Moravians came over not as charity colonists at the expense of the Trust, though the Trust did lend them money which they were later to return, but as servants of their patron Count Zinzendorf, under the Trustee ruling that anyone who cared to go to Georgia at his own expense and would take ten servants, might have a grant of as much as 500 acres of land. The Count received his grant on the Ogeechee River, but finding it inconvenient to leave Europe he secured his release from his obligation to go, and sent, instead, August Gottlieb Spangenberg and nine followers. They landed in Savannah in 1735, where they awaited the coming of others.

Another grant of 500 acres of land was secured, this time by Christian Ludwig von Zinzendorf, the eldest son of the Count; but he also secured a release from coming; and another group set out for Georgia on the last day of October, 1735, made up of men, women, and children, under the guidance of David Nitschman, the Bishop. The whole group of Moravians remained for the most part around Savannah, rather than take up the lands which the Trustees had so unwisely given them on the exposed Ogeechee frontier. In Savannah, stared at by the English, they made their friends among the Salzburgers who visited the town, and when the dangers of Spanish invasions from the southward set the Savannah militia to training, the Moravians standing on their rights refused to take part.

It became evident early to Spangenberg and Nitschman that the Moravians were out of place in Georgia, and they were confirmed in this opinion after visiting in 1736 their brethren in Pennsylvania. The next year with louder rumors about Spaniards marching against Savannah, there was more drilling and a census was taken of those who could be classed as fighters. The Moravians not only refused to march back and forth with guns in their hands, but they refused even to be counted. The feeling against them now became bitter, and there were threats that the Moravians would be killed if they did not help. They now sought the voice of the Lord that they might know what to do. The Lord speaking through lots, which the Moravians cast, advised them to "go out from among them." As they prepared to leave for Pennsylvania, the Savannahians turning Egyptian refused to let them depart until they had paid all money owed the Trust. Some began leaving in 1737 as the debt was reduced, and by the middle of 1740 every Moravian had departed for the North.

In all there had been only 47 Moravians in Georgia, 43 coming from Europe, one from Pennsylvania, one from North Carolina, and two born in Georgia. The Moravian adventure had been a misfortune for all concerned. It was foolish to send pacifists to a colony which undoubtedly would be forced soon into war, and it was doubly foolish to attempt to send these pacifists to the most exposed part of the colony. Instead of going to the Ogeechee, some of the Moravians had gone to the Savannah a few miles above the city, and there carrying out one of the desires that had impelled them to Georgia, the Christianizing of the Indians, they had set up a school for Indians at Irene.

As if to rectify somewhat the blunder they had made in sending the Moravians to Georgia, the Trustees in 1735, aided by a grant of £26,000 Parliament had made, decided to send to their Georgia Utopia an element which they had not contemplated in their original designs. The Spanish danger, apparent in the beginning, was becoming more ominous with the growth of the colony. The Parliamentary grant was a recognition of this fact. Oglethorpe, who was in England at this time and who had never been forgetful of the high excitement of an inevitable clash with the Spaniards to the southward, decided that some fighting men should now be sent to Georgia and that they should be planted on the most exposed frontier. So he sent Lieutenant Hugh Mackay into the Highlands of Scotland to recruit Scotchmen who had not helped their lot in their recent attempt to place the Pretender on the throne of England. One hundred and thirty of these hardy fighters with 50 women and children, such families as Dunbar, Baily, McIntosh, Mackay, and Cuthbert, were brought to Georgia and set down on the north bank of the Altamaha, as close to the Spaniards as they could go and still remain within the limits of Georgia as set by the King. They named their settlement Darien out of respect for the ill-fated attempt of Scotchmen to found a settlement on the Isthmus of Panama; but later for a few years, they called it New Inverness, as a reminiscence of their former surroundings in Scotland.

Bringing with them their minister, John McLeod, a native of the Isle of Skye, they took time to intersperse religious interests with their military activities, but the parsons never held sway here as extensively as in Ebenezer. Early they erected a fort with four cannon, and as other Scotchmen came in they spread out over the region and onto St. Simons Island, where they began the plantation régime, which blossomed forth so beautifully after the American Revolution.

The philanthropy of the Trustees was noble and extensive, but not broad enough to include the Catholics, whose persecutions had driven to Georgia the Salzburgers and Moravians, nor the Jews, whom the world had not yet learned to tolerate. So no Papist or Jew was allowed a place in Georgia; but in time this rule fell into disuse and both arrived and became valuable elements in the population.

The Jews were the first to appear and through such a manner as to lead the Trustees to demand their expulsion. When commissions to collect money for Georgia were being given out by the Trustees, three Jews secured them and instead of turning the money into the hands of the Trustees, they collected forty of their race in 1733, and unknown to the Trustees, sent them to Georgia. The Jewish collectors were called upon to remove this element which might prejudice the whole Georgia undertaking in the eyes of the English government and Englishmen generally. The impracticality of expelling them was soon evident, and Oglethorpe, who was willing to have his small group of settlers augmented from any quarter, allotted them land and defended them and his action before the Trustees. A few of them migrated to South Carolina, but a sufficient number remained to take some noticeable part in the affairs of Savannah and to collect enough furnishings to make a room a synagogue.

Though no other important separate groups of people came to Georgia for years after the arrival of the English, the Salzburgers, the Moravians, the Scotch Highlanders, and the Jews, yet constantly additions were being made to these peoples, and scattering elements from the nations of the earth came in. In that respect Georgia became a sort of cross-roads of the world, for within a half dozen years after the beginning, there could be found in the colony Piedmontese, Swiss, Salzburgers, Moravians, Germans, Jews, Scotch Highlanders, Welsh, and English. Georgia had as cosmopolitan a population as could be found in America.

CHAPTER IV

BUILDING A BUFFER AGAINST THE SPANIARDS

WHEN ONCE THE COLONY of Georgia was set going it became less a refuge for the unfortunate and more a buffer against the Spaniards. Whether the Trustees would have it so or not, the very existence of Georgia on land claimed by Spain inevitably made it so, and Oglethorpe, with all his commiseration for unfortunate people, looked upon the trend with pleasure. It was for this reason that he had settled the Scotch Highlanders on the Altamaha and had refused to remove them, in defiance of the wishes of the Trustees, who were more interested in their humanitarian project than in an imperialistic war.

Oglethorpe had scarcely set down his charges in Savannah, before he was looking, with the air of an invader, to the military defenses of the colony. He immediately fortified Yamacraw Bluff with five cannon, and then established Fort Argyle on the Ogeechee to the southwestward and settled ten families there, at a place where the Indians were accustomed to cross the river on their way to attack the Carolinians. In the early part of 1734 he set out down the coast to view his domain, to see how close the Spaniards were, and to locate strategic points to fortify. He selected a site for a settlement at the mouth of the Altamaha (later to be occupied by the Highlanders), and forgetful of where his dominions stopped, he crossed to St. Simons Island and indicated the future site of Frederica. He passed on to the next island, which he named Jekyl in honor of Sir Joseph, who had aided the Georgia venture with £500. On his return he viewed his defenses on the Ogeechee. As an outpost more for trade than defense, he established the next year up the Savannah the town of Augusta.

Having successfully planted his colony on Yamacraw Bluff and having viewed the possibilities of defense and offense too, Oglethorpe boarded a man-of-war in Charleston and sailed for his native land in May, 1734. To give the people of England a touch of the atmosphere of Georgia, he took back with him his friend Tomo-Chi-Chi with his wife, nephew, and five Creek chiefs with their attendants. Their visit created great excitement and interest from the nobility down to the rabble in the street who at times almost injured the red men in their stampedes to see them. Tooanahowi, the nephew, made proud the hearts of the clergy by reciting the Lord's Prayer both in his own language and in English. One great round of audiences, receptions, and celebrations marked their stay; and before they left, the poets had even begun to sing their glory. They visited the King, Oglethorpe's estate, the Archbishop of Canterbury, and the Georgia Rooms, in London, the home of the Trust where they were housed for a time. At Eton, Tomo-Chi-Chi received hearty acclaim from the students when he recommended that they be given a holiday. Sadness at the death, through small-pox, of one of the Indians and the fear that their stay was becoming too expensive to their hosts, led the Indians to return after four months, but not without £400 worth of presents and a vast admiration for the might and glory of England.

As a method of controlling the Indians in Georgia, this visit was worth much to England. Not only did the Creeks develop great respect for the English, but even the Cherokees were much impressed by the stories they heard from the Tomo-Chi-Chi tourists. Still remembering the visit that seven of their chiefs had made to London in 1730, with Sir Alexander Cuming, when they had acknowledged British supremacy, they now sent a letter to the Trustees, written in red and black characters on a buffalo hide, which fifty of their chiefs delivered to Oglethorpe in Savannah.

Had Oglethorpe's exploits in planting the Georgia colony
not seemed so remarkable, Tomo-Chi-Chi's visit would have
dimmed his reception. As it was, England received Oglethorpe
as a great benefactor and moral hero and an empire builder.
The new colony of Georgia now loomed into an importance
which overshadowed every other project of the day. Parliament
made the grant of £26,000, previously mentioned, to help
finance a great outpouring to Georgia, and within a short time
the Trustees had 1,100 applications. As the Spanish frontier
was assuming great importance now, a military tinge was given
to much of the activity on behalf of Georgia. Various sailings
were carrying people to the new colony: Tomo-Chi-Chi and
his party had returned with one group, the Scotch Highlanders
followed, and toward the end of 1735 Oglethorpe made ready to
return in what came to be known as "the great embarkation."

The flotilla of two vessels, like a military expedition, sailed
away under convoy of a man-of-war. On board were Oglethorpe, John and Charles Wesley, Charles Delamotte, a group
of Salzburgers under Von Reck, a few Moravians and many
other settlers. On board were also cannon, other munitions of
war, provisions, and tools. The voyage was long and stormy,
and to consume some of the time Oglethorpe exercised his men
at small arms practice and instruction. They reached Tybee
Island in February, 1736, and when Oglethorpe arrived in
Savannah, he was received in true military fashion with a
salute of 21 cannon.

Oglethorpe had hoped to induce most if not all of these new
colonists to go to the southern frontier to join the Highlanders
who had lately arrived; but the Salzburgers and the Moravians
naturally wanted to join their own groups elsewhere, and only
by hard pleading were the remainder steered to the southward.
As the captains refused to take their ships there, the settlers
were transferred to small boats and forced to row for five days
through the inner passage to the Altamaha. The little fleet
was held together by placing the food and strong beer in the

forward boats whereby none might eat and drink who did not follow.

Oglethorpe soon followed this army of occupation to direct their disposition. He laid out the miltary town of Frederica on a bluff on St. Simons Island overlooking the inner passage, and here he developed a Verdun for southern North America. This place became the most healthful of all the coastal towns, screened against a background of great live-oaks festooned with Spanish moss; and here the first alligators were seen and regarded as most outlandish monsters. The place took on a military air with its streets named for army officers, with a fort, magazine, barracks, and entrenchments and the martial bustle of drilling troops. The military soul of Oglethorpe was charmed with it all, and he made Frederica rather than Savannah his home.

With Frederica rising to dispute the passage of the Spaniards, Oglethorpe, in March, set out on an expedition to the southward accompanied by Tomo-Chi-Chi with 40 Indians and by Hugh Mackay with 30 Highlanders, "to see where his Majesty's Dominions and the Spaniards joyn." Passing by Jekyl, he landed on the northern point of Cumberland Island, and selecting a commanding position for a fort, named it Fort St. Andrews, and left Mackay with his Highlanders to build it. Continuing with his Indians, he passed the mouth of the St. Marys and came to an island which he named Amelia. He then proceeded to a small island, San Juan, near the mouth of the St. Johns River, and there Tomo-Chi-Chi showed him the very doors of the Spanish possessions, and so excited was the old chief that Oglethorpe had great difficulty in dissuading him from attacking the Spaniards immediately. Oglethorpe saw the great value of fortifying this place, for by so doing he could block the inner passage to Georgia and force the Spaniards out into the open sea, if they should attempt to attack Georgia. Here after close investigation Oglethorpe found "where his Majesty's Dominions and the Spaniards joyn." On his return to Frederica, the Indians gave a big war dance in his honor, and then departed for their homes.

To protect Frederica, Fort St. Simon was built at the southern tip of the island. On the southern end of Cumberland Island rose Fort William, and on San Juan Island frowned forth at the Spaniards, Fort St. George. Indeed, Oglethorpe was laying hold of his Georgia dominions and advancing claims to a great area beyond. He was using his best efforts, either to provoke a war with the Spaniards or so strongly to entrench himself that they would not dare attack him. To satisfy those who might have a keener conscience than his, Oglethorpe concocted a map showing one of the branches of the Altamaha debouching near the St. Marys, to prove that Georgia extended at least so far. And, indeed, was not Oglethorpe here allowing his interest in extending the British possessions, transcend his service merely to Georgia, for had not Charles II pushed his dominions as far southward as the twenty-ninth parallel?

Additional roads were now projected. They were largely for military purposes. Among the first labors performed by Oglethorpe's regiment was the cutting of a road down the center of St. Simons Island from Frederica to Fort St. Simon. A few years previously Hugh Mackay with the aid of Indians supplied by Tomo-Chi-Chi had cut a road from New Inverness to Savannah, which became one of the principal colonial roads. Another road cleared out in 1739 joined Savannah with Augusta. As war would come from the southward, this road was of little military significance, but it was serviceable in supplementing the river connections.

What were the Spaniards thinking of such bold activities, and how had they been regarding the English occupation of Georgia from the days Oglethorpe had landed his hordes on Yamacraw Bluff? In their most exhilarating moments they had never ceased to claim territory far enough north to include not only Charleston, but Augusta too. Was this not a fair claim with which to combat the English contention that St. Augustine was theirs? The Spaniards did not neglect to protest to England against establishing Georgia south of the Savannah, and even before a single settler had arrived in America, rumors were afloat in England that Spanish spies were closely watching every move.

The most ubiquitous and baffling spy of them all was an Englishman, John Savy, who had gone to South Carolina, where he had got into debt so heavily that he crossed over the Savannah. Leaving Georgia in 1735, he finally turned up in Madrid in the pay of Spain, under the name of Colonel Miguel Wall. His conscience finally revolting against the villainies he had seen and engaged in from Madrid to Havana, he turned up in London in 1737 and told all to his native countrymen.

Now that the policy of the English and the activities of Oglethorpe had goaded the Spaniards into strong protesting and spying, the Trustees began calling on Parliament for aid in defending Georgia. The defense of the colony, which the charter had saddled onto the Trustees, was becoming too much for them. Their purpose had been to carry out a great social experiment, not to fight a war. In 1735 under the advice of Oglethorpe, who was in England on his first visit, they asked the government for 24 cannon with all equipment that should go with them, four field pieces, 500 small arms, two flags, 50 barrels of powder, and other munitions of war. Early in 1737 after having fortified the coast almost to St. Augustine, Oglethorpe arrived in England on a second visit, largely to secure support for the war he was about to provoke with the Spaniards.

The Trustees, already smarting under the heavy expenses Oglethorpe had entailed upon them in promoting a war instead of helping the settlers, now decided to ask Parliament to take over the full expense of protecting Georgia. Alarmed by the confessions of Savy, made at this time, warned by Oglethorpe of the critical situation, and urged insistently by the Trustees, Parliament saw no other course than to accept the responsibility and expense of defending Georgia. Oglethorpe

was made commander-in-chief of all His Majesty's forces in
South Carolina and Georgia, money was voted, and he was
given permission to raise a regiment to take back with him.
So urgent was the situation that a company from the garrison
at Gibraltar was sent to Georgia immediately, and in the fall
of 1738 Oglethorpe followed with the regiment he had enlisted.
Mindful of the necessity of increasing the permanent population of the colony, Oglethorpe allowed those who would join
the regiment to take their wives and children with them to
occupy grants of land he would make them. This was, indeed
a military expedition—600 soldiers on five transports convoyed
by two war vessels. So sure were the Spaniards of Oglethorpe's
warlike intentions that they tried to induce the English government not to allow him to return.

His troops were a turbulent assemblage, giving him almost
as much concern as the Spaniards. It was flecked with Papists,
who denied the authority of the King, and with Spanish spies.
Before reaching Georgia, he discovered a plot to kill the officers
and hand over the regiment to the Spaniards. One conspirator
was tried and executed, and another, William Shannon, was
whipped and drummed out of the regiment. Shannon was later
discovered among the Creeks, arrested, tried, and finally executed. While inspecting his Gibraltar company, which had
been sent to Cumberland Island to strengthen Fort St. Andrews,
Oglethorpe was set upon by a group of malcontents who attempted to assassinate him with guns and swords. The ring-
leader was speedily shot. As if the soldiers were not creating
enough trouble, even the officers too often developed quarrels
which led to fights with fists and sticks, and now and then resulted in duels. Some of them were sent back to England for
trial.

In the meantime, negotiations between the English and the
Spaniards had been going as well in Georgia as in England.
When Oglethorpe had returned in 1736 from his first visit to
England, he had brought back with him Charles Dempsey, a

commissioner appointed by the British government to go to Florida to treat with the Spaniards. At the very time Oglethorpe set out on his trip to the mouth of the St. Johns River, bent on fortifying the whole coast, Dempsey and Major William Richards of Purrysburg left for St. Augustine. Though boat-wrecked on the way down, they finally reached St. Augustine, where they entered into conversations with Don Francisco Moral Sánchez, the captain-general of Florida. Suspicious that peace-makers were trying to cloak the activities of Oglethorpe and his Indians on the St. Johns, Sánchez detained Dempsey until Oglethorpe was able to demonstrate, by warding off Indian attacks against St. Augustine, his harmless intentions. Dempsey, Richards, and Major William Horton, who had followed, were then released; and it was decided to continue the negotiations at Frederica. As these English commissioners had seen the fortifications of St. Augustine, the Spaniards would now have a chance to inspect Oglethorpe's military town of Frederica.

Oglethorpe, who had the qualities of a great actor, decided to use the occasion of the visit of the Spanish commissioners to make a profound impression upon them. He had all the forts along the coast manned with whatever men could be found and as the Spaniards passed, every available gun was fired. When they arrived at Frederica, another great drama was enacted for them. In the midst of the conference, a group of Indians, apparently so enraged that they could not be restrained by Oglethorpe, burst in and began bitterly to berate the Spaniards for their cruelties. After much apparent effort, Oglethorpe quieted the Indians, and then reminded the Spaniards that he was doing all he could to keep the savages from attacking Florida, and he left the impression that the forts up and down the coast were for the protection of the Spaniards rather than for their harm.

In the treaty of Frederica, here concluded, in 1736, it was agreed that neither nation should occupy the mouth of the St.

Johns and that all boundary disputes should be left to the home governments. This treaty suited the English well enough, but Spain was so outraged at this apparent surrender of her rights that she repudiated the agreement; and inviting Sánchez to visit his home land, the King had him executed on his arrival. Don Antonio Arredondo, an able captain of engineers, immediately went to Frederica and informed the English that instead of the Spaniards receding to the St. Johns, Oglethorpe and his debtors must get out of all Georgia, for Spain owned the country as far as St. Helena Sound, beyond the Savannah. This was the situation in Georgia in the fall of 1736 when Oglethorpe made his second trip to England to ask that Parliament take over the defense of Georgia and give him a regiment.

Signs were multiplying that English and Spaniards must soon clash on the southern frontiers of Georgia. Not only was there no understanding on territorial division, but complications were also growing up in other quarters. An uprising of slaves in South Carolina in which twenty whites were killed, was laid to Spanish tamperings; and the temper of the Indian nations to the westward had been made uncertain by French and Spanish agents who had gone among them. One of the strangest characters ever discovered in the Indian country was Christian Gottlieb Priber, a German, who had originally intended to come to Georgia but who later turned up in Charleston only to depart soon for the Cherokee nation. He was a strange dreamer, who working himself into the confidence of the Cherokees, dangled before their imagination an elaborate communistic scheme of government embracing the arts of civilization. Desiring the competition of the French traders with the English, he was looked upon as a French spy, and was finally arrested in 1743 and imprisoned at Frederica. Here he escaped miraculously the explosion of an ammunition dump only to die a natural death shortly thereafter, but not before he had impressed upon his jailors the fact that he was an unusual man.

To cement English friendship with the Indians, Oglethorpe made good use of his interpreter Mary Musgrove, who saw to it that the Creeks came to Savannah occasionally to greet him. In 1738 a group appeared, swearing their allegiance to the extent of 1,000 warriors if necessary, but also informing him that they had been forced to resist much tampering from Spanish and French agents. A mighty gathering of Creeks, Cherokees, Choctaws, Chickasaws, and others, they said, would take place at Coweta Town on the Chattahoochee the next year, and they invited Oglethorpe to be present. This was a grand opportunity. Oglethorpe and a few retainers set out on horseback with Indian guides to ride more than 200 miles through trackless woods and across unbridged streams. In the midst of a great savage assembly, he explained away the grievance against dishonest English traders, cemented the friendship of the Indians, and induced them not only to re-affirm the old boundary of the Altamaha but to extend it to the St. Johns.

He returned by way of Augusta, and on reaching this outpost he was informed that England had declared war on Spain. Here he remained for a short time, first straightening out some misunderstandings with the Cherokees and then prostrated with a fever. On his return down the Savannah, he learned that his old friend Tomo-Chi-Chi, aged about a hundred, had died, and had expressed the desire to be buried near his white friends in Savannah. In a solemn procession Oglethorpe carried out a state funeral, buried the old chieftain in one of the town squares, and ordered a pyramid to be erected over his grave.

CHAPTER V

THE WAR OF JENKINS' EAR

THE WAR THAT now developed on the Georgia frontiers, known as the War of Jenkins' Ear, was precipitated by causes far wider than the quarrel between Oglethorpe and the Spaniards in Florida. At the end of Queen Anne's War, the British had secured through a clause of the Treaty of Utrecht, the right to supply the Spanish colonies with slaves and to send annually 500 tons of merchandise to their ports. The Spanish should have known that when once they opened a loop-hole in their colonial trade to the enterprising British merchants, 500 tons would be stretched into any amount the English could smuggle through. The Spaniards struggled valiantly to hold the English to the allotted tonnage, and in so doing they were not always gentle in dealing with English vessels they overhauled. Because of their preoccupation with the War of the Polish Succession, which broke out in 1733, their protests against the founding of Georgia and their measures against British smugglers were of little effect; but as they became less entangled in Europe and as the British became more menacing and disregardful of Spanish rights, they began to act with greater rigor. Off the coast of Florida they were said to have seized Thomas Jenkins, a smuggling Englishman, cut off his ears, and told him to take them and show them to his King. Jenkins appeared before Parliament to prove how brutal the Spanish were; and a report to the same body listed fifty-two British vessels which had been captured and plundered by the Spaniards.

With such provocation, it seemed that war was inevitable. Both sides began to prepare for it, but Walpole, much of a pacifist, was able to avert it for a time. In January, 1739, the

Convention of El Pardo was signed. For the illegal seizure of English vessels the Spaniards were to pay £95,000, and as for the boundary between Georgia and Florida, the Altamaha was to be considered temporarily the line of demarcation, until a joint commission could make a final settlement, and in the meantime neither side should increase its fortifications in the region between the Altamaha and the St. Johns. The agreement soon fell flat, as neither side was anxious to carry it out. England declared war in October, 1739, and the following month Spain accepted it.

This was the struggle for sea-power and world trade, which came just in time to start a war which the stress between Georgia and Florida would otherwise have precipitated. It was fought both on land and sea, the Georgian frontiers providing the principal land arena and the Caribbean Sea the water. Edward Vernon became admiral of the seas and General Oglethorpe assumed command of the land forces.

After burying Tomo-Chi-Chi, Oglethorpe made rapid preparations to enter the conflict and to assume the offensive. Counting on about 200 fighting men to be recruited from his Georgia colonists, he set Mary Musgrove to using her best graces in rousing the Indians, and he sent runners into the Creek country to call for 1,000 warriors. He, himself, set out for Frederica. The Spaniards were the first to draw blood, when they fell upon a small outpost of Highlanders on Amelia Island and slew two of them. Quickly retaliating, Oglethorpe hurried southward as far as the mouth of the St. Johns where he harried the country round about, but could find no Spaniards. Lieutenant George Dunbar proceeded on up the river to capture the two forts, Picolata and St. Francis, on the river directly to the west of St. Augustine. Having no artillery and finding them too strongly fortified, he withdrew. Oglethorpe with his Highlanders and Indians, in fifteen water craft, made a new attack on New Year's Day of 1740 and carried both forts. This was a blow of no mean importance to the Spaniards;

it cut their connections with their settlements in western Florida around Pensacola.

Having now cleared the way, Oglethorpe planned a grand descent upon St. Augustine, that Spanish stronghold which Drake had once sacked and which Governor Moore in Queen Anne's War had attacked. Beginning in 1735, under Governor Manuel de Montiano's régime, the fortifications had been so greatly strengthened through the engineering skill of Arredondo that Oglethorpe was to have a much more difficult task than any commander who had preceded him. Now that he was commander-in-chief of the royal forces in both South Carolina and Georgia, Oglethorpe made a trip to Charleston to ask for aid. Though enthusiastic at the founding of Georgia and lending a helping hand to begin with, South Carolina had seen Georgia assume such a prominent part in the management of affairs in the southeastern country as to leave her somewhat smarting and jealous of this upstart. After much haggling Oglethorpe was given the promise of a regiment of 500 men and a further promise of 100 more later, but with insufficient artillery. Colonel Alexander Vanderdussen was made the commander of the South Carolinians. They were to be enlisted for only four months, and the promise of plunder was largely responsible for their going at all.

By the late spring of 1740 Oglethorpe was able to collect 900 regulars and provincial troops and 1,100 Indians with which to invade Florida. The whole force was to rendezvous at the mouth of the St. Johns, the South Carolinians and the Highlanders marching thence across country and Oglethorpe taking his forces by water. The British navy provided nine small vessels to make it possible for a quick descent on St. Augustine by land and water.

As they moved southward, detachments on May 10th seized Fort St. Diego with more than fifty prisoners and when they came to Fort Moosa, two miles from St. Augustine, the Spaniards evacuated it and retired into the city. Oglethorpe having already largely lost the element of surprise was to suffer further disappointment when the prearranged signal to the fleet to begin the attack, failed to produce results. On account of the shallowness of the bar at the harbor's edge and because of the presence of Spanish galleys, the fleet had been unable to play its part. With all his plans awry, Oglethorpe now settled down to a siege, hoping to starve out the garrison. Again he was doomed to disappointment. A Spanish flotilla was able to slip in to aid the fort, and a detachment of Spaniards made a sally out and cut to pieces a group of Highlanders caught off their guard at Fort Moosa. There was now nothing left for Oglethorpe to do but give up the siege.

It was a most melancholy debacle. What of hopes, hard luck and the Spaniards had left, was soon destroyed by diseases that arose out of the pestilential mid-summer climate. To add controversy to defeat, the South Carolina troops were charged with failure to play a manly part in the expedition, with, indeed, playing so insignificant a part as not to lose a single man in action. Actuated by no friendship for Georgia, the South Carolinians charged Oglethorpe with incompetency and with trying to belittle their commander Vanderdussen.

Just before Oglethorpe's failure at St. Augustine, Admiral Vernon had suffered a melancholy reverse in his attempt to take Cartagena, on the north coast of South America. Suffering defeat on land and sea, the British now became quiescent while the Spaniards prepared to take the offensive. Oglethorpe marched his dispirited and disease-ridden troops back northward, and at Frederica for the next two months he lay sick of a fever. He still maintained his southernmost outpost on Amelia Island and when Spanish vessels seeking to spy out the Georgia coast came too close he chased them back to St. Augustine.

Knowing well that the Spaniards were preparing to make a grand descent on Georgia to destroy her, Oglethorpe kept a sharp lookout to the southward and made every effort to strengthen his position. As the British, who gradually renewed their offensive, after the Cartagena defeat, in fruitless attacks in the West Indies, failed to heed Oglethorpe's call for support, he was left largely to his own resources. He strengthened his string of forts down the coast, maintained good relations with the Indians, and, in desperation, swallowing his pride, called on South Carolina for more troops. Thoroughly disgruntled the South Carolinians turned a deaf ear, forgetful of the fact that if the Georgia defenses did not hold, they, themselves, would be the next object of Spanish wrath. These dissensions the Spaniards had sensed, and they counted on them as a very important element in their success. Indeed, it was a most restricted and petty point of view on the part of South Carolina, and it showed no great grasp of imperial demands on the part of the British government. Oglethorpe was left alone in Georgia to meet a major offensive by the Spaniards.

There can be little doubt that the Spaniards expected nothing less than a smashing victory against Oglethorpe's small army, the utter destruction of Georgia, and the retreat of South Carolina to the northward. So sure were they that these victories were written in the future, that in their preparations they swept their West Indian stations for ships and troops, and Arredondo, the engineer, prepared a lengthy document to prove Spain's claims to the South Atlantic regions as far north as St. Helena Sound.

In the early summer they began their active preparations to descend upon Georgia. They collected an army and fleet in Havana, sailed for St. Augustine, and from this point proceeded up the coast in 50 vessels with 1,800 soldiers and 1,000 seamen.[1] They either reduced or ignored Oglethorpe's little forts on the way up to make their attack upon his little Frederica Verdun. On July 4, 1742, they stood off St. Simons Sound, preparing to land on the island. They ran by Fort St. Simon

[1] This force has been variously estimated from 33 vessels and 2,000 men to 56 vessels and 7,000 men. The figures accepted here are those given by Herbert E. Bolton in *The Debatable Land*, page 94.

without difficulty and landed a few miles up the inner passage toward Frederica. To prevent themselves from being cut off and captured, the garrison in Fort St. Simon spiked their guns and retreated up the island. The Spaniards marched in, took possession, and made preparations to follow the retreating Georgians to Frederica. The road which the Georgia regiment had cut through the center of the island from Fort St. Simon to Frederica became the center of Oglethorpe's strategy.

Now developed marching and counter-marching up and down this road, which ended in the battle of Bloody Marsh and the discomfiture and retreat of the whole Spanish expedition. On the 7th of July a force of Spaniards marched up this road to within a mile of Frederica, but before they were able to get clear of the woods and deploy in the open savanna, Oglethorpe at the head of his rangers and Highlanders attacked them, captured the commander and either killed or captured most of this force of 170 regulars and Indians. The remnant retreated, followed by Oglethorpe's Highlanders and others. When the Georgians reached an open glade, they concealed themselves, while Oglethorpe returned to Frederica to bring down reënforcements. Another Spanish detachment came up, discovered and attacked the ambushed Georgians, and put them to flight. But a group of Highlanders under lieutenants Southerland and Mackay suddenly executed a flank movement, got in the rear of the Spaniards, and ambushed another open glade about two miles from Fort St. Simon. The Spaniards on their return obligingly marched out into this open glade and stacked their arms, the better to rest from the excitement of their victory. Now the Highlanders opened fire upon them and quickly rushed out into the open and before the mêlée was ended they had killed or captured about 200 Spaniards. It came to be called the battle of Bloody Marsh, and though it was a minor engagement, it helped to unnerve the main Spanish force and led to its ultimate return to Florida.

Deciding to take immediate advantage of news which had

reached him that the Spaniards were torn with internal dissensions and jealousies, Oglethorpe marched down the island with 500 troops, practically his whole force, and attempted to surprise the enemy. These plans were completely frustrated by the desertion of a Frenchman who carried to the Spaniards news of the weakness of Oglethorpe's forces. The situation seemed desperate, when Oglethorpe invented a stratagem which undoubtedly had a part in the final withdrawal of the Spaniards. He set loose a Spanish prisoner with a letter written to the French deserter, indicating that the Frenchman was not a deserter but a spy. In the letter the Frenchman was instructed to lead the Spanish fleet up toward Frederica where masked batteries could better destroy it, and to induce the Spaniards to remain on St. Simons at least three more days, for by that time reënforcements of 2,000 infantrymen and six men-of-war would arrive.

The Spaniards were not so gullible that some of them did not think of this letter as a stratagem of Oglethorpe's; but after a council of war had discussed not only the possibilities of English reënforcements, but the difficulties of the terrain where the fighting must be carried on, the strong resistance that Oglethorpe was able to offer, and the approach of the hurricane season, they decided to take their ships and sail away.

The withdrawal of the Spaniards was a remarkable move. Without a doubt they outnumbered Oglethorpe's forces four to one, but it must be remembered that the Spanish force was a motely aggregation, made up of regulars, volunteers, Indians, and Negroes. There was great relief not only in Georgia but throughout the English colonies in America. But nothing could better show the separate and independent existence of the English colonies, one from another, than this War of Jenkins' Ear. While Georgia was on the point of being snuffed out, the rest stood off afar and looked on. Even South Carolina, whose turn was next, refused to send troops to repel this great invasion until the Spaniards had retreated. Then a boat-load came in great haste, which led a Georgian to observe bitterly that the South Carolinians came only "after the Spaniards had been chased quite out of the Colony." Yet the other English North American colonies seemed appreciative enough of Oglethorpe's efforts. Every governor from New York through North Carolina congratulated and thanked Oglethorpe for delivering the mainland from the Spaniards. George Whitefield, man of God, was greatly impressed with the Spanish withdrawal, and saw nothing short of divine interposition. "The deliverance of Georgia from the Spaniards," he declared, "is such as cannot be paralleled but by some instance out of the Old Testament."

Irrespective of how momentous and significant were the results of this war, it was made up of a great deal of grandiloquent marchings back and forth, much mismanagement, bad luck, and disappointment on the part of both sides, so much as to make it appear at times like a comic opera. This characteristic was evident at the time, at least to a Boston rhymester who wrote:

> "From Georgia to Augustine the General goes;
> From Augustine to Georgia come our foes;
> Hardy from Charleston to St. Simons hies,
> Again from thence to Charleston back he flies.
> Forth from St. Simons then the Spaniards creep;
> 'Say Children, Is not this your Play, Bo Peep'?"

The withdrawal of the Spaniards in July, 1742 was the last act of Spanish Florida in the drama of the War of Jenkins' Ear. Oglethorpe remained in Georgia another year, and in March of 1743 took a small force and went to the gates of St. Augustine to harass and stir up the Spaniards, but they refused to come out to fight, and Oglethorpe returned, never again to molest the Floridians.

As the Spaniards would not fight and there was no more war in Georgia, Oglethorpe left his regiment and the defense of the colony in the hands of William Horton and sailed away for England never to return. He had now spent ten years of his life in Georgia; he had nursed the colony from infancy through strength enough to beat back unaided the strongest attack the Spaniards could launch against it. Furthermore, there had not always been agreement and coöperation from the Trustees and the British government; and the neighboring South Carolina for whose protection Georgia had been planted had ceased to be neighborly, and instead had persisted in a controversy which was to stretch out its length through a pamphlet warfare. He had not been properly supported in the war by either the Trustees or the British government and a military debt of £12,000 was returned to him unpaid. A disgruntled officer brought nineteen charges against his moral and military character which were answered in a court martial the following year, to Oglethorpe's complete exoneration. In England other interests than Georgia engaged his attention: a wife, whom he took the year after his return, and another court of inquiry to quash unfounded charges of disloyalty to George II. His interest in the Trust faded and he left Parliament in 1754 to settle down, to become an intimate of the literary men of his day, to grow so old as to make people start unbelievable rumors concerning his age, and to make them wonder how a person could still be as old as he was and remain alive. He lived to see his Georgia become an independent state and a part of a greater independent nation.

The War of Jenkins' Ear by 1744 grew into a greater war which evolved from European rivalries and dynastic ambitions, known in Europe as the War of the Austrian Succession but among the English colonists of America as King George's War. France now came in to dispute with England, and military activities died down completely on the southern frontier as the war raged around Cape Breton and in Acadia. The conflict was ended in 1748 in the Treaty of Aix-la-Chapelle. The Georgia-Florida struggle, by this time half forgotten, like all

other problems that this bifurcated war raised up to settle, was
left to help provoke future wars. Not until 1763, in a treaty
ending another war, were the Georgia-Florida troubles settled
—settled now by England taking possession of Florida.

Now that the war was officially at an end, the Georgia regiment, which for the past half dozen years had had nothing to
do beyond train its eyes toward Florida, was disbanded and
sent home, whether back to England or to settle in the colony. Only one company was left for the defense of the colony,
and South Carolina, smarting under a régime which had made
her a military appendage of Georgia, sought to secure control
of the Georgia defenses, now that there were no enemies in
sight. Frederica grew up, flourished, and died with the making
and the ending of the War of Jenkins' Ear. When the regiment
departed, few people were left, and however much the Trustees
might try to make it a great commercial port, its fortifications
and houses began to crumble, and prematurely it took on an
old age which made of it a ruin.[2]

Though Georgia's infancy was shot through with war, there
were bound up in her life the other concerns of a normal existence—religion, education, land, labor, making a living, and
laws and government.

[2] What was left when the Revolution came was demolished by the British, and
with the coming of independence, when the legislature attempted to revive it,
Frederica would respond to no stimulus.

RUINS OF THE BARRACKS AT FREDERICA AS
THEY APPEARED IN 1851
B. J. Lossing, *Pictorial Field-Book of
the Revolution*, II. New York:
Harper & Brothers, 1860

Top left: HERNANDO DE SOTO, WHO WITH A THOUSAND FOLLOWERS MARCHED ACROSS GEORGIA IN 1540, LOOKING FOR GOLD. *Top right:* NICOLAUS LUDWIG, COUNT ZINZENDORF, WHO SENT THE FIRST MORAVIANS TO GEORGIA IN 1735. *Bottom left:* PEDRO MENÉNDEZ DE AVILÉS, THE FIRST WHITE RULER OF GEORGIA, WHO VISITED THIS REGION IN 1566. *Bottom right:* TOMO-CHI-CHI, AN OLD CREEK CHIEF, WHO MET OGLETHORPE WHEN HE LANDED AND WHO ACCOMPANIED HIM TO ENGLAND IN 1734.

GENERAL OGLETHORPE AS AN OLD MAN

George White, *Historical Collections of Georgia*. New York: Pudney &
Russell, 1855.

CHAPTER VI

A PECULIAR COLONY

GEORGIA WAS A philanthropy, a military colony, and a commercial adventure. All three purposes were served in the rules set up for establishing, governing, and developing it; but the experiment in philanthropy was primary with the Trustees and loomed largest. The other ideas were promoted as far as they helped or did not hinder the first.

This colony was designed to be different from all other British colonies ever set up. As it was an experiment with people, those people must be selected, and the conditions surrounding them must be controlled. In addition to the selection of the people, the other elements in the experiment chosen for regulation were the system under which the people should hold their land, who should perform the labor, what crops should be grown, and what beverages the people should drink.

As land was fundamental, the Trustees worked out a system of holding it which they considered vital to their experiment. In the first place, the land should not be settled in a haphazard fashion, which had characterized the uneven and sprawling growth of most of the other English North American colonies. Settlement should proceed in an orderly and compact fashion into each large tract set aside for the purpose, and to insure compactness no person in the experiment should control more than fifty acres. The communal plan, suggestive of the New England colonies, was established, whereby the people should be grouped into villages, where each person should own a town lot and a garden, and farming land not far away. If the experiment was to have a chance, these conditions must be stabilized, and to effect this, the land must not be held in absolute ownership, for otherwise the person could sell, mortgage, or lose his land to others, and the conditions of the experiment would be changed by the coming in of people not selected by the Trustees or by the concentration of more than fifty acres of land in the hands of one person. A further purpose to be served in life tenure would be a guarantee that people who had already failed in the economic struggle for existence should not do so again.

Additional land regulations permitted inheritance only through *tale male,* meaning descending to the eldest son. Where an owner had no son, the land reverted to the Trust at his death, but his heirs should be paid for the improvements made upon it. All landowners must clear ten acres within ten years after the grant and must plant upon it at least 100 mulberry trees. Ten years after the grant the owner was required to begin to pay two shillings a year quit rent, which was a source of revenue the King claimed for himself. Though the philanthropic experiment was aided first by these land rules, yet commercial purposes would be served, especially the silk business; and the defense of the colony would be promoted, for fifty-acre tracts of contiguous territory made a compact settlement easy to defend, and the rule against women inheriting the land always insured a fighter for each tract.

The establishing of Savannah carried out clearly this land system. A tract of twenty-four square miles, 15,360 acres, was set aside, sufficient to accommodate 240 families, with 3,360 acres reserved for commons, roads, streets, and for other public purposes. The part of the tract to be occupied by the city was laid off into wards of forty houses each and the ward was divided into tithings of 10 lots. The streets were wide, with squares at intervals for market-places. The town holdings of each family should be a building lot and a garden on the edge of town, both together making five acres; and beyond the limits of the town should be the remaining 45 acres of the fifty acre grant where the mulberry trees should be planted and the farming operations carried on.

When Savannah should fill up or when the Trustees should accede to the desires of colonists who did not wish to settle there, they would begin other settlements spreading out around the Savannah area. These were little counterparts of Savannah, with ambitious city plans like Savannah. Frequently ten families or more would start such a community, and soon there were such places as High-Gate, where a dozen French families were settled, Hamstead, a German community, Joseph's Town, a Scotch settlement, Abercorn, Thunderbolt, Skidaway Island, Fort Argyle, and the fort on Isle of Hope. Where a fort was not the principal purpose of the settlement, the military tinge was generally present in some small fortification.

Mindful of the cost of such a well-worked out experiment where all the people should be given their passage across, their land, their farm implements, and their keep until the first crop should be raised, the Trustees in the interest of practicality provided for another class of settlers, who were called adventurers and who should meet their own expenses in coming to Georgia. These people might have as much as 500 acres of land if they should bring over as many as ten white servants. That the experiment might not be allowed to suffer too much from this extraneous element, the adventurers were not allowed to sell their land, and must agree to clear 200 acres and plant on the tract 2,000 mulberry trees, and promise not to leave for three years. Besides a charge of a pound and a shilling for the grant when made, the adventurer after ten years was required to pay 20 shillings quit rent the hundred acres.

This part of the Trustees' plan made it possible for people of high estate to come to Georgia and become a part of the colony. Many took advantage of it, so that before the Trust was ten years old, as much land had been granted to adventurers as to charity settlers and thereafter the proportion became much greater. As the land the former secured lay outside the tracts set apart for the orderly development of the colony, the adventurers spread out up and down the rivers and coast-line. They particularly coveted the islands. Even in the case of these adventurers, the Trustees exercised rather closely their right of selection, and no person who was interested in secur-ing land for speculation was accepted. Though they might secure as much as 500 acres, the average amount obtained was 220 acres. Thus, the speculating zeal which had gripped people in the older colonies was allowed no sway in Georgia, and when Carolinians and Virginians sought to come into this new colony-in-the-making, they found the door closed to them. And so, it came about that during the first part of Georgia's exist-ence, her settlers were recruited almost exclusively from Europe.

The white servants, often called indentured servants, whom the adventurers were required to bring over, were held for only a term of service, generally from four to fourteen years, most commonly seven years; and when they gained their freedom they became a part of the permanent population of the colony if they chose to remain. If they agreed to stay four years, the Trustees allowed them 25 acres of land at first and later in-creased it to fifty, and their former masters were required to give them certain farming implements and other materials necessary for a start. The Trustees, just as anxious to exercise the power of selection over the servants as over any other people who should come to Georgia, resolved at the beginning "That no Servant be allowed to go with any Persons to Georgia, till they are seen and approv'd by the Board." The adventurers were not alone in possessing white servants; the Trustees brought them over on their own account to labor under over-seers, and ship captains were allowed to land approved servants in the streets of Savannah for sale to the highest bidder.

The system of indentured servants was largely a failure, for they were generally discontented, and they expressed their malevolence toward their masters by performing less labor than was necessary for their keep, by stealing, by setting fire to fields, and by running away to South Carolina. Recruited from people too poor to pay their way to America, most of these servants came from England, Wales, and Germany. This element in the Georgia population was very small, being an insignificant part of the half million of indentured servants who came to America before the Revolution.

Also, by a law of the Trustees, which set Georgia apart from all the other English settlements, African slavery was prohibited. In establishing this policy, the Trustees were actuated by no feeling of commiseration for the slave or abolition sentiment, which was to arise with great force a hundred years later. Oglethorpe, as director and later deputy governor of the Royal African Company, spread slavery and made money out of the trade; and although he had taken an unusual interest in the case of Job, a slave in Maryland and the son of an African king, and had helped to restore him to the jungles, he never had for the slave any of the philanthropic feeling which he showed toward debtors and other unfortunates.

There should be no slavery in Georgia because it would introduce an extraneous element wholly incompatible with the experiment. In any event, only the adventurers could have expected to own slaves, for naturally the charity settlers, who were unable to pay their passage to Georgia, could have had no sensible expectation that the Trustees would in addition to all their charity bestow upon them slaves. If for no other reason, these settlers should at least bestir themselves enough to work for their own living in this Georgia garden. And to allow the adventurers to possess slavery would by degrading labor accentuate the difference between the adventurer and charity settler and retard the day when both should occupy the same high plane. In addition, slaves would weaken the colony, for they could not become soldiers but would become an object for the Spaniards to entice away to Florida or whip up into a servile insurrection in Georgia. And, indeed, slaves could not be used in raising silk and making wine, toward which Georgia was to turn her principal efforts. So, the Trustees decreed that any slaves found in the colony should be disposed of for the benefit of the Trust, unless they had escaped from South Carolina, and then they would be restored if claimed within three months and all costs were paid.

A ruling made in the beginning, but elevated into a law in 1734, which became effective the following year, prohibited the importation of rum, gin, or brandy, or strong spirits under any other name. All such spirits found in Georgia must be spilled, and the person bringing them in should be fined £5 more than their value. The law did not apply to wines and beer. Strong liquors as an element in this Georgia experiment, the Trustees felt, would set up a reaction certain to produce slow decomposition or an explosion. The effects of rum in England were known to all; it had been a potent force in propelling many an Englishman into poverty or the debtor's prison. Now, who would be so foolish as to restore it to the recuperating Georgians, especially when Oglethorpe believed its effects in Georgia were more deadly than elsewhere? He declared that rum had slain some of his settlers soon after their arrival, and the Indians complained that it was flowing from Georgia into their country, producing disorders.

The industrial and commercial plan to which Georgia should conform was another peculiarity, which, however, had not been first tried in Georgia. Here was the garden of Eden in America if it were ever to be found, and here should be made to flourish the vine and the mulberry and all the various plants for whose products England was now paying tribute to foreign nations. Here would the silk business at last succeed, first tried in Virginia and driven out by tobacco, and next, in South Carolina to be dethroned by rice and indigo. Foolishly was this will-o'-the-wisp chased down the Atlantic coast, and now the Trustees expected to find it in Georgia. On their common seal was a design of silk-worms surrounded with the motto *Non Sibi Sed Aliis*—indeed, here was altruism with a silken center.

A public garden on the eastern extremity of Savannah, ten acres in extent, was laid out, and here would be the nursery for all those plants that were to make Georgia bloom and prosper; and to find them, an agent was appointed to go to Madeira, the West Indies, the northern part of South America, and to the ends of the earth. Wine-making and all the other exotic occupations that had been wished on Georgia failed one after another, before the silk business ultimately fell. Georgia was expected to produce all the silk England needed, saving her the necessity of importing £500,000 of it from foreign countries, to set 20,000 of her own people to raising it, and to afford employment to 20,000 more in England. Among the first settlers was Nicholas Amatis, a silk expert from Piedmont, who came to start the business. Oglethorpe, practical with all his philanthropy, confessed he had no great interest or faith in making out of Georgia a mulberry forest, yet he carried out the rules requiring the planting of mulberry trees and made presents of these trees to the Salzburgers.

These industrious Salzburgers soon became the chief silk-producers in the colony, supplying more than half of all sent out. In 1735 a small amount which they produced was taken to England and it attracted so much attention that the Queen had it made into a dress which she wore on special occasions. In 1750 the Salzburgers produced over 1,000 pounds of cocoons, and the next year there was erected in Savannah a filature where the cocoons were unwound. In 1764 more than 15,000 pounds of silk were delivered to the filature, over half being produced by the Salzburgers. About this time the silk business in Georgia reached its climax, and thereafter it steadily declined. It was pushed out by the unfriendliness of the climate, the high price of skilled labor, the withdrawal of the bounty that had been placed on silk, and the advent of rice planting and other activities. By the outbreak of the Revolution the filature had fallen into disuse, and the war itself destroyed most of the silk business that was left.

These chimerical and Utopian business notions of the Trustees and of the mercantilists had no chance of succeeding, and the longer they were pushed the less foodstuffs were produced and the nearer the colonists came to starving. So close to the verge of hunger were they in 1739, on the outbreak of the war with Spain, that Oglethorpe offered a bounty on corn and potatoes. During the first decade the colony was forced to rely largely on importations of foodstuffs from South Carolina and elsewhere. Cotton, on which Georgia was later to base her existence, was not raised at this time, though as early as 1738 the Salzburgers grew a few stalks amidst the frowns of the Trustees. Apart from their fruitless efforts in exotic occupations, the people produced potash and rice, dug the native roots, sawed lumber and made staves for barrels, and engaged in cattle raising and fur trading.

The last two occupations were the most lucrative in early colonial times until the rise of the plantation system elevated rice planting into a major industry. Securing their first livestock from the South Carolinians, the Georgians began grazing their cattle up the Savannah, down the coast, and into the interior, and soon found themselves pushing uncomfortably close against the Indian frontiers. They had their cattle brands and their round-ups, suggestive of a business which was a century and more later to assume great proportions west of the Mississippi.

The Indian trade in furs was all-absorbing with many people. Here was easy money and exciting adventure. The fur trade loomed large throughout all America in colonial times, and long before Georgia had been conceived, the South Carolinians were active in this business far to the westward of the Savannah. When they were helping to promote the settlement of Georgia, the South Carolinians did not realize that they were promoting a strong rival in this business. One of the only three laws that the Trustees ever passed related to the Indian trade, and it provided for such regulations which to them seemed

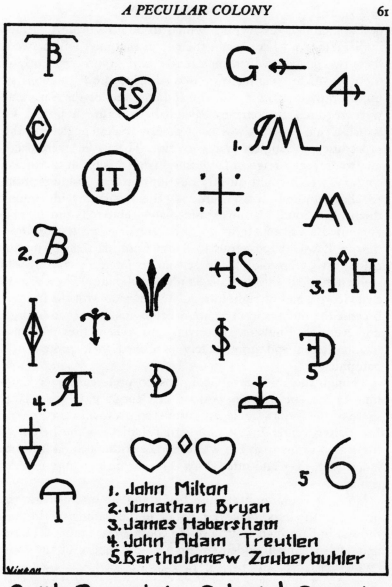

1. John Milton
2. Jonathan Bryan
3. James Habersham
4. John Adam Treutlen
5. Bartholomew Zouberbuhler

Cattle Brands in Colonial Georgia

desirable and necessary, but which to South Carolina seemed intolerable. And here began the rift in the good will between these two peoples, which manifested itself so inconveniently in the days of the Spanish war. According to the regulations set up, all people trading with the Indians west of the Savannah were required to come to Savannah to secure a license for which a charge of £5 was exacted. Any traders neglecting this procedure were subject to a £100 fine. These rules were necessary to prevent a reign of lawlessness from arising in the Indian country, which could quickly develop through dishonest traders cheating the Indians, murdering them, and carrying among them rum. South Carolina immediately objected, and in 1736 appointed a committee to go to Savannah to protest to Oglethorpe. It was preposterous to South Carolina that an upstart colony two years old should set out to interfere with an old well-established business of South Carolinians. They argued that Georgia had no right to regulate the trade with the Indians, because the Indians were a nation, belonging neither to Georgia nor even to England. Receiving no relief, they returned to Charleston and immediately published their protest in a pamphlet.[1]

Though the rules gave Georgians no preference over Carolina traders, the strategic position of Georgia gave her a large share of the Indian traffic. Augusta soon grew into the greatest fur-trading center in the Southern colonies. In the height of the season as many as 600 white traders with 2,000 pack horses laden with deer and otter skins came here to engage in their traffic.

Nothing could indicate the beginning or better mark the growth of the importance of Georgia in the trading world than the rise in Savannah in 1744 of the commercial house of Harris and Habersham, founded by Francis and James of the same

[1] One of these pamphlets is in the De Renne Collection of the University of Georgia Library. It is entitled *Report of the Committee Appointed to examine into the Proceedings of the People of Georgia, with respect to the Province of South Carolina, and the Disputes subsisting between the Two Colonies.*

names respectively. They provided the first organized exporting and importing business for the colony, and through their efforts Savannah became a port in reality, for up to this time Charleston had served Georgia very largely in this capacity. They were the first to charter vessels to carry away Georgia products, which at this time were tar, pitch, staves, rice, and deer skins. Their trade began with New York, Boston, and Philadelphia, but by 1749 vessels were sailing directly from Savannah to Europe.

Trade and economic development could not progress far before some form of money would be required. Apart from a few copper coins and, perhaps, a Spanish milled dollar now and then, the medium of exchange was a form of indebtedness called sola bills, which being peculiar to Georgia carried little respect and less acceptance outside. These were promises to pay made by the Trustees to anyone to whom they owed money. These bills could be passed on indiscriminately as money in the colony and would be redeemed when presented to the office of the Trustees in London. They were in denominations from £1 to £20. Oglethorpe was given the right to issue these sola bills in paying Trustee debts. When the King took control in Georgia, all of these bills which had not already been redeemed, were called in. Thereafter, in addition to some Spanish, Dutch, and English coins, provincial paper money made its appearance.

CHAPTER VII

THE UTOPIA FAILS

THE RUTS THAT nature had made for the people of the eighteenth century were so enticing that those who had been placed on high ground longed to return. Georgians did not want to be different from other people, and when philanthropic reformers sought to make their colony a Utopia, the Georgians became uncommonly discontented.

Although they liked wines and beer, they wanted to drink rum like other good Englishmen. Grog shops grew up on all -sides, making little or no attempts to disguise themselves. It seemed everyone drank rum, irrespective of the law, and when those who sold it were prosecuted, no jury could be found which would convict them. So completely did the jury system break down in this connection that the Trustees gave permission to try such cases without a jury; but this dispensation so obligingly given seems never to have been accepted, for one observer reported that "from high to low the magistrates drink it and are unwilling to enquire what others use it." So plentiful was rum that it flowed into the Indian country in such quantities as to cause some chiefs of the Chickasaws and Cherokees to complain in 1739 that "the smallpox and rum carried up last winter by unlicensed traders, had slain near one thousand warriors and hunters among them." South Carolina, which resented the rum law little less than the law licensing Indian traders, attempted to violate it by carrying rum up the Savannah in boats to land it on the Georgia side. Georgia in seizing this rum and spilling it out won additional ill-will from the South Carolinians.

The Trustees, who through fear of too much control by the

English government, had passed only three laws, now discovered when they attempted to get the rum law repealed that even three laws were too many for them to have passed. The Board of Trade objected to certain details regarding the repeal. Nevertheless, the Trustees in 1742 sanctioned the disregard of the law, which no one would obey, and allowed the importation of rum if it were paid for by the products of the colony. The trade in rum was brought about largely by a well-organized group of Savannahians with much support in other parts of the colony.

Many of the colonists were bitter against the prohibition of slavery and the peculiar land system which prevailed, and they also did not like the form of government to which they had been treated. They had a right to question the wisdom of the policy of the Trustees and secure its change if they could, but the lengths to which they went in their bitter complaints and their ceaseless attacks on Oglethorpe and the Trustees, marked them down as malcontents unappreciative of the favors they had received from the Trustees and disregardful of the honest intentions of that body. The malcontents broke out with greatest virulence at the beginning of the Spanish war, a time when Oglethorpe needed the undivided support of his colony, and many of the Georgians expended their strength opposing the Trustees while Oglethorpe and his English regiment and Indian allies fought the Spaniards.

They were disillusioned about this Georgia "garden of Eden," and they blamed the Trustees for all their ills. No one seemed to be prospering; the land was not fertile; there was little silk raised and no wine; rice and corn were grown only in small quantities, and cotton and indigo were curiosities; the olive trees died, and all the exotic plants which the Trustees' garden was to afford withered away; there was malaria in the swamps and the sun was hot; few people were coming to the colony and many were leaving; the people would not work for the land was not theirs; they did not like to plant mulberry trees; and they wanted more rights in the government.

The fight for slavery was carried on with great intensity. Many Georgians did not see why they should be forced to work in the hot sun, while across the Savannah the South Carolinians enjoyed their leisure while their slaves labored. The fight for slavery centered in Savannah. The Salzburgers, an industrious folk who had never seen a black man until they had left their European home, feared the Negroes and opposed the importation of slaves. The Highlanders, also a self-reliant and hardy people, objectd to slaves, and fearing nothing, placed their opposition on high humanitarian grounds which the rest of the world was not to attain for a century. They declared that slaves were a curse to the people who owned them, and that no one had the right to reduce people to slavery. Without waiting for the policy to be changed, many Georgians began to bring in slaves by stealth, and if apprehended, they returned them to the South Carolinians from whom they had hired them. Emboldened by the success of their plan, instead of hiring them for a few years, they hired them for a century and paid the full purchase price.

The land system was the source of unending complaint until it was changed. The people objected to quit rents, which were not due for ten years and which in actuality they never paid throughout the whole period of the Trust. They also objected to the rule against a woman inheriting land and, therefore, the loss of improvements on the land where there was no son. The Trustees soon became lenient on both these points, sometimes allowing a daughter to inherit the land and at other times paying for the improvements. The malcontents did not want the land divided into a small city lot, a garden nearby, and another tract farther away in the country. Also, they felt that fifty acres was too small, and that the land should be held in fee simple.

In 1738 the malcontents organized themselves for a campaign against the policy of the Trustees. One hundred and twenty-one Savannahians, including some of the magistrates, signed a petition demanding rum, slaves, and the absolute ownership of the land. The Trustees answered the petition with an expression of surprise at this amazing evidence of ingratitude, denied the petition, and dismissed the magistrates who had signed it. Oglethorpe strongly opposed the petitioners, and advised the Trustees not to grant it, observing that "The idle ones are indeed for Negroes. If the petition is countenanced the province is ruined." So bitter were the malcontents, headed by Pat Tailfer, against Oglethorpe and the other Trustees that they wrote a book against them with a mock dedication to Oglethorpe. They called the book *A True and Historical Narrative of the Colony of Georgia in America* and they carried it over to Charleston where it was published in 1741. Referring to Oglethorpe, they declared, "Under the influence of our Perpetual Dictator we have seen something like *Aristocracy, Oligarchy,* as well as the *Triumvirate, Decemvirate and Consular Authority* of famous Republics which have expired many years before us." In effect they became Spanish allies, as they spread the false report of Spanish victories.

Having decided to cease petitioning the Trustees, the malcontents determined to ignore them altogether and appeal directly to the British government. They sent Thomas, the wayward son of the venerable Secretary of Georgia, William Stephens, who laid their complaints directly before Parliament. This body gave a hearing in 1742, and upholding the Trustees, forced Stephens to fall upon his knees and receive the reprimand of the House.

As the Trustees saw their policy so strongly, so consistently, and so continuously opposed, they began to weaken in their insistence on it. Undoubtedly the colony was not prospering. Some critics averred in 1740 that it was reduced to one-sixth of its former population and that it was "in a starving and despicable condition." Having already receded on the rum prohibition, they next gave way on slavery. The demands for it

had become widespread, and when men like James Habersham, George Whitefield, and even the Salzburgers advised
the Trustees to grant slavery, they did so. Bolzius wrote in
1748, "Things being now in such a melancholy state, I must
humbly beseech your Honors not to regard any more our
or our friends' petitions against Negroes." The next year the
Trustees set up a system of rules permitting slavery and providing for its regulation. It was allowed in a limited manner
only and was tied into the system of indentured servitude. For
every four slaves, there must be one white male servant. The
planter should not have unlimited power over his slaves. He
must register them in the colonial records, see that they did not
work on the Lord's Day, cause them to attend Christian service, teach them the obligations of marriage and allow no marriages between the races, prohibit profane swearing among
them, and see that one female for every four slaves should be
taught how to wind silk. Thus, in their recession, the Trustees
still held partly to their ideas of philanthropy and silk.[1] Slavery, once let in, spread out over the land and became one of
the chief interests of the people. Under it the people grew
strong, but in the institution were the germs of destruction
of the very civilization it was building up.

The land system was the next stone to fall from the arch
which the Trustees had sought to construct in the New World.
The Trustees wrought the changes by degrees, first giving up
the *tale male* principle. The people, anxious for a complete
change at once, expressed great anger when news was received
that only this part had been changed. One Savannahian on
hearing the news, said that the whole announcement seemed
to be made up of nothing but *tales* and *males,* and that all the
lawyers in London could not make him understand it, and
another observed that these two words had been used so often
that the author should be committed to Bedlam for lunacy.

[1] The next year the Trustees incorporated these rules into a law and sent it to
the Privy Council for approval, but there is no evidence that it was ever acted
upon.

The Trustees' laws and regulations, like all others, were much more severe on paper than in action. Constantly violating them, people in Georgia built up estates far beyond the fifty acres allowed. Through inheritance, purchase, or a loosening system of grants, some of them secured as much as 2,000 acres. Finally in 1750, the peculiar rules were completely removed, and the people were permitted to buy and sell as they pleased.

The outbreak of Mary Musgrove was not a part of the Trustees' plan in Georgia, but it came as near wrecking the colony as any part of their mistaken philanthropy. Mary, after the death of her husband John Musgrove, had married Jacob Matthews, who also had died, but not before he with Mary's support had attempted unsuccessfully to secure a land grant and money from the Trustees. Then she married Thomas Bosomworth, a dishonest and unworthy man, who made a failure as minister to the colony and then sought to enrich himself by disrupting it. Taking advantage of Mary's position among the Creek Indians, he induced them to grant him the three reserved islands, St. Catherines, Ossabaw, and Sapelo. Then getting the Creeks to declare Mary their queen, he and Mary brought to the outskirts of Savannah in 1749 a menacing army of Indians to demand that the colony grant him the salary which Oglethorpe had promised Mary, but which he had neglected to pay. Only by the quick action of Noble Jones in calling out the militia was Savannah saved from destruction and the whole colony from great inconvenience. Balked in these efforts the Bosomworths carried on their fight for the next ten years both in Georgia and in England, until finally they forced a settlement which gave them St. Catherines Island, where they had long lived, and £2,100 in money. This was the most persistent and longest drawn out of the troubles that beset colonial Georgia.

Though land, slaves, rum, and Indian troubles played a great and somewhat devastating part in the lives of the people, there were other interests of a more constructive nature which engaged their attention. There were children to be educated, orphans to be cared for, and souls to be saved.

The Trustees, though interested in establishing schools, left the matter largely in the hands of the Georgians. They aided by making grants of money occasionally, while the S. P. C. K. and the S. P. G. took a more direct interest by rather regularly paying the salaries of the school masters. There was little effort made to set up schools outside of Savannah and the Salzburger settlements. One of the first schools established was at Irene, on an island about five miles above Savannah. Here the Moravians began educating Indian children in 1735 and continued the work until 1740, when they moved to Pennsylvania and the Indians went to the Spanish war. Here the Rev. Benjamin Ingham taught for two years, acquired the Indian language, and began writing a Creek grammar. In Savannah, Charles Delamotte opened a school where he not only taught the children to read, write, and "cast accounts," but also instructed them in the catechism. After Delamotte departed, John Dobell continued the school into a permanent institution, and it was ultimately made free to all. The Salzburgers began early to instruct their children. Christopher Ortman taught at Ebenezer for a time; but failing to please, he was dismissed and before long became an object of charity. After the Spanish war, John Ulrich Driesler set up as school master at Frederica; but he died within a year, and the town itself nearly disappeared.

In reality a school, though called an orphanage, was the institution at Bethesda, about a dozen miles from Savannah. Here was one of the most successful and satisfactory developments in colonial Georgia. It was the product of George Whitefield and James Habersham, two Englishmen who came to Georgia in 1737 and 1738, respectively. They were convinced before leaving England that Georgia needed such an institution, and although Whitfield came as a churchman to care for the religious needs of Savannah, he was soon more interested in the orphanage. Leaving Georgia the year after his arrival he returned to England, there to receive full ordination in the church and to raise money for his new venture. Receiving a 500 acre tract from the Trustees for the orphanage, Habersham remained in Georgia to gather together the children, instruct them, and build the orphans' house. Thereafter until 1744, when he developed the trading house of Harris and Habersham, he labored with these children, all of whom were not orphans, instructing them in religion, in learning, and in vocational subjects. Whitefield spent a great deal of his time travelling over England and America raising money, and finally was overtaken by death in Newburyport, Massachusetts. Besides the contributions he received throughout the world he secured an income for the orphanage from a plantation he purchased in South Carolina, where he could use slave labor.

Whitefield in 1764 tried to convert the orphanage into a college, as there was no such institution south of the College of William and Mary in Virginia. He petitioned the colony for 2,000 acres of land, on which he would place more slaves to supplement an income already as great as £1,000 some years. He would call the school Bethesda College in the Province of Georgia. The colony was agreeable, but the English government insisted on conditions which Whitefield refused to meet, and so the charter was never granted. Balked in this far-sighted move, Whitefield turned to developing it into an academy similar to the one Benjamin Franklin was promoting in Pennsylvania.

In his will Whitefield bequeathed the whole establishment to Selina, Countess Dowager of Huntingdon, an English lady, with the injunction that she turn it into a college; but before she was able to act lightning destroyed the building, and the Revolution soon made further progress impossible. After her death, Georgia diverted the property to a board of thirteen trustees, who continued the orphanage until 1808 when fire and hurricane destroyed it again. What was left was sold and the proceeds were turned to Savannah charity and education, and the orphanage was not revived until 1854, when the Union Society, a philanthropic organization which had arisen in 1750, assumed control.

In any undertaking so shot through with philanthropy as Georgia was, religion must inevitably play an important part. Though the Georgians were fit objects of missionary zeal and labor, the Indians in the early days of Georgia played even a bigger part in the missionaries' imaginations of what could be accomplished. On account of this divided purpose, the multiplicity of peoples who made up Georgia, the impractical men who came as missionaries, and the general perversity of human nature, it must be recorded that the work of the church in colonial Georgia was little less than a failure.

There was religious liberty in the colony as long as everyone remained a Christian and did not accept Roman Catholicism, but the Trustees and the organized religious agencies like the S. P. G. aided only the Church of England. Throughout the whole period of the Trustees, about £7,500 was spent on religion, which resulted materially in a religious structure being finished in Savannah in 1750 and a church or two among the Salzburgers; but spiritually the mass of the people seemed to be as perverse as ever. The succession of ministers to Georgia was hurried. First came Henry Herbert with the original cargo, who stayed a few weeks and died on his way back; then came Samuel Quincy, who resigned in 1735 and returned sick and dispirited; the next year came the Wesleys, John and Charles, like babes in the wilderness, the one, missionary to Savannah and the Indians, and the other, secretary to Oglethorpe, minister at Frederica, and Secretary of Indian Affairs. Charles, well-meaning but wholly unsuited for the rough surroundings, remained in Georgia less than three months. So tactless was he and so critical of everything he saw, that in less than a week he had fallen out with Oglethorpe and with most of the population of Frederica, and in a fit of despondency cried out, "I would not spend six more days in the same manner for all Georgia."

John remained longer and developed a correspondingly more bitter experience. He was opposed to remaining in Savannah, for he wanted to go among the noble savages of the wilderness to save their souls. Dissatisfied from the beginning, he fell in love with a parishioner, asked the Moravians what to do about it, and they after casting lots, advised Wesley to think no more of it. He incurred the ill-will of the rulers in Savannah, who indicted him on ten counts and allowed a suit for damages of £1,000. Bewildered, dispirited, and disgusted, Wesley, after repeatedly seeking to clear his name in a trial, fled Savannah by night in 1737, and returned to England.

William Norris came next, to fall out with Oglethorpe, and to stay "till vice got the victory," returning in 1741 under a cloud; then William Metcalf started for Georgia and dying on the way was succeeded by Christopher Orton, who arrived in time to die the next year. The next minister appointed was too practical to be religious, and too troublesome, dishonest, and grasping to remain as minister more than a year. This person was Thomas Bosomworth, who married Mary Musgrove and became so intent on enriching himself even to the disruption of the colony, that the problem he developed was not to be settled for years to come. Next and last in the hierachy under the Trustees came the good and gentle Swiss parson, Bartholomew Zouberbuhler, who was the most sensible and successful of all who served the Lord and Georgia.

Just as rum, slaves, and full ownership of land had been withheld from the Georgians, so was the government likewise. Though the government meant less to them than these other concerns, their complaints at times were loud enough to make it seem more important. The government of Trustee Georgia was elementary in the extreme; there was not even a person in charge who was called governor, nor a person acting under definite instructions of the Trustees. As Oglethorpe was present for most of the first ten years, he was looked upon as the head, and did exercise general civil supervision until the colony became embroiled in the Spanish war.

The Trustees had been so intent on the Utopian social experiment that they had neglected to study governmental needs; and they never learned until the last year of their control that they should give the people power, that they themselves should cease trying to control a situation about which they knew very little, and that so poor were their colonial advisers that the more they reported the less the Trustees knew. The government set up was designed for Savannah only, and as little settlements grew up elsewhere the Savannah government was extended over them if they were near, like Abercorn or Joseph's Town; but if they were far away like Ebenezer, the government was whatever the group selected, whether it be by ministers casting lots to learn the Lord's will or no government at all. The Savannah government was not set up until Oglethorpe had decided that he had the settlement well established. On July 7, 1733, he gave up his complete patriarchal sway and set up the rule the Trustees had provided. In this government, the people voted for nothing or no one; they were children and should take whatever was given them. This was unique among all the English colonies in America. The sum total of the establishment was a general court, consisting of three judges, called bailiffs, and a recorder. There were a few constables or conservators of the peace. That was all the government there was; but there were duties for it to perform, for people quarreled and fought and got into debt again and were thrown into prison, even in this land which was to abolish debt. But there were no lawyers, as it was contemplated that Georgia should be "a happy, flourishing colony . . . free from that pest and scourge of mankind called lawyers."

Some of those in authority were untrained, unlettered, cantankerous, and jealous of the others. To add to their dignity, the bailiffs were later given purple gowns trimmed in furs, a mace worth $500 to preserve order, and a seal worth $150 to impress their authority. Here was ample room for tyranny, and the people had reason to complain of it, John Wesley among the chiefest. The most unscrupulous of the bailiffs was Thomas Causton, whose authority was greatly increased by the fact that he was the Trustees' storekeeper, a position which made it possible for him to starve into submission those whom he disliked, for he could withhold from the poor and set exorbitant prices for those able to buy. His imperious and tyrannical terrorizations as a bailiff and his dishonesties as the public storekeeper, brought him finally to a day of reckoning before the Trustees in England, and while returning to Georgia in 1746 for evidence which he claimed would clear his name, he died at sea.

In 1737 the Trustees added another cog to their governmental machine, by appointing William Stephens secretary to the colony, to look after the records in Georgia and report all the details in the government of the colony that the Trustees might want to know. Otherwise he was without power.

When Frederica had been set up in 1735, the Trustees gave it a government similar to that in Savannah; and in 1741 when the southern part of the colony had grown populous and important with its soldiers and its war, they divided Georgia into two parts with Savannah and Frederica as the centers. Now, each part should have a government of its own, consisting of a president and four assistants. They really had little power, outside of being a court of appeals for the town courts. As the war was on when the Frederica division had been designated, it was not organized during the struggle, and at the end of the war in 1743 the two-county idea was given up and the whole government was centered in Savannah.

In 1741 Stephens had been made president of the Savannah county, and in 1743 when Oglethorpe returned to England and Frederica County was abolished, Stephens became head of the whole colony. From then on almost to the end of the colony under the Trustees he remained the chief official in Georgia. In 1751 having grown old and feeble, he asked to be relieved. The Trustees, recognizing his long and faithful service, granted his request and put into the office of the presidency Henry Parker, who had been a bailiff in early Savannah, and then an assistant under Stephens. The Trustees at this time appointed to the office of Secretary James Habersham, the orphanage builder and the merchant.

The year before they gave up their charter the Trustees decided to test out the Georgians with a little more government. They knew that the King would automatically fall heir to Georgia in 1753, and should they give up the colony in a condition void of all evidences of self-government, they might be considered as suggesting a continuation of such a situation. They also felt that South Carolina, who had already begun to show her desire to get back that land beyond the Savannah which had once been hers but was now Georgia, would have less chance of destroying the colony, if it should be granted more government. So an assembly was called in 1751 in Savannah, to be attended by delegates in varying numbers from all the towns and groups of families in the country as large as ten. They had no authority to pass laws, but only to make reports on their respective parts of the colony, make suggestions for the Trustees, and debate measures for the betterment of the colony. They met with Francis Harris as speaker, and recommended among other things that Savannah should have a new wharf and that ships should not dump ballast into the river. They also asked that the charter be renewed to prevent South Carolina from annexing the colony and that the people be given the right to make their own laws.

Though the Trustees did not accept all the recommendations made to them, they were well pleased with this first experiment in the direction of popular government. They made preparations to have the assembly meet the following year, and better to control the membership and set standards to be met, still thinking in terms of silk, they decided that no one should serve who did not have 100 mulberry trees growing and produce fifteen pounds of silk yearly on each fifty acres of land he possessed. Another act of the Trustees was to carry out the recommendation of the assembly to organize the militia. All people owning 300 acres of land were made cavalrymen, who must appear at each muster, mounted. All other able-bodied men belonged to the infantry. In June, 1751 the first military review was held, in Savannah, with Noble Jones as commander, when about 220 infantrymen paraded. As the defense of the colony was now in her own hands since the disbanding of Oglethorpe's regiment, the militia organization was doubly important.

As was their custom, the Trustees asked Parliament in 1751 for an appropriation to help maintain Georgia. Having already done much more for Georgia than it had ever done for any other American colony, Parliament refused to give further help. The King was then approached for aid, but the answer was returned that Georgia should get no further help until the Trustees gave up their charter. As the Trustees had a year of official life left, they entered into negotiations with the King's agents and agreed to give up their charter at once, surrendering it June 23, 1752.

There was much anxiety among Georgians about this time over the ultimate disposition of the colony. They sought to have the charter renewed, for fear that the King might give them a less desirable government, or what was infinitely worse in their eyes, that South Carolina might swallow up the colony. The Trustees were properly watchful, and before they surrendered their rights in Georgia, they secured the promise of a separate colonial status for the Georgians.

The Georgia experiment had failed, but enough had been salvaged to be handed over to the King to make possible a permanent colony. Every distinctive feature had been abandoned, before the Trustees finally gave up their charter; and had it lasted much longer the Trustees, themselves, who one after another had been losing interest, would have faded away. After the first decade people had shown little concern and had quit giving money for Georgia.

Georgia had never been a distinctive debtor colony. The total number of people who came over on the charity of the Trustees was 2,122, of whom 1,026 were foreign Protestants. And charity settlers did not necessarily mean debtors; as previously noted, probably not a dozen had been in jail for debt. In fact, it had never been a distinctive charity colony, for not half the people who came to Georgia came at the expense of the Trust, and it has been estimated that two-thirds of the charity colonists left. The population of the colony under the Trust fluctuated widely. During the first six years, about 5,000 people came to Georgia, but with the violent discontent that broke out around the time of the Spanish war, so many left that the colony became almost extinct in the early 1740's. As the experiment was gradually given up with the coming of rum, slaves, and the ownership of land, the colony began to gain strength, so that when it was handed over to the King, there were more than 2,000 white people and about 1,000 slaves. Yet twenty years of effort on the part of the Trustees settled only 153,000 acres—an area about as large as a tract fifteen miles square. Outside of the first few years of the colony's existence, the greatest growth came during the last two years, after slavery and the ownership of land had been permitted. In fact, during the negotiations of the Trustees with the King and after the colony had been given up, but before it had been transferred, land was granted so rapidly as to suggest that the Trustees were trying to grant away as much of the land as possible before the King should have a chance to assume control. Incidentally, the Trustees were showing consideration for a great many of their friends in Georgia who, they believed, deserved this reward. All the members of some families, including minors, were granted 500 acres each. During the year 1752, 106 people were given 500 acre grants, 55 were given 100 acre grants, and 41 received 50 acres. There were various other amounts given, such as eight people receiving 800 acres each, and fourteen receiving 200 acres each. Nearly 75,000 acres of land were granted away this year.

The Trustees had never ceased to regard with suspicion royal authority, for in developing Georgia they had a purpose different from what King and Parliament wanted. Hence it was that they never designated a governor for Georgia, because such an official must meet the approval of the King; instead they allowed Oglethorpe to act for ten years in that capacity, though never in name, and after him they appointed presidents to rule Georgia. Furthermore, the Trustees passed only three laws, for laws also must be approved by the King; instead, they governed by rules and regulations, which needed no royal approval. In fact, the Trustees had sought to set up a Georgia which had all but disappeared by the time they gave up their charter.

So King and Parliament were now confronted with the task of re-founding Georgia, a Georgia that was to be after the pattern of other British colonies on the Atlantic seaboard, the Georgia which lasted and grew into a state in the American Union. This new Georgia was not the colony which knew Oglethorpe, and Oglethorpe showed no interest in this new departure—though it was much less a departure from what he had wanted than from the Utopia which the Trustees had planned. The "Father of Georgia" had been dead a year before the *Gazette of the State of Georgia,* June 8, 1786, recorded his passing, in seven words: "General Oglethorpe, died August last, aged 103," in which both the date of his death and his age were misstated. Actually he died on June 30, 1785, and he had lived only 89 years. But as Georgia grew older and more

reminiscent it delighted to recall its heroic days under Oglethorpe, not the period of royal control under the King's governors, whose "mighty deeds" had been discredited by the
Revolution. So, Oglethorpe, who began as the "Father of
Georgia," a hundred years later was wearing that title again,
perhaps nevermore to be deprived of it.

CHAPTER VIII

GEORGIA BECOMES A ROYAL PROVINCE

KING GEORGE II was not puzzled over what he would do with Georgia. The English government was too practical to attempt any further experimenting; neither would it grant any more colonies to William Penns or Lord Baltimores. And above all, it would set up no self-governing colonies like Rhode Island and Connecticut with which to be bothered. Georgia should be a royal province like Virginia or New York, and the King would manage it to suit himself.

Georgia was now to pass from a mere settlement which could scarcely be called a colony into a province with all the governmental machinery which any other royal colony had. The pattern already existed and with a few changes it should be made to fit Georgia. There were to be a governor, a general assembly, and courts; and now for the first time would Georgia learn what a fully organized government was like, and for the first time have a part in it.

Never before had Georgia had a governor, for Oglethorpe had had no title and those to follow him under the Trust had been called presidents. The governor being the civil ruler and the military commander of all forces on land and water bore the grandiloquent title, "Captain-General and Governor-in-Chief of His Majesty's Province of Georgia, and Vice-Admiral of the Same." He was appointed by the King and stayed only as long as the King desired. As for his powers, he could convene, prorogue, adjourn, and dissolve the general assembly and veto their acts; he could appoint all officers not elected by the people or designated by the Crown; he presided over the court of appeals; and he controlled the granting of land.

Next in importance was a group of twelve men, appointed by the King, and called the Royal Council. They had a mixture of powers and duties unlike any body in America today. They advised the governor as a sort of privy council or cabinet, they served as the court of appeals, and they sat as the upper house of the general assembly.

The lower house was known as the Commons House of Assembly, and consisted of nineteen men, elected by the people. Any law passed by the general assembly not only could be vetoed by the governor, but it could be vetoed by the King. Here for the first time the people of Georgia were given a part in the government. Anyone owning 50 acres of land might vote for an assemblyman, and anyone owning 500 acres of land might serve as an assemblyman, if he could secure the election. These qualifications were not hard to meet, as land was easy to obtain; and yet those who lived in the towns and made their living there in businesses and who did not want to be bothered with owning 50 acres of land in order to vote and 500 to hold a seat in the assembly complained much at these qualifications. Later the law was changed to allow city dwellers to vote if they paid a tax on property equal in value to 50 acres of land, and to hold seats in the assembly if they paid a tax on property worth £300. Also the *viva voce* method of voting, used in the beginning, was changed to the ballot.

A Georgian might go through life without having any dealings or great concern with the governor, the council, or the Commons House of Assembly; but few could hope to escape the courts, for here their fundamental rights were guarded. Below the court of appeals, which was made up of the governor and the council, were the general court, consisting of a chief justice and three associates, a court of admiralty, and minor courts held by the local justices of the peace, called courts of conscience. For the common man these last-named courts were the most important, for here all his petty disputes were settled, and the justices, likely unlearned in the law, used the rule of their conscience. Georgia was largely a counterpart of England in the law and justice dealt out.[1] Although there were courts, Georgia had been a blessed land, so simple in its life and structure, as not to need lawyers. But the year that brought in the new government, brought also the first of the lawyers, and within five years they had multiplied so fast that they were important enough to be referred to as "the bar."

Though the King secured Georgia in 1752, he was not ready to assume control for two years. During this interregnum the Trust officers, at the behest of the King, continued to rule the land. William Stephens, who had given up the presidency in 1750 to Henry Parker, two years later had died at the age of eighty, and was buried in Georgia soil—a former member of Parliament and a loyal officer of the Trustees. Parker also soon died, and Patrick Graham became the president, and it was he who handed the colony over to the first royal governor.

The chief officials of the King's new government were Capt. John Reynolds, governor, William Clifton, attorney general, William Grover, a graduate of Oxford University, chief justice, and James Habersham, secretary. The King, still considering Georgia a military province, had picked an officer in his navy to be the first governor. Reynolds, true to his calling, came to Georgia on a man-of-war, and was received in Savannah with great rejoicing, for the people now believed that they were about to enter into a new life.

Reynolds was indeed entering into a new life, and bold was he to attempt it; for one long versed in politics might well have hesitated. Here was a new government to be instituted from top to bottom, an assembly must be convened and tamed, the Indians must be weaned away from the ingratiating French, and an eye must be kept on the southern border to note what the Spaniards were doing. Yet no violent break of a fundamental nature was to be made with the past. The property of

---

[1] Some of the details of this governmental scheme were not developed until after the government had been set up and the general assembly was in operation.

the people still remained their own with all grants of land made by the Trustees confirmed; but the land system was somewhat changed. Now the quit rents would be two shillings the hundred acres and, unlike in the days of the Trustees, they must be paid, and for every 100 acres of land owned five acres must be cleared.

The first assembly met in Savannah in January, 1755, and after some turbulence was soon grinding out laws, and one of the first it passed provided punishment for anyone denying the validity of those laws. It reorganized the militia, provided for roads and bridges and passed a slave code. This slave code became the basis for all further laws concerning slavery, and it was much more severe than it came to be through the following century of modifications. No less than ten crimes were listed punishable with death, such as murder, rape, poisoning a white person, setting fire to property, and inciting an insurrection. A bounty was offered for the scalp of any slave who should run away to Florida, a barbarous law soon to be dropped. No slave might leave a plantation without a permit; slaves might not assemble in unusual numbers; not more than seven might travel along a road together; slaves might not possess beer or spirituous liquors, nor be allowed to keep a boat or neat cattle; they must not be taught to read or write, nor must they beat a drum, blow a horn, or make any unusual noises. Yet all was not set down to the detriment of the slaves: They must not be made to work on the Lord's Day, nor more than sixteen hours a day, and they must be properly clothed and fed. If the government should exact the life of a slave, the owner and the injured party should receive £50, and if a person should kill a slave he should suffer a fine of £50. To attract settlers to Georgia a law was passed in 1758 forbidding slaves to engage in carpentry, masonry, bricklaying, and similar skilled professions.

The general assembly spent some of its time effectively in passing needed laws and it spent a great deal of time quarreling

Top left: JAMES HABERSHAM, MANAGER OF THE BETHESDA ORPHANS HOME, MERCHANT, AND ACTING COLONIAL GOVERNOR. *Top right:* JOHN WESLEY, FOUNDER OF METHODISM, AND MINISTER OF THE CHURCH OF ENGLAND IN GEORGIA, 1735-36. *Bottom left:* GEORGE WHITE-FIELD, PROGRESSIVE PREACHER AND THE FOUNDER OF THE BETHESDA ORPHANS HOME. *Bottom right:* NOBLE JONES, FRIEND OF OGLETHORPE, MILITARY OFFICER, SURVEYOR, COUNCILLOR, AND TREASURER OF THE COLONY.

Top: MIDWAY MEETING HOUSE, BUILT IN 1792 TO REPLACE THE ONE DESTROYED BY THE BRITISH IN THE REVOLUTION. *Bottom:* JERUSALEM CHURCH, BUILT BY THE SALZBURGERS AT EBENEZER BEFORE THE REVOLUTION.

with Governor Reynolds, who was more accustomed to giving orders on a ship than trying to handle unbridled and inexperienced legislators. He neglected the forms of law in attempting to control the assemblymen; he flouted the courts by ordering a man hanged two days before the time appointed; he even quarreled with his councillors; and in trying to cover up the traces of his illegal doings, he foolishly had the legislative minutes altered. He soon dissolved the assembly and set out to get another one which would do his bidding. In this work he made good use of William Little, a ship surgeon, whom he had brought along to be his private secretary. He delighted to honor Little with most offices which the law allowed him to fill, and Little for all these favors, using the methods current in England for controlling Parliament, secured the election of men who would obey the behest of the governor, and obtained for himself the speakership. So bitter did the people become against Little that a grand jury presented his holding the speakership as a public nuisance.

Reynolds made himself unpopular in Savannah by attempting to move the capital to a bluff on the south side of the Ogeechee River about fourteen miles from its mouth. Here he sought to develop a town which he called Hardwicke, in honor of the Lord High Chancellor of England. It seems that the governor had developed a dislike for Savannah when at the first official meeting he held, the building used as a capitol fell down and forced him to move to another. He boomed Hardwicke by laying out a town where 27 lots were soon taken up and by granting in the vicinity 21,000 acres of land; but it never became the capital and never developed into a town of any consequence.

In sending a martial man to be the first royal governor of Georgia, the King may have had the feeling that the new governor might have duties more military than civil, for relations with France in America at this time were fast approaching a crisis. On the upper Ohio River and along the Canadian

border English and French outposts were approaching nearer
to one another, and their traders and land speculators had already come into grave misunderstandings. About the time
Reynolds arrived, George Washington clashed with the French
in western Pennsylvania, and now, in 1754, war broke out
which in America was called the French and Indian War, but
which two years later spread over Europe in what came to be
known as the Seven Years' War.

It was fortunate for Georgia that the greatest strains and
stresses were in the north, but the southern border was not
free from dangers of conflict. The French were entrenched not
far away in Mobile and New Orleans; and the Spaniards, who
were not involved in the war at the beginning but entered it
later, were an ever-present threat in St. Augustine. When the
war was a year old, the British government sought to raise two
regiments in America and called upon Georgia to do her part.
Weak, surrounded by wavering Indians and potential and present enemies, and being well weighed down with troubles of
her own, Georgia replied that she could assume no part in the
war until it came to her own borders. Believing his biggest
problem was setting the colony into a proper state of defense,
Governor Reynolds enrolled in the militia 750 men, and equipping them as well as he could, ordered them to be drilled six
times a year. He worked out an elaborate system of forts to
be strung down the coast from Savannah to Frederica and then
up the Altamaha and Oconee rivers and across to Augusta.
It was an effective military precaution, but Georgia was unable
to pay for it, and England refused to meet these additional
expenses. The governor became even more unpopular for
worrying the people too much about soldiering when they saw
no war near.

In the face of his unpopularity and the expensive uncertainties of warfare, Reynolds had the temerity to ask the Board of
Trade to increase his salary. Plainly this naval captain had made
a failure in trying to govern a civil people. He was recalled in

1756 and allowed to resign. He was restored to his old position in the navy and later became an admiral.

And now in the midst of a war, which had not yet spread to the southern border, instead of replacing Reynolds with another military man, the King sent Henry Ellis, an explorer, to be governor of Georgia. Ellis had once tried to find the Northwest Passage, and though, like all the others who had attempted this feat, he had failed, yet his work was considered so valuable that he had been made a fellow of the Royal Society. He arrived in Savannah in 1757 and the people cheered; and a group of schoolboys in military formation welcomed him. Even the Indians were on hand to assure him "that they would brighten the chain with their Friends the English, and make the Path bloody with their Enemies, the *French* and their *Indians.*" To mark the contrast in their affections, the Georgians burned in effigy William Little, the former henchman of Reynolds, "a tyrant in himself, and a promoter of it in his master."

Ellis remained only three years, but he was well liked by the people. Ill-health, produced by the enervating climate, drove him from Georgia. The fact that the trouble-maker William Little attempted to discredit him in the beginning by trying to disrupt the first assembly only endeared him to the people. He endangered the friendship of Savannah, however, when he continued to flirt with the idea of moving the capital to Hardwicke on the Ogeechee.

The war that was flourishing in the northern colonies still kept away from Georgia's doors, but signs of its nearer approach were becoming evident. No one knew when the secret diplomacy and family compacts in Europe might land Spain in the conflict, and then war like that which had troubled Oglethorpe would return; but the old General, no longer much interested in Georgia, would not return to fight it. Before leaving England, Ellis had secured the promise of 500 muskets for the defense of the colony, and various presents for the Indians, and soon after arriving he made a tour of inspection to the southern border. He recommended the building of some log forts, and this the assembly did. It also forbade Georgians driving their livestock across the border to sell to the Spaniards or send foodstuffs with which to feed them. Here was an embargo against a power yet friendly. Throughout this time Ellis was corresponding with the Florida governor seeking to maintain friendly relations, but well might the Spaniards be suspicious of the Georgian.

The greatest immediate danger to Georgia was the Indians, who almost surrounded the colony and who could muster 8,000 warriors. As if this danger did not exist, England called on Georgia again, in 1757, for aid against the French in Canada. After pleading poverty, the general assembly recited in the rejection of the call how plentiful the savages were, how the colony was without artillery or troops, and how it had no war vessels to protect its coast. To ward off the Indian danger rather than wait and fight an Indian war, Ellis took part in a conference with Governor William H. Lyttleton, of South Carolina, and Colonel Henry Bouquet, the commander of the King's forces in southern America, where it was decided that the main Indian chiefs should be invited to conferences in Savannah and Charleston. The conference which took place in Savannah in October, 1757, was made up of a strange mixture of stageplay designed to win over the Indians through fear and favor.

These preparations and activities were as near as Georgia came to war under the régime of Ellis. In 1760 he returned to England with the good will of the Georgians, later to be appointed to the governorship of Nova Scotia, which he filled through a deputy. He spent his old age in southern France and died in Naples.

To succeed Ellis, the King appointed James Wright, long associated with the government of South Carolina, able, successful as an executive, and a patriotic Britisher. He arrived in 1760, and befittingly enough, this same year George III succeeded to the throne of England, and in Savannah he was proclaimed king—the first and only time such a formality ever took place on Georgia soil, for the colony arose under George II and disappeared under George III. Of the three colonial governors, Wright was the most successful despite the fact that he had the most difficult position to fill, and he was the best liked, even though he was finally driven out in the Revolution.

Becoming governor at the most active part of the French and Indian War, he arrived in the midst of the Cherokee War, which was the southern phase of the French and Indian War, but whose field of operations did not extend into Georgia. Caused by ill treatment some Cherokee warriors had received from the whites, and by the inciting activities of the French, this war which broke out in 1758 lasted until the fall of 1761. It raged on the northern and eastern borders of Georgia from Fort Prince George in South Carolina to Fort Loudoun in eastern Tennessee, and was characterized by brutalities on both sides equally reprehensible. Oconostota, the implacable enemy of the British, and Attakullakulla, the loyal friend, each played his part in the struggle.

Wright looked well to good relations with the Creeks and was able to maintain them, but scarcely had the Cherokee War ended and relieved Georgia of one major concern, before another dangerous situation developed: Spain entered the war to help France. The French privateers which had been raiding the coast and even entering the Savannah River to capture people and threaten the destruction of Savannah, despite all the fortifications Wright had been able to throw up there, were now joined by many Spanish raiders. The opposition was too much for the one little Georgia gunboat which Governor Ellis had provided before his departure. Georgia was now the most exposed part of the English mainland possessions, and had the war not conveniently come to an end in 1763, the Spaniards

might have wrought much more havoc than they were able to
do in the days of Oglethorpe.

The Treaty of Paris made remarkable and fundamental
changes on the Georgia border. The Spaniards having foolishly
entered the war after the French had been defeated, gained
little more than an opportunity to take a seat at the peace
table, there to give away whatever England should demand of
them. Florida had long been troublesome to the English; now
they would have it for themselves, and in return they would
give back to Spain, Havana, which they had recently taken.
France sought to save Florida for her ally Spain by offering
England Louisiana instead. England, mindful of the dangerous
nuisance Florida had been in the hands of Spain, insisted on
Florida and forced her way.

Now the century-old dispute with Spain over the southern
boundary of English possessions was settled; there remained the
internal British problem to decide where Georgia should leave
off and where Florida should begin, or whether all of Florida
should be added to Georgia to make it one colony. The St.
Johns River had long been considered the proper dividing
point between Georgia and Florida, and so the Board of Trade
fixed the southern boundary of Georgia at a line drawn from
the mouth of this river westward to the confluence of the Flint
and the Chattahoochee rivers. James Grant, the newly appointed Florida governor, raised many objections to this line.
He claimed that the better part of Florida lay north of the
St. Johns River and that the line from the mouth of that river
would soon leave the river flowing up from the south, and be
an object of continual dispute for years to come. He suggested
the St. Marys River and a line drawn from the headwaters
of that river to the confluence of the Flint and the Chattahoochee. Such a line would be short and easy to find. Grant's
argument prevailed; the St. Marys line, which required a hundred years of searching before it was located, was accepted;

and Georgia was deprived of a considerable area which she had long coveted and which Oglethorpe had sought to conquer.

Even with the loss of territory which they considered their own, Georgians gained by the Treaty of Paris that peace of mind which came from thinking they knew where their southern boundary was. In his Proclamation of 1763, which established this line, the King set up another line which proved to be of no immediate inconvenience to Georgians, but which might become very troublesome when once they should fill up the coastal regions and start migrating to the westward. This was the so-called Proclamation Line, which forbade all colonists from New Hampshire to Georgia to make settlements or purchases of land west of the sources of rivers running into the Atlantic Ocean. At this time, it had not been determined how far west Georgia should go, but in 1764 the definite limits of Georgia were laid down in a commission to Governor Wright. The Mississippi River was made the western extremity, and the original northern boundary remained unchanged, but the southern boundary was made the 31st parallel from the Mississippi to the Chattahoochee and thence down the river to meet the line from the St. Marys River. Thus was Georgia greatly enlarged to embrace most of the region which was years later to become the states of Alabama and Mississippi.

There remained for immediate settlement the claims of the Creek Indians to this southern region, and while this agreement was being sought Georgia took advantage of the opportunity to push the Creeks back all along her northern and western edges that there might be room for growth, now that the Spaniards and French had been got out of the way. The year that saw peace with France and Spain also brought an agreement with the Creeks. A great meeting, in which other than Georgia problems were dealt with, was held in Augusta, attended by 700 Creeks, Cherokees, Choctaws, Chickasaws, and Catawbas, and by the governors of Georgia, South Carolina, North Carolina, and Virginia. John Stuart, Superintendent of

Indians Affairs for all the Southern colonies, was also present. In this treaty Georgia pushed the Creeks back of a line running up the Little River a short distance, thence southwestward to the Ogeechee and down this river to a point near the original treaty line of 1733, and thence southward down the coast to the Altamaha. Two years later it was extended to the St. Marys.

Georgia now had definite limits in which to grow and prosper, and she was not to be disturbed again until the Revolution came down upon her.

CHAPTER IX

GROWTH UNDER THE KING

GEORGIA HAD a great deal of trouble in finally establishing undisputed possession of the regions lying south of the Altamaha River. Though it was outside the original limits of the colony, Oglethorpe had attempted to lay hold on it to the exclusion of the Spaniards; but as the war ended without a settlement of the boundary, this territory became a sort of neutral ground or a no-man's-land, until the Treaty of Paris in 1763 settled the question by awarding all Florida to England. Before Spain had been pushed out, and while this region was in dispute, it became a refuge for malcontents and outlaws, and even after Spain had given it up, the actual ownership of the land was complicated by the claims of South Carolina.

As a freebooting disturber south of the Altamaha, Edmund Gray held a position of preëminence. He had drifted down from Virginia about the time the King had taken over Georgia, had got himself elected to the assembly from the Augusta region, and by playing the rôle of a great man with vast influence had sought to disrupt the colonial government. Failing, with a group of followers he took refuge at a point which he called New Hanover, about thirty miles up from the mouth of the St. Illa River, a name which busy people later merged into Satilla. There in 1755 he set up a trading post where he trafficked and plotted with the Creeks and drew unto himself adventurers and outlaws to the number of 300. Governor Reynolds objected to their presence, and his successor Governor Ellis sought to dislodge them, but Gray paid little attention. The Spaniards came up to enquire why Gray was on land they claimed, but they threw out the hint that if he would acknowledge himself to be under the authority of Spain, he might remain. Thus did Gray's gang become a pawn in the jig-saw diplomacy of England and Spain. Georgia insisted on Gray's departure, South Carolina with a hazy claim to this region objected to his presence, and the Board of Trade in England in 1758 so insistently ordered him out that he left only to return soon thereafter. The next year he so ingratiated himself with England when he led a group of his Creek allies against the Cherokees that he was permitted to make his settlement on Cumberland Island undisturbed.

Scarcely had Gray's disruptive schemes been settled before a much more serious descent was made on the trans-Altamaha country. Beginning about 1760, when it became evident that Spain would be forced out, South Carolina laid claim to this region and set about appropriating it in the first of the great land speculations which were to dog the progress of Georgia for the next half century. The legal basis of South Carolina's claim rested on the fact that Georgia had been originally that slice of South Carolina between the Savannah and Altamaha rivers, and since at this time those boundaries had not been changed, South Carolina held that the territory to the southward should continue to be in her possession. Fearing no doubt that Georgia would secure this region when the treaty of peace should come, Governor Thomas Boone, of South Carolina, granted 343,000 acres here to 200 important South Carolinians. Such prominent men as Henry Middleton and Henry Laurens were given great tracts. The whole procedure was undoubtedly a great speculation, for there was little probability of these people settling the land.

After the Treaty of Paris had given this region to Georgia, Governor Wright strongly objected to South Carolina's attempt to strangle the growth of the young colony by preëmpting all this fertile land. As South Carolina did not even deign to receive his complaints, he carried his fight before the British government. He declared that South Carolina's seizure of these lands was "the death wound or destruction of Georgia." The Board of Trade declared this veiled theft unwarranted, but finding that the grants had been completed, it left the subject to the two colonies to work out an agreement. In 1765 the Georgia assembly passed a law confirming these grants if the South Carolina owners should conform to the Georgia rules relative to clearing and settling the land and if they recorded with the Georgia government the proof of their grants with the limits. Many of the South Carolinians completed their grants according to Georgia law and received patents for them. Twenty tracts, for the most part of 1,000 and 2,000 acres, were perfected during the four years directly preceding the Revolution.

There was much value in Georgia's knowing at last the exact limits of her territory, and to what extent she could lay hold on it. She could now go forward in her development. Up to this time there had been considerable progress in settling the colony. The abandonment of Georgia by the Trustees emphasized a new era, which was already in the making. It would have been difficult at this time to find a single ear-mark of the Georgia Utopia, so enthusiastically planned twenty years previously. The people now owned their land and black slaves worked in the fields. Charity was no longer dispensed, and the original English charity settlers had largely disappeared. A new class of debtors, Georgians, had arisen who had never known English debtor prisons, but who were fast becoming acquainted with Georgia prisons. Georgia was now like other English colonies. Laws were passed to prevent masters of vessels from carrying away from their debts these Georgia debtors; and conversely, laws were passed to relieve Georgia debtor prisons, even as England had acted twenty years before. By an act of 1766 any debtor so abject in his poverty as not to be able to pay for his own upkeep in jail, should receive from his creditor seven shillings a week. Thus should the Georgia creditor pay for the luxury of having vengeance on his debtors, and if he should refuse to make payment of the seven shillings, the debtor should be allowed his freedom.

To take the place of the selected unfortunates with whom the Trustees had expected to settle Georgia, other people from a wide variety of places and conditions came in. In this new era, the first and the most valuable group to come were about 350 South Carolinians, who had lived in that colony long enough to take on the name but were not typical South Carolinians. They were a peculiar people who had come in the great migration to Massachusetts in 1630, but who had grown dissatisfied after a generation or two there and had moved on to South Carolina. On the Ashley River these Puritans built up their own little community and remained a few more generations before deciding that the land of Canaan lay on beyond the Savannah. They sent out their spies and found that the land was good. So in 1752 they crossed over into Georgia and settled on a tract of 32,000 acres, which they had not seized through fire and sword but by agreement with the Georgians. This land lay south of the Ogeechee, midway between the Savannah and the Altamaha rivers, and so they called their settlement Midway. They brought with them 1,500 slaves and set them to clearing out rice and indigo plantations. Within three years most of these Puritans had arrived, but a few kept drifting in for the next decade. They were a religious people and maintained the Congregational form of church government. They followed their wisest counsellors and the best impulses their conscience afforded, and thereby laid the foundations for an influence in colony and state which was to show itself in an amazingly large number and variety of intelligent leaders.

Rich in wisdom and good citizenship, they became also wealthy in worldly goods. At first, they traded overland with Savannah, up the old military road Hugh Mackay had built, but progress demanded a seaport; and so they built Sunbury, which soon became so important that it was declared a port of entry in 1761. During the year 1762, it was visited by 56 vessels.

Another group who came to Georgia a few years after the arrival of the Puritans were the Acadians, a people who came in greater numbers than the Puritans, but who came under different circumstances and passed on into nothingness, leaving scarcely a trace. These Acadians had been driven out of Nova Scotia by the British at the beginning of the French and Indian War, and dispersed to the uttermost parts of the British possessions. Two ships laden with 400 of these unfortunate French refugees landed in Georgia, a dangerous addition to the weakest colony already beset by French perils. Georgia received them hospitably but with no charity. Attempts were made to induce them to enter into indentured servitude, but in a strange land, they could never be content. They slipped away to South Carolina and thence to Louisiana, France, St. Domingo, and into an oblivion which completely swallowed them up.

The end of the French and Indian War gave a throbbing impulse to people both in the colony and outside to push forward the settlement of Georgia. As was characteristic of a great part of the history of America, land speculation and actual desire for settling were so mixed up that at times it was hard to discover the true nature of any attempt to get land. There were good examples of both at this time, the South Carolina push representing the one, and the Puritan migration the other. Even more speculative than the South Carolinians were certain noblemen and commoners in England. In 1764 Denys Rolles and a group of associates attempted to secure possession of all that part of Georgia south of the Altamaha with an extension on into Florida. Their purpose was to develop great plantations of silk, indigo, and cotton, to exploit the timber resources, and to seize the Indian trade. The Board of Trade refused to permit this chimerical speculation, but Rolles, not to be put off so easily, petitioned for Cumberland

Island, where he would develop another Garden of Eden, as wonderful as Sir Robert Montgomery years before was going to make. This scheme also failed to attract the Board. But within less than six months along came Alexander Montgomerie, tenth Earl of Eglintoun, who wanted a grant to a great region embracing parts of Georgia and Florida. He made the most amazing promises such as bringing over within ten years, 100,000 settlers; and hoping to help his petition, he begged the privilege of putting at the head of "this great and expensive undertaking" a member of the royal family. His petition also failed to win approval.

Another speculation, not located in Georgia but engaged in by a Georgian, was the attempt of Jonathan Bryan, who had long been prominent in the colonial government, to get control of the so-called "Apalache Old Fields," which lay south of the Georgia border and were stretched into a speculation to include about 5,000,000 acres. Bryan, working in conjunction with a group of East Floridians, planned to develop in this region a vast cattle-raising, agricultural, and trading business. As this speculation was attempted just before the Revolution broke out, Governor Wright, well suspecting the loyalty of Bryan, was able to dissuade the Indians from agreeing to the grant.

Apart from bubbling speculation, there went on a steady push into Georgia. About 160 Germans under John Gerar William DeBrahm came in 1751 and settled at Bethany and during the next few years a great many more followed. A group of Irish Protestants settled at Queensbury on the Ogeechee in 1768; and about the same time a colony of Quakers secured a grant of 40,000 acres north of Augusta and settled a town near the Little River, which they called Wrightsborough, in honor of the governor.

Land was being granted so fast that the Indians were soon pushed back in another treaty. It was now becoming popular in South Carolina and far up in North Carolina and even in

Virginia to set out for Georgia, a young colony with a great future. If the Indians were in the way of this migration, then they must be made to move. It happened, too, that many Indian traders had, perhaps, through design, got the Indians deeply in debt, so deeply that it seemed that they could never pay out. These debts amounted to £40,000 or £50,000. The simplest solution would be to call the tribal representatives together and announce to them that the forests they inhabited were entirely too extensive for their needs, and that by giving up a great deal of their surplus hunting grounds they could secure release from their debts. Cherokee and Creek chieftains met Governor Wright and John Stuart, the Indian superintendent, at Augusta in 1773 and agreed to give up two great tracts of land. The Creeks and Cherokees ceded a region extending up the Savannah River beyond the Broad almost to the junction of the Keowee and the Tugaloo rivers and westward to embrace a great extent of country, called the New Purchase, which later came to be called Wilkes County. The other tract, which the Creeks ceded, lay between the Ogeechee and Altamaha rivers.

In return for this land which the Indians gave up they were to be relieved of the debts they owed to the traders, chief among whom were George Galphin and James Jackson and Company; and the British government pledged itself to meet these obligations. All seem to have secured settlements except George Galphin, an Irishman to whom the Indians owed almost £10,000. Galphin had set up his trading house at Silver Bluff, below Augusta, just across the Savannah River in South Carolina, where he carried on trade operations from Charleston to St. Augustine and Mobile. As the Revolution soon came, Galphin's claims were disallowed because the British held that he had supported the Revolutionists, but after the war the Georgians refused to pay on the ground that the debt was an obligation on the Federal government. This troublesome problem was dragged out and the claim was not paid until 1849, long after the death of Galphin. When finally settled it amounted to over $234,000.

Immediately after the treaty had been signed, Governor Wright issued his proclamation informing the people up and down the Atlantic that the land was open for settlement and that it could be had on attractive terms in lots varying from 100 to 1,000 acres. There were to be no quit-rents for ten years. He also proclaimed the fertility of the land and the fact that it would produce fine crops of wheat, corn, tobacco, and hemp. Settlers rushed into this New Purchase, as it was called, so fast that they crowded the Indians into a hostility, which nearly provoked a war. In 1774 Governor Wright and John Stuart held a conference with the Creeks in Savannah, and succeeded in quieting them. As the northern tract was the more accessible, it began filling up rapidly, especially in the Broad River Valley, where a great many Virginians came. At the confluence of the Broad and Savannah rivers, Fort James was erected to protect the incoming settlers, and soon a town was laid out at this strategic spot, and called Dartmouth.

Georgia was fast growing completely away from all recognition of her former self. Instead of a few discontented charity colonists with a good sprinkling of foreigners, hovering along the coast, by the time of the Revolution a great influx of people from the colonies farther north had greatly changed the character of the population as well as its location. Up the Savannah and westward, the course of empire took its way in Georgia. Instead of having about 3,000 white people and 2,000 slaves as when the King took over the colony, it had about 50,000 people with almost half slaves when the King was forced to give it up. The greatest growth had followed the end of the French and Indian War.

Of all the purposes which were held out in the founding of the colony, only the commercial one seems to have succeeded. The people busily set about using common sense in doing whatever could be best done in Georgia. They found it easy to raise rice on the swampy coast, and farther inland they raised wheat, corn, peas, and indigo. The great forests of tall pines, which seemed to cover the whole country below Augusta, were a perfect invitation to the people to get from them tar, pitch, and turpentine, and from these trees and others the sawmills cut lumber, shingles, boards, and staves. Through the cleared fields as well as the more open woodlands, roamed great numbers of cattle and hogs, growing into wealth for the people. Horses were bred in numbers sufficient to meet the needs of farmers and planters. Many people traded with the Indians and brought in deer skins.

As for mining, there was none, and as for manufacturing there was very little. Said Governor Wright in 1766, "There are no Trades, Works, or Manufactures set up, or about to be set up in this Province that I know of, which are or may prove hurtful to Great Britain." Georgia was a perfect and obedient child of the English mercantilists. She bought in England nearly every manufactured article she needed. Only Negro shoes and rough cloth were made in the colony. Rum, sugar, coffee, and slaves she bought from the West Indies, and according to Governor Wright these articles came from the British possessions as the law directed. Flour, biscuits, and certain other food products came from the northern colonies, and though this was legitimate trade it was pernicious, for it took most of the money Georgia could lay hold on. This was true because Georgia had little that the northerners wanted except money; as for the West Indians, they were glad to receive Georgia lumber, rice, pork, horses, cattle, and other products for their sugar and rum and pay for the excess in gold and silver. Almost everything which Georgia produced she exported in varying amounts; but rice, indigo, lumber, naval stores, deer-skins, beef, and pork were the staple articles for which Georgia was known. To promote the good name of the colony and protect it from its dishonest traders, a law was enacted in 1766 to set up an inspection for beef, pitch, tar, turpentine, and fire-wood. The Georgians were not a seafaring people, and therefore not owners of many ships; still they possessed 36 small craft amounting in all to about 2,000 tonnage.

In fact, Georgians were more closely allied economically, socially, and sentimentally with the West Indies than with the northern colonies. Within one year (1773-1774), eighty-eight West Indians vessels came into the Savannah port. This trade with the West Indies brought Georgians most of their gold and silver coins; their trade with the northern colonies took most of this money away from them. As early as 1764, voices in Georgia were raised against this northern trade, and the question was asked and for the next hundred and fifty years reiterated why Georgians could not produce their own flour and butter.

Georgia exported a great variety of products from her fields and forests. During the 1760's and 1770's, ships carried out of the port of Savannah such articles as these: silk, leather, timber, lumber, shingles, staves, hoops, handspikes, spars, oars, pitch, tar, turpentine, cedar posts, cord wood, pink root, lime, Sago powder ("proper for fluxes and other disorders in the bowels"), indigo, cotton, rice, peas, corn, potatoes, oranges, orange juice, tobacco, ground nuts, candles, tallow, beeswax, myrtle wax, honey, straw, reeds, canes, horses, oxen, cattle, sheep, hogs and hog products, turkeys, geese, chickens, deer skins, beaver skins, raccoon skins, otter skins, cow hides, cow horns, and sturgeon. There were no exports of the products of the buffalo herds which roamed over Georgia when the colony was first settled, for they had soon been exterminated. The buffalo was "this awful creature" which Mark Catesby, an English naturalist, had seen back about 1722 when he was wandering through that region later to be Georgia and which he further described as so large that its skin was "too heavy for the strongest man to lift from the ground."

Though Georgia was still a land of opportunities where no one with any ambition and a common amount of ability need be a ne'er-do-well, yet these same opportunities made it possible for some to get far ahead of others. In 1773 there were 1,400 plantations made up of 120,000 acres. As this averaged less than 100 acres to the plantation, it is evident that the mass of the people were small farmers. The fact, however, that there were some plantations or holdings by the same man which amounted to over 25,000 acres, the average size of the Georgia plantation must recede to even smaller proportions. There were, in fact, some very great planters in Georgia at this time, though there could not have been many. James Habersham, one of the most important men in colonial Georgia, owned about 200 slaves and land sufficient to make 700 barrels of rice or more. James Wright, though governor and an honest man, found ways to secure twelve plantations consisting of more than 19,000 acres on which he worked more than 500 slaves; and perhaps the largest land holder in colonial Georgia was John Graham, with more than 26,000 acres.

People could farm and trade and progress to no great degree unless they had money. Under the Trustees the people had their sola bills, but such unusual money disappeared with the other peculiarities of the Trustees. The year the Trustees gave up Georgia, Parliament passed a law forbidding the colonies to issue paper currency, and now is seemed that Georgia was to struggle along with a few stray Spanish coins, depreciated South Carolina currency, and whatever English currency she could secure. Through special arrangements Georgia was allowed in 1755 to issue £3,000 in paper currency, and thereafter at intervals the colony increased her supply. In some instances the English authorities winked at violation of the law and in others they allowed a loose interpretation of the English prohibition.

As the cost of government was not great, the raising of money with which to meet it was easily accomplished. The total expense of carrying on the civil establishment varied little throughout the royal period, amounting generally to about

£3,000. The total income when the Revolution broke out was a little more than £5,000 and, it was derived almost entirely from taxes on general property. The chief method used in appraising land for taxation was to note the kind of timber found growing upon it.

Just as government was simple and inexpensive, the people's tastes and wants in other fields were as plain. There was not a printing press or newspaper in the colony for the first thirty years of its existence. There were, indeed, books, for many had been sent over at the beginning and later, and others had been written by people in Georgia. The malcontents got out their books and pamphlets, and Thomas, the son of good old William Stephens, wrote various books, including his *Castle-Builders; or, the History of William Stephens, of the Isle of Wight, Esq.* These books were published in London, or sometimes with more convenience in Charleston. In fact, Charleston was the local printing metropolis for Georgia until James Johnston, "skilled in the art and mystery of printing," set up a shop in Savannah. In 1762, the assembly to dignify its enactments by having them printed, passed a law encouraging the establishment of a printing press in the colony, and the same year appointed James Johnston as official printer. From then on he printed the laws of the colony, and in 1763 began the publication of the first newspaper in the colony, the *Georgia Gazette*.

With the coming of royal control, which made possible the exploitation of Georgia's natural resources, the more fortunate settlers, and especially the officials, began to take on the ways of wealth and culture. Savannah now became a social and an intellectual center of the colony, as it had from the beginning been the governmental center. These wealthy Georgians had their town houses as well as their country mansions and their plantations, bearing such names as Hermitage, Valambrossa, Hope, Silk Hope, Isle of Hope, Wormsloe, Cedar Grove, Laurel Hill, Orange Grove, Mulberry Hill, Wild Horn, and

Lee Hall. In going back and forth they used their chariots, phaetons, and riding chairs. The richest man in the colony was Governor Wright and John Graham was reputed to be second. The latter had an English gardener and twenty-three house servants. His properties were worth £40,000 with an annual income of £4,000. Wealth like this made possible the sale of a half pew in Christ Church for £50.

They dressed in the finest garments and jewelry to be got in England: silk and thread mits, wigs and bags for them, "cherryderry jackets," white lamb gloves, "black shammy [chamois] gloves," satin bonnets, painted hose, silk breeches (as well as the "everlasting and honeycomb" variety), gold and "barleycorn" necklaces, silver earrings, gold rings set with amethysts and diamonds, and gold and silver breastpins. They also had their smelling bottles, tooth pick cases, silver seals for letters, silver cork screws with pearl handles, wine glasses and decanters, playing cards and fiddle strings, silver-mounted small swords, "sand glasses from 2 hours to ¼th of a minute," mahogany and walnut furniture, and "Hogarth's prints in neat gilded frames." The wealthy who feared the wrath of storms bought "machines for preventing houses from being struck by lightning, after the newest and best manner."

There was some visiting to the other colonies, especially to the British West Indies. The people danced, sang, played cards, drank coffee and tea, attended horse races, read books provided by the Library Society or bought at the shops, and celebrated various historical, religious, and patriotic days, such as St. George's Day, St. Patrick's Day, Guy Fawkes Day ("being the anniversary of the Gunpowder Treason"), and the King's birthday as well as his accession to the throne. The St. Andrews Club saw to it that St. Andrews' Day was properly observed. But the King's birthday was the greatest occasion of the year, when amidst flags fluttering on the forts and from the mastheads of all the ships in the port, the governor and high officials marched to Fort Halifax to drink the King's health while

cannon boomed and the rangers fired three volleys from their
small arms. The procession then returned to the council house
to enjoy an elegant banquet. In the evening there were bon-
fires and illuminations, "and the night was concluded with all
possible demonstrations of joy."

But there was "another half" in Georgia who did not enjoy
these luxuries and evidences of culture. They were the ne'er-
do-wells and unfortunates to be found in all times and places,
and a middle class who did not care for these fineries. At the
bottom were the Negro slaves who did not count as part of
the citizenry, yet they were something more than property.
They rode horses now and then as did the white people, and
so reckless were these horsemen at times that the grand jury
presented as a grievance the fact: "the white people, as well as
negroes, are suffered to ride on horseback at a gallop through
the streets of Savannah, to the great danger of its inhabitants."
And it was all too common a custom for those who had no
horses to ride to steal them. For this crime some were hanged,
some were pardoned, and some made their escape as did William Saxe, who was reputed to have broken jail twenty-eight
times.

In keeping with the general policy of the British government, Georgia established in 1758 the state religion of England. The colony was divided into eight parishes and each one
was given a name reminiscent of early Christianity. There was
St. Paul (Augusta), St. George (Waynesborough), St. Matthew (Ebenezer), Christ Church (Savannah), St. Philip (Hardwicke), St. John (Midway-Sunbury), St. Andrew (Darien),
and St. James (Frederica); and when the regions south of the
Altamaha became a part of the colony in 1763, four additional
parishes were created, St. David, St. Patrick, St. Thomas, and
St. Mary. In each parish a church should be built, except in St.
Paul (Augusta) and Christ Church (Savannah) where churches
already existed, and a tax should be levied to pay the salaries of
the clergy, who should receive £25 a year, to provide charity

for the poor, and to pay for all other parochial needs. Wardens and vestrymen were provided and records of births, marriages, and deaths were to be kept.

There was no forced membership in the Church of England. A Georgian could belong to any of the numerous sects which had grown up in Georgia, such as Lutherans, Congregationalists, Presbyterians, Baptists, and Hebrews, but no one was relieved from paying taxes for the upkeep of the established Church.

Though colonial Georgians were never so completely saturated with religious zeal as many New Englanders were, the laws of the colony could not be blamed for this condition. In 1762 an act was passed "for preventing and punishing vice, profaneness and immorality, and for keeping holy the Lord's day, commonly called Sunday." Among the requirements here recorded was compulsory attendance on public worship, and as Indian dangers increased, the compulsory carrying of firearms to church. To further guard the morals of the people, lotteries and other forms of gambling were forbidden.

In the beginning the Georgians were a peculiar and chosen people, with the Trustees to watch over them as fathers over their children and with Parliament to shower upon them money. As time went on they began to follow after strange gods and to cast aside their peculiarities, and by the outbreak of the Revolution they were much like the people in the other colonies. They were, indeed, the youngest colony and the weakest, and they were not so lost to the feelings of gratitude as not to remember the favors that had been granted them in their early development. Otherwise they had come to be typical English colonists.

CHAPTER X

THE RISE OF DISCONTENT

WHEN THE GEORGIA experiment was started, there was little reason for anyone to predict that this colony would soon be like the other British colonies on the North American mainland. If later there were to be an "Original Thirteen" to band themselves together to oppose the mother country, it might well have been inferred that Georgia would not be among them. Nova Scotia or either East or West Florida might have made the thirteenth. Georgia had been the pet of English philanthropy and of the English Parliament; a million dollars had been expended upon her in addition to all the charity that had gone along with the founding and early development of the colony. Gratitude might well have made Georgia the last stronghold of British loyalty in America.

That opposition to the mother country grew up here along with the other revolting twelve, must be attributed to a complexity of causes. Conspiring together to produce this result were a spirit of independence produced by unwise and tactless treatment by the mother country, an isolation by 3,000 miles of ocean, an organized campaign of persuasion carried on by the other twelve, and the world-wide characteristics which makes people complain and magnify human ills. To counterbalance the large number of Georgians who, because of the youth of the colony, had been born in England and who, therefore, had not lost their English sympathies, was the fact that a great many of those colonists most indebted to England had left, and there had come in from the provinces to the northward a great many settlers who were accustomed to thinking of themselves as American more than English.

The French and Indian War left England with a heavy debt. In seeking ways to meet it, she naturally looked toward her colonies, for the defense of whom much of her debt had been incurred. The more she studied her American colonies, the more she was convinced that these colonies should help meet the imperial debt. And in future colonial defense, she resolved that the colonies should provide the soldiers or pay the cost of British troops. In raising this money, various forms of taxes might be used, and at the same time the whole colonial commercial system could be rehabilitated, for the independent disposition of the colonies had caused them to set at defiance any English trade regulations which they did not like.

Georgia, conforming unusually closely to the pattern English mercantilists had set up for the colonies, produced raw materials and left England to manufacture them. Furthermore, she had few ships to be tempted to violate English navigation regulations, and she could not be expected to get greatly excited when smuggling New England merchants and traders should be caught and tried for their crimes. Not only did the enforcement of the navigation laws not upset Georgians, but even the imposition of the first tax law on the colonies did not in the beginning provoke them.

Relying on the simplicity of its collection and its small amount, two years after the war had ended, England set up a stamp tax. According to the law, all papers used in legal transactions as well as in printing should have attached to them a stamp, and these stamps, or paper with the stamp impressed on it, should be sold by British agents sent out for that purpose. The Georgians at first felt that this tax was "as equal as any that could be generally imposed on the Colonies"; but even so, it was too much for James Johnston, printer, to pay, for in December, 1765, he discontinued publishing his *Georgia Gazette*. It was poverty, not protest.

News of the stamp law had reached America long before the stamps could be got ready and sent over. Opposition sprang up almost everywhere outside of Georgia. The tax might not be very burdensome, but the fact that Parliament had proceeded to tax the colonies without first asking them about it, was held to be an intolerable tyranny. Virginia would do something about it, so would Massachusetts. Excitement grew and spread, and a Stamp Act Congress was called to meet in New York City in 1765. Georgia's original acceptance of the law did credit to her loyalty to the government of which she was a part, but now with the colonies to the northward stirred up, she would also get excited. Even staid conservative James Habersham said that the colonies should have been consulted before the law was passed and that it was an insult to common reason to argue that they were represented in Parliament, as some metaphysicians were attempting to prove. In pursuance of an invitation to send delegates to this congress, Alexander Wylly, the speaker of the Commons House of Assembly, issued a call to the assemblymen to meet in a convention in September in order to pick delegates. Sixteen members met in Savannah, but Governor Wright, on hand to look loyally after the King's business, used such great tact and telling arguments that he persuaded the convention not to send delegates.[1] They did, however, send an observer to bring back a report on what the congress should do. The denunciations of the tax made by this Stamp Act Congress reached Georgia in due time and aroused the people considerably.

South Carolinians took it upon themselves to instruct the Georgians in the proper reception to give the stamps, and there was an outcry against Georgia in some of the other colonies because she had sent no delegates to the Stamp Act Congress. Georgians needed from others no instructions on their duty; they would decide for themselves whether they liked stamps. Some of their own leaders soon came to the conclusion that it would be an intolerable burden to buy the stamps, as it would carry out of the colony much of their money. Organized

[1] Virginia, North Carolina, and New Hampshire likewise did not send delegates.

opposition soon developed not only in Savannah but throughout the colony, promoted on the part of some as much by the
excitement of an organization as by hatred of the stamp tax,
for only a very few people would ever have occasion to buy the
stamps. This organization had the resounding title of Sons of
Liberty, or Liberty Boys, called by their enemies "bonfire
brethren," and was a part of such an organization extending
throughout the twelve colonies to the northward.

In December the first stamps arrived on board the *Speedwell*.
They were unloaded and placed in the royal warehouse awaiting the coming of the agent who should sell them. Two hundred of the Sons of Liberty, who had a name and an organization but nothing to do, immediately became active. They
assembled in Savannah and threatened to seize the stamps and
destroy them. Governor Wright set 40 soldiers to watch the
warehouse, and the excitement grew. Rumors were soon afloat
that James Habersham was the stamp-agent, that various other
Savannah merchants were the agent, and the threat was made
that if each did not clear himself, "the fatal consequences that
may arise from this you may judge." Three of the accused
offered a reward of £50 for the name of the person who started
the slander, and Governor Wright offered an equal amount for
the conviction of the offender. A day or two before the time
set for beginning the sale of the stamps, which happened to
be the anniversary of the accession of George III, a day always
celebrated in the colony, "about seven o'clock that night the
effigy of a stamp-officer was carried through the streets, and
afterwards hanged and burnt, amidst the acclimations of a
great concourse of people of all ranks and denominations assembled together on the occasion." So reported editor Johnston
of the *Georgia Gazette*. When the agent arrived he dared not
offer the stamps for sale until the city should become quiet.
Threats were heard against the agent and even against the
governor, and rumors were soon coming in that 600 Liberty
Boys were gathering in various parts of the colony to march on

Savannah. The agent now slipped away and the stamps were taken for safer keeping to a fort on Cockspur Island, where they remained for a short time before being reloaded on the *Speedwell* to be taken out of Georgia forever.

Even this spirited resistance did not meet the full approval of the South Carolina censors who had elected themselves to pass judgment on what Georgia should do. They were so enraged at the Georgians for allowing a few ship captains to clear their vessels on stamped paper that they attempted to cut off all trade with Georgia, and threatened to burn any ship coming from that "infamous colony," which should attempt to enter a South Carolina port, and to put to death any South Carolinian who traded with a Georgian.

The overzealous attitude of South Carolinians was somewhat due to the lack of tact and ability in managing them displayed by the royal governors of that colony. During the single administration of Governor Wright in Georgia, there were six changes in the governor's chair in South Carolina. Wright had with considerable tact and discretion refrained from calling out the Georgia troops to put down the Liberty Boys, for he had a total of only 150 soldiers scattered among five forts and posts over the colony, and if he had called out the militia, he declared, "I should have armed more against me than for me." With a charitable feeling toward his Georgians, whom he loved, Wright claimed they had been stirred up against the stamp tax by outsiders. "They did not think of it," he said, "till spirited on by our Northern Neighbors who never let them rest, or gave them time to cool off." Where Georgians' hearts lay at this time was well illustrated in their reaction to the passing of their good parson Zouberbuhler and of Champernoun Williamson, unknown otherwise than as a Son of Liberty, both of whom died a few days apart in December, 1766. The Parson got a line or two in the *Gazette,* merely recording his death; the Liberty Boy drew a fat paragraph followed by a poem, the ships in the port hoisted their flags, minute guns boomed while he was being buried, and the populace beat their breasts in anguish.

The discontent, first shown in a persistent manner in the stamp act disturbance, was not to be completely allayed by the repeal of the act the year after its passage. Even as tactful and well-liked a governor as Wright could not prevent a querulous and vigilant Georgia from keeping the agitation going. Yet when he called the assembly together in July, 1766, to inform them that the act had been repealed, they thanked the King for giving up the stamp tax and expressed their relief that they in their excitement had passed no resolutions derogatory to him. The opposition to the governor and the King lay throughout the colonial régime in the Commons House of Assembly, as might well be expected. The councilmen, appointed by the King at the instance of the governor, with few exceptions upheld the mother country; but many of the assemblymen, elected by the people, were Sons of Liberty, whom the governor chose to call "Sons of Licentiousness"; and as the contest became more bitter when the Revolution drew nearer, they showed little respect for the governor.

Out of the stamp act controversy arose the dispute over who should be the colonial agent, an official maintained in London to guard the interests of the colony. William Knox, who had chosen to uphold the position of Parliament in the dispute, the Commons House of Assembly dismissed from office, and appointed another in his stead. Governor Wright refused to confirm the new appointee and for three years Georgia was unrepresented. An agreement was reached in 1768, when Benjamin Franklin, an agent for Pennsylvania, agreed to act also for Georgia. His services were so acceptable that he became a hero for a colony which he never visited, and when the colony became a state it remembered him by giving his name to a county and to a building in its first education institution.

Another dispute in the long course of agitation which resulted in the Revolution centered around the refusal of the

Commons House of Assembly to pay for the support of the few British regulars in the colony; but when the threat was made to withdraw them, the assembly made the appropriation.

The repeal of the stamp act in 1766 resulted the next year in Parliament's passing the Townshend act levying a tax on glass, lead, paper, and tea. Now unstamped paper would bear a tax, and in addition the other articles would be taxed. There was immediate opposition in the commercial colonies to the northward, and especially did Massachusetts and Virginia object to these new taxes. In answer to a letter received from Massachusetts, seeking to arouse opposition in Georgia, the assembly in the latter part of 1768 passed resolutions of agreement with the plan being worked out whereby the colonies would refuse to import goods from England. Governor Wright, who had warned the assembly when it came together, to waste no time in opposing the new tax law, now dissolved the assembly. Before adjourning, this body sent to the King a friendly and humble message pledging its support but begging for a redress of its grievances.

The Georgia merchants and people generally were getting excited and they were beginning to express themselves in meetings apart from their Commons House of Assembly, which the governor dispensed with at his pleasure. In September, 1769, the Savannah merchants met to condemn the British tariff act and to warn the people that it would drain all the money from the colony, as the tariff tax must be paid in gold or silver. Shortly thereafter another meeting of protest was held in Savannah, presided over by Jonathan Bryan, a member of the council, whose boldness thus shown caused the King to dismiss him from office. At this meeting the non-importation agreement was adopted, placing Georgia in line with the other colonies. They resolved to engage in manufacturing and to buy no British goods except certain necessities which they enumerated and upon which they set a price, to buy no more slaves from the British, and to refuse to carry on business with anyone in Georgia who did not sign this agreement. A citizen gave this serious and prophetic warning in the *Gazette:* "How long designing men may be able to impose, or how long the remonstrances of the Americans may go unconsidered, it is impossible to determine—*Tho' every year a new act should be made, or repealed, matters can never continue easy while the claim is kept up to tax the Americans where they are not and cannot be represented;* but, if providence does not deny them the blessing of increasing and multiplying as much as they have done, our children may see the greater part of the British nation settled in America, and, if they are but virtuous, all the powers of oppression on earth joined together cannot hinder them from being free."

Good relations between Georgia and the King were fast becoming imperilled. Laws passed by the assembly were disallowed with greater frequency, and long and inexcusable delay marked the course of every law submitted. The disallowance of laws distinctly advantageous to the growth of the colony brought the suspicion that the King was trying to destroy its strength. Not only was the royal approval withheld from certain land laws and laws for the better control of slaves, but the King refused to grant full rights to the regions annexed to the colony at the end of the French and Indian War. After waiting six years to have these four southern parishes given representation, the assembly in 1769 exempted them from all taxes until this right was granted to them, and thereby they cleverly applied the principle of no taxation without representation, which they argued England had violated in the stamp act. The next year the King assented, and this colony of a colony was incorporated fully as a part of Georgia.

As the loyal agent of the King in Georgia, Governor Wright upheld fully the royal authority, but all the tact and persuasion he could command did not prevent outbreaks in his Commons House of Assembly. Noble Wymberley Jones, son of Noble Jones, took a course in the rising discontent, which led him far from the loyalty instilled into his father by a residence in the colony since the day of its founding. So, when the assembly made Jones speaker in 1770, Governor Wright resenting this rebellious disposition, informed the assembly that he would not be allowed to serve. The assembly was incensed at this interference and so informed the governor, whereupon Wright dissolved the assembly.

Governor Wright, having long wanted to visit England to enjoy the royal approval which he knew awaited him, left the next year, and when he returned in 1773, he was Sir James Wright, for the King had bestowed upon him a baronetcy. During his absence, James Habersham, who had lived long and loyally in the colony, was made acting governor, only to run into the same troubles with the assembly which had beset Wright. Among the instructions he had received was the injunction to prevent Jones from serving as speaker of the assembly, if it should be so obstreperous as to elect him again. Upon the first opportunity, it elected Jones, and Habersham vetoed its action. Having had no fear of the governor, it would now not be pushed aside by an acting governor; it rebelliously elected Jones a second time, and Habersham rejected him again. Determined never to surrender its right, the assembly elected Jones a third time, but seeing the futility of the procedure, he refused to accept, and thereupon the assembly elected Archibald Bulloch. Knowledge of the third election of Jones did not reach Habersham until some time later when he was examining the minutes, and so exasperated was he on learning of this persistency that he forthwith dissolved the assembly when it refused to strike out the minute recording Jones' third election.

Up to this time there was no widespread opposition either to King or Parliament, and indeed there had been little differentiation in the minds of Georgians between these two governmental authorities. As the struggle became more bitter, they were going to attack specifically that authority which could

JUDGMENT DAY OF TORIES

This old print represents a mob preparing tar and feathers for their victim while
he remains suspended in the air.

Top left: ANTHONY WAYNE, COMMANDER OF THE AMERICAN FORCES IN GEORGIA WHEN THE BRITISH EVACUATED SAVANNAH IN 1782. *Top right:* NATHANAEL GREENE, COMMANDER OF THE DEPARTMENT OF THE SOUTH IN 1780 AND LIBERATOR OF GEORGIA FROM THE BRITISH. *Bottom left:* LACHLAN MCINTOSH, BORN IN SCOTLAND, BRIGADIER IN THE REVOLUTION, AND THE DUEL-LIST WHO KILLED BUTTON GWINNETT. *Bottom right:* ARCHIBALD BULLOCH, PRESIDENT OF THE SECOND PROVINCIAL CONGRESS AND FIRST "PRESIDENT AND COMMANDER-IN-CHIEF OF GEORGIA."

be opposed with least danger to themselves of being classed as traitors and rebels. As most British action took place in the name of Parliament, that body received their first blows; and long did they protest their loyalty to the person of the King and their respect for him. But in the end they attacked all British authority and accepted *rebel* and *traitor* as badges of distinction.

By this time a division in Georgia sentiment was evident. The old men, who had been born in England and who had come to Georgia to grow up in the service of their King, could never pull themselves out of their loyalty to him; the younger men who had no sentiment born of a residence in England and who had minds which looked forward more than backward, were ready, if provoked, to attack England. Noble Jones remained loyal; his son, Noble Wymberley, became a Revolutionary leader. James Habersham could never turn against his King; his sons, James, John, and Joseph, early joined the Revolution. Fathers supported England, sons opposed her; and a war broke out which has come to be called the Revolution, but which was in fact a civil war, not only because different parts of the same empire were fighting each other but also different groups, within the colony.

CHAPTER XI

THE GEORGIANS REVOLT

EVENTS WERE moving swiftly in England and in her American colonies. British stamps were forgotten with the coming of the tariff taxes which Charles Townshend had devised, and soon all taxes were removed except the tariff on tea. The American colonists had become so upset and excited that they called, in 1774, a congress of all the colonies, which has come to be known as the First Continental Congress. This Congress met and resolved that no English colony should either buy anything from England or sell anything to her, and that the next year a second congress should meet. What would Georgia's reaction to this movement be?

These were momentous developments which propelled Georgia into the maelstrom, and she had to decide for herself how she would get out. Conscious that the oppressive measures which England had instituted against the more rebellious colonies in the North endangered the liberties of all, four Georgia radicals, Noble W. Jones, Archibald Bulloch, John Houstoun, and George Walton, called on every patriot in all Georgia to come together, July 27, 1774, at a tavern in Savannah kept by Peter Tondee, a carpenter and a graduate of the Bethesda orphan school. At this meeting a committee of thirty-one was appointed to frame resolutions; but being far from representative of the whole colony, this group hesitated to adopt a policy. Instead, it called another meeting for the following August 10th, to be made up of delegates from all the parishes, in the same number as existed in the Commons House of Assembly. As this gathering was not a mass meeting like the preceding one, no one was allowed in Tondee's Tavern except the 26

delegates who appeared. They took a bold stand in their resolutions of condemnation of the British government and support
of the colonial position. To build up a revolutionary organization, they appointed on a general committee all people who
had attended both Tondee Tavern meetings, and declared that
any eleven of these might be considered empowered to correspond with the other colonies. Another committee was appointed to collect provisions to be sent to the patriots in Boston,
and so prompt was this committee in setting to work that soon
it had collected 579 barrels of rice. Although there was patriotic
determination enough in these meetings, no action was taken
toward sending representatives to the First Continental Congress, which was to meet in Philadelphia the following September, for the mass sentiment in Georgia was yet to be
determined.

Governor Wright had watched this revolutionary outburst
at the Tondee Tavern meetings and had used great skill in
preventing any definite action. Now and later he pointed out
the fact that Georgia alone of all the English colonies had been
the object of great consideration by Parliament, that she had
received from that body £200,000, that she was young and
without England unprotected against the 10,000 Indian warriors who could swoop down upon her, that if she chose to
rebel against England she could be easily overrun and con-
quered by the strong English forces in St. Augustine, and that
after all, Georgia's rights were not being violated, for she had
no charter under the King. He influenced counter meetings in
Savannah, into which Noble Jones and James Habersham,
acting as managers, collected almost a third of the people, and
got resolutions passed decrying all agitation against England.
Governor Wright, himself, had forbidden the second Tondee
Tavern meeting when he heard it was to be held, and had
declared he would arrest all who should take part in that
illegal gathering. Soon afterwards he began a systematic propaganda over the colony to arouse the people against the agitators,

and manipulated petitions from Wrightsborough, above Augusta, to the St. Marys, praying that the agitation should cease. About the time when the First Continental Congress was meeting, without Georgia delegates, 100 people signed a communication published in the *Georgia Gazette,* sharply condemning the Tondee Tavern meetings. In the contest to organize the mass of Georgians, it began to look as if Governor Wright would succeed in smothering out the agitators; and, indeed, he did succeed in preventing delegates from going to the First Continental Congress.

Though Wright had made the course of the Revolutionists much more difficult, he had not succeeded in silencing the agitation. In January, 1775, they held the first of a series of meetings, which they dignified by calling provincial congresses, and which were ultimately to absorb the authority of the colony and drive Wright out. In this First Provincial Congress only four parishes were represented, and so it could scarcely claim to speak for the whole colony. It met at the same time the Commons House of Assembly, called by Governor Wright, was scheduled to meet and, indeed, as almost all of the delegates to the congress were members of the Commons House of Assembly, that meeting of the congress could be considered a caucus of the assembly. If the congress could manipulate the assembly to the extent of having it adopt the congressional program, then would the voice of the Revolutionists appear to be the voice of Georgia. In pursuance of this policy, the Provincial Congress elected three delegates to the Second Continental Congress, to meet the following May, and passed a modified adherence to the non-importation association, and it reported this action to the assembly. In the meantime the assembly had been working on a set of patriotic resolutions which should end up with the appointment of the delegates to the Continental Congress. When Wright heard of what was about to transpire, he adjourned the assembly before it could fill in the names of the delegates, but it succeeded in passing the resolutions condemning England. It did not, however, pass the non-importation resolutions, so it was a question as to whether Georgia was in the association, since only a modified agreement had been passed by a congress made up of only four of the eleven parishes. This was the last meeting of the assembly, for later, both in the following May and November, when Wright sought to re-convene it, he found it impossible to secure a quorum.

Up through January, 1775, when the First Provincial Congress had adjourned, the gains of the Revolutionists in Georgia had not been impressive. Archibald Bulloch, Noble W. Jones, and John Houstoun, the three delegates elected by the First Provincial Congress, refused to go, for they felt that since the assembly had not acted on their election and since the body which had elected them represented only four out of the twelve parishes, they could not presume to represent Georgia. Yet they felt that Georgia should be condemned rather than excused for not associating completely with the other colonies, and in a note to the President of the Continental Congress, they said, "The unworthy part which the Province of Georgia has acted in the great and general contest leaves room to expect little less than the censure or even indignation of every virtuous man in America." Outsiders generally and especially the South Carolinians looked upon Georgia's course as timid and pusillanimous, and when in May the Second Continental Congress met with Georgia unrepresented, it declared her unworthy of respect and forbade all trade with her.

Though a great many Georgians who were later to become Revolutionists felt that they should at this time be careful and deliberate, the South Carolina Puritans, who had settled at Midway, in St. Johns Parish, were boldly determined from the beginning to join the other colonies in opposing England. Disappointed that the Tondee Tavern meetings had failed to send delegates to the First Continental Congress, these Puritans announced that they would dispatch representatives if they

could get a majority of the parishes to unite with them. Failing
in this move, without waiting for the united action of the
colony they entered, December 1, 1774, the non-importation
association, recently established by the Continental Congress.
And when the First Provincial Congress met the following
January the St. Johns delegates sought, before their entry, to
force that body to adopt the association. On the refusal of the
Provincial Congress to commit itself, the St. Johns delegates
refused to become a part of that body.

Thoroughly exasperated at the timidity of the colony, these
Georgia Puritans, who had always lived much unto themselves,
determined to secede from Georgia and form an alliance with
South Carolina, whence they had come twenty years previously. They sent a delegation to Charleston in February to
bring about a union, but South Carolina, circumspect in her
own proud stand and contemptuous of Georgians, refused to
enter into an agreement, for she was determined that the whole
colony must fall under the ban of trading with South Carolina.
She did, however, recommend the Puritans to the Continental
Congress, and in March, they elected Lyman Hall as their
delegate to the Second Continental Congress. Hall took with
him as good will offerings 160 barrels of rice and £50, to be
presented to the Massachusetts sufferers. He joined in the deliberations of the Congress but did not vote.

In breaking off commercial intercourse with Georgia, South
Carolina declared that she considered Georgians "unworthy of
the rights of freemen, and as inimical to the liberties of their
country," and she threatened to hold the Georgians to account
first, if the British should spill the blood of a patriot on American soil. With this threatened invasion of Georgia by South
Carolinians, Governor Wright found himself in a precarious
situation. He called on the British government for troops, but
it failed to send them, because either it did not want to endanger the loyalty of Georgia or it was unacquainted with the
need for additional forces, since Wright's letters in passing

through South Carolina had been opened and their meaning changed.

The news of the battle of Lexington reached Savannah on May 10th and stirred up a wild commotion so uncontrolled that it resulted in a raid on the colonial powder magazine, led by Noble W. Jones, Edward Telfair, Joseph Habersham, and John Milledge. They seized the powder stored there, and the tradition is that part of it was included in a shipment of rice and money sent to Massachusetts about this time and that it was used in the Battle of Bunker Hill. Such recklessness would inevitably propel Georgia into revolution. Governor Wright offered a reward of £150 for the arrest of the raiders. Having tasted excitement, the Revolutionists would now push on through. On June 4th, as was the custom, Savannah made preparations to celebrate the King's birthday by placing on the river bluff cannon to be fired; but the celebration was greatly marred by the work of malcontents, who spiked twenty-one guns and rolled them down the bluff. On June 5th the Liberty Boys erected a pole and celebrated the birth of liberty.

Not only were increasing disorders and growing excitement leading to a condition of uncertainty, but the ostracism and isolation imposed upon Georgia placed a humiliation on the malcontents and a destructive inconvenience on the merchants and traders. Having reached the end of endurance, a group of outraged Georgians met in Savannah at the liberty pole on June 22nd, and appointed a council of safety, consisting of sixteen members headed by William Ewen, whose task it was to awaken the colony to its duty and to cultivate an understanding and good feeling with the Continental Congress and with the other colonies. Events now moved so swiftly that within a month the Revolutionists snatched the whole government from the hands of Wright and joined the other twelve colonies to make up the Original Thirteen.

On July 4th, the Second Provincial Congress met, attended by more than 100 delegates from every parish in the colony—

at last, the people were aroused. After electing Archibald Bulloch president and George Walton secretary, they adjourned from Tondee's Tavern to the Meeting House, where the Rev. Dr. John Joachim Zubly preached them a sermon "on the alarming state of American affairs." Making amends quickly for the timidity of the past, they entered with a whole soul into the non-importation association, elected delegates to the Second Continental Congress, issued various menacing petitions and flaming addresses, informed Governor Wright of what they had done, and making provisions for future meetings, adjourned on the 17th.

In entering into the association, they pledged themselves to import nothing from England and to give up the custom of wearing mourning, as the cloth for it could be had only in England, to drink no East India tea, to promote manufactories and the raising of sheep, and to appoint committees all over the colony to see that these rules were obeyed. A special secret seven was set up to find out everything the Provincial Congress should know. To be delegates to the Continental Congress, they redesignated Bulloch, Jones, and Houstoun, and added to the number Lyman Hall for the bold spirit he had shown by already attending, and the Reverend Zubly, for the excellent sermon he had preached and the various patriotic pamphlets he had written. Any three attending would be considered a quorum.

In a set of resolutions adopted on July 10th, they stretched taut the lines that held the colony to the mother country, as they set forth the political philosophy of the Revolution, which was fast becoming common speech from the St. Marys to the Androscoggin. In these resolutions, filled with such expressions as "despotic Ministry," "corrupted Parliament," and "army of mercenaries," they were careful to say nothing against the King, for they were not yet come to the point where they wanted independence. In a direct petition to the King for a redress of their grievances, they expressed great respect for him but detestation for the bad advisors with whom he had surrounded himself. Whatever might be the fate of this petition, they felt that they could "unrestrained, apply to the great and merciful Sovereign of the whole earth" and pray Him that the wicked might be removed from the King and that his throne might be established in righteousness. In an address to the people, with startling directness, they announced, "A civil war in America is begun," and recounted how the despicable British had spilled the blood of their fellow-men, and also how the Americans had well defended themselves and had stood up against the best British regulars.

They informed Wright what they had done and why. The people had been goaded into setting up this new governing body by his continual proroguing and dissolving the assembly, and after all, this Provincial Congress was much more representative than the old assembly had ever been. Wright was helpless; he had attempted in May and was to attempt again in November to reconvene the royal assembly, but without avail; his power was gone and the troops he called for with which to maintain his authority the British did not send. In August the Revolutionists seized the militia organization and expelled every officer who would not sign the articles of the non-importation association; they seized the custom house and took control of the port; and lastly they took over the courts of justice. Only the personal respect in which he was generally held guaranteed Wright his freedom in the colony. Dispirited and defeated, he asked to be recalled, but the government for which he had worked so loyally for the past fifteen years allowed him to remain to suffer the humiliation of arrest and imprisonment.

The British government was working cleverly though futilely to salvage Georgia from the wreck of its American empire and add her to those colonies which were to remain loyal, the Floridas, Quebec, Nova Scotia, and St. John. Therefore, it would not provoke further trouble in Georgia by sending

Wright troops. Near the end of 1775, when Parliament passed the Prohibitory Bill, breaking off trade with the rebellious colonies, it debated seriously whether Georgia should not be excluded from these penalties; but ultimately Georgia was grouped with the others, and Wright was ordered to enforce not only the terms of this law but to confiscate the property of all Georgians who did not give obedience to England. But before these orders reached Georgia, not only had British authority disappeared but Wright had fled.

For the purpose of observation and securing food, two British war-vessels and a transport laden with troops anchored off Tybee early in 1776. News of their arrival produced great excitement in Savannah, where an attack was momentarily expected. To prevent Governor Wright from communicating with them and securing their aid, on January 18th the council of safety ordered his arrest as well as the detention of all others who had not signed the articles of the non-importation association, unless they gave their parole not to take up arms against the new Georgia government. Joseph Habersham and a small following boldly entered the governor's mansion, where they found Wright holding a conference with his council, and before he could realize the purpose of the visit, they arrested the governor while the councilmen fled. They took his parole and left him in the mansion, on his honor not to communicate with the war-vessels. Wearied with his detention and fearful of the menaces of the Liberty Boys, on the night of February 11th he made his escape, and took refuge on the ships at Tybee, soon to sail away for Halifax, but not until they had had a brush with the Georgians. The Georgians were glad to be rid of their former governor, whom they did not wish to harm.

In the meantime, the Revolutionists had consolidated their government. They made permanent the Provincial Congress; they apportioned its membership among the different parishes and made it a larger body than the old assembly had been; and they gave the right to vote to all who had paid a tax. They set up a committee of fifteen to act as a court of appeals; and to concentrate and maintain a continuous authority which could act quickly at all times, they made permanent the council of safety. In December, George Walton succeeded William Ewen as the president. The council now exercised full authority when the Congress was not in session. It borrowed and printed money, collected provisions and munitions of war and kept close track of the herds of cattle in the colony, commissioned officers of the army and navy, watched the Indians and sent them presents, gave permission for people to enter and leave the province, prevented the price of goods from rising on account of the non-importation association, directed the raising and movement of troops, granted letters of marque, and provided for the election of new provincial congresses.

With Georgia engaged in such marked Revolutionary activities, the South Carolinians soon lost their contempt for Georgians and began to work in harmony with them, and Georgia reciprocated by sending South Carolina 5,000 pounds of powder and a brass field-piece. In fact, complete accord had been established by autumn of 1775. The Continental Congress also welcomed the new Georgia that had arisen and in November ordered the recruiting of a battalion of continental troops for its defense. Lachlan McIntosh became colonel of the battalion, Samuel Elbert, lieutenant-colonel, and Joseph Habersham, major.

The life taken on by the Revolutionary government formed in July, 1775, was soon evident. It was now necessary to blockade Georgia against all trade prohibited by the non-importation association and to prepare the colony for war, if unhappily it should come. In July, 1775, news reached the rebels that a British ship laden with powder was off the coast. The Provincial Congress commissioned Oliver Bowen and Joseph Habersham and placed them in charge of a boat to assist the South Carolinians who had also spied the British ship. The combined forces of the Georgians and Carolinians captured the vessel and secured 9,000 pounds of powder, 5,000 pounds of which they sent to the Continental Congress. Two months later the Georgians captured another British vessel laden with 250 barrels of powder, and about the same time they turned away a British vessel attempting to sell slaves.

To protect the beef supply against British raiding vessels, all cattle was ordered removed from the sea islands, and to gain war supplies which could not be manufactured in Georgia the council commissioned Captain Bowen to trade with French and Spanish West Indies, and Captain Pray was ordered to voyage to the Dutch possession of St. Thomas to obtain small arms, swivel guns, ammunition, and as many seamen as he could induce to return with him. To meet the expenses of these preparations the Second Provincial Congress voted £10,000 to be redeemed three years after reconciliation with England. Beginning in early 1776 Georgia exempted from the provisions of the non-importation association all vessels bringing in a certain amount of powder and other specified munitions of war, and to supervise the systematic arming of the colony a committee consisting of Samuel Elbert, Edward Telfair, and Joseph Habersham was appointed.

The first actual clash with the British took place in March, 1776, when the British war-vessels anchored at Tybee, finding it impossible to secure provisions, determined to seize a fleet of eleven rice ships tied up and detained at the wharf in Savannah. Fearful that the British would attempt to seize them, the Georgians erected fortifications, and swore to burn the city and the rice vessels before they would permit their capture. The warships sailed up the river, slipped by Hutchinson Island, and seized a few of the rice vessels before the Georgians could prevent it. Failing in their efforts to treat with the British, the Georgians, now aided by a force of South Carolinians, boarded some of the boats and set them afire. The British made away with two, but six were left and these the Georgians dismantled to prevent their escape. There had been much firing of cannon and small arms, but only a few people were killed or wounded in this comic-opera, "Battle of the Rice Boats." With this first flash of war extinguished, the position of Georgia was still precarious, for the only troops in the colony were Colonel McIntosh's battalion of 236 men, 60 mounted men on the Florida border, and a few more scattered on the western frontiers to watch the Indians.

The Third Provincial Congress met in January, and was still in session when the attack was made on Savannah. In great fear it fled to Augusta, and there, to make more efficient the working of the government, changed the framework. On April 15, 1776, this Revolutionary government adopted the first written fundamental document ever made by Georgians. It was a short text of eight rules and regulations, rather than a well-developed constitution. It was designed to be temporary, to await the advice of the Continental Congress and the exigencies of the times. There should now be a president and commander-in-chief of Georgia, elected by the Provincial Congress for a term of six months. The Provincial Congress and the council of safety should be continued, but the latter should be composed of thirteen men in addition to the delegates to the Continental Congress. The council should have no law-making power, but its advice the president must both seek and follow. Courts were organized, salaries were fixed, and all the old laws not inconsistent with new conditions were to continue. Thus was another definite step taken to consolidate Revolutionary government in Georgia, and to lead farther away from England. The Provincial Congress elected Bulloch, who had been president of the two previous congresses, the first president and commander-in-chief.

The tide of time had set in toward a complete and irretrievable break with England. A movement which had started out to secure rights claimed in the British Empire was fast propelling the American colonies into a demand for independence. The mother country had sought no understanding with her aggrieved colonies, but with a policy of blood and iron, sprinkled with contempt, she had alienated from many almost every filial feeling. War had set in, battles had been fought, and blood was being shed. The colonies had united under George Washington as commander-in-chief, who soon found himself vigorously defending New York City; and yet the colonies were still in the British Empire.

Georgia, which had been the last to join in the movement, was not in the early stages actuated by any desire for independence. Her first delegates to attend the Continental Congress included one who was as loyal to the colonial position as any one in Georgia, as long as the movement did not lead outside the Empire, but who could never fight for separation. Of the five appointed, Bulloch, Houstoun, and Zubly took their places in Philadelphia in September, 1775, but Zubly, as honest and fearless as anyone in Georgia, abandoned his seat when the drift toward independence set in. He returned to Savannah and his congregation, to be banished the next year with half of his property confiscated. In February, 1776, the Georgia delegates were Bulloch, Houstoun, and Hall, who had been re-elected, and George Walton and Button Gwinnett, who were to take the places of Jones and Zubly. On these men would rest Georgia's decision in the momentous question of independence, for no instructions were given to them. They were asked to remember that Georgia was surrounded with dangers on all sides, and that the closer the union with the other colonies the better. They should, therefore, "propose, join, and concur in all such measures as you shall think calculated for the common good and to oppose such as shall appear destructive."

When independence was voted in the Continental Congress the three Georgians present to sign the declaration were Button Gwinnett, Lyman Hall, and George Walton. On August 10th, a messenger reached Savannah with a copy. Archibald Bulloch, who had been elected president of Georgia, read it to the coun-

SIGNATURES OF THE
GEORGIA SIGNERS

cil and then repaired to the public square where the document was read to a gaping multitude, and then to the liberty pole it was carried to be read again and be emphasized by thirteen booming cannon. So compelling were its words that mobs of people hurried to the battery to hear it read a fourth time, to be followed by a salute from the siege guns there. That night a great funeral procession carried through the streets of Savannah an effigy of George III and buried it with high mockery. As the news spread, the outlying parishes held their celebrations.

Georgians had been slow to rebel in great numbers against the British Empire, but when once aroused they could become as stormy and uncontrolled as any Revolutionists in America. They had not waited for the Declaration of Independence to be signed before they began their patriotic extravagances. The Rev. Haddon Smith, rector of Christ Church in Savannah, had the previous year refused to observe the fast ordered by the Continental Congress, and to add to his contumely he made slighting remarks about the Provincial Congress. For this rebellion against rebellion, he was at once published as a public enemy, and a vigilance committee ordered that he desist from further preaching. In June, 1775 a Savannahian named Hopkins saw little sense in a liberty pole meeting at that time and said so. The patriotic fervor aroused led to his being tarred and feathered and dragged up and down the streets of the city for four or five hours. James Johnston, whose Revolutionary sentiments were difficult to discover, found it necessary to suspend his *Georgia Gazette,* February 7, 1776. A month before the Declaration of Independence, the council of safety listed and published as dangerous to liberty the names of forty-one people, and so sweeping were its patriotic suspicions that it included Edward Telfair, who was later to establish a reputation equal in patriotism to any Revolutionist in Georgia and to be rewarded with the governorship of the state. The intolerant extremes to which the patriots went at times led to the development of bitter enmities which were to devastate Georgia, and drive conservative support to the British armies. Colonel Thomas Brown, the scourge of upper Georgia in the Revolution, had been early driven into the arms of the British by the patriotic outburst of Augustans who tarred and feathered him and dragged him through the streets. Daniel McGirth, whose name became a terror wherever he went, left the Georgia forces because an unjust demand had been made that he surrender his horse, Gray Goose. Escaping prison, he rode away on Gray Goose to harry Georgians with fiendish delight. Undoubtedly, Georgia had got into the hands of the extreme radicals.

Although the other colonies in the beginning were much disgusted and bitter at Georgia's tardiness in joining the Revolution, they might well have pondered whether the value to be got out of it would not be much more for Georgia than for themselves. She was so weak and exposed that she might well have been considered more of a liability than an asset. She had only about 50,000 people, including Negro slaves. If every Georgian had cast his lot with the Revolution, she could not have afforded more than 5,000 fighting men. There were 10,000 Indian warriors in the tribes to the westward who had long been friends of England. They could not be blamed for not understanding why they should suddenly become the allies of a people who themselves scarcely knew why they had changed their allegiance. With Georgia out of the rebel movement, an easier boundary for the latter to defend would have resulted, the Savannah River. Indeed, Georgia had more to gain than to give in entering the Revolution; and the protection she received in a union with others, she was not soon to forget.

CHAPTER XII

THE WAR OF THE REVOLUTION

ALTHOUGH FEW celebrated battles were fought in Georgia, the Revolution produced here as great a devastation as beset any other part of America. Added to the fighting brought on by invading armies of British regulars was a bitter civil war among Georgians, provoked by the refusal of many people to join the Revolutionists. It was the good fortune, however, for Georgia to remain, for the first three years, far away from the area of the major campaigns. Not until the war had run its course through the battles of Trenton and Princeton, Brandywine and Germantown, Valley Forge, and Saratoga, did the British, dispirited and defeated in the North, turn their attention to the South.

Georgia did not wait, however, for the British to transfer the war to the South before she began military activities. By the perversity of fate, in every war that had taken place in her history, it had been her misfortune to have the enemy owning Florida and entrenched in St. Augustine to threaten and harry her southern frontiers. Every Tory in Georgia and the southeast and every enemy of the Revolutionists, together with runaway slaves and hostile Indians, looked to Florida as a haven, whence, organized as Florida Rangers, they could harass Georgia. By the beginning of 1776 these forays had become so troublesome that Captain John Baker, with seventy mounted volunteers from St. Johns Parish, made a swift march to the St. Marys to surprise a fort there which Governor Wright's brother had constructed. Aided by a British war-vessel the fort withstood the attack, and Baker was forced to retreat.

Nothing seemed to be left for Georgia to do but play again

at the century-old game of attempting to take St. Augustine. The Continental Congress had early recognized the advantage of possessing this stronghold, and on New Year's Day of 1776 recommended the project to Georgia, South Carolina, and North Carolina. In pursuance of this idea, as well as to promote the general defense of Georgia, Jonathan Bryan, John Houstoun, and Lachlan McIntosh went to Charleston in June to confer with General Charles Lee, who was the commander of the Continental troops in the Southern Department. Presenting the exposed situation in Georgia, surrounded as she was by hostile Indians and Florida Rangers, they convinced Lee that a strong attack should be made against Florida immediately. The Continental Congress now came to the rescue of Georgia by appropriating $60,000 to be used in raising and maintaining two additional battalions of Continental troops, the building of four galleys to protect the coast, and the construction of a fort at Savannah and one at Sunbury.

General Lee brought together a considerable army in Savannah which he reviewed in August, on Yamacraw Bluff. Commanded by Robert Howe and William Moultrie these troops were marched off for Florida, but before the end of September the whole force was back again, without ever having got much further south than Sunbury and without seeing the enemy. The whole expedition was a complete fiasco, owing to lack of transportation, lack of equipment, faulty management, and the hot climate. The troops, which had been strung out down the coast, were returned, and Georgia was left defenseless, as the fall of New York required concentration of efforts in the North.

Georgia had never since the arrival of Oglethorpe been able to become reconciled to St. Augustine in the hands of an enemy. She would not be now. Charles Lee and all his lieutenants might falter, but Georgia would do what had up to this time been the impossible, and the man who would do it was Button Gwinnett. In the early part of 1777, President Archibald

Bulloch had died and Gwinnett was made president and commander-in-chief of Georgia. To make people long remember
his term of office, and also to eclipse his enemy, Lachlan
McIntosh, Gwinnett decided not only to capture St. Augustine
but to conquer all Florida and annex it to Georgia. In addition
to a desire to gratify an ambition for military glory, President
Gwinnett wanted to punish the Florida Rangers, who in February had captured Fort McIntosh on the Satilla River and
had threatened Fort Howe on the Altamaha before they were
finally driven back into Florida. As he proceeded to get his
expedition ready, he decided to be content with less, and as an
unkind fate would have it, he was ultimately forced to accept
nothing. The great descent on Florida was planned with Sawpit
Bluff on the St. Johns River as the rendezvous. Colonel John
Baker with the Georgia militia should go by land and the
Continental troops under Colonel Samuel Elbert were to go by
boat. As might have been expected, the forces were unable to
time their arrival properly, and as a result each was forced to
fight the enemy without the aid of the other. By the end of
May, the expedition had met with complete failure and was on
its way back, and Gwinnett was thoroughly discredited, not
only as "Commander-in-Chief" but also as "President."

Not only because it had become a habit to attempt to invade
Florida, but also for other reasons, the Georgians again, in
1778, made ready for their annual descent. So bold had the
Florida Rangers become that they had carried out their raids
to the banks of the Altamaha River, and had actually sent their
spies into Savannah. Exasperated at this condition, the council
promised anyone who would raise as many as fifteen men a
"roving commission," which entitled him to plunder Florida
at will and to keep all that he should take. It also gave permission for Georgians to occupy any lands they pleased in
Florida north of the St. Johns River, and if they could maintain
their position for three months, then they should have a permanent grant of 500 acres. To add to the Florida dangers, a

South Carolina Tory, named Scophol, had marched across the Savannah below Augusta, and had plundered his way across Georgia to Florida, drawing after him every Tory and malcontent who would follow, until he had collected a horde of 500 or 600 men. The Scopholites were a terror and a menace to Georgia.

John Houstoun, now head of the Georgia government, decided to destroy the British power in Florida, and he, himself, would command the Georgia troops to make sure that the expedition would be a success. At Fort Howe on the Altamaha, the forces should assemble, 2,000 and more. Colonel Samuel Elbert commanded the Georgia Continentals, General Robert Howe, now commander of the Southern Department, led the Continental regulars, Houstoun brought up his militia, and Commodore Oliver Bowen commanded the Georgia navy. Colonel Elbert, while waiting at Fort Howe for the troops to collect, sent a force down the Altamaha in April and captured three British vessels near Frederica. By July the expedition had scattered itself from Savannah to the St. Marys, but nowhere had it been able to concentrate, for Houstoun refused to take orders from Howe, and Commodore Bowen refused to take orders from either. Finally Howe decided to abandon the expedition, and on July 5, 1778, he wrote from Fort Tonyn, a stronghold on the St. Marys which the British had abandoned, "In short, if I am ever again to depend upon operations I have no right to guide, and men I have no right to command, I shall deem it then as now I do, one of the most unfortunate accidents of my life." This expedition had been torn to pieces by jealousies between Continentals and militia, lack of preparations, swampy country, and the hot pestilential climate.

The British retreated beyond the St. Johns, and so sure was Houstoun that he was responsible for their flight that he decided to march on without Howe and take St. Augustine. On second thought, he concluded to return, but for months thereafter there were rumors that St. Augustine would soon be taken.

For three years Georgia troops had been marching up and down her coast in a border war-game, half-comic though tragic enough. By the middle of November, 1778 disquieting rumors reached Georgia that the full power of the British Empire would be sent against her, and in the operation an army from the North and troops from Florida would form a vise which would close down upon her. Scarcely had the rumor reached Georgia, before the Florida forces had set out—a land army of 100 British regulars and 300 Indians and Scopholites, commanded by Lieutenant-Colonel Mark Prevost and an expedition of 500 men by water under Lieutenant-Colonel L. V. Fuser. These two forces were to join in the Midway settlement and march upon Savannah to assist Colonel Archibald Campbell, who was sailing from New York with 2,000 regulars. The British hoped to retrieve in the South their Saratoga disaster, by conquering Georgia and continuing a triumphal march northward.

The forces from Florida made their appearance first. Prevost reached the Altamaha by the middle of November, and before the end of the month he had swept on up to Midway. In an attempt to drive him back, General James Screven was killed in a fierce engagement. The main forces of the Georgians quickly fortified the Ogeechee and took up a position there. Prevost had expected the aid of Fuser but, discovering that he had not made his appearance before Sunbury according to plans, retreated to Florida, burning stacks of rice and devastating the country as he marched back. Before leaving Midway, he burned the Meeting House. Scarcely had Prevost disappeared, before Fuser landed 500 men near Sunbury and demanded of Colonel John McIntosh and his 200 defenders that they surrender the post. McIntosh answered, "Come and take it," but Fuser, finding that Prevost had retreated, did not accept the challenge. Instead, he sailed down the coast and landed on St. Simons Island. For this answer, the Georgia assembly voted McIntosh a sword, with his defiant words written upon it.

In the latter part of December the long expected grand assault upon Savannah was made. Colonel Campbell landed more than 2,000 troops a few miles down the river and made preparations to seize the city, defended by General Howe with a few more than 600 troops. As Savannah was well protected by impassable marshes the British had no easy task before them. But Howe, failing to take the good advice given him to secure certain passageways across the marshes, made it possible for an old Negro to show Campbell a little-traversed passageway and thereby give the British an important advantage. The British were upon Howe before he knew it, driving the Americans through the streets in great confusion and out through the swamps and rice fields. More than half of the Americans were killed, drowned, or captured, whereas the British lost only a half dozen killed and nine wounded. Howe with a few soldiers made his escape into South Carolina and ordered the troops at Sunbury and Augusta to follow him. Thus would he have entirely abandoned Georgia to the British; but the forces at Sunbury and Augusta chose to await the British.

Wright soon returned as royal governor and sought to supplant the Revolutionary government, even as it had supplanted him in 1775. He was rewarded for a time with almost equal success.

The defeat at Savannah was as amazing as it was melancholy. Howe was bitterly assailed for his incompetency, which almost bordered on treason. Many people felt that he could have withstood an indefinite siege, if he had properly guarded the approaches to the city. A court martial tried and acquitted him, but he lost his military reputation, which he did not regain by wounding General Christopher Gadsden in the ear in a duel provoked by the General's harsh criticism.

The British now made haste to seize all Georgia. Colonel Augustine Prevost, in early January, sailed up from Florida with

2,000 troops and laid siege to Sunbury, defended by Fort Morris and 200 troops commanded by Major Joseph Lane. Little fighting was required to take the place, for the Americans lost only three killed and six wounded, and the British casualties were only one killed and three wounded. Fort Morris, which the British renamed Fort George, and much war material fell into the hands of the British. Again had disaster overtaken the Revolutionary cause in Georgia.

Colonel Prevost marched on to Savannah to take charge while Campbell swept all before him up the Savannah River. Savannah had fallen on December 29, 1778; on January 2, Ebenezer was occupied. Though the majority of the Salzburgers supported the Revolution, Pastor Christopher F. Triebner upheld the British, but this support did not prevent the conversion of Jerusalem Church into a hospital and horse-stable and the ultimate extinction of Ebenezer as a town. The British continued on up the river, opposed by John Twiggs and Benjamin and William Few with the small forces they were able to collect, and before the end of January, Campbell had seized Augusta. Well might the Georgians have despaired, for not a place of importance was left to them throughout the state.

Flushed with victory, Campbell sent out his raiders northward into Wilkes County, and their appearance led many of the defenseless people to flee into South Carolina. It seemed that the British had completely snuffed out all opposition; but an amazing bit of life was smouldering which in less than a month was to flare up with such force as to compel the British hastily to abandon Augusta. Elijah Clarke, John Twiggs, and John Dooly, rousing the frontiersmen of Wilkes and the regions to the southward, and assisted by Colonel Andrew Pickens with a group of South Carolinians, fell upon an army of 800 British led by Colonel Boyd on Kettle Creek, completely dispersed it, and killed Boyd. In the latter part of February, Campbell moved out of Augusta toward Savannah, and hope rose high among the patriots.

After the disgrace of Howe, General Benjamin Lincoln was placed in charge of the Southern Department. With headquarters at Purrysburg, in South Carolina, he began preparations to drive the British out of Georgia, or confine them to the coast. At this time the British had about 4,000 troops in the state, made up of loyalists from New York, New Jersey, South Carolina, and Georgia, of Florida Rangers, and of a few Hessians. Lincoln hoped to concentrate about 8,000 troops, but in the midst of his preparations, in early March, 1779, General John Ashe, with a detachment of 2,300 men, allowed himself to be attacked at Brier Creek, on the point of land made by its junction with the Savannah, and here being surprised by a force under Mark Prevost, he suffered a most humiliating defeat. The whole army was scattered, with many men killed, drowned, and captured, and most of the remainder fleeing to their homes. The only forces which made an effort to fight were those led by Samuel Elbert.

The British had made a good beginning in their plan to subdue the southern states, one by one, on their march northward. Georgia was prostrate, and unless a strong effort were made to reclaim her, the people who had not fled would reconcile themselves to British rule again. In the fall of 1779 a bold move was made to oust the British from Savannah by calling to the aid of Georgia a French fleet, since France, in a treaty the previous year, had agreed to come to the rescue of the Americans. Count d'Estaing had sailed for America with the hope of bottling up the British fleet in the Delaware River, but before he arrived the British made their escape, and so after a fruitless cruise off the north Atlantic coast, he sailed for the West Indies, where he won easy victories. In high spirits he willingly listened to the pleadings of the Georgians, and agreed to come and drive the British out of Savannah and give them back their city. He arrived on the coast of Georgia September 1st, sailed up the Savannah, and without waiting for General Lincoln to come with his American troops, de-

manded the surrender of the city. General Augustine Prevost
cleverly asked for and secured a short delay, not to consider the
demand, as Count d'Estaing thought, but to give a British
force in South Carolina under Colonel John Maitland time to
slip into the city. Lincoln arrived about the same time, and the
French and American armies laid siege. As three weeks and
more of siege operations produced no evidences of success,
Count d'Estaing became impatient, for he feared the inroads
of disease, the dangers to his fleet of the autumn hurricanes,
and the approach of British war vessels. He ordered a grand
assault for October 9th, which resulted in a dismal failure. The
gallant Count Pulaski fell mortally wounded and Sergeant
Jasper, of Fort Moultrie fame, met death. More than a thousand Americans and French were killed or wounded. The
British casualties were about 150. There were about 6,500 allies

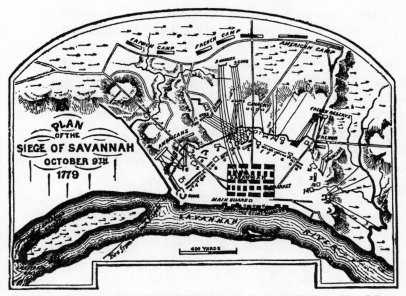

B. J. Lossing, *Pictorial Field-Book of the Revolution*, II. New
York: Harper & Brothers, 1860.

engaged, while the British numbered about 2,500. To the French the Savannah misadventure was calamitous enough, but to Georgia it was a catastrophe.

Lincoln with his remnant of an army, leaving Georgia to her fate, retreated into South Carolina, in an attempt to save that state; but within six months Charleston had fallen and the British seemed well on their way toward crushing out all opposition in the South. Georgia now swung backward swiftly into a state of nature, more savage than brute creation. The customs of civilized beings disappeared as a war of extermination began, in which Whigs and Tories, with fire and sword, fought and plundered each other. The weaklings fled the state, and only those who were strong in their hatreds and their muscles remained. Guerrilla warriors and unvarnished murderers sought vengeance among themselves, which too often bore no recognizable relation to the Revolution itself. Added to the murderous warfare were starvation and small-pox. In this welter of barbarism, arose heroes and heroines whose meed of good deeds made them shine the brighter by contrast. Some were more mythical than real, but the fame of all grew with time. Elijah Clarke and his son John never gave up the fight, though forced to flee the state; John Twiggs, Benjamin and William Few, James Jackson, and others rallied small groups who fought and ran in order to fight again; John Dooly harried the British until he was foully murdered in bed by marauding Tories, but his son later amply avenged him by an equally foul murder of nine Tory prisoners without hindrance from his officers. Patrick Carr, a real Irishman in the flesh, did valuable service as a partisan warrior and developed a halo of heroism so extravagant that tradition made him count life a failure since he had killed with his own hands only a hundred men. History records little more than the fact that Robert Sallette lived, but tradition made of him a person much more remarkable than many Robin Hoods and Dick Turpins combined. Times that produced such men would be indeed remiss if they did not produce remarkable women. Sarah Gilliam Williamson, wife of Micajah, never found it necessary to leave her plantation while her husband was fighting with Elijah Clarke; and if Aunt Nancy Hart were half what tradition has made of her, she was largely responsible for the rescue of all upper Georgia from the Tories.

To make possible these American heroes, it was necessary that British and Tory fiends arise. Acting the part well, emerged James and Daniel McGirth, Thomas Brown, and Colonel Grierson.

With the British power strongly radiating out of Savannah, two areas of cyclonic disturbances developed, one down the coast in the Midway region and the other north and west of Augusta centering in Wilkes County. The greatest patriotic

NANCY HART ATTACKING THE TORIES

George White, *Historical Collections of Georgia*. New York: Pudney & Russell, 1855.

strength lay in this upcountry, where the last remnant of the Revolutionary government took refuge, and thus did Wilkes County become all that was left of Revolutionary Georgia, in strange striking contrast to South Carolina where the up-country was Tory. As the patriots flitted through the forests organizing themselves and attacking their enemies, it was fitting that Spirit Creek, below Augusta, should have been their gathering place. In the last days of 1779 the Revolution-ary government ordered six forts to be built in Wilkes so the people might "enfort themselves," and when these forts were finished each was manned by thirty men.

After the fall of Charleston in May, 1780, the British re-occupied Augusta, as Andrew Williamson turned traitor and handed it over without a struggle, accepting in return a com-mission in the British army. The city was delivered to Thomas Brown, who had lived there at the outbreak of the Revolution and who had been tarred and feathered and dragged through its streets for lack of patriotic zeal. Now he took vengeance, tardy though terrible. He scourged and murdered the patriots living there and confiscated their property, and he harried and devastated all the surrounding country. So barbaric were his cruelties that Elijah Clarke was temporarily forced to suspend his military activities in order to lead into the mountains of East Tennessee for safety 400 women and children. He then resumed his fighting in South Carolina.

In the fall of 1780 Clarke was back in Wilkes preparing to wrest Augusta from the British. In an attack in September he failed as British reënforcements came up. Of the thirty wounded prisoners he left, Brown hanged thirteen on his stairway where he could watch them and the remainder he handed over to his Indian allies to scalp and torture to death. But the next year the embittered Georgians rejoiced, for they took Augusta as well as their revenge. With the aid of an American army under Light-Horse Harry Lee and Andrew Pickens, the Georgians, led by Clarke, invested the city in May and gradually tightened their grip. Soon they captured a part of the city and made prisoner Colonel Grierson, whose fiendish barbarities had so enraged the patriots that a soldier shot him to death and although it was common knowledge who did it, the officers were never able to find out officially. The last refuge of Brown's forces was Fort Cornwallis, and the better to attack it, General Lee constructed a tower by which to elevate his cannon. The city was taken and James Jackson was awarded the honor of commanding it.

It was about this time that a Tory song was written called "The Volunteers of Augusta" and sung to the tune of "The Lilies of France." Calling for retaliation and revenge, the first four stanzas are:

> Come join, my brave lads, come all from afar,
>   We're all Volunteers, all ready for war;
> Our service is free, for honour we fight,
>   Regardless of hardships by day or by night.

> #### Chorus
> Then all draw your swords, and constantly sing,
> Success to our Troops, our Country, and King.

> The Rebels they murder,—Revenge is the word,
>   Let each lad return with blood on his sword;
> See Grierson's pale ghost point afresh to his wound;
>   We'll conquer, my boys, or fall dead on the ground.

> Then brandish your swords, and constantly sing,
> Success to our Troops, our Country, and King.

> They've plundered our houses, attempted our lives,
>   Drove off from their houses our children and wives;
> Such plundering miscreants no mercy can crave,
>   Such murdering villains no mercy shall have.

> Then chop with your swords, and constantly sing,
> Success to our Troops, our Country, and King.

> Then think not of plunder, but rush on the foe,
>   Pursue them, my boys, with blow after blow,

Till in their own bed we see them all welter
Or behind the Blue Mountains retreat for a shelter.

Then chop with your swords, and constantly sing,
Success to our Troops, our Country, and King.

The chief activities of the patriots in the region south of Savannah were confined to the water. The guerrillas on land became privateers on sea, and many Georgians took their vengeance as well as valuable property as they harried British commerce or beat back marauding vessels from Florida. The Georgia privateers made the rice vessels on the Ogeechee their special object of attack and often they were successful. The regularly commissioned naval vessels were commanded by Commodore Oliver Bowen until 1778, when, for too independent a disposition, the assembly declared him in high contempt and suspended him. Edward Telfair was the chief boat-builder of the Georgia Revolutionists. The last important ship in the Georgia navy was the *Sailors' Delight,* both bought and sold at auction the last year of the war.

General Lincoln, captured at the fall of Charleston, was succeeded as commander of the Southern Department by Horatio Gates, who signalized his services by fleeing from the enemy 180 miles in four days; and in December, 1780, Nathanael Greene was put in command in the South. In March of the next year he fought Cornwallis at Guilford Courthouse in North Carolina, and set him on the road to his ultimate defeat at Yorktown in October, while Greene marched back into South Carolina to clear out the British there. In the meantime, the Georgians after the fall of Augusta had been pressing the British hard and were restricting their sphere of influence as they converged on Savannah. Colonel James Jackson raised his Georgia Legion and carried his fighting to the banks of the Ogeechee and to the southward, while Colonel Twiggs pushed the British into Ebenezer. With the surrender of Cornwallis, the chances of the British to reconquer America had perished, and it was now only a matter of waiting for time to run its course. To speed the time and assist Jackson and Twiggs, in the spring of 1782 General Greene sent Anthony Wayne to Georgia with a force of Continental troops. Sir James Wright, who had been back in Savannah playing as governor since its capture in 1778, now made every effort possible to have re-enforcements sent, but Sir Guy Carleton in New York ordered the evacuation in May, and Wright was soon in communication with Wayne trying to secure the best terms possible for those people who had chosen to support his government. The Georgia governor, John Martin, anxious to save for the rebuilding of his state as much property and as many people as possible, gave the British merchants ample time to dispose of their goods at a fair price, and promised that he would recommend to his government the granting of oblivion to all the loyalist militia who were not guilty of murder. War criminals must not be allowed to depart, but must submit to trial in the Georgia courts.

In July the British marched out and General Wayne allowed James Jackson the honor of taking possession of the city for the Americans. The Georgians did not assist the British in evacuating the city; otherwise they would not have permitted the removal of much property plundered throughout the state, including 5,000 slaves. The treaty of peace was not signed for more than a year (September 3, 1783), but the Georgians, at last rid of the British, set about building on the ruins of seven years a new commonwealth.

CHAPTER XIII

CIVIL GOVERNMENT DURING THE REVOLUTION

GOVERNMENTAL CONDITIONS in Georgia during the Revolution were accompanied by almost as much disorganization as characterized military affairs. Not only did the British in re-establishing their royal authority attempt to impose upon the people another government, but the patriots, or Whigs, as they chose more often to call themselves, torn with internal dissensions during the darkest days, set up two Revolutionary governments. Thus a people badly in need of law and order found themselves beset with three governments with none of them able to afford either.

The declaration of the colonies in 1776 that they were forever independent of the British Empire, made it necessary for them to build with greater permanency in their governmental organization. Georgia's rules and regulations, by which in February the government of the presidency was set up, had been designed as temporary; so now President Bulloch called an election for a convention which would, while it sat, not only govern the state but also make for it an instrument of government, which was to be its first real constitution. This assembly met in October, 1776, and continued until the following February. It did a remarkable work, for now for the first time was the detailed organization of Georgia reduced to paper, and a chance given for the new Revolutionists to set down and try out their new ideas and principles.

Levying or not as they pleased or were able to do, upon the past governmental experiences of Georgia and of the other colonies and upon the theories and practices of governments and philosophers as far back as Plato and Aristotle, these

Top left: ELIJAH CLARKE, UNYIELDING SOLDIER OF THE REVOLUTION. *Top right:* BENJAMIN LINCOLN, BORN IN MASSACHUSETTS THE YEAR GEORGIA WAS FOUNDED, COMMANDER OF THE DEPARTMENT OF THE SOUTH IN 1778, AND A LEADER OF THE UNSUCCESSFUL ASSAULT ON SAVANNAH THE NEXT YEAR. *Bottom left:* CHARLES HENRI, COUNT D'ESTAING, COMMANDER OF THE FRENCH FLEET IN AMERICAN WATERS, WHO UNSUCCESSFULLY ATTACKED THE BRITISH IN SAVANNAH IN 1779. *Bottom right:* COUNT CASIMIR PULASKI, POLISH FRIEND OF AMERICA, WHO WAS KILLED AT THE SIEGE OF SAVANNAH, 1779.

Top left: JAMES JACKSON, BORN IN ENGLAND, SOLDIER IN THE REVOLUTION, MEMBER OF THE UNITED STATES HOUSE OF REPRESENTATIVES, GOVERNOR, AND BITTER FOE OF THE YAZOO LAND FRAUD. *Top right:* GEORGE M. TROUP, WHO AS GOVERNOR NEARLY PRECIPITATED A WAR WITH THE UNITED STATES IN HIS ATTEMPT TO DRIVE OUT THE CREEK INDIANS. *Bottom left:* GEORGE R. GILMER, TWICE GOVERNOR, A MEMBER OF THE UNITED STATES HOUSE OF REPRESENTATIVES, AND THE GARRULOUS BUT LOVABLE AUTHOR OF *Sketches of Some of the First Settlers of Upper Georgia. Bottom right:* JOHN FORSYTH, GRADUATE OF PRINCETON, MEMBER OF THE UNITED STATES HOUSE OF REPRESENTATIVES AND OF THE SENATE, MINISTER TO SPAIN, GOVERNOR, AND SECRETARY OF STATE UNDER ANDREW JACKSON.

constitution-makers boldly labored and produced a detailed framework of government. They set up and separated the executive, legislative, and judicial authorities, and added an abbreviated bill of rights, including the principles of the writ of habeas corpus, freedom of the press, trial by jury, and prohibitions against excessive fines and bail.

Remembering their experiences with Governor Wright, these constitution-makers divided the executive authority between a governor and a council and stated that he should exercise that authority only with the advice of the council, who should be in constant attendance at his residence. He should be elected by the House of Assembly, hold office for only one year, and might not succeed himself for two years after the end of his term. His power was further weakened by the prohibition against his vetoing bills, granting pardons, or remitting fines. No one was allowed to be governor who had not lived in the state three years and who would not swear to give up his authority when his term of office should expire. The governor, besides being given the title of *Honorable,* should also be captain-general and commander-in-chief of the state's army and navy.

The council was a group which the House of Assembly selected from its own membership, taking two councilmen from each county which sent up as many as ten representatives. Such counties would, therefore, lose two of their representatives, but would gain two councilmen. All other counties were unrepresented on the council, but when their population should grow to 100 voters they would reach the council stage. All counties with as many as ten voters should have one representative and their representation should increase according to a fixed scale. Not only did the council keep constant watch over the governor, but it likewise reviewed all bills passed by the House of Assembly and returned them within five days with its comments. The house, though forced to listen to the advice of the council, was not forced to accept it. In the absence of the governor, the president of the council should assume his duties.

The chief source of authority was the legislature, consisting of only one body, called the House of Assembly, which in a sense was an oligarchy having not only complete legislative power but by indirection much of the executive as well. Any person was eligible to the assembly who had lived in the state a year, who was a Protestant and 21 years old, who owned 250 acres of land or property worth £250, and who could swear that he had not secured the office by fraud or bribery. The assembly should last for only one year. In addition to county representation, cities were also given membership in the assembly.

The judiciary should consist of a superior court for each county, composed of at least four justices, and minor courts, called courts of conscience. There was no supreme court; and the judicial authority which the colonial council had possessed was not continued with this new council. There was, however, a chief justice, elected by the House of Assembly, as indeed were all the other judges, who should attend and preside over the various superior courts, and in a sense, give a semblance of uniformity to judicial procedure and interpretation.

The right to vote was given to all white males who owned property worth £10, or who had a mechanic trade, and who had lived in the state six months. Voting should be done by ballot. Anyone who was fortunate enough to have these qualifications and who should not have enough interest in his government to vote, should be fined £5.

Now that the authority of the Church of England was acknowledged no more than the authority of the King of England, the Georgians abolished the parishes and established for purposes of local government eight counties, and to emphasize what they were thinking about most, in naming the counties, they dethroned the saints who had presided over the old parishes, and erected Liberty. Now arose Wilkes, Richmond, Burke, Effingham, Chatham, Glynn, and Camden, all old friends of the colonies, and the name Liberty, itself, appropriately alighted on a county composed of the former parishes of St. John, St. Andrew, and St. James. As the churchmen had not been conspicuous in the fight for independence from England, the power of the church was destroyed by abolishing the tax for its support and the granting of religious liberty to all, and by excluding from membership in the House of Assembly all clergymen.

In the midst of war, these constitution-makers thought of schools and provided that each county should set them up, but that the state should support them. The cheap trappings of titles of nobility should not be worn in Georgia, and no one might through the principle of entail maintain great family holdings. Anxious to play her part in the new confederation of states that was being formed, Georgia provided that her delegates should be appointed annually and should not only serve in the Confederation Congress but should also be members of the state assembly.

This constitution could be amended only by a difficult process. Petitions from a majority of the counties, signed by a majority of the voters in each county and stating the definite change wanted, must be sent to the House of Assembly, which should call a convention whose sole power consisted in making only the changes specified in the petitions.

This constitution was finished in February, 1777, and without taking time to submit it to the people, the convention declared it adopted. Before it could be carried into operation President Bulloch died, and to fill the vacancy the council of safety designated Button Gwinnett. Having been ambitious for military glory and having had his hopes thwarted by the preferment of Lachlan McIntosh, Gwinnett now as head of the state decided to carry out his Florida invasion, previously mentioned, and in doing so took special pains to ignore McIntosh. Then, failing in his expedition, he sought next to be elected governor under the new constitution, but the assembly decided on John

Adams Treutlen, a patriotic Salzburger. These reverses greatly pleased McIntosh, who showed his pleasure so exuberantly that Gwinnett challenged him to a duel. In Savannah, twelve feet apart, they savagely fought it out according to the gentleman's code. Both were wounded, and after four days of intense suffering, Gwinnett died for the want of medical care which science had not then developed. Great excitement prevailed, for the duel emphasized factional differences that were arising among the Whigs. Lyman Hall and the more radical element demanded the trial of McIntosh and secured it. Though he was acquitted, McIntosh left the state because of bitterly hostile public opinion. He was given a command in the North, and his leaving put Georgia in charge of Howe, who was soon to show his incompetency by giving up Savannah to the British.

Since the constitution required the election of a governor at the first meeting of each legislature in January, Governor Treutlen, who had been chosen in May, served scarcely more than a half term; but during that time he succeeded in crushing an attempt of South Carolina to obliterate Georgia as a state and re-annex her. South Carolina's contempt for Georgia, born almost as soon as Oglethorpe had set up the colony, had not abated even though Georgia had entered the Revolution with vigor after a late start. In the latter part of 1776, South Carolina resolved to absorb the regions beyond the Savannah, and to carry it out she appointed William H. Drayton and John Smith to forestall Georgia's making a constitution by appearing before the convention and showing the Georgians how foolish it would be for them to attempt to establish a state. In the latter part of January, 1777, they applied for permission to address the convention and were admitted. Drayton recalled how Georgia had at one time been a part of South Carolina and how, if now she should be re-annexed, she would prosper uncommonly. The expense of government would be reduced and she would not be expected to help pay any of South Carolina's public debt; her land would become much more valuable, her currency would be greatly helped, her trade would flourish, and Savannah would become twice as prosperous; and boundary disputes would automatically disappear. If Georgia should fail to grasp this argument, then South Carolina would build a great city across the river from Savannah, and in many other ways would sap the strength out of the upstart state of Georgia.

Drayton was expecting too much from human nature when he asked people who held the reins of authority and were busily constructing a new government, to give up their offices and silently disappear into oblivion. Naturally they resented the arrogance of such requests, but it was also natural to expect a few Georgians to agree with Drayton. Refusing to accept as final the convention's rejection, Drayton began to correspond with various Georgians and to send them petitions to be circulated, demanding that Georgia join South Carolina. When Treutlen became governor, he resolved to put an effective stop to Drayton's insidious work. On July 15th he issued a proclamation in which he charged Drayton and others with "unlawfully endeavoring to poison the minds of the good people," and "by letters, petitions and otherwise, daily exciting animosities among the inhabitants, under the pretense of redressing imaginary grievances." He offered a reward of £100 for the arrest of Drayton or any of his accomplices.

Drayton, safe in South Carolina, issued a stinging and satirical answer to Treutlen's proclamation, in which he called Treutlen a Tory and a buffoon, and his proclamation, "a compound of nonsense and falsehoods." Property and life, he declared, were unsafe in Georgia and its burlesque government was "a disgrace and detriment to the American cause."

The new government under Treutlen gained strength as it grew older. In January, 1778, John Houstoun was elected governor; but he foolishly set out on his St. Augustine venture and soon added more weakness than strength to his government. With the governor in the field, the council decided to forego its constitutional right and duty of advising with him, by declaring that full executive power should be vested in him. This unconstitutional abdication of power was as much a recognition of the disorganization that was setting in as it was an effort to strengthen the governor.

Amidst the alarms of a British advance on Savannah, a legislature was elected in early December, 1778, which was to meet in the following January to elect a new governor. Before that time arrived, the British had captured Savannah and scattered the Whigs in every direction. The last entry in the council minutes recorded the disaster which had overtaken the state: "The Town of Savannah being taken by the British Troops, on the twenty eighth of December put a final end to public business of a civil nature."

The British now feeling that they had demolished the civil as well as the military power of the Whigs, set about reclaiming Georgia and setting up the old royal government. They called upon all citizens to deliver up their arms and munitions of war and to take an oath to support George III and "solemnly disclaim and renounce that unlawful and iniquitous confederacy called the General Continental Congress." They ordered the confiscation of the property of all men who remained obdurate. On March 15, 1779, a board of commissioners was set up to ferret out the property of those who refused to take the oath, with the promise that revenues from it should be used, instead of taxation, in carrying on the military operations and the royal government. Furthermore, there should be no added taxation by Parliament. Only the Tories should be allowed to engage in business and trade. To break up thoroughly the rebel government, a reward of ten guineas each was offered for the arrest of the Whig assemblymen. A society called "The Friends of Constitutional Liberty" was set up in Savannah to patrol the city and watch for rebel activities. The *Georgia Gazette,* now re-enforced with the word *Royal,* re-appeared on January 21, 1779, and soon was running under the management of the versatile James Johnston, whose ability as a printer was equally good whether he be Whig or Tory.

The military officials began this work of rehabilitating British civil authority. Soon Lieutenant-Colonel Mark Prevost was made lieutenant governor and ordered to set up a government. In July Sir James Wright returned to continue the work he had left off three years previously, and Chief Justice Anthony Stokes and other old royal officers drifted back to take up their former duties. Before Sir James could proceed far in re-establishing his old government, the Count d'Estaing attack on Savannah directed the attention of all Tories to the defense of the city. Wright forsook governmental activities for the time, vigorously to aid in beating off the Whigs. With the rebels scattered, he now set about extending his authority over the state, by spreading proclamations of forgiveness to all who would lay down their arms, by putting under a bond of good behavior those who were lukewarm, and by threatening to prosecute for high treason those who continued to resist. Many Georgians, despairing of victory, ceased their opposition and accepted Wright's government.

After almost a year of effort Wright set his government going, in name at least. In May, 1780, a royal assembly was elected, which met in Savannah soon thereafter, and although a quorum did not appear, Sir James decided to let it sit and transact business. On July 1st it passed a law disqualifying for holding office 151 rebels listed by name and a great many others by description. Later laws were passed confiscating rebel property.

This royal government, though at times stronger than its rival and always more stationary, was never able to approximate the strength it possessed in colonial times. It was a mere incident in the military policy of England of reconquering her former colonies, and therefore received little aid apart from this purpose. Sir James frequently complained of being left almost wholly unprotected, and finally when Savannah was evacuated by the British he went out with a complaint that no effort had been made to strengthen his government.[1] Although his power nominally extended to Augusta during the intervals when the British held that city, the boundary line of any effective authority which he could exercise did not reach north of Hudson's Ferry on the Savannah, about half the distance to Augusta.

On the fall of Savannah, the Whig government fled to Augusta, where it attempted to reorganize itself and continue its existence. It was particularly unfortunate for the patriots that the British invaded the state and upset the government just at the time when a transition had to be made from one administration to another. The assembly, elected in December, 1778, to meet in the following January to choose a governor, was so scattered that a quorum could not be collected. A few members came together, but did not feel that they could validly elect a new governor; and as Governor Houstoun's term had expired, the state was now left without an executive head. They did, however, on January 7th, select a provisional committee to act as a council until a fuller assembly could be got together to give it definite power. Within a few weeks the assembly, augmented with increased membership and courage, clothed the council with executive power, whereupon the latter elected William Glascock its president, who thus became the highest executive officer in the state, though not termed governor. Before the end of the month the British seized Augusta, and the remnant of the Whig government was forced again to flee. By July the British were out of Augusta and the Georgia government came to life again in a meeting of the assembly which elected a supreme executive council to take the place of a governor and to exercise all executive power. It consisted of

[1] Sir James deserved well of the British government. He worked long and faithfully for royal interests in Georgia, and had his advice always been followed, he might have saved his colony for Britain in the Revolution. After he left Georgia never to return he devoted much of his life to pushing the claims of expatriated Georgia loyalists to recompense for their losses, and when he died the British showed their high regard for him by burying him in Westminster Abbey—a unique honor for a former governor of Georgia.

nine men with self-perpetuating powers. The Georgians hoped that it might continue to rule, even if every other part of the government passed out of existence. This council had the right to elect the state's delegates to the Continental Congress, though in fact they were elected by mass meetings of patriots, and these delegates were also to help keep governments in Georgia going, for they were given power to borrow money, regulate the militia, appoint judicial officials, and set up local government. The constitution had broken down completely and the state was now in the hands of a small group of dictators, as, indeed, necessity demanded.

The supreme executive council immediately ordered the county treasurers to bring their funds to Augusta, as there was "the utmost distress for cash," and knowing that it had no power to enforce its demands, it threatened to call upon the state of North Carolina to assist in ruling Georgia. Still the supreme executive council raised little money and was soon forced to permit its troops to collect their salaries by plundering the Tories. The council organized July 24th with Seth John Cuthbert as its temporary president, who gave way a few days later to John Wereat as the permanent head.

Dissensions, already evident in the Whig ranks, soon broke out in a government set up to oppose the supreme council. George Walton, Richard Howley, George Wells, and others by devious methods resolved themselves into what they claimed to be a constitutional assembly and proceeded to elect Walton governor. This action was to forestall the meeting of the assembly called by Wereat for January, 1780, according to the constitution. Here were two governments, in addition to Wright's in Savannah, quarrelling over a duty which neither was able to perform. Wereat's supreme council was conciliatory, and claimed no powers beyond what had been given them by the old assembly and disclaimed any ambitions to belabor an already fading cause. Yet the Walton faction continued to charge them with violating the constitution and with Toryism, and it carried on what little government there was outside of Savannah. The Continental Congress, refusing full trust to either faction but fearful of the extinction of Georgia, placed in the hands of General Lincoln and Joseph Clay, a member of the supreme executive council, $500,000 to be used in rescuing the state.

The assembly met in January according to Wereat's call, and it seemed that after a year of civil turmoil the state could not get back on its constitution. Under the influence of the Walton clique, it elected Richard Howley governor and did him the additional honor of electing him to the Continental Congress. It also declared that the government under the supreme council had been illegal and that all of its acts were void. About this time the British were closing in on Charleston, and Lincoln stripped Georgia of its defenses to aid in protecting South Carolina. The Georgia government that had seemed to start well was now fast descending almost to the point of extinction. The assembly resolved that in the absence of the governor the executive council and its president should have full powers of government; and fearing the fall of Augusta, admitting that it could "be surprised by twenty men; by which the Members of Government might be Massacred or captured," it fixed as the future capital Heard's Fort, far up in the backwoods of Wilkes County. As the days became darker, Governor Howley decided to leave Georgia to her fate while he sought safety in states farther north and in attendance on the Continental Congress. On his departure George Wells, who was the head of the executive council, became the chief executive of the state.

The failure of the patriots to work in harmony was pathetic. The fires of hatred kindled by the McIntosh-Gwinnett duel were still burning, and when in the latter part of 1779 McIntosh returned to Georgia, Walton forged letters to the Continental Congress deprecating McIntosh's return. The forgery was soon detected, which added further to the quarrel between the two factions. Wells, who was a member of the Walton clique, which had defied the supreme council, seems to have been a late convert to the Revolution and in addition was overbearing in his manner. For these and other reasons, somewhat obscure, the fiery patriot James Jackson, early in 1780 fought him in a duel and killed him. It was a savage encounter, fought without seconds, in which both were wounded. When found, Wells was dead and Jackson was lying upon the ground dangerously wounded in both knees. Indeed, one of the besetting weaknesses of the patriots in Georgia was their inability to bring about coöperation either in civil government or in military affairs. Army life was riddled with threats and encounters, some of which were aired in the executive council meetings, as in the instance where an officer quarreling with another whipped out his sword and threatened "to make Sun and Moon Shine thro' him, or Words to the Effect."

With George Wells, the chief executive, dead, the council elected Humphrey Wells, who gave way after two days to Stephen Heard, February 18, 1780. Charleston fell in May and soon thereafter Augusta came into the hands of the British again, and the fragments of the Georgia government retreated deep into the forests of Wilkes to the frontier at Heard's Fort which had been previously designated the capital, and now Wilkes became the state of Georgia as far as the patriots could control it. As Lord Cornwallis harried South Carolina and Major Patrick Ferguson marched into the upcountry, there was danger that Whig Georgia would become completely extinct.

As time went on, the government maneuvered its base of existence from one fort or fortified place to another through Wilkes and Burke counties, and finally came to rest again in Augusta after the British had been expelled from that place in June, 1781. In August an assembly was got together which elected Nathan Brownson governor, and at last the solid foundations began to be laid, on which an enduring government was to be based. The assembly immediately made preparations to collect the Georgians who had fled the state. Those in South Carolina were ordered to return within thirty days; those in North Carolina, within sixty days; those in Virginia, within ninety days; and those who had fled farther northward, within four months. If they did not return within these limits to help drive out the enemy, they should have their property taxed three-fold. In January, 1782, a new assembly met in Augusta and elected John Martin governor, and under him the government gradually crept down the Savannah to Ebenezer as the British were driven back, and finally when the British evacuated Savannah in June, 1782, the Georgia government occupied its original capital, using the old silk filature as a meeting place. In January, 1783, the assembly elected Lyman Hall governor, who had been among the first to enter the Revolution, and in notifying him, promised him every aid to "establish *Whigism* on a permanent basis." Realizing that the state had been governed without regard to the constitution since the fall of Savannah in December, 1778, this assembly now declared that all governmental acts coming within that period, "founded in good Policey and the real interests of this State," should be considered valid.

The Whig government had dragged out a life so stormy, and most of the time so feeble, that it had passed few laws. As the assembly had been generally non-existent, most of the actual rules and regulations for carrying on the war were issued by the council, which served not only as the whole government but also acted as a sort of Red Cross organization. It spent much time procuring and sending corn, rice, salt, and other necessities to the destitute Whig families; it even assumed responsibility for a fifteen year old girl who had been paralyzed. It also settled disputes among the people, granted them permission to trade or do other things, and looked after the wealth of cattle in the state to see that unscrupulous persons did not steal them and change the brands. It even acted as a supreme court.

The most far-reaching laws passed during the Revolution dealt with that class of people who had not taken up or who had given up the patriotic cause; and through their severity, confiscated the property and banished many whose presence in peacetime might have done much to help rehabilitate the state. The first of these acts was passed March 1, 1778, and through its provisions 117 Georgians were declared guilty of treason, their property was ordered confiscated, and they were banished from the state with the penalty of death promised if they returned. To execute this law, a board of commissioners was appointed in each county. The state was soon overrun by the British and the full execution of the law became impossible. Many people through choice or stern necessity joined the British or acquiesced in their rule, and thereby laid themselves open to charges of high treason. To reclaim as many of this class as possible, the assembly in August, 1781, granted forgiveness to all who would join the Whig armies by October 1st.

To deal effectively with all who had laid themselves open to high treason from the beginning, including the 117 listed in the first confiscation law, the assembly passed an act May 4, 1782, giving their names and providing by elaborate arrangements for the confiscation of their property through a central board of commissioners. All persons named were banished from the state, and if they returned or remained they should be imprisoned until an opportunity came to send them to the British dominions beyond the seas. If they should persist in returning, they should suffer death without benefit of clergy.

The patriots drew a distinction in the degree of guilt that might adhere to Georgians in their support of the British. The original and habitual British supporters should be dealt with most severely; those who through the exigencies of circumstances supported the British, should be dealt with more leniently. To take care of this situation, the assembly passed an act in August, 1782, which set up three classes of people to be dealt with, and which listed the names in each class. As these people were not considered too despicable to be reclaimed for the state, none was to be banished and their property should not be confiscated. The first class, numbering 15, should be taxed or amerced 12% of their property, the second class, numbering 21, should pay 8%, and the third class, numbering 63, should expiate their sins against the state by either joining the state military forces or providing a substitute.

Not until the British were largely cleared from the state could the various confiscation laws be actually enforced. Shortly before the British evacuated Savannah, commissioners were selected to proceed with the confiscation and sale of all kinds of property of the loyalists. They moved from one part of the state to another, selling this property to those who had fought for independence, whose patriotism generally greatly exceeded their purse. The patriots now received their reward. Thousands of acres of land of James Wright and of the other loyalists were sold to Samuel Elbert, James Jackson, James Habersham, Jr., Elijah Clarke, Richard Howley, and to many other patriots. Agents of the commissioners scurried around over the state ferreting out cattle, farm implements, and other property of the loyalists, all of which was offered for sale.

The enthusiasm of the people to buy this confiscated property greatly exceeded their ability, with the result that a law was soon passed allowing them two months in which to decide whether they would restore the property to the state or pay for it. One half of the payment must be in gold or silver and the other half in Georgia paper currency. Out of particular respect for certain heroes, the state made them gifts of land now and then. It gave large plantations to both Nathanael Greene and Anthony Wayne, and it presented to Count d'Estaing four tracts of 5,000 acres each. Some of this land was confiscated and some of it was part of the great domain which the state already owned. To Elijah Clarke the state gave the plantation of Thomas Waters, a particularly notorious Tory.

The rigors of confiscation and amercement were somewhat

lightened as the hysterical hatreds of the Revolution died down. Undoubtedly the excitement of war had led to mistakes; these should be righted. Sir Patrick Houstoun, the elder brother of Governor Houstoun, had suffered confiscation of his property by both sides; but he was later relieved of his penalties. James Johnston, printer, finally elected to be a patriotic Georgian, and was relieved of his burdens. For twenty years after the Revolution, special acts of the assembly were passed to excuse people from banishment, confiscation, or amercement. But with all the amends which the state tried to make, it drove from its borders hundreds of people who had at one time been valuable citizens. Many of the Georgia Tories first fled to Florida, but when England gave this province back to Spain in 1783, these and other Georgia refugees went to the Bahamas and other British West Indies and to far-away Nova Scotia and Upper Canada. Loyal to the end, one of them in taking his leave could not refrain from making this frank but defiant farewell statement: "I do not pretend to excuse myself, but will own that I have done as bad nearly as my power would allow; but this I can assure you, all good men, that you have men among you, called *good Whigs,* who are as great villains as HENRY COOPER."

Land, confiscated or otherwise, was used not only to reward the faithful after the war but also to stimulate patriotism during the struggle. In 1776 the state offered 100 acres to anyone who would enlist for three years or the duration of the war. The next year the assembly passed a law, setting up a headright system, designed primarily to bring in settlers, who would incidentally increase the fighting population. By this law every free white person or head of a family should have 200 acres of land and 50 additional acres for each member of his family and also 50 acres for each slave not exceeding ten. He must pay the nominal sum of two shillings the hundred acres and must settle the land within six months. If a settler should build a grist mill on his land he should have 100 acres additional; if a sawmill, 500 acres; and if an iron works, 2,000 acres. A land office was set up and it was expected that a great migration would start into an attractive country, though one that must be defended. War soon scattered the settlers, and as the patriots were pushed farther up into the frontiers of Wilkes County, the assembly early in 1780, in order to strengthen this last stronghold, allowed people nine months in which to make their settlement, and cleverly excused them from all military service except to defend their homes. It was in this law, passed January 23rd, that a town was provided for, to be the last rallying point for Georgians and to be called for the last hope of the Revolution—Washington.

In 1781 the assembly allowed all soldiers who should hold out to the end, 250 acres of land free from taxation for ten years, provided they could not be convicted of "plundering or distressing the country"; and later it extended this right to those who had fled the state but who had continued to fight. During the next few years bounties of land were granted to the Continental soldiers who had served in Georgia and to those Georgians who had served in the state navy. There were 4,381 soldiers and sailors who received grants of Georgia land.

As land was about the only wealth in Georgia which could not be carried off or destroyed, it became an important factor in the financial affairs of the state during the war. The poverty of the state was distressing. It was useless to levy taxes, for they could not be collected. As a medium of exchange the state began early to issue large amounts of paper currency; but it became so worthless that it was soon of no use. Attempts were made to bolster up the value of these paper notes by securing them with property confiscated from the Tories, but the amount issued was too great. In 1783 the assembly established tables of depreciation, which through a sliding scale made the value of the notes almost vanish with the passing of time. One of the most acceptable forms of currency which came to be used was the Negro slave. Now and then the governor's salary was partly paid in slaves; James Jackson's Georgia Legion received slaves as part of their recompense; and various other obligations of the state were met with slaves, as in the case of a patriot who received Negroes for 367 gallons and three quarts of whiskey furnished General Wayne's troops, "at a time when the army was suffering greatly for liquor." In order that the mythical treasury of the state might be kept filled with Negro currency, confiscating agents were kept busy detecting Tory slaves. In addition to slaves, the state used for money anything else which had value. For discovering a conspiracy against the state in 1782, David Davis was rewarded with "a Compleat Suit of Clothes, a good Horse Saddle and Bridle, a likely Negro and three hundred Acres of Land."

Apart from meeting governmental needs the state had little use for currency, as there was little commercial activity. At the beginning of the Revolution, trade with the British was prohibited through patriotism, and debts to British merchants were confiscated. When soon thereafter starvation threatened the people of the state, the exportation of salt, rice, and other foodstuffs to the other states was prohibited periodically. In May, 1783, the state, considering the war ended, removed all restraints from trade.

The war had been unusually destructive in Georgia as it developed through the bitterest partisan struggle into a war of extermination of both life and property. Half the property in the state had been destroyed, the institution of slavery was upset, and the people were torn asunder through hatreds and suspicions. For years thereafter, the word Tory was the most devastating charge that could be fastened by one politician upon another, and more than one aspiring Georgian was destroyed by it. Robbers and murderers after the close of the war continued to infest the highways to such an extent as to endanger the life of the government. In 1782 the council voted a half dozen cartridges to each member for his personal safety; and for "the more effectually expelling and totally annihilating those enemies to mankind (those hellish and diabolical fiends) from the face of the earth," it offered ten guineas each for their dead bodies, "or good and sufficient proof that such of the under mentioned persons are absolutely and bona fide killed," and then listed the names of twenty-two people.

Slavery well-nigh disappeared during the war. The British enlisted in their army any slaves they could induce to join them; and the patriots used them for road making and labor battalions and for manning the galleys on the coast. Upset and unattached, many fled the state for South Carolina or made their escape into the British possessions of Florida. After the war many of them collected in the Savannah River bottoms and marauded the countryside until 1786, when a force of Georgians, South Carolinians, and fifteen Catawba Indians stormed their stronghold and killed or captured most of them. A few days later one of the Negro leaders was found and taken to Savannah, where he was tried and hanged. The editor of the *Gazette* remarked, "It is, perhaps, the wish of interest, as well as of philanthropy, that they were all in Africa."

Sometime before peace with England had been made, the Georgians set about establishing an understanding with the British authorities in Florida. Now and then during the latter period of the Revolution they made agreements relating to trade and the recovering of runaway slaves, and in 1782 three commissioners were appointed to bring about peace on the St. Marys. The next year Elijah Clarke was allowed to cross into Florida to search for horses which had been plundered from him. In the general peace arrangements of this year, England gave up Florida to the Spaniards, and so keen was the Georgians' hatred of the English that they looked upon this transfer to their old enemy as a blessing; and to show their friendship for their new neighbor, the governor of Georgia sent the new Spanish governor a message of congratulations.

With the ghost of South Carolina's absorption plan laid, on the northeastern boundary, and with the Spanish friendly on the south, Georgia was now left to deal with the wreckage which the Revolution had left her.

CHAPTER XIV

CONSOLIDATING THE STATE

GEORGIA WAS now an independent state, and as far as England's recognition was concerned, she was an independent nation, untrammeled by any obligations to any other nation or state. Georgia, however, had no desire to be an independent nation, for the protection which she hoped to secure from a union with the other revolting colonies had been one of her principal considerations in entering the Revolution. In 1778 the Articles of Confederation were adopted by Georgia and ten other states, but they did not go into effect until 1781, when Maryland, the last of the thirteen, acceded to them. Though the states were almost independent nations under this form of government, Georgia was jealous of this connection, weak though it was. About this time, when Georgia and South Carolina were under the heel of the British, there were rumors that England might offer independence to the other colonies and retain the ones she had reconquered. This rumor greatly upset the Georgia delegates in Congress. They bitterly condemned the suspected movement to drop Georgia from the Confederation, and they reënforced their argument with a recital of the sacrifices the state had made for independence and the great strength it would add to the Confederation through its fertile lands, good harbors, and wealth of timber.

Though the state was not excluded from the Confederation, it was sometimes remiss in assuming its rights in the new government. Frequently it had no delegates in Congress, either because those elected were not interested enough to make the trip or because the state did not have enough money to pay their way to the national capital. In 1784 though six were elected, the state provided money sufficient for only two of them. Yet Georgia was conspicuously honest in meeting the requisitions levied upon her by the Confederation government. In 1783 she set up a fund composed of money and credits secured from the sale of confiscated property, which amounted to £108,889, and from this sum she expected to receive enough interest to meet her obligations to the Confederation.

Though Georgia favored an effective union, she was no less interested in maintaining her rights to separate existence as a state in that union. During this Confederation period (1781-1788), she in her semi-sovereignty officially signed herself, "The State of Georgia by the Grace of God Free, Sovereign and Independent." She exercised the full right to decide who might become her citizens, and to be certain that no Tory should slip in, she sent to the other states the names of all her former citizens now banished and asked for similar lists from them. In the beginning she received provisionally as citizens all who appeared before the council and received its approval, or who might be passed by certain other officials. Naturally many people came without reporting to anyone. Not until 1785 did the state pass a definite naturalization law. According to this law aliens might be domiciled and given civil rights by registering with a court. To become a citizen a person must reside a year in the state, after which he must procure from a grand jury a certificate stating that he was an honest man and a friend of the government, and this transaction must be recorded in the superior court. Thereupon he must swear allegiance to Georgia by which automatically he became vested with all the rights, liberties, and immunities of a citizen, except that he must reside in the state seven years before he should be eligible to hold office. All people who had fought against Georgia or the United States were barred from citizenship. Out of special regard for France, still an ally, the law made it possible for a Frenchman to become a citizen and be immediately eligible for office after three years' residence in Georgia, or if he should marry an American, only one year's residence was necessary. Now and then favored individuals were given a short-cut to citizenship by special acts of the assembly, which invested them with immediate citizenship.

The state passed not only naturalization laws but also patent and copyright laws. Any person might copyright his books, maps, or other literary products by registering them with the secretary of state. He then had the exclusive right to sell his products for fourteen years, renewable for fourteen additional years; but his prices must be reasonable, or his copyrights would lapse. Patents were granted by special enactment. In 1788 Isaac Briggs and William Longstreet were given a patent for fourteen years on "a newly constructed steam engine, invented by them."

Exercising the rights of sovereignty, the state passed a tariff law in 1784 which operated not only against foreign countries but also against the other states.

As tariffs raised little revenue, the state was forced to resort to other devices. As long as the confiscated property held out it afforded the greatest reservoir from which the state secured funds, but soon, much against its will, the assembly was forced to levy taxes on the people. In 1783 a tax of twenty-five cents was placed on each 100 acres of land, town lot, or slave; and a poll tax of one dollar was levied on each free Negro and a two-dollar tax on each idler, who was described as a male over 21 years of age who did not follow some lawful occupation or trade, or who did not cultivate or cause to be cultivated five acres of land. As the tax law was passed each year, the rate as well as the general system changed with time. Soon the tax rate was thirty-five cents on each hundred dollars' worth of land and the land was classified for valuation according to its location and the kind of timber which grew upon it, as sea island, salt marsh, tide swamp, river swamp, pine lands, pine barren lands, oak and hickory lands, and lands of various other descriptions—a system borrowed from colonial times.

The financial chaos which marked the Revoltuion continued throughout the Confederation period, with many kinds of certificates of credit issued by various state officials, such as the governor, the speaker of the assembly, and the auditor. In 1786 a large issue of paper money was made, and the notes were printed in the English notation despite the fact that the American decimal system had been established the year previously. When the Federal constitution went into effect in 1789, this paper money became unconstitutional; but Georgia did not disrupt her finances further by complying literally with the new provision. She extended the time for the withdrawal of this state paper for five years, during which period she accepted it in payment of all state debts.

With the coming of Federal coins, after 1789, Georgia passed a law fining anyone who clipped them or any other coins that circulated in the state, £100 for the first offense and for the second offense death without benefit of clergy. As little Federal money was coined until 1795, various kinds of metallic money circulated in Georgia, and in 1794 the Spanish milled dollar was by special law legalized as money and its value established. Not until the next year did the state go on the decimal basis, when a law was passed declaring that the notation should be dollars, desmes (a tenth part of a dollar), and other minor coins.

In addition to exercising the fundamental powers of sovereignty, the early assemblies went to the other extreme and wasted their time with many inconsequential things which minor officials should have done. They passed special acts granting divorces, changing the names of people, allowing certain persons to practice law, pardoning people convicted of crimes, and settling a great variety of particular cases which later regulations placed under the authority of the executive and judicial departments.

During the eight years of the Confederation, Georgia gradually added strength to her governmental life. When she emerged from the Revolution, her government had been almost extinct. She did not even have official records of her laws, or the papers of her governors, or the decisions of her courts. During the British occupation her official papers had been meagre and scattering; and her records prior to the occupation had been spirited away just before the fall of Savannah in 1778. John Milton, the secretary of state, had gathered up the most important papers in his office and some of the governors' papers and had fled with them to Charleston. When that city fell, he carried them on to Newbern, in North Carolina, and when the British were on the point of overrunning that state he took them on to Maryland. Continually harassed by the absence of her records, Georgia in 1784 promised to pay a suitable sum of money or to grant not over 1,000 acres of land to any responsible person who would bring them back. Ultimately the state recovered all of these documents.

Nationalism grew strong with the Georgians, and when the Confederation asked for more powers, Georgia readily gave her consent. Nevertheless, the Confederation soon proved to be a failure, and when in 1787 a constitutional convention was held in Philadelphia to strengthen or remake the government, Georgia elected six delegates to go. Only four ever attended; they were William Few, Abraham Baldwin, William Pierce, and William Houstoun, and only Few and Baldwin signed the new constitution. Though the Georgians did not take a prominent part in the convention, Abraham Baldwin on one occasion saved the convention from disruption by producing a delay through a tie vote he manipulated. The Georgians favored an "energetic and formidable" government, and for this reason and the fact that the state was large in area, they voted generally with the large states. Mindful of the labor supply necessary to develop their vast resources, they opposed the restriction against importing slaves from foreign countries.

A copy of the new constitution reached Georgia in October, 1787, and on the 26th a convention was called to meet in Augusta on Christmas day to consider the document. Three other states ratified it earlier, but Georgia was the first Southern state to do so, and none adopted it with greater joy or unanimity of feeling. After the convention had ratified it by a unanimous vote, January 2, 1788, a cannon shot boomed out for each of the thirteen states, though two were to hesitate long before they should accede to the new union.

The reception Georgians gave Washington on his tour through the state in 1791 might well have convinced him not only of the high personal esteem in which they held him but also their extreme loyalty to the national government. Additional proof was to be seen in the fact that they had named a town for him in 1780 and had by 1786 begun to celebrate his birthday, February 11th—for neither they nor Washington had yet dropped the ten days to make it the 22nd, a change which calendar reform had decreed in 1752.

Although Georgia had helped to produce a strong union of the states, she soon felt the power of that new government to such an extent that she defied it. Two cases arose before the United States Supreme Court in 1792, in both of which Georgia was a party and in both a loser. In one, Georgia *vs*. Brailsford, she saw her law confiscating British debts so interpreted as to restore to Brailsford, a British merchant, money which she had expected to keep. The case was finally decided against her in 1794 by the verdict of a jury—the first time this procedure had ever been used in the United States Supreme Court. In the other case, Chisholm *vs*. Georgia, she indignantly refused to appear before the Supreme Court to defend herself in a suit instituted by a South Carolinian, claiming that it was the right of no individual to humiliate a sovereign state by suing it. Other states had supinely allowed themselves to be sued in the Federal courts by individuals from another state, but Georgia was the first to resist it. The decision was handed down in

1793 but the judgment, which was adverse to the state, was not rendered until the next year. So excited did the Georgians become that the assembly formulated an act declaring that anyone who should attempt to enforce this judgment should be hanged, but it did not become a law, as the state was then on the point of receiving satisfaction. Other states besides Georgia were aroused by this decision, and a movement to amend the Federal constitution was begun, which resulted in the eleventh amendment being added in 1798. This amendment denied the right of an individual to sue a state. Thus, Georgia early set herself up as a guardian of the rights of the states.

Now that Georgia was a member of a new union with a new fundamental framework, it was necessary that she reconsider her own governmental structure. The constitution of 1777 had been made when little sustained effort could be given to anything else than to war and defense. As this document was the result of the first effort at constitution-making, it was naturally elementary and transitional. Disregarding the manner required by the constitution for its amending, the legislature in the latter part of January, 1788, named three "fit and discreet" persons from each county to meet in Augusta for the purpose of making any changes deemed necessary. In November the new constitution was completed, and copies of it were scattered over the state to be read by the people. Instead of the people voting for this new document, they were required to elect delegates to meet in January, 1789, to accept or reject it. This convention, instead of either accepting or rejecting the constitution, made various alterations, which necessitated the calling of a third convention. This last convention met in May and adopted the new constitution and celebrated the event by firing eleven cannon shots, one for each state in the union at that time. Thus occurred a peaceful revolution in the Georgia government which paralleled the change in the national government.

This constitution of 1789, though making a more complete

and elaborate government, had the distinct merit of being less than half as long as the constitution of 1777. One of the most important changes related to the governor. His powers were increased and the method of his election was altered. His term was lengthened from one year to two, and he could now veto bills and grant reprieves and pardons to all except traitors and murderers. He was elected by the senate, a new body set up by this constitution, from three names sent to it by the house. Being a more important official now than in 1777, he was hedged about by more definite qualifications. He must be thirty years old, and must own 500 acres of land or have other property worth £1,000. Feeling their age and the importance that went with it, the Georgians now required the governor to have resided six years in the state before his election.

In providing for the legislature, Georgia fell into line with the other states by erecting a body with two chambers, a senate and a house of representatives. The qualifications for membership in the house were reduced from the ownership of 250 acres of land to 200 acres, or other property from £250 to £150. The required term of residence in the state was increased from one year to two, and the religious qualification was removed. The term of office remained the same, one year, and the age requirement was continued at twenty-one. The senate was composed of one senator from each county, to serve for three years. The qualifications were ownership of 250 acres of land or £250 of property, and the attainment of the age of twenty-eight.

The qualifications for voting showed the growth of democracy. Any citizen twenty-one years of age who had paid a tax the year preceding the election should be allowed to vote, and the method should be by ballot. Had the women been politically minded, they could have voted, for the constitution by inference or inadvertence gave them the right. The other features were much like the old constitution, except this new one showed unmistakably the influence of the new Federal constitution.

The eighteenth-century Georgians were certain that governmental institutions were like fast-growing children and that they frequently must be given new garbs. The constitution of 1789 provided for a convention five years later, to be composed of three men elected from each county, who should by a two-thirds majority vote decide whether the constitution needed amending, and if so, to proceed to make those amendments by a majority vote. This convention met in 1795 and decided that the senators should serve for one year instead of three, that the governor should be elected by a joint ballot of the house and senate, that the assembly should meet in January instead of November, and that the capital of the state should be Louisville. It also reapportioned the membership among the counties, and provided for another similar constitutional convention to be elected in the same manner three years later.

Back of these arrangements for the frequent amending of the constitution lay a fundamental cleavage of interests which had developed before the close of the Revolution, a cleavage between the fast-growing frontier upcountry, with its liberalism and ambitions to inherit the earth, and the stable coast country, with its conservatism and its determination to hold what it had. The welding of these two interests into a unity was long deferred. The clash between them first came to an issue in the location of the capital. The upcountry looked with hostility on the return of the capital to Savannah at the end of the Revolution, and it laid plans to fight for relocation. So insistent was the demand that the government be moved that the legislature adjourned in 1785 to meet in Augusta. In 1786 Augusta was made the temporary seat, until three commissioners, appointed this year, could fix a site within twenty miles of "Galphin's old town," and erect "a seat of government and the university." This new town should be called Louisville; but so slow had the state officers been in moving to it that the constitution-amenders of 1795 decreed that they must make the change before the next meeting of the legislature. Savannah, bereft of her ornament, attempted to hold most of the state records, claiming they were in fact much more the records of Chatham County than of the state. In the struggle that ensued, Governor Edward Telfair dismissed the chief justice and all the associate justices of the Chatham County superior court, and gained the bitter ill-will of the people of Savannah. Nevertheless, he secured the records and brought them to Augusta in two covered wagons protected by four armed guards.

Even more bitter and important than the fight over the location of the capital was the question of representation in the legislature. With the fast-growing upcountry, the coast could not hope long to maintain its control of the state. Since the constitution named the counties and fixed their representation, it became necessary, with the growth of population and new counties to amend the document frequently if democracy were to be served. In this last amending, the up-country had forged ahead in the number of representatives in the house, and it had won an additional victory in the change to election of the governor by a joint ballot.

The amending convention, scheduled to be elected in 1797, met the following year, and turned out to be one of the most important constitutional conventions ever held in the state. Instead of amending the old document, it produced a new constitution, almost four times as long as the old, and of such excellence that, with twenty-three amendments as time went on, it continued until the outbreak of the Civil War. Much of it was the work of James Jackson, who seemed to be as able as a constitution-maker as he had been intrepid as a soldier. Maintaining the fundamental framework of the old document, it filled in and rounded out the government with various changes and additions. Provision was made for the representation of new counties as they might be formed and a schedule of apportionment was set up for the increases of population in the old counties. Every county was allowed at least one representative and no county might have more than four. The shift of control into the hands of the planter class was clearly indicated by the adoption, for purposes of representation in the legislature, of the federal ratio of five slaves to three whites; yet the new constitution embraced more democracy when it permitted voting without reference to the ownership of property or the payment of a tax. The amendments of 1795 relative to the term of senators, the election of the governor, and the time of meeting of the general assembly were continued in this new document.

Though the government seemed complete in all other respects, it still eschewed a supreme court and abolished the old chief justiceship. The verdict of the superior court was final in each county, and under whatever circumstances errors might be corrected, the local judicial autonomy of the county was strictly guarded. The early decision against Georgians in the United States Supreme Court made them wary of setting up such an instrument of possible tyranny in their own midst. To bring uniformity in the application of state law, the superior court judges established the custom of holding a yearly conference, at which they discussed difficult points of law and constitutional questions. Not until 1835 was the constitution amended to set up a supreme court, and not until ten years later was the court finally organized.

To preserve the purity of elections the constitution required each member of the legislature to swear that he had not used illegal means in winning his office, and if it should be proved that he had offered or accepted a bribe or treat or had canvassed for the election, he should be disqualified. Religious freedom was guaranteed to all; and the foreign slave trade was prohibited, despite the fact that the Federal constitution guarded it against Congress for ten more years. On account of a trick in the title of the Yazoo land fraud act, which was still fresh in the minds of the constitution-makers and especially of James Jackson, the legislature was forbidden to include in a law matter different from what was indicated in the title. The evil of the legislature granting divorces was partly remedied by a provision prohibiting such action until a verdict had been secured before a superior court, and then two-thirds of each house was required. A section was included which did much to save the legislature from wasting its time on special legislation, by forbidding it to change the names of persons or do many other acts which could be done better by other agencies.

During this period of constitutional growth, the state was electing as its governors a variety of men, Revolutionary officers such as Samuel Elbert and James Jackson, a Scotch merchant in Edward Telfair, an Indian fighter in Jared Irwin, a land speculator in George Mathews, who slipped into office before he had fulfilled the residence requirement, and a politician in George Walton. James Jackson was first elected in 1788, but he refused the honor. In the latter part of 1794 there was an interregnum, which might have developed trouble had it been longer and had there been better means of communication in the state. The constitution-amenders of this year, in ordering the meeting of the legislature to take place in January instead of November, left this space of two months free from a governor, but George Mathews, whose term ran out in November, held on until a new governor was elected, and therefore served two months longer than his constitutional term.

When she took up her position in the new union in 1789, Georgia had greater potentialities than immediate importance. There was little chance that she would afford a president soon; the highest position one of her sons attained in the national administration before the end of the century was that of the postmaster-generalship held by Joseph Habersham who took office under Washington in 1795 and continued until 1801. She received three congressmen under the constitutional apportionment, but by the first census, taken in 1790, she dropped back to two. Her first congressmen were elected from districts, but the practice was allowed to vary until 1843, when a law of Congress required all the states to use the district method of election. One of the first contested elections to come before Congress was the dispute between James Jackson and General Anthony Wayne to a seat in the second Congress. Gross frauds had been practiced by Thomas Gibbons in favor of Wayne, without the latter's knowledge, and out of the bitterness that arose a duel resulted between Jackson and Gibbons, in which neither was hurt.[1]

By the end of the century, Georgia was politically and constitutionally established both within her own borders and in the nation; but territorially she still had a stubborn fight to wage before she could finally take possession of what she claimed to be her own. Her hardest struggle was with the Indians and with the complications which their occupation of most of the state produced. During the Revolution the Indians, though under the influence of the English, did not give Georgia a great deal of trouble. In 1777 the Cherokees had gone on the warpath, but most of their depredations were in South Carolina; and toward the end of the war the most hostile of the Cherokees established a menacing group of towns on the Chickamauga Creek, near Lookout Mountain. In 1779, after the British had upset Georgia, the Creeks were incited to attack; but an expedition under Andrew Pickens with 200 South Carolinians, aided by Elijah Clarke and John Dooly with Georgia troops, soon quieted them.

The departure of the British troops at the end of the Revolution did not mean peace in Georgia, for the Indians now be-

---

[1] Gibbons was an able Savannah lawyer, whose patriotism during the Revolution had not been conspicuous enough to prevent him from being attainted for high treason. He secured restoration to citizenship, became mayor of Savannah, and served in the legislature before he moved to New Jersey where he became interested in the steamboat business and became involved in the famous lawsuit, Gibbons *vs.* Ogden.

came more than ever the pawns of personal aggrandizement and foreign aggressions. The Spaniards, now back in Florida, carried on an insidious and unending campaign to incite an Indian conflict with Georgia. The English and the French were also interested participants wherever possible. To make the situation worse for Georgia, the Indians were controlled by unscrupulous half-breeds who plotted with and accepted bribes from all who would deal with them. The most notorious of these Indians was the Creek chieftain, Alexander McGillivray, whose father was a Scotchman, whose maternal grandfather was a Frenchman, and whose ancestry otherwise was Creek. Most of the time until his death in 1793 he was in the pay of the Spaniards. Another, more romantic and more evanescent but less powerful, was William Augustus Bowles, a Marylander by birth, a British soldier until he threw his uniform into the sea and joined the Creeks, after the Revolution for a short time an actor and portrait painter in the Bahamas, then, finally, a pirate with a Creek crew, and a rival of McGillivray.

There were many lesser figures, banished Tories, outlaws, and adventurers. Near the end of the Revolution a group of these dangerous characters led by Thomas Waters settled among the Cherokees on the Etowah River at the mouth of Long Swamp Creek and carried out a reign of terror on the frontiers of Wilkes County until the combination of Clarke and Pickens went against them in the latter part of 1782, broke up the settlement, and forced upon the Cherokees a treaty, which they had no right to make, ceding lands from the Tugaloo to the Chattahoochee.

Georgia under the Confederation, being independent in almost all respects where she cared to be, took up the Indian problem as her own business and began to make treaties without any consultation with the Confederation government. The right to make such treaties was not granted by the Articles of Confederation to the states; neither was it clearly denied. The state appointed an Indian Board in 1783, including Clarke,

Top: A RICE MILL ON THE SAVANNAH RIVER. THE RICE FIELDS DISAPPEARED WITH THE PASSING OF SLAVERY. *Harper's New Monthly Magazine,* May, 1853. *Bottom:* TOBACCO ROLLING. TOBACCO CEASED TO BE AN IMPORTANT CROP IN GEORGIA BY 1860, BUT IT RE-APPEARED IN THE TWENTIETH CENTURY. Edward King, *The Southern States of North America.* London: Blackie & Son, 1875.

Top left: JAMES M. WAYNE, GRADUATE OF PRINCETON, MEMBER OF THE UNITED STATES HOUSE OF REPRESENTATIVES, AND JUSTICE OF THE UNITED STATES SUPREME COURT, 1835-67. *Top right:* HENRY STEVENS, BORN IN ENGLAND, ANTE-BELLUM LUMBERMAN AND MANUFACTURER OF CLAY WARES. *Bottom left:* RICHARD PETERS, BUILDER OF ATLANTA, PLANTER, AND INDUSTRIALIST. *Bottom right:* MARK A. COOPER, MEMBER OF THE UNITED STATES HOUSE OF REPRESENTATIVES AND PIONEER IRON INDUSTRIALIST.

Lachlan McIntosh, Twiggs, and others, which made a treaty with the Cherokees at Augusta in May, confirming Clarke's Long Swamp treaty, and in November the Board, somewhat reconstituted, induced the Creeks to give up any claims they had to the territory. Out of this region, the state, the next year, laid out Washington and Franklin counties.

Having embarked on the treaty-making business, Georgia decided to end each war against the Creeks with a treaty which would push them further westward. In 1785 the clash of war was stayed long enough for a treaty to be made at Galphinton, under which the Creeks ceded to Georgia a great region south of the Altamaha extending to the Florida boundary; and the next year the Creeks were punished again in a short war, and made to re-affirm the Galphinton treaty in an agreement made on Shoulder-Bone Creek. This treaty was later repudiated by the Indians.

At this same time, Congress had its agents out looking for Indians who would make treaties with them. In the latter part of 1785 Benjamin Hawkins and other Congressional agents made at Hopewell, in South Carolina, a treaty with the Cherokees, establishing about the same line from the Tugaloo to the headwaters of the Oconee which the Georgians had made in their treaties of 1783, and strangely enough the Cherokees were given by this treaty the right to send a deputy to the United States Congress.

Indian relations were soon in the worst possible situation, largely because of the fact that Congress had declared void the treaties of Galphinton and Shoulder-Bone. The Creeks, now emboldened by their apparent alliance with the United States against Georgia, fell upon the Georgia frontiers, and in the course of two years (1787-1789) killed 82 people, wounded 29, and captured 140. They put to the torch 89 houses, and carried off many horses, cattle, and much other property. In addition to the small raiding parties active against the Creeks, Georgia, despairing of any protection from the United States,

called for 1,500 volunteers, and declared all Creeks not members of friendly tribes outlaws, and subject to be shot by anyone
on sight.

Georgia was coming to feel bitter toward the Federal government not only for its lack of protection to the state but also for
what appeared to be actual aid to the Indians. While the
United States was guarding her northwestern frontier, the
southeast was being left defenseless, the Georgians felt. In 1789
the old *confederated* United States went out of existence, and
the *federated* United States arose just in time to save a tottering nation. The new government immediately took up the
Indian troubles in the southeast and in September sent to
Georgia a commission, including General Lincoln. The commission tried to make a treaty with McGillivray, but the clever
old half-breed with 2,000 warriors back of him drawn up on
the Oconee, decided to end the talk and not resume it until next
spring. This commission, before returning to New York, in-
vestigated Georgia's treaty-making, and declared that the state
had been honest and open in its dealings with the Indians.

The next year McGillivray, with twenty-three kings, chiefs,
and warriors, was induced to go to New York, where at the
cost of much money and many presents, he agreed to the Treaty
of New York. The Creeks gave up all their lands east of the
Oconee and of a line drawn northward through the Currahee
Mountain to the Tugaloo—the old line set up by the treaty of
1783 and re-affirmed at Hopewell in 1785. To add definiteness
and permanency to this line, wood-choppers the next year
should clear a swath along it twenty feet wide. All their lands
west of this line the United States solemnly guaranteed to the
Creeks, and declared outlaws any whites who should go beyond
this boundary. And to add further to the permanency which
was to be given to the Creek occupation of this land, the United
States would make the Creeks herdsmen and cultivators instead of letting them remain "in a state of hunters," by furnish-

ing them free "useful domestic animals and implements of husbandry."

This treaty shocked the Georgians into a daze, out of which they finally emerged only to enter a rage. It was unthinkable to them that a government of civilized white people would definitely hand over to the savages for permanent occupation all of Georgia excepting a small eastern strip, and, to fix their minds against ever being induced to move, would attach them to the land as farmers. This treaty marked the entry into the heart of Georgia of a gall-like bitterness against the United States government which tinctured her relations with the Federal government in a deep and lasting way.

The treaty was a failure from the beginning. The line was not clearly marked for years, and neither Georgians nor Creeks cared to know where it was. Completely ignoring the treaty, each side carried on hostilities against the other until in 1793 Governor Telfair called a council of war in which it was determined to raise a force of 5,000 infantrymen and cavalrymen to crush forever the Creeks. President Washington became alarmed and strenuously protested against this war Georgia was making. Out of respect for him but with much bitterness the Georgians desisted. George Mathews, becoming governor this year, made a tour of the Indian frontier and recommended to the Federal government the building of small forts every twenty miles and garrisoning them with infantrymen and cavalrymen.

In 1796 the United States made another effort to settle the Creek troubles by sending Benjamin Hawkins and two other commissioners to Colerain on the St. Marys River, where they made a treaty with 123 kings, chiefs, and warriors in the presence of thirteen Indian agents, army officers, interpreters and citizens. This treaty merely confirmed the pre-existing treaties and gave the United States the right to a few five-mile-square tracts of land in the Creek country for army posts and trading stations. Georgia prevented the ratification of this treaty until the United States agreed that no invasion of Georgia's rights was intended by securing these tracts from the Creeks rather than from the state. The treaty was ratified in 1797. In addition to Indian agents already provided for, in 1796 the United States set up the factory system of trading with the Indians, whereby through licenses and fixed and reasonable prices traders were less likely to stir up warfare. One of the first factories or storehouses was set up at Colerain.

Though peace had been established with the Creeks, not to be seriously interrupted until the outbreak of the War of 1812, Georgia looked upon the Federal government more as an enemy than a friend in these dealings with the Indians; and she had come to feel that if the Indians were ever driven out of her borders she would have the task of doing it.

To tame and reduce to order a people who had just passed through the disintegration of warfare and whose numbers were being constantly increased by restless immigrants, was a difficult task. Robbers infested the state and made it necessary for the people to go armed; less dangerous but almost as troublesome mobs of people attacked land offices in their impatience to secure holdings; and the mass of rough frontiersmen developed sports and methods of settling their arguments which ultimately called for laws to curb them. The Georgia gentlemen settled their arguments in duels, but the vigorous backwoodsmen gouged it out. The state finally developed sentiment against each and embodied this sentiment in laws. The law against gouging came first, in 1787; not until 1809 was a legal blow struck at duelling. The anti-gouging law declared that the "savage custom of biting and gouging" must stop. To cut out the tongue, put out an eye, slit the nose, or otherwise mutilate the body carried a fine of £100 and two hours in the pillory or 100 lashes on the bare back for the first offense, and death for the second. The punishment for duelling was merely the denial of the right to hold office.

Vagabonds were intolerable in a growing state like Georgia,

where laborers were in great demand. Hence, they should be arrested and hired out to anyone who would pay their wages, which should be given to their families, or to themselves if they had no families; and if they were so vile that no one would hire them, then they should receive thirty-nine lashes on their bare backs at the public whipping post. Though Georgia was thoroughly committed to slavery, she believed that grave dangers might arise in promoting this institution. The slaves she had she would keep, but she questioned the wisdom of bringing in more. In 1793 she forbade the importation of slaves from the West Indies and Florida, and five years later she extended the law to include all foreign countries. This law antedated by a few months the provision in her constitution of 1798, prohibiting the foreign slave trade. By this law, to bring into the state a slave from abroad subjected the importer to a fine of $1,000; and by this same law, to bring in for sale a slave from any American state was made a crime carrying a fine of half that amount. At this time a great many Georgians believed that the slave trade was "not consistent with the principles of benevolence and humanity, or consonant with the true interest and prosperity of the State." To produce a supply of free labor, the state encouraged white indentured servants to come from Europe.

Economic progress blossomed forth in rice plantations on the coast and in large tobacco fields extending farther into the up-country; and after 1793, when Eli Whitney invented the cotton gin, cotton fields began to appear in greater numbers and to greater extents. Here was ample proof that Georgia's chief interest was in agriculture. To guard the quality of her tobacco, she set up inspectors; but she felt that cotton need not be examined, for in 1797 she repealed the cotton inspection law of the preceding year as "an unnecessary burthern on the planters of that article." Georgians soon restored from the devastations of the Revolution their wealth of live-stock. Large numbers of cattle, properly branded, grazed in the fields and woodlands; but when livestock wandered so far away as to become classed as stray, the law required that it be taken up and held a reasonable time for the owner, and if he did not appear it should be sold for the state. In early Georgia, as ever in frontier regions, to steal a horse was a most despicable and destructive crime and carried punishment with death. As for the wild life in the forests, Georgia saw the value of conserving it as early as 1790, when she passed a law punishing anyone who should hunt deer by fire-light in the night, with a five pound fine or thirty-nine lashes "well laid on" the bare back. The earliest routes of travel were on the rivers and coastal waters; but land passageways were necessary as the people drifted farther to the inland, and so the colonial trails were developed into roads which would accommodate wheeled vehicles, and new roads were laid out. Before the end of the century there was a network of roads connecting Savannah, Sunbury, Darien, Augusta, Washington, Louisville and other points; but the regions south of the Altamaha were still forced to depend for the most part on their water routes. At the intersection of roads, the law required signs directing the traveller. The first bridges were built by private endeavor and tolls were required for passage. Wade Hampton was given the right to erect a toll bridge across the Savannah at Augusta and to collect a toll from all who crossed, excepting the professors and students of the Academy of Richmond County. Stage coaches were soon rumbling over rough roads, and the right to establish lines between the various towns was granted by the state to private companies for a period of years. To keep in repair the "several roads, creeks, causeways, water passages and bridges," all males between the ages of fifteen and fifty, white and black, slave and free, were required to give to them not over twelve days' labor annually. Anyone living within seven miles of a route was held liable to work.

Georgia was overwhelmingly rural in her development; but a few towns naturally grew up. Savannah and Augusta in 1794

organized fire companies for their protection; but this precaution did not prevent in Savannah two years later, "the most
extensive and disastrous conflagration, ever experienced on this
continent." She called upon the city of New York for aid, and
induced Georgia to set aside for the relief of sufferers a part
of a tax imposed on the importation of slaves.

In the development of the general character of the people,
various organizations grew up before the end of the century.
The Savannah Association of Mechanics was incorporated in
1793, and a similar organization in Augusta grew up the following year. The Masons, who had been in the state since 1735,
secured in 1796 the incorporation of their Grand Lodge; and
the Union Society, an old organization in Savannah designed
to aid widows and to provide schooling for poor children, was
incorporated in 1786. The state's conscience varied on the subject of lotteries, but during this period they were allowed for
such purposes as raising money for churches, hospitals, schools,
libraries, and improving the navigation of the rivers.

A scattered population like the Georgians could support few
newspapers. James Johnston, since colonial days, had supplied
the people with their news. On January 30, 1783, he began the
first newspaper in the independent state of Georgia, naming it
the *Gazette of the State of Georgia,* and publishing it in Savannah. The next printing center to develop was Augusta, where
in 1785 the *Augusta Gazette* began. It was followed the next
year by the *Georgia State Gazette or Independent Register,*
which changed its name four years later to the *Augusta Chronicle and Gazette of the State of Georgia.* This paper has continued, with an abbreviated name, down to the present. In 1799
the *Augusta Herald* appeared. A town that could boast of being
the capital of the state might well be expected to have a newspaper, and so the third printing center to appear was Louisville. Here, in 1798, news from the remotest parts of the earth
was printed for the Georgia frontiersmen in the *State Gazette
and Louisville Journal,* later changed to the *Louisville Gazette*

and Republican Trumpet. Before 1810, newspapers had also arisen in Athens, Sparta, Petersburg, and Milledgeville.

As the state emerged from the Revolution, it seized upon religion and education as particular objects of its concern. Governor Lyman Hall in a message to the legislature in 1783 declared that the most certain way to tame the wild and unbridled nature of a people fresh from the devastations of war and influenced by residing in a region made savage by both man and nature, was to summon to their aid religion and education. The assembly, quickly seizing this point of view, called upon the people to meet in their churches and to make preparations to resume their religious activities. But as war had left few churches or congregations intact, it became the first duty to organize them. The legislature now began to incorporate various groups, but so poverty-stricken were the people that the state government in 1785 started out on the mistaken policy of granting financial support to organized religious denominations. It soon discovered that such aid would be repugnant to the political principle of the separation of church and state, and so it contented itself by granting congregations police protection against anyone attempting to disturb public worship.

The small Jewish synagogue in Savannah, established in colonial days, continued to exist; but its growth was confined to those who were born in the faith. The Salzburgers brought Lutheranism to Georgia in 1735, and it was they who kept this religion going. Never entering the evangelical movement in the up-country, this church confined its activities to Ebenezer and Savannah. The Catholics, having been excluded from the colony, did not enter Georgia in sufficient numbers to form a congregation until near the end of the century. In 1796 settlers from Maryland, who had come to Wilkes County, established a church at Locust Grove, near Washington; and in 1801 the Catholic Church in Savannah was incorporated by an act of the legislature. The Episcopal was the original church in Georgia, established by law soon after the Crown took over the colony from the Trustees; but when the War of the Revolution came, this Church of England became unpopular as merely another trapping of Great Britain. Its aristocratic background kept it from spreading as a church for the mass of the people, and so slow was its growth that it did not attain sufficient importance to be erected into a separate diocese until 1841, when Stephen Elliott, Jr., was consecrated its first bishop.

The churches that fought hardest the devil and one another for the control of Georgia were the Presbyterians, the Baptists, and the Methodists. Presbyterianism was brought to Georgia by the Scotch Highlanders, and in colonial times four distinct centers of this faith grew up. In 1735 the Scotch established their church at Darien under John McLeod; in 1752 the South Carolina Puritans set up their meeting house at Midway as a Congregational group, but they soon merged into Presbyterianism; three years later the Independent Presbyterian Church at Savannah was founded; and toward the end of the colonial period when settlers were beginning to flock into the upcountry and locate homes on Brier and Beaver creeks, Presbyterian communities grew up there. This faith was early carried to the people by such evangelists as the Reverend John Springer, who, under an immense poplar tree near Washington, Wilkes County, was ordained in 1790; and the Reverend John Newton, who as the first Presbyterian evangelist to enter Georgia, established Beth-salem in 1785, near Lexington. Since the days of Oglethorpe there had been a few Baptists in Georgia, and in 1770 Daniel Marshall crossed over from South Carolina and began preaching north of Augusta. Two years later he organized on the banks of the Kiokee the first Baptist church in Georgia. Prophets of this faith spread out over the state until ultimately they succeeded in gathering into their fold more converts than any other organized religion was able to secure. Virginians and Carolinians brought Methodism to Georgia when they began pouring into the up-country after the Revolution. Among the first to cry out the message of this church were Thomas Humphries, manly in appearance and earnest in demeanor, and John Major, known as the "weeping prophet." In 1788 Francis Asbury, the wandering bishop, held the first conference of Methodism in Georgia. The camp-meeting method of promoting religion, which had been hit upon about this time on the Kentucky frontier, was taken up by the Methodists and welded into their sharpest weapon against godlessness in Georgia.

Forced by the correct principle of statecraft to give up direct aid to religion, the government went forward with unusual zeal in establishing educational institutions. The constitution of 1777 required the legislature to erect schools in every county, and now that peace had come it became possible to carry out the requirement. A committee in February, 1783, recommended the setting aside of certain lots in Augusta and "the erecting a University or Seminary of Learning." For reasons unknown to the legislature the following July, the recommendation had not resulted in a law. So now, spurred on by a message of Governor Hall, this body passed a law on the last day of the month, which provided for academies in Augusta and Waynesboro, and endowed them with city lots and other lands. In 1786, the legislature sought, without success, to locate the university at Louisville.

With her position in the Union assured, with her constitutional framework established, and with the foundations of her social and economic order laid, the problem of the best use to which Georgia could put her vast territorial resources still remained uppermost.

CHAPTER XV

LAND SPECULATIONS AND SETTLEMENTS

THE REVOLUTION left Georgia impoverished in every way except in her land, which could not be destroyed. In her public domain she had unmeasured wealth, only dimly realized at the time; yet she was sufficiently aware of its value to make use of it in settling many of her debts; and some of her citizens as well as people from other states saw in it such possibilities for future wealth that they carried out speculations as amazing as they were bold and gigantic.

Georgia at the end of the Revolution claimed the same boundaries which Governor Wright had claimed following the French and Indian War. Outside of Virginia with her immense claims, Georgia came next in area among all the American states; but she was destined to have long controversies before she should succeed in fixing her accepted limits. The disputes that developed first, and became most important, were with South Carolina and with the Federal government.

The controversy with South Carolina waxed hot the quickest and was settled first. The main dispute was over the identity of the Savannah River in its upper stretches, for a considerable tract of land was involved in whether the Tugaloo-Chattooga fork was the main stream or whether it was the Keowee, or, indeed, whether the river should not be considered at an end where these two streams met and the name Savannah ceased to be applied. To complicate the settlement still further, South Carolina injected a preposterous claim to the southern part of Georgia—a revival of early colonial claims. In 1785 South Carolina appealed to the old Confederation Congress for a court of arbitration, provided for under the Articles; but before this court could be organized, the two states by direct negotiations settled their troubles. In 1787 commissioners met at Beaufort in South Carolina, and agreed that the Tugaloo-Chattooga branch of the Savannah should be considered the main stream, and that the boundary should extend up this stream to its northernmost spring, provided it were not north of the 35th parallel, which was the North Carolina boundary. In return for this large cession, South Carolina gave up her foolish claim to the southern part of Georgia. Assuming that the Chattooga took its rise about a dozen miles south of the North Carolina line, instead of north of it as is the fact, South Carolina this same year granted to the United States this narrow strip extending all the way to the Mississippi, territory which really belonged to Georgia and which the United States restored to her in 1802. Not until 135 years later was the dispute over the Savannah River settled in all its aspects, when in 1922 the United States Supreme Court ruled that the middle of the Savannah was the boundary, except where there were islands, and there the boundary should run midway between the islands and the South Carolina shore, thus giving all the islands in the Savannah, Tugaloo, and the Chattooga rivers to Georgia.

The dispute with the United States involved the vast western stretches of Georgia extending to the Mississippi. The United States claimed this region as part of the legitimate spoils of the Revolution, won not by Georgia, but by the combined efforts of all. Hence, it should belong to no one state but to the common country. Like the other states with western lands, Georgia relied on her colonial limits and refused to give way. This dispute was complicated by the claims of Spain concerning the boundaries of West Florida, which arose out of a bit of secret diplomacy of the Revolution. In the secret treaty made between England and the United States in 1782, before England knew whether she could retain West Florida or not, she agreed to make the 31st parallel the northern boundary of that province, if she should decide to part with it. If she should keep it, then the line would be 32 degrees and 28 minutes, which passed through the mouth of the Yazoo River and which was the boundary at that time. Spain in the general treaty of 1783 having secured West Florida, discovered this chicanery, and now claimed the latter line, which extended the region as far north as Vicksburg. So it now turned out that territory which later was to become the southern part of Alabama and Mississippi was being claimed by Georgia, the United States, and Spain. Finally, in 1795, the United States forced Spain to give up her contention, but Georgia still claimed it.

The United States had been asserting a more particular claim to this region between 31 degrees and 32 degrees and 28 minutes, as she held that since this territory had been a part of West Florida and not a part of Georgia under England, it could not now be validly claimed by Georgia. In 1787 Congress appealed to Georgia to cede all her western territory to the national government, and the next year, Georgia agreed to give the United States that part south of 32 degrees and 28 minutes, but on such terms as to cause its rejection. In 1790 the United States set up the Territory South of the Ohio and included in it not only what is now Tennessee but also the hazy strip that South Carolina had ceded to her and the part of Georgia's western lands claimed by Spain, and still occupied by her. In 1796 Tennessee became a state and the Territory South of the Ohio became moribund. Though Spain had agreed in 1795 to give up her claim, she did not move out until 1798. With the departure of Spain, the United States the same year erected this region, south of 32 degrees and 28 minutes, into the Territory of Mississippi and authorized the appointment of three commissioners to try to induce Georgia to give up all her territory west of the Chattahoochee. Both of these territorial governments had been set up without the consent of Georgia. The final settlement of the dispute was made in 1802, after Georgia had got so involved in the gigantic Yazoo land frauds that she was willing to let the United States have the territory in order to get out of this difficulty and secure other advantages.

Following the Revolution, land filled the minds of everyone and it seemed to carry that magical spell which produced land-rushes no less intensive than were the gold-rushes of a later generation. The mania to get hold of large tracts of land was so widespread and devouring that the officers of government forgot their public trust and dishonestly or foolishly flung open an empire to wild speculation. The movement was nation-wide, but Georgia with her wealth of land became an outstanding example of it.

A Georgian in 1787 took a witty and sarcastic fling at specu-lators, in a mock announcement of land for sale:

"*Halloo, Halloo, Halloo*

"The subscribers will sell on most moderate terms: Ten mil-lions of acres of valuable *pine barren* land in the province of Utopia, on which there are several very sumptuous air castles, ready furnished, that would make commodious and desirable habitations for the gentlemen of the speculative class.

"The celebrated island of Atlantis, too well described by the ancient speculator Plato, from whom the subscriber purchased it, to need a description now.

"All his water and wind mills on the River Lethe and on the Mountains of Parnassus and Olympus.

"One hundred millions of acres in the state of Terra Incog-nita, and elsewhere, too tedious to particularize.

"Also that incomparable and most famous riding horse Pega-sus. He would be an excellent nag for riding express, and for that purpose he is recommended to the purchaser or purchasers of the foregoing. Herachitus, junior."

In the beginning Georgia attempted to use her lands wisely, by rewarding those who deserved well of the state and by grants to actual settlers. Besides granting Count d'Estaing his 20,000 acres and Nathanael Greene and Anthony Wayne their plantations, the state rewarded its own heroes with land. It

made frequent grants to Elijah Clarke and probably aggra-
vated the land fever which had seized him and which characterized important later acts of his. By 1785, it had granted
him 5,875 acres in Wilkes and 1,150 acres in Washington
County. To Stephen Heard it gave 2,343 acres in Wilkes; and
to numerous other Georgians of some note it gave moderate
amounts of land. To John and George Galphin, sons of George,
it granted 15,000 acres out of respect for their father and out of
a sense of obligation in disallowing a private treaty they had
made with the Creeks. To Hester and Mary, daughters of the
brave General Screven, Georgia gave 1,000 acres apiece.

The most valuable use to which the state could put its land
was to grant it to actual settlers, and important efforts were
made to accomplish this end. During the Revolution the state
passed land laws primarily to secure soldiers through the encouragement of immigrants; and in 1783, the main provisions
of the land act of 1777, setting up the head-right system, were
continued for peace-time. The head of a family could have
200 acres for himself and 50 acres for each member of his
family, but no family should have more than 1,000 acres.
There was no cost except office and surveying fees for the first
200 acres, but additional land should cost from a half-shilling
to a shilling an acre, depending on the amount. It was distinctly stated that the person must settle on his land and cultivate three acres out of each hundred. This was the head-right
system and no fundamental changes were made in the land
system for the remainder of the century, though in the creation
of each new county the head-right system was re-enacted with
a few minor changes.

The executive council granted land until 1789, when it went
out of existence with the new constitution of that year. Thereafter, a justice of the peace could issue land warrants and the
justices of a county constituted a land court which met monthly
and confirmed land grants, which were then signed by the
governor. This system made it easy for people to secure land,

but also it apparently guarded well the state's public domain.

Under this system a great migration of people set into Georgia, which filled up so rapidly that there was constant pressure against the Indians for more land. About the time the Revolution broke out it was estimated that the number of people in the state was 50,000, with near a half slaves. Although many settlers came to Georgia during the first few years of the war, the conflict later became so destructive that the population must have been greatly reduced when peace came. When the first Federal census was taken in 1790 there were 82,548 people in the state, which represented an impressive growth; but during the next ten years almost as many people came to Georgia as were here at the beginning of the decade. The number in 1800 was 162,686. Most of these people were coming into the up-country, and of them the two most distinct groups, which tended for a long time to remain distinct, were the Virginians, who settled in the Broad River country, and the North Carolinians, who settled in that part of Wilkes County around Washington. The old colonial town of Dartmouth on the point of land between the Broad and Savannah gave place to a new town which the Virginians built up and called Petersburg, named for the town they remembered back in Virginia. Petersburg soon became a great tobacco center with 900 inhabitants, but with the coming of cotton by the end of the century, it rapidly declined and finally disappeared completely. Lisbon, first called Lincoln, on the right bank of the Broad, attempted to recapture the glory that was once Petersburg's but it, too, passed away.

To take care of the governmental needs of this fast-growing population, the state began to create new counties; and during this period when counties were set up for good reasons, the growth of the state could readily be measured by the increase in counties. The constitution of 1777 had created eight counties, and thereafter until 1790 only three new counties were set up. This was the period when the conservative coast still held principal sway and hesitated to increase the power of the upcountry by making new counties. It was during this period that Wilkes County extended widely over the upcountry and contained almost half of the population. But beginning with 1790, the movement for new counties swept all before it, and within the next ten years the number was more than doubled —the total created during this decade being thirteen.

In these new counties conditions were primitive, and justice was rude but swift. For ten years after the Revolution, most of the counties had neither courthouses nor jails. Trials were held in some private residence or under a tree, and prisoners were chained to posts or trees or penned in log houses. Soon after the war a court session being held in Wilkes under a tree was broken up when the jury, seated on a log, made a quick attempt to destroy a passing Tory.

While Georgia was rapidly being filled with sturdy settlers, amazing land speculations were rife. Much of this speculation was born in dishonesty, bribery, and other illegality or in gross carelessness of state officials. The Yazoo Fraud because of its immensity and far-flung consequences became the best-known, but up to the end of the century the land dealings in the state were shot through with fraud. Grants to any one person were limited by law to 1,000 acres unless exception was made by special legislation, but in spite of the law speculators were able to secure vast tracts. The heyday of the speculator began in 1789, when Governor Walton began signing warrants for as much as 50,000 acres for one man; Governor Telfair signed warrants for 100,000 acres to one name; and when George Mathews, a considerable speculator himself, became governor, he was willing to sign warrants for any amount. Richard Dawson was able to accumulate warrants calling for 1,500,000 acres; thirty-five people secured grants for one-third as much land as had been occupied since the landing of Oglethorpe. The fraud that permeated the whole movement is eloquently shown in the fact that from 1789 to 1796 more than three times as much land was granted as existed in the entire state reclaimed from the Indians. The twenty-four counties existing in 1796 contained about 9,000,000 acres; yet the custodians of Georgia's future had issued warrants for 29,000,000 in these same counties.

The methods of making grants are well illustrated in what happened in Montgomery County, where 7,436,995 acres were granted despite the fact that the total area of the county was only 407,680 acres. This was a part of the Great Pine Barrens Speculation, which reached far beyond the limits of Georgia. Since warrants could be issued by county officials, later to be countersigned by the governor, a group of speculators got control of the county government and without going through with a survey issued warrants to themselves to their hearts' desire, filling in as boundaries and markers fictitious streams and trees. These warrants, calling for millions of acres of land which did not exist, they took to Philadelphia and sold to other speculators and to unsuspecting buyers. Robert Morris, signer of the Declaration of Independence and chief financier of the Revolution, entered into speculation in his old age and acquired hazy rights to 2,000,000 acres of Georgia, all of which he lost in the bankruptcy which overtook him. A hundred years later, people were still attempting to locate their lands in Georgia, by looking for streams which did not exist and for walnut, oak, and hickory tree markers in a land where only wire-grass and pine trees have ever grown.

Speculators, connived at or aided by the state government, were not only raiding Georgia's land, vacated by the Indians and organized into counties; but they saw their most gigantic opportunities in lands still held by the Indians and especially the great expanse of the state's western lands whose ownership was clouded in the disputes of Georgia, the United States, and Spain. Elijah Clarke, who already owned many acres and who, no doubt, was vaguely aware that the state had granted away much more land than there was outside of the Indian country, decided to relieve the state of re-granting its lands still further by invading the Creek territories. Aided by the bitterness that arose after the treaty of New York in 1790, and making use of a motley assemblage of adventurers which he had collected to assist the French in their chimerical scheme to wrest Florida from the Spanish, in 1794 he marched his land-hungry followers across the Oconee River and settled down on lands which were guaranteed to the Creeks. His movement became especially menacing when it appeared that he had become filled with grandiloquent ideas about setting up another government, and was proceeding to organize a military régime. This trans-Oconee republic loomed so large in its possibilities for evil that President Washington became alarmed and ordered a tolerant Georgia government to break it up. Clarke was finally forced to desist, and a land-grabbing scheme different from the general pattern came to an end.

Speculations in Georgia's western lands began almost as soon as independence came, and the part the state took in them laid many of its officials open to faithlessness to the trust the people reposed in them, or at best to stupidity or lack of foresight. The first important scheme was a speculation around Muscle Shoals in the big bend of the Tennessee River, promoted by William Blount, John Sevier, and the evanescent State of Franklin. Blount and others visited the Georgia assembly in 1784 for the purpose of having a new county laid out there, and in a rather surreptitious manner the state erected a county which it called Houstoun. In return for aid that Georgia expected the State of Franklin to give her in her war with the Indians, large grants of land in this new county were promised to the Franklinites. Before this bubble got caught in a web of Spanish intrigues and blew up, another scheme was started farther west.

In 1785 Georgia established Bourbon County to the extent of locating its boundaries and appointing a number of justices of the peace and other officers; but she deferred the opening of a land office and the granting of land, for this new county embraced largely the western part of the region which Spain was claiming. To avoid an open conflict with the Spaniards in Natchez, she abolished the county three years later.

Perhaps Georgia felt that she could never assimilate her western lands and unify this vast region into the state, and perhaps she felt with so many authorities asserting claims, she might ultimately lose this small empire. Whatever the reason, she was constantly busied with her western lands. Having offered the southern part of this region to the United States in 1788 on terms which Congress rejected, and seeing Spain still astride it, the next year Georgia decided to sell three vast tracts of this western region to three groups of speculators who had organized for the purpose of buying them. These groups came largely from three states, whose names were attached to the companies, and as some of the land wanted lay in the vicinity of the Yazoo River, this name was added to the companies. They were the South Carolina Yazoo Company, led by Thomas Washington, alias Walsh, who was later hanged in Charleston for counterfeiting; the Virginia Yazoo Company, with Patrick Henry among the group; and the Tennessee Yazoo Company, with Zacariah Cox at the head. An attempt was made to organize a Georgia company, but the Georgians made their start too late to be included in the hasty legislation which set up these companies. They bargained for three separate rough designations of territory which it was thought at the time would amount to about 15,000,000 acres, but which was later estimated at 20,000,000; and for this they agreed to pay a total of $207,000, within two years, after which the title of the land should pass to them. A dispute soon arose over what should be used as money, when the Virginia Company began to gather up the worthless Georgia paper with which to make payment. The results was the refusal of Georgia to deliver title to the land on the ground that the terms of the sale had not been complied with. The South Carolina Company brought suit in the Federal courts to force Georgia to make delivery, but the eleventh amendment which Georgia had fortunately inspired was ratified in time to cause the dismissal of the case. After the United States secured this land, in 1802, the South Carolina Company sought unsuccessfully to secure a settlement from Congress.

It might seem that Georgia having escaped selling a vast amount of her land at about a penny an acre, would have been slow to part with a greater area at even a smaller price; but there took place a second Yazoo sale in 1795, which her faithless officials were induced to make through bribery. This time four companies were organized, each being allotted a roughly defined tract at a definite price. As these boundaries had not been surveyed it was not known how many acres were being sold, but the estimates ran from 35,000,000 to 50,000,000, and the total price offered by the four companies was $500,000, or about one to one and a half cents an acre. The companies were the Georgia, the Georgia Mississippi, the Upper Mississippi, and the Tennessee, with the first-named as the principal one.

Bribery and fraud appeared in the title of this act, in its body, and accompanied its passage. The title, made up of involved and muddling phrases, did not refer to the sales, and as a clever bribe to the people when they should learn the contents of this law, it set aside in each tract land sufficient to total 2,000,000 acres to be allotted to the citizens of Georgia on a scale worked out for each county and at the same price charged the companies. The trusted representatives of the people of Georgia and of other states swarmed into Augusta to hurry this law through the legislature. James Gunn, a United States senator from Georgia, was one of the chief lobbyists. Bribes of land, as much as 75,000 acres to one person, of slaves, of barrels of rice, and of money were freely handed to those legislators whose conscience inclined them against the bill. Some who were too honest to vote for the bill were induced to go home. Another company of Georgians was hurriedly organized, called the Georgia Union Company, who seeing the absurd price being offered for the land and convinced that the legislature was determined to make a sale, offered $300,000 more for the land, but their offer was rejected.

Governor Mathews, whose record in land dealings was shady, was prevailed upon to veto the bill, but the Yazooists soon executed some parliamentary maneuvers and made some changes which induced the governor to sign the bill.

Bitter opposition had had time to develop, even with the quick passing of the bill, and William H. Crawford, just getting started in politics, attempted to induce Governor Mathews not to sign the bill. As soon as the people discovered what had been done, a veritable cyclone of anger and resentment swept over the state. They protested individually and collectively, grand juries made presentments against the faithless legislators, and one enraged community drove out of the state its venal political servant. President Washington was indignant at what had happened and prepared to take action, and James Jackson, a colleague in the United States Senate of the faithless Gunn, resigned his seat to return to Chatham County to run for the legislature.

In the election, the corrupt legislature was turned out and a new group assembled in Louisville, the new capital, determined to wipe out every vestige of the shame that had been heaped upon the state. A rescinding act was quickly passed in 1796, which departed from the general nature of a law to argue for pages against the wickedness and unconstitutionality of the Yazoo act. The legislature declared that this act was not "democratical," that it attempted to set up in America an aristocracy, that under a false title, it disposed of "an enormous tract of unascertained millions of acres," and that it accepted $300,000 less than it might have got. Therefore, the Yazoo act was null and void; and to show its utter contempt for what had been done, the two branches of the legislature would meet three days later utterly to rub out every word of this infamy and publicly burn the act. Furthermore, every reference to the Yazoo infamy should be expunged from all the records of the state, and any state official who should ever take note of it in any way should be fined $1,000 and rendered incapable of holding thereafter any office of trust or profit in the state.

At the appointed time, a fire was built in front of the capitol building and as the house and senate solemnly filed out and took their places around it, the messenger of the house consigned to the flames the act as he spoke these words: "God Save the State! And Long Preserve her Rights!! And May every Attempt to Injure Them Perish as these Corrupt Acts now Do!!!" This was not the only burning exercise the legislature participated in. A year later, when it was discovered that a mortgage book had nineteen pages devoted to the Yazoo sales, the pages were torn from the book and brought into the hall of the house where, in the presence of the senate, they were consigned to the flames, and a page pasted in the book explaining what had been done.

To place beyond the reach of all future legislatures the right to tamper with the Yazoo lands, the constitutional convention in 1798 forbade the sale of western lands to companies or individuals until these regions should be laid off into counties, and it declared forever void the Yazoo act.

Such were the expressions of an indignant and outraged people in their collective capacity. James Jackson felt so keenly on the subject that he took it as a personal insult for anyone ever to refer to the Yazoo act, and to vindicate his wounded honor in such a breach, he fought at least four duels. For fighting a harmless duel with Gunn, his former colleague in the United States Senate, he needed little reason other than the former's unseemly activity in getting the act passed. With Robert Watkins he fought three duels. The first was a savage encounter immediately after the passing of the rescinding act, in which Watkins used not only his pistol but also a dagger, and failing in each attempt, he tried to gouge Jackson, who almost miraculously escaped death. The second duel was fought over a dispute in the constitutional convention of 1798 concerning the Yazoo act; and the third arose over the inclusion of the Yazoo act in a *Digest of the Laws of the State of Georgia,* which Watkins published in 1800. Though this digest had been ordered by the legislature, Jackson, now as governor, refused to allow Watkins to be paid for his labor, and ordered another to be prepared by Horatio Marbury and William H. Crawford.

The Yazoo companies, making the best of their bargains, paid most of the money immediately, and began re-selling their lands and organizing subsidiary companies. Many New Englanders especially became interested in these Georgia lands. The speculation fever was greatly heightened soon after the Yazoo act, by the signing of the treaty with Spain which removed one uncertainty and greatly increased the value of the land. By the rescinding act and the constitution of 1798, ample provision was made for returning all money paid in by the companies. Knowing a good bargain when they saw one and refusing to admit that Georgia could withdraw her sale, many of the Yazooists declined to call for their money, and insisted on having the land.

By this time Georgia had become involved in such complications that she seized the opportunity to appoint three commissioners to meet three provided for in the Congressional enactment of 1798, to make a final settlement of her western territory. In 1802 James Jackson, Abraham Baldwin, and John Milledge met the United States commissioners, James Madison, Levi Lincoln, and Albert Gallatin, and agreed to give up all Georgia's territory west of the Chattahoochee and of a line described as running north, from near the mouth of Uchee Creek to the Tennessee line. In return Georgia was to receive $1,250,000 and that part of the South Carolina cession to the United States which lay east of Georgia's western boundary. Strangely enough, James Jackson permitted the Yazooists to be included in the agreement to the extent that they should receive 5,000,000 acres of land or the proceeds from the sale of 5,000,000 acres. In this agreement was also a clause which led later to a long and most bitter quarrel with the United States. It was in essence a contradiction and abandonment of the Indian policy established in the treaty of New York of 1790, for now the United States promised to secure for the state all Indian lands at her "own expense . . . as early as the same can be peaceably obtained, on reasonable terms." It was agreed that one state should be formed out of this western cession; but time produced two instead of one.

Georgia was now relieved of her Yazoo complications, and the final settlement left $184,515 in the Georgia treasury which the Yazooists had not called for and which now the United States claimed and applied on her debt to Georgia for the western lands. The interest on this amount was long in dispute and as late as 1817 Georgia was maintaining that she should not be charged with it.

The Yazoo dispute became a national issue after 1802, and for a dozen years it disrupted and embittered national politics, with John Randolph, applauded by the Georgians, successfully preventing Congress from granting any relief to the Yazooists. Unable to get around the fiery Randolph, the Yazooists betook themselves to the Supreme Court in 1809 and won a decision the next year in the celebrated case of Fletcher *vs.* Peck, in which the court declared that the Yazoo claims were valid; for Georgia, in passing her law of cession, had made a contract which bribery could not affect, and from which she could not withdraw without the consent of the Yazooists. Emboldened by this decision, the Yazoo supporters in Congress in the absence of Randolph, forced through a final settlement in 1814, amended the next year, which gave the claimants $4,282,151.12½.

Much of the history of state and nation continued to be made around the subject of land, but in Georgia the days of gigantic frauds ended with the Yazoo trouble. Not all land speculations were fraudulent or reprehensible. It was an age in which the most honest attempted to grow rich in land speculations; and the fact that trickery, fraud, and bribery characterized many transactions should not stigmatize all who dealt in land. As bad as the Yazoo speculations were, they were made to appear worse and more unusual by being bandied around in the jig-saw puzzle of early Georgia political factionalism.

CHAPTER XVI

DEVELOPING NATIONALISM

No STATE ENTERED the Union with greater enthusiasm than Georgia, and although the national government had vexed her in the Treaty of New York and in the three Supreme Court decisions, Chisholm *vs.* Georgia, Brailsford *vs.* Georgia, and Fletcher *vs.* Peck, her pleasure in being associated with the other states was not lessened. The honor of the United States was her own honor, and when France in 1798 forgot the respect that was due an independent nation, Georgia no less than the national government resented the insults.

The French troubles were largely settled for a time, in a treaty made in 1800; but in the Napoleonic wars which soon began to shake the established order of all Europe, there arose troubles with England which were destined ultimately to draw into the maelstrom the United States. Britannia ruled the waves in too arbitrary a fashion to please the American ship-owners, whose vessels were darting in and out of the warring countries, carrying on a most lucrative trade. French decrees and British orders in council looked equally bad on paper, but the British sea-power was successful in translating them into more troublesome action. For this reason, England instead of France became the enemy which goaded America into war. Furthermore, Georgians had not forgotten the hatreds produced by the devastations of the Revolution, nor were they oblivious to the gallant efforts of Count d'Estaing and his French to drive the British out of Georgia.

But England was not now injuring Georgians directly, for they were not engaged in the carrying trade; the searching of a New England Yankee ship and removal of sailors was no loss to Georgians. This they understood; but they saw a right violated and the nation insulted, and they felt as much resentment as if they had been personally injured and insulted. They were Georgians, but they were also Americans. In 1807, the British war vessel *Leopard* fired on the American naval ship *Chesapeake,* and British sailors boarded and searched the American ship and took off four sailors under the claim that they were British subjects and their allegiance was indefeasible. Georgia, with the rest of the nation, became much excited. The Savannahians held a meeting of hot indignation, and demanded preparations for war. The state immediately laid in a supply of 10,0000 stands of arms, twelve field pieces, 700 pairs of horseman's pistols, and a great deal of ammunition and other war equipment, and she turned into an arsenal the old state capitol at Louisville.

England, paying little attention to American remonstrances, continued her lawless course. In 1809 Georgia declared she believed fully in the villanies and despotism of the British and that she stood by the national government in its refusal to submit indefinitely to British insults. And two years later, when the nation had worn thin the last fragment of its forbearance, the Georgia senate declared that the state stood ready for war, "with stern and unwavering contempt of individual danger," and that if the United States considered her honor "to have been outraged beyond the tardy remedy of negotiation," then Georgia would, "with proud alacrity," fly to her aid.

In his message to the legislature in November, 1811, Governor David B. Mitchell called upon that body to make preparations to fight England. He reminded the Georgians that their state stood exposed on almost every frontier and that they should take quick action in looking forward toward any eventuality. When war was declared the next year, Georgia gave it her hearty support and anxiously awaited any opportunity to go forward in it. Governor Mitchell referred with scorn to the New Englanders, who refused to support the war, and to the minority in Congress, who were wholly lost to a sense of patriotism. In 1807 Georgia had thanked the eccentric John Randolph for his fight against the Yazooists in Congress, and had named a county for him; in 1812 Randolph, just as eccentric, refused to become enthusiastic for the war to such an extent "as to render his name odious to every republican citizen," and Georgia now removed his name from the county. She re-named it for the gallant Jasper, who had fallen in the Revolution; and not until 1828, when she had long forgotten about this British war, did Georgia again name one of her counties for Randolph. As a blow to British manufactures and an encouragement to domestic industry, the members of the Georgia legislature resolved to appear in full suits of homespun, made within the state.

The enthusiasm of Georgia for this war was not measured alone by the indignation she felt at the insults Britain had heaped upon the United States nor by any tender pity she might have had for the New England shippers, despoiled of their vessels. She had a more immediate interest which touched her closely. Not since the first day of her existence had Georgia been free from the actual menace or at least the rivalry of the region beyond her southern frontier. Florida had always been a disturber of her peace, and in her attempts to end the evil, her efforts to capture St. Augustine had become almost a habit. In the Revolution, the British had made it a retreat from which to issue in their raids against Georgia; and when peace came, she had handed it over to the ancient enemy and disturber of the peace, the Spaniards. It then became a refuge for many Tories driven out of Georgia, who added more spleen to the ill-will already existing. Fugitive slaves from Georgia found here a ready relief from their enforced labor, and in alliance with hostile Indians found it easy to harass the Georgia frontiers.

In a war with England, the Georgians felt it ought to be an easy opportunity to secure Florida as part of the spoils of a conflict in which, true enough, the Spaniards might not become direct participants, but a conflict, nevertheless, in which their powerful ally England would be a participant. The United States was not oblivious of these feelings and her policy was not free from this influence.

Hence it was that in pursuance of a secret act of Congress, President Madison appointed in January, 1811, George Mathews, the former Georgia governor, and John McKee, an Indian agent, commissioners, with vague and elastic powers to take advantage of any opportunities that might come of directing Florida toward the United States. Mathews, in 1812, before war with England had been declared, engineered a mock revolution among former Georgians and others living south of the St. Marys River, and declared the Republic of East Florida. With the aid of an American fleet, which had been stationed at the mouth of the St. Marys, he seized Fernandina, on Amelia Island, and marched southward, followed by some American troops, to capture St. Augustine. He failed in his attempt, and soon the United States, alarmed by the vigor of his actions, recalled him, and appointed Governor Mitchell to manage the Florida business. Mitchell, neglecting his official duties as governor of Georgia, gathered up a few companies of Georgia militia and betook himself to the St. Marys, where he entered into a fruitless correspondence with the Spanish governor. Being no less anxious to secure Florida for the United States than had been Mathews, he invaded Florida with his Georgia troops; but in October, 1812, he was recalled, and the United States withdrew as fast as convenient from an adventure which she could not well defend.

Georgia was painfully disappointed at the refusal of the United States to follow up her lead in seizing Florida. She declared that Florida was a never-ending menace to her and that she had already suffered depredations affording sufficient cause for seizing this "corrupt and corrupting province." She had much in mind declaring war on Florida and taking it for herself, for she argued that the Federal constitution allowed a state to declare war to protect itself from invasion or imminent danger of it. As the first act in the drama, a mob in Savannah seized and destroyed a vessel laden with provisions for St. Augustine; but Georgians generally contented themselves with arguments. For almost ten more years they were to endure this Florida menace.

The war with Great Britain was confined largely to the northern borders of the United States, the West, and to the sea. Georgians had practically no contact with British troops, though they saw some bloody encounters with the Indians before the war was over. The United States early called on Georgia for 3,500 troops to be detached from the state militia and to be held in readiness. By November, 1812, ten companies had entered actively into the service of the United States. As Georgia had no munition factories, she found it difficult to secure swords, pistols, and other equipment. To supply this need, Governor Mitchell set up a sabre factory in Milledgeville which could make five dozen sabres a week; he also made preparations to have pistols made in the state.

The first alarms of war to reach Georgia were rung out by the Creeks. In the fall of 1811 Tecumseh, one of the ablest Indians of all North America, visited the Creeks and Seminoles and fired them with his plans of federating the Indians from Canada to Mexico, and regenerating their ancient powers and virtues. They plotted war against the whites. Not all of the Indians wanted to depart from the civilization the United States was trying to impose upon them. The Lower Creeks, who lived principally in Georgia, remained friendly, but most of the Upper Creeks, who were chiefly in Alabama, decided they would rather revert to pristine barbarism, bedaub their faces with war paint, and kill each other and any one else who might get in their way. These "red-sticks" made threats against the peaceably inclined Indians, and scared some of them into going to Milledgeville to secure the protection of the Georgia government.

Supplied with British arms and ammunition from Pensacola, the "red-sticks" burst upon Fort Mims, on the lower Alabama River, in August, 1813, and massacred 400 people. The frontier was now aflame with an Indian war. Into the fray came Andrew Jackson and his Tennesseans, with an expedition from New Orleans, and a force of Georgians. In September, John Floyd was ordered with 3,600 Georgia troops to rendezvous at Fort Hawkins, on the Ocmulgee, to prepare to go against the Creeks. Hindered by the lack of subsistence and transportation, he gradually made his way to the Chattahoochee where on the west bank he constructed Fort Mitchell, from which he moved against the Creeks. He fell upon them at two of their towns, Autossee, and Tallassee, on the Tallapoosa River, defeated them, and burned the towns. A few days later in a clash with them at Chalibbee, Floyd was badly cut up, though the Indians suffered considerable losses which they concealed as they retreated from the field.

In the meantime, General Jackson had been dealing with the Creeks, and in March, 1814, he broke their power in his victory over them at Horseshoe Bend. Five months later, he gathered together on the banks of the Alabama the defeated braves and forced them to sign the treaty of Fort Jackson, by which they gave up nearly all of their lands in Alabama and the southernmost part of Georgia in a strip about 70 miles wide. This treaty strategically cut off and isolated the Creeks from the Spaniards and Seminoles in Florida and the Choctaws and Chickasaws to the westward, but in doing so it secured most of the cessions in Alabama and left the heart of Georgia, from the Ocmulgee to the Chattahoochee, still in the hands of the Creeks. That part received by the Georgians, they considered worthless. The treaty had the additional defect of taking a great deal of territory from the friendly Creeks, whom it, however, attempted to recompense in the peculiar provision that each friendly Creek who had taken an active part in the war should have one square mile of land surrounding his home and improvements, which should "inure to the said chief or warrior, and his descendants, so long as he or they shall continue to occupy the same." Indian agent Benjamin Hawkins, who took part in making the treaty, was chiefly responsible for allowing the Creeks to keep their large holdings in Georgia.

The Georgians were deeply disappointed by this treaty. They had good reason to expect the United States to use this opportunity more fully to carry out the promise she had made in 1802, to remove the Indians from Georgia. Instead, the Indians had been left in Georgia and removed from Alabama, where the United States was under no obligations to act.

Peace with the Indians turned Jackson toward Florida and then New Orleans, and led the Georgians to look more closely to the defense of their coast, which they feared might be raided by the British war vessels at any time. At the beginning of the war, the Georgians, feeling that their coast was in great danger, provided for the organization of a company of militia in each coastal county, and Savannah stationed fast boats around the inlets to report speedily the first appearance of the British. Toward the end of 1814, when attack seemed more imminent, the troops around Fort Hawkins, now under the command of General David Blackshear, who had just set out to join General Jackson, were ordered to hurry to the Georgia coast. They had gone as far as Fort Early, on the Flint, before they were turned back. The path cut across the state to Darien by these forces came to be called Blackshear's Road.

The long-expected attack of the British came in the early part of 1815, when Admiral Cockburn made a landing on Cumberland Island and around St. Marys on the mainland, and began to pillage the country. Fearing that Savannah might be attacked next, Peter Early, who had succeeded Mitchell as governor in 1813, hurried with 2 000 troops to the defense of that city. As the Treaty of Ghent, ending the war, had been signed in December, 1814, all of these operations, including the victory at New Orleans, were needless; and when the news arrived, all fighting ceased.

This second war with Great Britain was a useless struggle, which settled nothing, and ended with each side restoring all its conquests. With the fall of Napoleon, Europe had peace, and England no longer in a struggle for her existence had no need to disregard American rights in defending herself.

Yet Americans assumed that they had won a glorious war, and with the self-confidence, if not national arrogance, that followed the treaty of peace, they for the first time began the development of a rampant nationalism. Now they had a soul which they could call their own. In this new movement, Georgia was in the forefront; her patriotism was unsurpassed. When in the latter part of 1814, news reached America of the preposterous demands of the British in the peace negotiations then going on at Ghent, Georgia resolved that the war should be continued with greater vigor, and during the struggle she passed resolutions of thanks and praise for American victories and victors. In 1817 she appropriated $10,000 to be used as gifts to the widows and children of Georgia soldiers killed in the war. In 1816 David B. Mitchell, now governor again, joined the national chorus of praise for the might of America. After telling how sordid were the monarchies of Europe and how stupid, ignorant, and prejudiced their people were for enduring their evils, he recounted how the American army, hastily collected and untrained, "gave the enemy in our recent contest, such proof of republican energy, as made them glad to withdraw their royal mercenaries from the conflict, under a succession of disasters which confounded themselves, and astonished all Europe."

The Treaty of Ghent ended the war with Great Britain, but there could be no end to the warfare that had been going on along the Florida border while Spain continued to allow that province to be a refuge and prey for freebooters, outlaws, adventurers, marauding Indians, and runaway slaves. Conditions were fast becoming intolerable for the peace of Georgia and the dignity of the United States. Near the end of the war, Colonel Edward Nicholls had landed a force from British war vessels and built on the Apalachicola River, about sixty miles south of the Georgia border, a fort which he provisioned with more than 700 barrels of powder, many guns, and other war equipment. This fort he handed over to the Seminoles and Creeks as a stronghold from which they could make raids across the border into Georgia. When peace was declared, Nicholls departed and soon a thousand or more runaway slaves from Georgia, who had laid hold of the river valley, seized the fort, and continued plundering the Georgia frontier.

As a defense, General Jackson, whose command included these regions, ordered the building of Fort Scott, in the southwest corner of Georgia on the point of land where the Flint and the Chattahoochee flow together. In attempts to provision this fort, it was found that the Apalachicola fort, or Negro Fort, as it now came to be called, stood in the way. The United States, therefore, in 1816, decided to demolish it, even though it was in Spanish territory and an invasion of that territory would be necessary. General Edmund P. Gaines, commanding on the Georgia frontier, sent Colonel Duncan L. Clinch with a force down the Apalachicola to invest the fort, while a naval expedition came up the river from the Gulf of Mexico. A joint attack was made which came to a most sudden and remarkable conclusion when one of the war vessels made a lucky shot of a red-hot cannon ball into the powder magazine of the fort. The fort was blown into fragments and more than 300 of the people in it were killed. This part of the Georgia frontier was thereafter free from molestation.

The year following the destruction of the Negro Fort saw another disturbance on the opposite end of the Georgia frontier. Here on Amelia Island, Sir Gregor MacGregor, an adventurer who claimed to be a Scotch nobleman, aided by Baltimore adventurers, seized Fernandina. He soon decided to leave, only to be followed immediately by Louis Aury, a French sailmaker turned freebooter. The United States took alarm at the menace these piratical expeditions held out for the Georgia frontiers, and for the nation as a whole. Toward the end of the year 1817, it sent troops to take possession of Amelia Island, and with their coming Aury fled.

It was evident that the whole Florida province was in a state of turmoil, which Spain was either unable or unwilling to control. To deal with the Indians, who were marauding the Georgia borderlands unceasingly, General Jackson carried out his famous invasion of Florida, in which he did not hesitate to capture two Spanish forts and hustle off to Havana their garrisons, seize the Spanish governor, hang two British subjects, and raise the American flag over the province.

Protests and demands for indemnity were soon flying to and fro among the United States, Spain, and England; but the dispute finally narrowed down to the United States and Spain, in which the former demanded that Spain must either adequately control Florida or give it up to the United States. In 1819 a treaty of cession, whose negotiation was aided by John Forsyth, the United States minister to Spain and a Georgian, was agreed upon. The transfer took place two years later, when Jackson was made governor of the new Florida Territory, and a problem which had plagued Georgia for almost a century was finally settled. John Clark, the governor of Georgia, could now rejoice that Florida would "no longer be the rendezvous or asylum for the smuggling and piratical adventurer of every nation, nor the secure retreat for the lawless and ungovernable of our state." Georgians were particularly pleased that "Old Hickory" should become the first governor of the territory south of them.

Though Georgia was now relieved of an enemy in Florida, she was still vexed by the uncertainties of her Florida boundary line. Apparently the location of the line was simple enough, for

in 1764, the boundary had been described and the description
had never been changed. It ran in a straight line eastwardly
from the junction of the Flint and Chattahoochee rivers to the
head of the most southern branch of the St. Marys River and
down that river to the sea. The only point about which there
could be a dispute was the most southern branch of the St.
Marys, and it was in the fixing of this location that the trouble
lay. This line had merely been described, but never run; and
in 1795, when Spain withdrew her advanced claims to the
northern part of West Florida and accepted the 31st parallel,
the commissioners did not run the line east of the Chattahoochee. They did, however, locate what they considered to be
the most southern branch of the St. Marys and did erect a great
mound of earth at its head, which they called Ellicott's Mound,
after the American commissioner. For years Georgia denied
that this was the true head of the St. Marys, but in 1819 commissioners which she had appointed to run the line accepted
Ellicott's Mound. As the United States did not act, the line
could not be fixed at this time. A few years later, in 1828, after
Thomas Spalding, representing Georgia, and Thomas Mann
Randolph, acting for the United States, had surveyed a line
the previous year, Georgia changed her mind again, and now
claimed that Ellicott's Mound was incorrect as it marked the
northern instead of the southern stream of the St. Marys. Not
until 1859 was the line finally run and fixed, with the acceptance of the mound, which by that time had grown famous,
and not until 1866 did Georgia find time to signify her agreement. The early drifting of settlers into the disputed region
made an agreed line a necessity, and the tardiness in establishing it was a considerable hindrance to law and order there.

Fighting the second war with Great Britain and getting the
Spaniards out of Florida relieved Georgia of one of her major
disturbances; but there was another which was even more vexatious and devastating. She still had her Indians, which the
United States had promised to remove; but presidents came
and went and still Georgia had her unwelcomed Indians.

CHAPTER XVII

PUSHING AGAINST THE FRONTIER: CREEKS AND CHEROKEES

THE ORGY of land speculations which characterized Georgia for twenty years following the Revolution, brought the people to their senses by the beginning of the new century. The vast stretches of her public domain west of the Chattahoochee had been given up in 1802, and it was now easy for the most stupid to see the desirability of using sound judgment in disposing of her remaining lands.

By the terms of the cession, the United States promised to remove the Indians from the state as fast as it could be done peaceably and on reasonable terms; and with commendable speed she bought from the Creeks, a few months after the agreement, a long strip of land directly west of the Oconee, in a treaty which James Wilkinson, of shifty fame, Benjamin Hawkins, and Andrew Pickens made with them at Fort Wilkinson. Now possessed of new lands, Georgia decided to adopt a new land policy. No longer would she grant away through fraudulent officials three times as much land as she actually owned.

She determined first that her land was valuable only when it was occupied by citizens, that it should be disposed of in small tracts, and that it should be granted free of charge except for a few necessary expenses. This decision was of great importance, for she might have held her lands for a price and been slow to part with them as they increased in value. In this way she could have slowly built up a vast endowment, either in land or money, which might ultimately have relieved the people of taxation, as Governor George M. Troup later thought possible. Or she might have reserved certain portions of the land, while at the same time permitting a relatively rapid settlement, and later disposed of these lands at a high price. Governor John Clark believed that "liberal reservations" should be made by the state.

Georgia accepted a different philosophy on the greatness of a state, and staked her future in her people instead of in reserved lands. Governor Troup declared, "Men and the soil constitute the strength and wealth of nations, and the faster you plant the men, the faster you can draw on both." The United States, not as liberal as Georgia, in the disposal of her lands charged a price never less than $1.25 an acre. In one distribution alone, that of 1827, if Georgia had sold the land at the price charged by the United States, she would have received for it almost $6,000,000.

Her new land policy, called the land lottery system, was begun in 1803 in a law laying out three counties from the lands secured from the Fort Wilkinson treaty. The main features of this new policy were to be continued throughout the settlement of the remainder of the state, as one Indian cession followed another until the last Indian had left. It thus happened that Georgia developed two distinct land systems: the head-right system east of the Oconee River and the land lottery system west of it. By this law, the land was divided into parcels of 202½ acres (45 chains square), which was the size generally adhered to except notably in the gold regions, where it was 40 acres; and after having been surveyed and properly charted, it should be offered to the public in the form of a lottery, in which each citizen should have one chance, and if he were the head of a family, two chances. Widows, orphans, and Revolutionary veterans also were given varying chances. As there were many more citizens in every lottery than there were parcels of land, it naturally happened that many people drew blanks, and, therefore, received no land. In surveying these lots, the small tracts that were left here and there with less than the 202½ acres, were known as fractional land, and they were reserved by the state and sold for a price.

The progress of settling the state westward was marked by one Indian cession after another, with the territory secured being immediately laid out into counties and surveyed into lots, followed by a land lottery. From 1800 to 1809, fourteen new counties were erected; from 1810 to 1819, nine counties; from 1820 to 1829, twenty-nine counties; and from 1830 to 1839, seventeen counties. These counties represented definitely the rapid filling up of the best Indian lands; thereafter the counties which were created resulted from the growth of sparsely settled regions, or too often from political barter. During the first four decades of the nineteenth century, the state grew in population from 162,000 to 691,000. Being a frontier state filling up with settlers, it grew much faster than the country as a whole. The decades in which its growth was most marked were from 1800 to 1810, when it was 55%, and from 1820 to 1830, when it was 51%.

The spreading out of a people into a new land is accompanied by failure and death as well as by success and progress. Settlements grow up, develop boundless ambitions and dream of their coming greatness, and by tricks of fate, aided by popular whims and economic laws, sink back into nothingness. The law of the survival of the fittest works inexorably here, and towns, dead and forgotten, are left as mute evidence of dismal failures. Hardwicke, which in colonial times had ambitions of becoming the capital of the province, struggled on until it was declared the county seat of Bryan County in 1793; but life would not take hold of it, and by 1824 there was only one family remaining. Though efforts were made in 1866 to revive it, failure resulted, for it seems to have been decreed from the beginning that it should be one of the dead towns of Georgia. Sunbury, on the coast, grew up in colonial times, and became a rival of Savannah. It suffered the devastations of the British during the Revolution and of a hurricane a few years later, and with the

progress of settlements to the westward, Riceborough super-
seded it as the county seat in 1797. Then Bermuda grass and
weeds, followed by stray cattle, took possession, and Sunbury
became only a memory. Jacksonborough was a thriving town
in 1799, when it became the county seat of Screven County, and
it could at one time boast of being the home of John Abbot, an
authority on lepidopterous insects of Georgia; but its dream of
greatness ended in 1847 when Sylvania became the county
seat, and it soon died. So, too, was the fate of Hartford in
Pulaski County, of Salem in Clarke County, Jeffersonton in
Camden County, and of other towns now dead.

The recession of the Indians developed into prominent towns
and forts which had their day, and then night came. Fort
James, Fort Barrington, Fort Early, Fort Lamar, Fort Hawkins, Fort Lawrence, Fort Perry, Fort Scott, Fort Wilkinson,
Fort Wayne—all and more came and went. Francisville, where
the old Horse Path from the Ocmulgee to the Chattahoochee
crossed the Flint, built by Francis Bacon, who married Jeffer-
sonia, the daughter of Benjamin Hawkins, thrived until it became the victim of an era when railroads came and left it to
sleep unto death.

The progress of the state was always westward, west by north
more during the first half of the century and then west by
south. The coast, left behind by the westward migrations, grew
slowly but surely; and, somewhat contemptuous of the grasping uplanders, thinking herself denied by them her proper
position she became a state unto herself. Having seized the
capital from Savannah at the end of the Revolution and moved
it to Augusta, preparatory to taking it westward to Louisville,
by 1804, the westward moving people considered Louisville too
far east and legislated into existence the town of Milledgeville,
making it the capital. The old statehouse at Louisville, first
turned into an arsenal, was then sold at auction.

Just as the onward sweeping population moved the capital
with it and left once ambitious towns to die, so at the same

time it laid the foundations of more important towns which
were destined to grow great. Among such towns were Macon
on the Ocmulgee and Columbus on the Chattahoochee, the one
laid out in 1823 and the other five years later. The one early
became a great cotton market, and the other developed into a
manufacturing center. Towns in their infancy were generally
ruled by three or five commissioners, who passed laws, levied
taxes, and imposed fines; and not until they should become as
populous and important as Savannah or Augusta did they develop mayors and councils.

After 1803, the settling of all unoccupied lands west of the
Oconee could legally proceed only through the land lottery
system; but the lands elsewhere not yet occupied might proceed

EMBRYO TOWN OF COLUMBUS ON THE
CHATTAHOOCHEE

Mrs. Basil Hall (author) and Una Pope-Hennessy (editor), *The
Aristocratic Journey*. New York and London: G. P. Putnam's Sons,
1931.

under the head-right system or under special arrangements. An example of the first was Walton County, laid out in 1803 on the northern borders to take care of settlers whom Georgia considered within her limits. A few years later when the boundary line was surveyed, it was found that the settlement lay in North Carolina, and Walton County thereupon disappeared. Taken care of by special laws was a group of settlers who had obtruded themselves into the Cherokee country and had set down on a strip of land extending southwest of the Tugaloo River, and called Wafford's Settlement. In 1804 the United States made a treaty with the Cherokees, who ceded a strip four miles wide and about twenty miles long, designed to include these settlements. Georgia finally annexed them to Jackson County.

Georgians were as hungry for land in the nineteenth century as they were in the eighteenth, but now they were forced to be contented with 202½ acres apiece instead of small empires. Though the size of their holdings secured directly from the state was smaller, they were no less insistent on having them; and this surge against the frontier for more land led the state almost to the verge of war against the national government.

The United States, never quite making up her mind on what ultimately should happen to the Indians, had particularly muddled the problem in Georgia. By the Treaty of New York, and by the common tenor of most of her treaties, she led the Indians to believe that the lands they were allowed to hold should remain to them forever, and to emphasize their permanent occupation, she promoted their becoming farmers and their taking on the civilization of the whites. By the agreement made with Georgia in 1802, when she gave up her western lands, the United States promised to remove every Indian from the state as soon as it could be done peaceably and on reasonable terms. Though in actual wording there was no conflict of promises, in principle there was an absolute conflict. Out of this troublesome situation arose a contest with the United

States, which embittered the Georgians more than any other problem which had ever arisen.

The United States having promised the Indians one thing and Georgia another, immediately set out to satisfy both. For a decade and a half, neither seemed to find much at which to complain; for the United States began making treaties with the Indians, in which she obtained important cessions, but at considerable monetary costs exacted by the occupants. The Creeks being more directly in the way of Georgia's westward march, were the first to feel the pressure. In addition to making the cession in 1802, in which they had allowed the whites to gain a foothold on the west banks of the Oconee, they, three years later, retreated to the Ocmulgee, but they retained fifteen square miles east of the river, where the United States should be allowed to erect a fort and trading station, just across the river near the point where Macon later grew up. For giving up this land to Georgia, the United States paid the Creeks more than $200,000.

Then came the war with Great Britain and the Indians, out of which the treaty of Fort Jackson grew, a treaty which greatly displeased Georgia, because it secured only that "sterile and unprofitable territory," isolated by ungranted Indian lands on the north and still menaced by Spanish Florida on the south. Perhaps as a sop to Georgia, the United States appointed Governor Mitchell the Indian agent in 1817; and the next year it attempted to pacify the Georgians by paying the Creeks $120,000 to give up about 1,500,000 acres in two tracts, one south of the Altamaha and the other around the headwaters of the Ocmulgee. But as long as the heart of Georgia, from the Ocmulgee to the Chattahoochee, remained in possession of the Creeks, Georgians would not be satisfied. In 1819 she chided the United States for being so slow in fulfilling a promise long overdue: Georgia had "waited the tide of events, and observed the march of time for seventeen years"; she had seen two states made out of the territory which she had given up in 1802;

other states had been relieved of their Indians and were growing great, while Georgia, to whom the United States owed particular obligations, was languishing because she could not take control of her own possessions.

Despite the chidings of Georgia, the United States seemed anxious to placate the state and carry out her promises. In 1821 she secured from the Creeks the great stretch of territory from the Ocmulgee to the Flint, with the exception of the

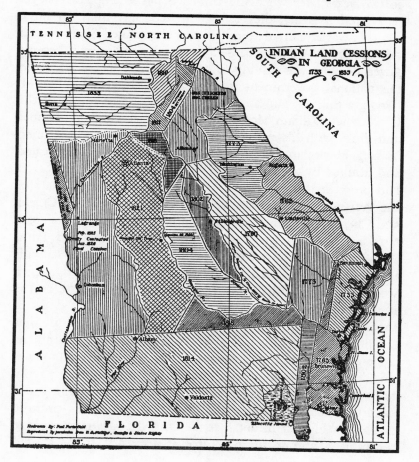

Indian town of Buzzard-Roost, one thousand acres around Indian Springs, and a small tract including William McIntosh's home. For this area the United States paid the Indians $200,000, and assumed the debts of the Creeks to Georgia for depredations they had carried out, to the amount of $250,000.

By this time the Creeks had come to see that the next demand for territory would likely send them completely out of Georgia and on their way to lands west of the Mississippi; and so two years later when the United States attempted to negotiate another treaty, they refused to cede any more territory. Georgia was equally determined that the United States should put the Creeks out, and this same year (1823) a man became governor, who was willing to carry the state into a war with the national government if necessary. This was George M. Troup, a militant and amazing character, a first cousin of the Creek chief William McIntosh, somewhat eccentric in manner and dress, with his curly sandy hair, blue eyes, and dignified bearing. He declared that Georgia had been outrageously treated and insulted by the halting fashion in which the United States had proceeded in carrying out her promise to rid the state of the Indians. Georgia was more dead than alive with the Creeks and Cherokees holding her best lands. Troup made bitter protests and charged the Federal government with bad faith. President Monroe answered Georgia's intemperate attacks with the declaration that the United States had never pledged her word to put the Indians out except with their consent, and if it were impossible to induce them to go, the United States should not be blamed for the failure. He assured Georgia that the president would continue unceasingly to urge the Indians to go on peaceable and reasonable terms. Troup refused to take this declaration as an answer, and he chose to direct his reply to John C. Calhoun, the secretary of war. In a most biting and sarcastic letter, he argued that if the government's promise meant anything, it meant that the United States must remove the Indians, and do so with force, if necessary. If the United

States were going to back out of its bargain made in 1802, then it should give Georgia the $5,000,000 it had showered on the New England Yazooists, and restore to Georgia the states of Alabama and Mississippi.

Although the Creeks had held a council at Broken Arrow, in Alabama, in 1824, in which they reaffirmed their intention never to part with another inch of their lands, President Monroe, genuinely desirous of appeasing Georgia, appointed in December, 1824, two Georgians, James Meriwether and Duncan G. Campbell to treat with the Creeks for the cession of their lands. Soon thereafter they met Creek representatives in a council, but found them adamant against further cessions. Yet in February following, they induced 400 chiefs and headmen of the Lower Creeks to negotiate a treaty at Indian Springs, in which they agreed to give up all their lands in Georgia and in return should receive an equal amount of land in the West and, in addition, $400,000.

The Upper Creeks, warlike and definitely opposed to leaving for the West, refused to attend the Indian Springs negotiations, and on hearing of what had been done, they decreed death against William McIntosh, the Lower Creek chief, who had been mainly responsible for the treaty. A party of 170 braves carried out the sentence by attacking McIntosh at night in his home on the Chattahoochee. They set fire to his house, drove him out into the yard, shot him down and stabbed him to death.

Not only was a great commotion raised among the Indians, but also the strained relations between Georgia and the United States became more tense. The Indian agents had been for years unsympathetic with Georgia, and she had come to look upon them as the chief promoters of hostility between the state and the Indians. They had appeared to be almost as much opposed to the Treaty of Indian Springs as were the Upper Creeks, and Troup felt strongly the suspicion that these agents had been helpful in stirring up the Upper Creeks to murder

McIntosh and other chiefs. Though the treaty had been ratified by the Senate and signed by the president, Monroe sent agents to Georgia to investigate, and soon Troup was in a heated battle with them. The Georgia governor declared at this time, "I verily believe that, but for the insidious practices of evil-minded white men, the entire nation would have moved harmoniously across the Mississippi."

No doubt, President Monroe was glad to hand over the presidency to John Quincy Adams, on March 4, 1825, if for no other reason than to be relieved of the Indian troubles in Georgia. Troup was now in no mood to compromise with a New England Adams; neither was the new president inclined to bow to Georgia. Declaring that the treaty had not been properly negotiated, Adams disallowed it, and forbade Troup to begin surveying the land.[1] Troup, enraged by these attempts to deprive Georgia of her spoils of victory, bitterly declared in May that if Adams continued the course he had set out on, nothing but war could result, for when people ceased to be masters they became slaves. In a heroic mood, he informed the legislature that it was "not too late, to step forth, and, having exhausted the argument, to stand by your arms." He continued his plans to survey the land, and made preparations for war.

Adams, fearful of starting a civil war, gathered together at Washington a group of chiefs from both the Upper and Lower Creeks, and by corrupting them and using chicanery, got them to agree to the treaty of Washington, in January, 1826, whereby they ceded all their lands in Georgia excepting a small strip west of the Chattahoochee. Troup was utterly displeased with this treaty, as it did not provide for a cession of all the Creek holdings. He ordered surveys to be made for the whole region without reference to the reserved strip. Such a move was in high contempt of the United States and of its chief executive,

---

[1] Nevertheless, this treaty was officially published in *Indian Treaties, and Laws and Regulations Relating to Indian Affairs* (Washington, 1826), a work authorized by the Department of War.

and brought down the threat by Adams to use the United States army to restrain Troup's surveyors. Troup declared that Georgia was ready for war. In February, 1827, he defied James Barbour, secretary of war, saying, "You will distinctly understand, therefore, that I feel it to be my duty to resist to the utmost any military attack which the government of the United States shall think proper to make on the territory, the people, or the sovereignty of Georgia, and all the measures necessary to the performance of this duty, according to our limited means, are in progress. From the first decisive act of hostility, you will be considered and treated as a public enemy, and with the less repugnance, because you, to whom we might have constitutionally appealed for our own defense against invasion, are yourselves the invaders, and what is more, the unblushing allies of the savages, whose cause you have adopted." He ordered the immediate liberation of any surveyor who might be arrested, called for the Georgia troops to hold themselves in readiness to march on short notice, and began to establish depots of arms and ammunition.

President Adams hurried a treaty with the Creeks, which was made in November, 1827, and which ceded the last vestige of Creek lands in Georgia. About the same time the United States Senate appointed a committee, headed by Thomas Hart Benton, to investigate the trouble, and in a long report it practically justified Georgia's course. Troup denied that he had any desire to break up the Union, but that, on the contrary, he was helping to guarantee it by seeing that the rights of all should be respected—and in determining what the rights of the states were, the Supreme Court could not be allowed to be the arbiter. Though Troup had whipped up much excitement in the state to support his contest with the United States, his political enemies declared that he had employed threats and wild language more to cement his party following than actually to provoke a war. It was also observed that Troup and his Georgia followers would have likely been forced to fight a civil war alone, had a clash come, for the rest of the South did not become greatly excited.

Georgia was forever free of her Creeks, except for an exciting invasion which a group from Alabama carried out in an attempt to join, in 1836, the Seminoles in Florida. They burned the village of Roanoke, in western Georgia, and seized a few steamers on the Chattahoochee, before General Winfield Scott with Federal forces was able to subdue them. Though no longer troubled by the Creeks, Georgia still had her Cherokees, of whom she had long been trying to rid herself.

The Cherokees, living in the mountainous part of the state to the northward, had not got in the way of the Georgians as quickly as had the Creeks; but Georgia was no less conscious of their presence and no less determined that they also must go. In response to the policy, advocated by Jefferson as early as 1803, that the Indians should ultimately be removed to the regions west of the Mississippi, a group of Cherokees had left in 1809 to spy out this new land, and soon returned with a favorable report which led a few to migrate. In 1817 and 1819 they made treaties giving up small strips in northeastern Georgia, and a large number departed, but these were mostly from Tennessee where they had made larger cessions. It seemed that the Georgia Cherokees were less desirous to go than those living in North Carolina, Tennessee, and Alabama.

In 1824, seeing how the Creeks were being pushed out, the Cherokees adopted a definite policy against leaving, and in a memorial to Congress presented by John Ross, George Lowery, Major Ridge, and Elijah Hicks, declared that they knew what the western lands were like—a barren waste with neither trees nor water. There they could engage only in the chase and warfare, and as they had decided to quit those occupations forever, it had now become "the fixed and unalterable determination of this nation never again to cede one foot more of our land." As in the case of the Creeks, there developed a party among the Cherokees, who saw the futility of attempting to hold out

against Georgia, and who, therefore, argued that the Cherokees should remove as soon as convenient. This lack of harmony among the Cherokees complicated the problem and led
to a long and painful struggle before they were finally forced
out.

The United States government, by unwise acts, made more
difficult the fulfillment of its promise to Georgia. With one
hand it tried to remove the Indians and with the other it
planted them deeper into the Georgia soil. In the treaties of
1817 and 1819, it allowed all Cherokees who wanted to become
citizens of the United States and who were considered capable
of managing their property to receive 640 acres of land and remain in Georgia. It had also, in its efforts to civilize them,
aided them with the implements of a stable society, and had
helped the American Board of Commissioners for Foreign Missions to Christianize and educate them. To pamper them in
the importance that they were taking on as a nation apart from
Georgia and in no wise under her control, the United States
received Cherokee delegations with all the pomp given to
diplomats of foreign nations.

Under such benign influences the Cherokees began to take
on a national consciousness and to consider themselves forever
implanted in the lower ramparts of their beloved Southern
highlands, in a region which had been claimed by Georgians
from the day George II had granted it in 1732 but which had
belonged to the Indians from time out of mind. They numbered about 14,000. Most of them lived in Georgia, and they
owned in 1825 1,277 slaves. Sequoyah, a remarkable Cherokee,
invented in 1825 an alphabet; the next year a printing press
was set up at New Echota, their capital, which began printing
a newspaper, the *Cherokee Phoenix*. The following year they
took a long step toward political stability by constructing themselves a constitution and modelling it slightly after the Federal
document. A representative of the United States made a trip
through the Cherokee country in 1829, and declared that, "the

advancement the Cherokees had made in morality, religion, general information and agriculture had astonished him beyond measure. They had regular preachers in their churches, the use of spirituous liquors was in a great degree prohibited, their farms were worked much after the manner of the white people and were generally in good order."

This threat of being deprived of a great part of her domain by an alien and semi-barbarous people appeared intolerable and unthinkable to Georgia; she would resist it to the uttermost limits. Apparently no further dependence could be put in the promise of the United States to remove the Indians, for, going on the assumption that it was not bound to use force, it had not been able to make the Indians cede additional territory for almost a decade. So Georgia started out on a policy which ignored the United States and its futile treaties and which came near ignoring the existence of the Cherokees. John Forsyth, former minister to Spain and now governor, put a swift end to this new nation trying to erect itself in the state of Georgia. He recommended to the legislature that it extend the laws of the state over the Cherokee country, since it was as much a part of Georgia as was the remainder of the state, and that body proceeded to do so on December 20, 1828. Two years later it forbade the Indians to play longer with their make-believe government. Now, there was no longer a Cherokee nation nor were there treaty rights; if the Indians wanted to remain in Georgia they must do so in competition with the whites. Georgia hoped that this new policy of hers would drive them west of the Mississippi.

Georgia, having assumed the government of the Cherokee country, soon found work to do. An Indian named George Tassel or Corn Tassel was tried for murder in Hall County in 1830 and sentenced to be hanged. Interested friends of the Cherokees had his case carried to the United States Supreme Court on a writ of error; but Georgia, resolving not to be bothered with Federal courts, ordered the sheriff to hang Tassel.

George R. Gilmer, who was now governor, declared that he would resist all interference with the Georgia courts.

The Cherokees could get no consolation or sympathy from the imperious Andrew Jackson, president of the United States, for he had been long advising them to accept the inevitable and leave. Even with Georgia ignoring the Cherokee treaty rights, Jackson would not act. With the support of outside friends, the Cherokees sought to have Georgia restrained by the United States Supreme Court, which was dominated by the strong nationalist, John Marshall. In 1830 they sought in that court, through their counsel, William Wirt and John Sergeant, to prevent Georgia from carrying out her laws in the Cherokee country. In this case, known as the Cherokee Nation *vs.* Georgia, John Marshall held that the Cherokees had no right to bring this suit, not because he did not sympathize with them, but because they were neither citizens nor a foreign nation. Identifying the Indians legally for the first time in American history, he declared that they were a nation subject to the authority of the United States and were its wards. It was clear that the court supported the position of the Indians in their quarrel with Georgia, but it was unable to act in this case, as the suit was not properly before the court. But soon a time would come when it could act.

In July, 1829, gold was discovered in northeastern Georgia, and a stampede set in which filled the diggings with a wild and lawless population. To control them, Federal troops were marched in, and were marched out again when Georgia indicated to her friend, President Jackson, that she did not want them, and that she would manage the region. In 1830 she required all white people in the Cherokee country to secure before March 1st of the following year, a permit to reside there. Though designed primarily to bring to order the lawless gold-diggers, this law also touched the missionaries, who had been working among the Cherokees from the beginning of the century. Even if their own sympathies had not inclined them to the Cherokee position, they would have found it politic in their work with the Indians to agree with them. As a result, the missionaries had become a pernicious influence in the three-cornered imbroglio among Georgia, the Cherokees, and the United States. They had steeled the hearts of the Indians against removal and had brought down upon themselves the hatred of Georgia.

Headstrong and unwise, some of them showed their contempt for Georgia by refusing to call for permits, and invited arrest. The most prominent among them was Samuel A. Worcester. They were tried before Judge Augustin S. Clayton in the Gwinnett County superior court, and released on a technicality, though Judge Clayton was fully determined to resist the Federal government on the main issue. Governor Gilmer, seeking diligently to avoid trouble, begged the missionaries either to accept a permit or to leave the state within ten days. Fanatically indignant that they should be asked to obey the laws of Georgia, they ignored Gilmer's pleas, and as a result, got themselves re-arrested by the Georgia militia and rather roughly handled before they were brought before the Gwinnett court again. Eleven people were arrested, three being missionaries, Samuel A. Worcester, Elizur Butler, and James Trott. They were tried in September, 1831, convicted, and sentenced to four years in the penitentiary. Still desirous of being lenient with them, Governor Gilmer offered each a pardon if he would swear allegiance to Georgia and leave the Cherokee country. All agreed with the exception of Worcester and Butler, who decided they would try to become martyrs.

Besides becoming martyrs, they also hoped to get their case and that of the Cherokee nation before the United States Supreme Court, which they believed would order Georgia out of the Indian country. Worcester, not being an Indian, had the right to bring a case before the court. He entered suit for his freedom in 1831, on the ground that he had violated no law, as Georgia's enactments dealing with the Cherokees were void.

The case, known as Worcester *vs.* Georgia, was heard the next year, with Wirt and Sergeant appearing for Worcester. John Marshall now decided that the Georgia acts were void, that she should stop bedevilling the Cherokees, and that she should free Worcester. Wilson Lumpkin, who was now governor and who had important ideas about the Cherokees, paid no attention to Marshall except to say that Georgia would not notice his decision; and President Jackson, who had no love for Marshall, the Indians, or the missionaries, refused to enforce the decision. The missionaries now learning for the first time the astounding fact that Georgia was more powerful than the United States Supreme Court, thought better of their earlier refusal of a pardon, and in January, 1833, accepted the clemency offered by Governor Lumpkin.

Before the Cherokee troubles were finally settled, Georgia had one more tilt with the Supreme Court, over James Graves, in a case similar to Tassel's. Again she flouted the authority of the Supreme Court and ordered the execution of Graves.

In the meantime, Georgia by other acts was bringing the Cherokee problem to a swift conclusion. In 1831 she ordered the Cherokee lands to be surveyed, the next year she laid them out into ten new counties, and the following year she granted them all away in a lottery. In 1834 she allowed the whites to go in and occupy their holdings, and gave the Cherokees two years to get out of the way. Not only were the Cherokees maneuvered out of Georgia, but the United States was forced into a corner where it was necessary for her to act. Most of the Cherokees were wise enough to see that they should make a treaty and leave as soon as possible. Their representatives went to Washington in 1834 and made a treaty, but a faction, headed by John Ross, a Scotch half-breed, refused to accept it, as they were determined never to leave Georgia. The next year another treaty was made, but the Cherokees refused to accept it in a council they held at Running Water. In December of that year, United States commissioners came to New Echota, the Cherokee capital, and made a treaty with the faction led by John Ridge, Major Ridge, and Elias Boudinot, who saw the futility of holding out longer. The Ross followers refused to appear and opposed the treaty. By this treaty the Cherokees agreed to give up all their lands and in return to migrate to lands in the West and receive $5,000,000.

In 1838 the Cherokees, rounded up by the hard methods of the United States troops under General Scott, set out for their western home, giving up forever the Georgia hills, which they had so well loved and for which they had fought so long. A small group were able to elude the law and the army and finally to gain a legal footing in a reservation in western North Carolina, where they have ever afterwards kept alive their ancient manners and customs.

Georgia's long struggle with the Indians was of widespread interest, not only to her own citizens but also to the people of the United States. It upset Congress frequently and brought into play the oratory of Clay, Webster, and Calhoun as well as the heated clashes of others. It became a subject of angry conversation among abolitionist groups and Northern sewing circles, and led to the widening of the ugly rift of sectionalism, which slavery had already created. Georgia heard enough to make her resent Northerners coming south to exploit these troubles. Mistaking John Howard Payne's visit to the Cherokees as outside meddling, she invaded Tennessee to arrest him, and held him prisoner until his mission was better understood.

Though Georgia was not the only state to have Indians, she had greater difficulty than any other in getting rid of them or settling the question of their status, despite the fact that the United States was under special obligations to her to remove them. Through treaties negotiated by 1832, Mississippi had been given the promise of freedom from her Choctaws and Chickasaws; Florida, from her Seminoles; and Alabama, from her Creeks. Georgia still had her Cherokees, with a few in North Carolina, Tennessee, and Alabama, and it seemed to her that she was destined to have them forever. She acted vigorously throughout the whole contest, and early took the lead in a struggle which she carried on with such success that it was unnecessary for the neighboring states to raise the issue.

It had happened that more through natural developments than design, the United States had cleared out most of the Indians from the states north of the Mason and Dixon Line and of the Ohio River, while they still remained in great strength in the South. This led Georgia to charge sectional partiality.

With the Indians finally out of the way, Georgia was for the first time in her existence master of her own territorial destiny. Now she was unshackled; with exuberance and enthusiasm she could now go forward.

CHAPTER XVIII

PARTY POLITICS

IN THE BEGINNING, Georgians had less interest in politics than was later to characterize them and all other Americans. In a new and rapidly developing country, the average citizen is impelled more by the desire to accumulate wealth than to seek office, unless, indeed, the office can be readily used to advance his economic position. So it was then, that Georgians looked upon office-holding as a burden, and only through a sense of strong patriotism and public duty could they convince themselves that they should accept the task. The difficulties and dangers of travel also deterred some. Frequently Georgians elected to the council refused to serve or later resigned; and as likely as not anyone elected to Congress before 1789 would never attend.

Interest in the control of the government naturally increased and grew with the development of political parties, state and national. Though the outlines for parties were dimly evident from the beginning, they did not become clear-cut and bold until about the end of the century, and though logic might well require party arrangements for state affairs to be somewhat different from national interests, the tendency has always been, in the American states, to merge them unreasonably. In Georgia, however, very early there developed party organizations, names, and activities for state affairs which at times bore little or no relation to the nation.

It was rather natural for Georgia to embrace the national party organization which grew up around Thomas Jefferson, for its principles appealed to frontiersmen everywhere. In addition, its leader was a Southerner; and though sectionalism was not yet a powerful political weapon, the Southern states were already conscious of a unifying force among themselves, evidenced and aided by slavery and their geographical position. Federalists were weak in Georgia and soon died out, for they had taken their origin in such a peculiar manner as to make their principles bear little relation to those of Alexander Hamilton and the national Federalist party. They had little or no desire to elevate the nation at the expense of the states or to see the select and educated few do the ruling; for, though they were the few in Georgia, they were not the educated. They were produced by local conditions, and when they disappeared, there was none to dispute the universal sway of the Jeffersonian Republicans, until the "reign of Jackson" led to the rise of the Whigs. Georgia cast her electoral vote for Washington twice, for Jefferson three times, and twice each for Madison, Monroe, and Jackson.

The Georgia Federalists had their rise in the scramble for land that set in immediately after the Revolution. The more conservative leaders organized themselves around James Jackson, who carried out a fierce attack against the Yazooists and land grabbers in general, calling them Tories, Federalists, or any other names that suggested themselves. His enemies charged that his vehemence was designed more to build up a party organization than to save the state's patrimony. He succeeded well in both, for land frauds ceased in Georgia, and he developed and brought to his standard such strong leaders as William H. Crawford, George M. Troup, David B. Mitchell, and Thomas U. P. Charlton. They very cleverly and effectively embraced Jefferson's doctrines, declared themselves to be the Jeffersonian party in Georgia, and thereby left their opponents no choice except to become Federalists if they desired to have a national standing. There was the remarkable development of each party in Georgia into a contradiction of the national party. The aristocratic element, as far as one had arisen in Georgia, found itself in the democratic Jeffersonian party, while the democratic frontiersmen were forced by circumstances into the aristocratic Federalist party under Hamilton.

Federalism could not long thrive in Georgia; the opponents of James Jackson soon forgot the harsh things he had said about them, and giving up their unnatural connection with Federalists, went into the Jeffersonian party. Georgia now had only one national party; but for years she was to have two bitter state parties, who fought violently for public offices.

Before James Jackson passed from life in 1806, he had organized a well-led party, with William H. Crawford controlling the upcountry element and Troup, the coast. With the extinction of Federalism in Georgia, the Jackson followers continued the aristocratic tradition, while their opponents, whether rightly or not, claimed to represent the cause of the small farmers and frontiersmen. There was much re-arranging of party allegiances. It was not so simple a development as the mere passing of the former Federalists into a local party to oppose James Jackson and his followers. The difference in the economic background of these two parties, whatever it might have been, bore little relation to their doctrines or beliefs, for they were based largely on personalities rather than principles. Soon after the second war with Great Britain, these two parties became particularly active, and then they took on the names of their leaders, George M. Troup and John Clark, the son of Elijah.

From the beginning of the nineteenth century on down until the names of Troup and Clark were on the tip of every Georgian's tongue, the Jackson party ruled the state; and as the legislature during this time elected both the governor and the United States senators, the party that controlled this body controlled the two most coveted offices in the gift of the state. Hence it often happened that a party leader had his choice of the office he would have. In later times the governorship became distinctly a stepping-stone to the United States senate, much to the detriment of the well-ordered government of the state.

In 1801 Jackson left the governor's chair to become United States senator, and after David Emanuel, president of the state senate, had occupied the chair for a short interim, the legislature elected Josiah Tattnall to rule the state. Within a short time Tattnall, prostrated by disease, sought health in the Bahama Islands, but he soon died in Nassau. The Jackson party filled the vacancy by electing in 1802 John Milledge, a friend of education and a descendant of one of Oglethorpe's original settlers. Re-elected, he continued to serve until 1806, when he was advanced to the United States senate to fill the vacancy left by the death of Jackson. But the Jackson party went marching on with the election of Jared Irwin, who had been governor once before; and in 1809 David B. Mitchell, a Scotchman and a Jackson leader of long standing, became governor and remained long enough to get Georgia into the War of 1812. He gave way in 1813 to Peter Early, and then after two years returned to the governorship for two more years.

By this time the party of opposition was gaining strength, and under the skillful leadership of John Clark, it began to do battle with the Jackson group, now led by George M. Troup. For years these two men contended with each other for the mastery of the state, and after each had won the prize and lived his day, the parties continued under new leaders but under their old names. Since they were simply two great personal followings, avowedly so, they needed no principles; but outside observers who were not accustomed to such frankness, still looked for the principles which separated them, and were forced to give up the riddle in the spirit of old Hezikiah Niles, of Baltimore, who in his *Register* exclaimed, "We know not what they differ about—but they do *violently* differ."

Under this régime of personal politics, there grew up many political tricks and methods of controlling the voters, which remained as a heritage for the days when measures instead of men should enlist the support of the people. As these contests gave the people an outlet for their fighting instincts, their leaders must be brave, whether morally or not made little difference, but physically, absolutely. The rough petty frontier politician gouged his way to victory, but the gentleman fought it out in duels. James Jackson came to be known as the "prince of duellists," and perhaps it was his good marksmanship which had much to do with his political success. His ally, William H. Crawford, was little less mixed up in the duelling business. In 1802 he fought and killed Peter Lawrence Van Allen, a Dutch New Yorker and a Clark follower, and two years later he was saved by a board of arbitration from fighting a duel with John Clark himself. In 1806 these two came together in a duel which no one could prevent, fought at the High Shoals of the Apalachee, in the Indian country. Clark wounded Crawford in the wrist. Not being contented with injuring his political and personal enemy so slightly, Clark challenged Crawford to another duel, which was refused. Having no respect for Judge Charles Tait, a one-legged Troup party leader, Clark horse-whipped him and was fined $2,000 for the pleasure got from this encounter. John Murray Dooly, a Clark follower, and a most proficent wit, joked himself out of a duel with Judge Tait by showing the public how unfair the match would be with the judge wearing a wooden leg. Though the law said in 1809 that no one associated with duelling in any way should be allowed to hold an office of trust or profit, the people liked fighters, and as a result, Georgians fought duels for a half century longer.

It was necessary to amuse Georgians, not convince them, if their votes were to be secured; hence the rise of shooting matches, gander-pulling, pole-climbings, and horse-races. Another method of securing votes was the barbecue, where roasted pigs, calves, and sheep were much more convincing than any amount of dry argument. In an age when fighting, organized or unorganized, was dear to the hearts of the people the militia muster became a first-rate political instrument. The laws of the state had elaborately organized the people into major-generals and divisions, brigadier-generals and brigades, and regiments, battalions, and companies, with their proper officers. All male whites between 18 and 45 years of age, with the exception of government officials, millers, ferrymen, ministers, students, "post riders, madmen and ideots," belonged to this army, and to prove their soldierly qualities and make themselves more efficient, they mustered twice a year as battalions and four times as companies. No person who expected to go far in politics neglected to get himself made a colonel, at least.

The two parties took advantage of each other in every way which they could discover. It became a Georgia tradition, though wholly erroneous, that Jesse Mercer, in the guise of preaching the funeral sermon for Governor Rabun, who had died in 1819, made the occasion memorable by using most of the time to castigate the Clark party. The Troup party early managed to fill the board of trustees of the University with their own members, and not until the Clarkites in 1830 threatened the destruction of the school, did they secure representation on the board. Garrulous but lovable George R. Gilmer was elected to Congress in 1828, but neglecting formally to notify Governor Forsyth of his acceptance, reached Washington to discover that the governor had declared the place vacant. And so ran the course of party politics in Georgia.

Georgia see-sawed back and forth between Troupers and Clarkites in the governor's chair. In 1819 Clark was successful by a majority of thirteen in the legislature, and two years later secured re-election by a majority of only two. At the following election, in 1823, Troup came in, but by the slim majority of 85 to 81. If Clark had not previously believed that the people instead of the legislature should do the electing, these dwindling legislative majorities were convincing enough. Since the Clarkites were the common people, they could particularly and appropriately argue for more democracy. In 1824 the constitution was changed to allow the people to elect the governor, and in the election the following year, Troup was able, with all the Indian excitement he could stir up, to win a re-election by a majority of only 600 in a total vote of 40,000. As Troup refused to permit himself to be run for a third term, his party selected as their candidate John Forsyth, one of the ablest men the state ever produced. Forsyth had already sat in both branches of Congress, and had been minister to Spain from 1819 to 1823, during which time he negotiated the purchase of Florida. The Clark party failing to induce their strongest man, Duncan G. Campbell, to run, nominated Matthew Talbot, who had nearly defeated Troup in 1823, but Talbot died only a few days before the election and left Forsyth unopposed. As governor, Forsyth had the Cherokees to deal with, but before this problem could be settled, his term of office expired, and he soon re-entered the national arena, becoming secretary of state in 1834 and serving until 1841.

In the election of George R. Gilmer in 1829, there were signs of the disintegration of the Troup and Clark followings. Clark removed himself from Georgia politics by going to Florida to live, and Gilmer on taking office declared that he would not be governor of any party but of all Georgians, and that the people in their voting ought to begin to consider principles rather than men. This advice of Gilmer's was not necessary, for Georgians were at that time being perplexed with problems so difficult of solution as to cause them to forget their petty personal jealousies. Getting rid of the Indians was troublesome enough, but a greater danger was arising which was to hang over Georgia and the other Southern states for many years, like a threatening cloud. This was the tariff, and it was soon to become so cataclysmic as to shatter all party lines and forever destroy Troupers and Clarkites.

Following the second war with England, Georgia in her exuberant nationalism had favored a protective tariff as a great patriotic American move against the degenerate nations of

Europe; but the tariff, when once saddled upon the nation, became an old man of the sea around its neck, which Georgia and the rest of the South began to try to shake off. The tariff acts of 1816, 1824, 1828, and 1832 came streaming along, and instead of the rates becoming less they were made successively higher. The South not developing into a manufacturing region, saw that a protective tariff was a great detriment to her, for it increased the price of everything she bought but did not raise the value of what she sold. It took money from the pockets of Southerners and put it into the pockets of Northerners, and therefore she branded it as legalized robbery.

Georgia, in a set of resolutions in 1828, protested against the tariff as oppressive and unconstitutional; and an excitement was soon whipped up which caused the people to forget for the time their Indian troubles. Each succeeding legislature thundered out its protests, but the nation's tariff policy continued unshaken. Thereupon, leaders over the state, especially the Troupers, began suggesting that Georgia should refuse longer to obey the tariff, that she should nullify it and submit no longer to this species of robbery. This nullification movement took life following the commencement exercises of the University of Georgia in August, 1832, an occasion which always brought together the political leaders of the state no less than the educational leaders. A meeting in the new chapel laid the foundations for a campaign throughout the state to induce the people in the following October to elect delegates to go to Milledgeville to nullify the tariff. The leaders in this nullification movement were William H. Crawford, John M. Berrien, and Augustin S. Clayton.

Great excitement swept over the state, as the campaign for delegates progressed. Many people, especially the Clarkites, came to the aid of John Forsyth, who opposed the nullifiers, and argued to the Georgians that nullification would mean war, bloody civil war. The convention met in Milledgeville in November with 131 delegates from 60 out of the 80 counties.

South Carolina, who, herself, was about to nullify the tariff, had her representatives present and attempted to stampede the convention into nullification. The resolute determination of John Forsyth to prevent it found expression in his withdrawal from the convention, followed by 50 other delegates. The remaining delegates, sobered by this bold move, passed resolutions of fiery opposition to the tariff but they fell short of nullification. South Carolina, disappointed that Georgia had not set the nullification ball rolling, held her convention a short time later and passed her famous ordinances. Only through the hard work of Forsyth, did Georgia escape the position in history which came to South Carolina. Wilson Lumpkin, who had been elected in 1831 as a Troup man, at this time expressed the opinion of the majority of Georgians, when he said to the legislature: "The mystical doctrine of nullification, as contended for by its advocates, has only tended to bewilder the minds of the people, inflame their passions, and prepare them for anarchy and revolution. Wherever it spreads, it engenders the most bitter strifes and animosities, and dissolves the most endearing relations of life. I believe nullification to be unsound, dangerous and delusive, in practice as well as theory."

The legislature resolved against nullification, but it still believed there was nothing more iniquitous than the tariff. New parties and new names now arose, parties based on measures instead of men; and the settlement of the nullification controversy marked the beginning of Georgia's entry into national politics through two parties instead of the one which she had been previously embracing. The Troupers, who had been for the most part nullifiers, resented Andrew Jackson's rough handling of South Carolina in breaking up nullification, became his enemy and the enemy of the strong nationalism which the president was showing, took the name of State Rights Party, and soon embraced the Whig Party and its name. The Clarkites, largely the anti-nullifiers, supported Jackson, took the name Union Party, and soon began to carry the banner of the Democrats. There was much rearranging of party allegiances in Georgia for the next few years, and the evolution of Whigs and Democrats was not so simple as the mere passing of all Troupers into State Rights men and then to Whigs, and all Clarkites into Union men and Democrats.

For the next ten years the conservative party dominated Georgia, first under the name of Union and then Democratic. Lumpkin's conservatism got him re-elected in 1833, and two years later a straight-out Union candidate, William Schley, became governor. Then came Gilmer again in 1837, who was in turn succeeded by Charles J. McDonald after a hard fight against Charles Dougherty, an extreme State Rights man. McDonald was re-elected and served until 1843, when for the first time the Georgia Whigs elected their candidate for governor, George W. Crawford. The Whigs continued their rule for two more years in the re-election of Crawford. In 1847 the Democrats returned to power with George W. Towns, and through two successive terms he held sway, until the accumulating woes of a distracted country burst forth in 1850 and came near breaking up the Union. How Whigs and Democrats in Georgia reacted to the perils of these times will appear hereafter. But it should be remembered that by this time, the Whigs had become the conservative nationalistic party, while the Democrats fought for state rights and various measures looked upon as radical and dangerous.

Before 1824 Georgia nationally was likened by one of her citizens to the handle of a pitcher—all on one side. But in this year the "era of good feeling" under President Monroe ended, when a regiment of favorite sons rebelled against the nomination of William H. Crawford by the Congressional caucus. Georgia cast her electoral vote for her distinguished citizen, despite the opposition of the Clark party. John Quincy Adams finally secured the election, but his handling of the Indian question so enraged Georgia that she indicated her desire for

Andrew Jackson two years before the election. She voted for Jackson because of his rugged nature and frontier background, and she voted to re-elect him in 1832 because he had allowed her to have her way with the Indians. Just as James Monroe had recognized Georgia and had found an excellent secretary of the treasury for eight years in William H. Crawford, Jackson complimented Georgia and received excellent service in return through the appointment of John M. Berrien to the attorney-generalship in 1829, and John Forsyth to the secretary-ship of state in 1834, and James M. Wayne to the Supreme Court in 1835.

Georgia liked Jackson, but she had no faith in his ability to pick a successor, and so she refused to vote for Martin Van Buren in 1836. True enough, the Jackson party in Georgia, the Democrats, supported him; but because of their dislike for the little New Yorker, and because of Jackson's high-handed treatment of South Carolina in the nullification business, enough Georgians went over to the Whigs to carry the state for that party for the first time. Thereafter, until the Civil War, she voted for the Whigs twice, and for the Democrats four times. In state affairs, the see-sawing back and forth between Whigs and Democrats was almost as marked; there was no solid Georgia, politically, in ante-bellum times.

For the two decades preceding the Civil War, Georgia took a more prominent part in national affairs, and her state politics were more closely than ever tied up and intertwined with the nation. Sectionalism was beginning its withering work, and in the contest Georgia stood in the forefront.

CHAPTER XIX

TURNPIKES, RIVERS, CANALS, AND RAILROADS

IN 1800 the Georgia of the white man was only a narrow strip of land, scarcely more than sixty miles wide at any point, extending up and down the Savannah and the coast, from the Tugaloo to the St. Marys; and although she claimed territory westward to the Mississippi, and succeeded in establishing undisputed ownership in 1802 as far as the Chattahoochee, she passed through a long struggle before she was able to take possession of it. Her expansion over this great region, completed in 1835, was almost equivalent in extent to the founding of a half dozen Colonial Georgias.

One of the first and most important tasks in laying hold of this region was to provide transportation facilities. If economic development was to pass beyond a primitive society in this new land, communication among the people and outlets to markets would be necessary, and in the older part of the state, the small beginnings would need to be carried forward. Nature had blessed Georgia with a net-work of rivers, which lent themselves to the first transportation needs of the settlers, and with the early efforts to remove snags and sand-bars, they became the first highways of trade. The movement to put the rivers into a fit state of navigation by requiring the labor of the people living along their banks, soon gave way to the plan of granting charters to companies to improve the rivers and to charge tolls. The Oconee Navigation Company received a charter in 1810 for the purpose of putting the river in order as far up as Barnett Shoals, near Athens. The great expense of such undertakings soon put a stop to them, and convinced the people that if the rivers were ever to be made navigable and kept so, the state would be compelled to do it.

Born of the new life that gripped the state following the second war with Great Britain, Georgia began an ambitious program of river improvements in those regions reclaimed from the Indians. In 1817 she appropriated $10,000 each for the Ocmulgee and Oconee, $5,000 each for the Altamaha and Broad rivers, $3,000 for the Ogeechee, a like amount for Brier Creek, and $20,000 for the Savannah. At the same time, she set up a permanent internal improvement fund of $250,000, to be invested in "bank or other profitable stock."

The improvement of the Savannah River offered difficulties beyond the mere work of removing snags and sandbars, for South Carolina had an equal interest in the navigation of the river and Georgia felt that she also had an equal obligation in bearing the expense of improving its navigation. The two states were never able to come to a final agreement, largely because South Carolina was more interested in the river north of Augusta than in the lower stretches. This policy was largely determined by her fear of helping Savannah at the expense of Charleston, if she aided in improving the lower stretches of the river; and when the Charleston and Hamburg Railroad was projected to touch the Savannah opposite Augusta, she was definitely determined to aid no projects which would not act as feeders for this road.

River fever was running high, and now that money had been provided, it was seen that a program of orderly development should be worked out. In 1820 a committee of the house of representatives made a long report and recommended to the legislature the appointment of a topographical and civil engineer who should survey the rivers and develop a program of work.

By this time, settlements had spread far away from the river banks, and if all the population were to have a chance to get to market, then other means than rivers were necessary. The only other ways of travel were by canals and turnpikes. The state was promoting turnpikes by granting charters to private companies, both for the purpose of building them and for running stage-coaches over them, and in 1821 it did the unusual act of lending $3,000 for five years to a turnpike company. As time went on, the stage companies with their monopolies over their respective lines connected all the principal towns of the state, with Milledgeville as the hub or center of the network. Georgia was also being aided with turnpikes and having her enthusiasm whetted for more of them by the Federal government under its policy of providing military roads and post roads. In 1808 Albert Gallatin worked out such a plan for the whole nation and in 1816 John C. Calhoun greatly elaborated it. Under these plans, Georgia received various Federal highways. In 1811 one was built from Milledgeville westward across the Chattahoochee, and in 1815 the Federal government ran a road from Athens northward through the Cherokee country into Tennessee.

Besides the main roads, which were classed as turnpikes, there were various other roads which were little better than trails. Some of them were not passable for wheeled vehicles. A peculiar kind of highway, which existed in Georgia for a time, was the tobacco road. As such roads were constructed for the purpose of rolling great hogsheads of tobacco to market, they followed the ridges to avoid crossing water courses. One of these roads ran from the upcountry tobacco regions down the ridges to a point below Augusta, where the tobacco was loaded on boats on the Savannah.

Settlers back of the rivers might depend also on canals, but in Georgia, as well as throughout the South generally, their construction was greatly retarded by the high river banks, frequent floods, and by the porous soil that prevailed in many places. Canals played practically no part in Georgia's efforts to get to market. In 1818 three canals were chartered. Two of them, near the mouth of the Altamaha River, were of no importance. The third, connecting the Ogeechee River with the Savannah above the city of Savannah, was the only canal in the state ever to attract much attention or to cost much money. At first little was done toward constructing this waterway; and so, in 1824, it was re-chartered and enough enthusiasm was stirred up to cause it to be finished in 1831, after the state had aided to the extent of buying stock in it to the amount of $44,000. The dream of extending it to the Altamaha was never realized, and after the railroads came it was abandoned as having been a failure from the beginning.

Transportation speculations set in after the opportunities for cheap lands had passed, and the ambitious who would become great business men and promoters of mighty undertakings turned to projects for roads, canals, and railroads. With the impressive, though hazy, title of the Mexican Atlantic Company, a group of Georgians in 1825 secured the right to construct some sort of transportation route across the state, "between the waters of the Atlantic Ocean and those that flow into the Gulf of Mexico." A canal was suggested, but it might be a railroad, though all ideas concerning the latter were at that time very dim. This very year Thomas Spalding had sought to obtain from the legislature a charter to build a railroad from the Ocmulgee (draining into the Atlantic) to the Flint (reaching the Gulf of Mexico), at the point in central Georgia where these rivers flowed less than fifty miles apart. This was in pursuance of a far-flung plan of his to bring together the Mississippi Valley and the Atlantic Seaboard without the hazards of storms, pirates, and attacks of warring nations that beset the route around the southern tip of Florida. The legislature refused to grant the charter, but instead chartered the Mexican Atlantic Company. Two years later, Spalding and some associates were given permission to cut a canal or build "a railroad of wood" from the Ocmulgee to the Flint, but they must do the former within ten years or the latter within five, or they should lose their rights. Spalding tried heroically for years to finance this road, but it ended in failure after a few miles of grading had been done. These were the days when charters were easy to get and difficult to comply with, and as a result, most of the projects never got beyond the paper on which they were written.

With the enthusiasm for transportation developments widespread, the legislature in 1821 increased the internal improvement fund to $500,000, and in 1825 created a Board of Public Works whose duty it was to employ "artists, agents, and labourers" to make surveys and estimates for canals, roads, bridges, and all other means helpful in developing transportation. The board was specifically instructed to investigate the possibility of building a canal across the state as centrally located as possible, to join the Tennessee River, and to run from the main stem subsidiary canals. Exciting rumors of railways, though they were little understood, induced the legislature to give the additional instructions to the board to call to its aid "all men of science" necessary to investigate "artificial railways," with the view to substituting them for canals. Georgia was determined not to be caught behind the times in any new ways of travel or transportation. Hamilton Fulton, an Englishman, was appointed chief civil engineer. Immediately, he divided the board into three divisions and set them severally to studying the northern, central, and southern parts of the state. The northern division, under Wilson Lumpkin, had the most difficult task, as it was forced to contend with the mountains. A canal route was surveyed to connect with the Tennessee through Chickamauga Creek, but soon dissensions arose over the possibility of constructing a canal. Some members held that a turnpike or inclined planes and a railway would be the only feasible means of securing passage through the mountains. By the end of 1826 the board was discredited and abolished and Fulton was dismissed.

Centralized control had been tried and had failed; the state now went back to local boards for each piecemeal project.

But in 1828 the legislature in looking back over the past thirteen years, determined that the state had spent $321,500 on
rivers principally and that the money had been all but wasted.
The next year the state appointed two superintendents to
improve the rivers and turnpikes and to make a greater use of
slave labor which had come to be employed during the past
few years. Heretofore, the policy had been to hire slaves, but
now the state adopted the policy of buying slaves outright. It
came into the possession of 190 slaves before it definitely decided in 1833 to sell all of its "public hands."

The craft which plied the rivers went through an interesting
evolution. As the original canoes and batteaux were of little
commercial value, the pole boats made their appearance. They
were propelled by poles, generally in the hands of slaves, and
could be navigated upstream as well as down. With the rise of
cotton plantations, large flat-boats or cotton-boxes were used
to float bales of cotton to market, but these craft had the dis-
advantage of being only one-way boats. At the end of their
journey they were broken up into lumber and sold. The coming
of the steamboat marked the outstanding importance of the
rivers as highways of commerce; and to Georgia goes the credit
of making some of the earliest experiments in this form of
navigation.

In 1788 William Longstreet, of Augusta, was given a patent
by the state on a steam-engine, and two years later he attached
it to a boat and was able to force the craft up the Savannah at
the rate of five miles an hour. He was unable to make his
steamboating of much commercial value until about 1808; but
the preceding year Robert Fulton had run his *Clermont* up the
Hudson and convinced a doubting world. Fulton took out
patents and attempted to control the steamboats on all American waters; but soon his attempted monopoly failed everywhere
except in the New York waters. In 1814 Georgia granted a
steamboat monopoly on all Georgia streams to Samuel Howard
for a term of twenty years, provided he should put a boat in

active operation within a period of three years, and at least one boat on each river within a period of ten years. The year before his time was to expire he got together a boat which he called the *Enterprise* and proudly sent her up the river to Augusta.

As steamboating was an expensive business, especially in Georgia, where skilled mechanics were few and iron works non-existent, Howard formed a company in 1817 called the Steamboat Company of Georgia, and secured a new charter and monopoly. It seems that the state soon regretted its liberality, for the following year it chartered the Savannah River Navigation Company for the purpose of bringing about cheaper transportation between Savannah and Augusta and to guard against the evils of monopolies "by means of which, capital and business are engrossed by a few, and regular trade and fair competition are destroyed." The charter did not designate the method of propulsion to be used, but the monop-

Steamship
SAVANNAH
"First across the Atlantic"

THE *SAVANNAH* WAS THE FIRST STEAMSHIP TO CROSS THE ATLANTIC OCEAN. · · · · SHE SAILED FROM SAVANNAH, GEORGIA, ON THE 22 ND. OF MAY 1819, AND REACHED LIVERPOOL, ENGLAND, ON JUNE 20 TH, HAVING BEEN 14 DAYS UNDER STEAM, THE REST OF THE TIME UNDER SAIL AS THEY FEARED THE FUEL MIGHT GIVE OUT. · · THE PADDLE WHEELS WERE MADE TO FOLD UP LIKE A FAN, AND TO BE LAID ON DECK WHEN NOT IN USE.

AFTER LEAVING LIVERPOOL THE SHIP VISITED COPENHAGEN, STOCKHOLM, ST. PETERSBURG, CRONSTADT AND ARENDAL IN NORWAY. SHE THEN SAILED TO SAVANNAH IN 25 DAYS, STEAMING ON THE PASSAGE 19 DAYS.

© 1931 by A J Robinson

Courtesy of the American Steamship Owners' Association, New York City.

oly granted Howard prevented the use of steam. The riddle was answered when in 1820 the *Genius of Georgia* silently glided up the Savannah to Augusta. It was propelled by 19 horses walking on an endless belt; it was a team-boat. This clever use of horse-power was soon given up, and the team-boat disappeared as a lost wonder of the world; for the United States Supreme Court, in the famous case of Gibbons *vs.* Ogden, deciding a suit brought by the governor of New Jersey against Thomas Gibbons over the navigation of New York Bay, declared that no state could grant a steamboat monopoly on its waters.

In the meantime, steamboats began making their appearance on other Georgia rivers, and especially after the Gibbons *vs.* Ogden decision in 1824. In 1819 the *Georgia* had steamed up the Altamaha and Oconee rivers from Darien to Milledgeville, but not until ten years later did a steamboat reach Macon on the Ocmulgee. The regions surrounding the Chattahoochee and Flint rivers had scarcely been recovered from the Indians before steamers began to ply those rivers. In 1828 the *Steubenville* reached Columbus, and soon boats were carrying large amounts of cotton out of western Georgia. Some of the steamers carried as many as 1,200 bales at a time.

Steamboats had been used on the rivers and inland waters of America more than a decade before anyone was bold enough to attempt to cross the ocean in a craft propelled by steam. Just as Georgia was a pioneer in applying steam to navigation on rivers, she also made the first successful attempt to send a steamboat across the ocean. In 1818 the legislature, "with the view of making a laudable and meritorious experiment . . . to attach, either as auxiliary or principal, the propulsion of steam to sea vessels, for the purpose of navigating the Atlantic and other oceans," incorporated the Savannah Steam Ship Company. The company provided a boat, with auxiliary steam power, which they called the *Savannah,* and the next year they sent it to Liverpool. It thus became the first vessel aided by steam power to cross the Atlantic.

As Georgians were not a sea-faring people, it was remarkable that they should make such progress and take even another forward step in the evolution of ships. In 1834 Gazaway B. Lamar, a banker and cotton merchant of Savannah, had John Laird, of Birkenhead, England, manufacture for him iron plates which were riveted together in Savannah into the first iron vessel ever seen in American waters. He called it the *John Randolph*. It was as great a wonder to see iron float as it had been to see a boat go without sails.

Georgia's progress in internal improvements was not very impressive, but she was the gainer, for soon railroads were to come and largely supersede rivers, canals, and turnpikes. The money which she might have spent on such public works, she now luckily held ready for railroads, and in this latest form of transportation she early assumed a commanding position in the American Union.

In 1833 the Charleston and Hamburg Railroad, which had been under construction for a few years, reached the bank of the Savannah opposite Augusta, and afforded ocular proof to any Georgians who would look, that railways were practical. Indeed, such proof was not awaited by citizens of Eatonton, who secured a charter in 1831 to build a railroad to Augusta, nor did Thomas Spalding, who had got a charter four years earlier for his Ocmulgee and Flint Raiload, need proof; but the first charter to produce a railroad in Georgia was secured by Athenians in 1833. A company was organized, with James Camak as president, and called the Georgia Railroad, to build a railroad between Athens and Augusta. For the first few years this little college town found no sympathy in Augusta for the project, as the Augustans felt that they might become only a way-station on a railroad line which would carry passengers and freight from Athens to the sea at Charleston. Aided by the banking privileges allowed it in 1835, the road was pushed along with vigor and in 1841 it reached Athens. After the road had been built and its value seen, Augusta got control of it, and made John P. King the president; and then Athens, for years thereafter, complained of the harsh treatment she received from the Augustans. At Union Point this road sent off a tentacle to the westward, reaching for the banks of the Chattahoochee. For a few years the branch from Union Point to Athens was served by horse power, and when steam was applied, it was through a small locomotive weighing about three and a half tons.

The coming of railroads was of extreme importance; on them awaited the rise and fall of cities, and the growth and decline of whole sections. No city in Georgia saw more clearly the dangers and the advantages than Savannah. With the Georgia Railroad virtually an extension of the Charleston and Hamburg, Charleston would have a rail connection with the heart of upper Georgia and would thereby drain away traffic which Savannah had been accustomed to get. Fearing this would become a major disaster to her, citizens of Savannah made quick efforts to extend her commercial influence. In 1833 they secured a charter to run a road to Macon, in the heart of the state, and two years later they got the additional right to engage in the banking business. At this time W. W. Gordon became the president of the company, which was known as the Central of Georgia Railroad and Banking Company, and did much toward pushing forward the work. After a hard financial struggle, it reached Macon in 1843, and tapped the rich cotton trade of central Georgia. As time went on, it built short feeder lines, aided the construction of longer lines, bought or leased other roads, and by the outbreak of the Civil War had become one of the greatest corporations in the South.

Savannah with its Central of Georgia Railroad and Augusta with its Georgia Railroad became great rivals, and around these two rivalries much railroad development centered. Each built up its system and gathered around it its satellite roads, and so jealous were they of their respective spheres of influence that not until 1854 did they connect their systems, when a line was run through "no man's land" from Millen to Augusta. The two parent stems ran for a hundred miles paralleling each other at a distance not greater than fifty miles.

Apart from the local restricted view of serving certain cities and sections of the state, the railroad builders of Georgia carried out a dream of vaster possibilities, which John C. Calhoun and Robert Y. Hayne were seeking to realize for the economic glory of South Carolina and of the South as a whole. The rich Ohio River Valley and the Middle West must soon reach the outside world by a method quicker than the waters of the Mississippi. A railroad to Cincinnati would build up a commercial and political alliance which would drain the wealth of those regions to the southward. The South Carolinians sought in vain to use their Charleston and Hamburg Railroad and extend a line through the ramparts of the Southern highlands up through western North Carolina, eastern Tennessee, and Kentucky, and thereby make Charleston the outlet.

Georgia was much interested in the movement but not in the route South Carolina sought. Early there had been hazy plans to extend the Georgia Railroad on beyond Athens across the mountains, but this idea soon gave way to a more practical scheme. The route which Wilson Lumpkin had chosen for his canal now came to be looked upon as the ideal route for the railroad to the Middle West. In November, 1836, an enthusiastic railroad convention was held in Macon, which decided that the railroad should be built from the Chattahoochee to the Tennessee, where there would be excellent chances for further connections, and it boldly declared that the state should construct the road.

Not waiting for enthusiasm to wane, these railroad dreamers, aided by various local interests hoping to secure branch lines, hurried through the legislature the next month a law providing for the construction of this road by the state. While South

Carolinians held conventions and made speeches, the Georgians set their surveyors to work, and by 1839 they had 2,000 laborers digging with fair prospects of having 100 miles graded by the end of the year. In 1851 the work was finished and the state of Georgia now found itself in possession of a railroad, which it named the Western and Atlantic, running from the Chattahoochee to Chattanooga.

The southern terminus was located through a chain of circumstances. In order that this state road should not have its southern end dangling in a wilderness, the Georgia Railroad should extend its line from Union Point westward toward the Chattahoochee and a Central of Georgia Railroad connection in Macon should be extended northward, and the point where the two roads should meet would be the beginning of the Western and Atlantic. At this point was a little postoffice called White Hall, which was renamed Terminus, later called Marthasville, to honor Governor Lumpkin's daughter, and finally, Atlanta. The Macon extension, first known as the Monroe Railroad and later the Macon and Western, with the aid of Northern capital reached the meeting place in 1846. The Georgia Railroad had arrived the preceding year.

Here a great city was soon in the making, the outgrowth of its geographical position and of the enthusiasm of its promoters. Its possibilities were evident from the beginning, and the spirit of progress which seized the people led them to dream and work in harmony for the glory of Atlanta. A noticeable sprinkling of Northern capital and Northern settlers soon appeared and began to add a bustle not characteristic of Southern cities. As its location was the resultant of economic forces recognized by converging railway lines, it looked to the railways for its future greatness. As the tendency in the transportation development of the South was to build a system of railways roughly paralleling the coast, connecting the fall-line cities, and another system farther inland, connecting Piedmont cities, Atlanta took the lead in promoting the latter roads. To secure

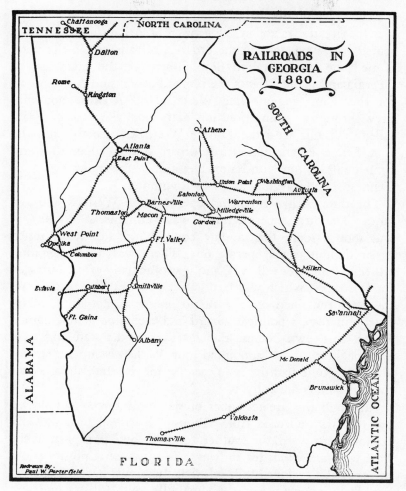

RAILROADS IN GEORGIA .1860.

connections with Montgomery and regions to the westward, the Atlanta and West Point was started in 1845 and finished eight years later. Connections with the South Carolina and North Carolina cities to the northeastward were planned and much agitated, but little was accomplished before the Civil War put a stop to further railway construction.

It was the Western and Atlantic Railroad, however, which was the greatest factor in the growth of Atlanta. It also represented a master stroke in the progress of railroads in the state. It tied the transportation development of the Southeast to Georgia and made Atlanta the railroad center and basing point for the whole region. The Western and Atlantic not only drew through its connections in Chattanooga the trade of Nashville, Louisville, and the Middle West, but also through the East Tennessee and Georgia Railroad, completed in 1855 and connecting Dalton with Knoxville, it drew the traffic of eastern Tennessee and Virginia as far as Richmond.

The state both owned and operated the Western and Atlantic. The first superintendent was William M. Wadley. It was soon evident that a state could build a railroad much easier than it could operate one. There was much agitation either to lease it or sell to it, and it was actually offered for sale for $1,000,000, which was less than it had cost. For seven years the offer remained open with no one to accept until, fortunately, in 1857, a political wizard and economic genius named Joseph E. Brown became the governor of the state and took hold of the road. He appointed John W. Lewis superintendent and by 1860 he had the road earning for the state about a half million dollars annually.

Although the greatest lines of economic forces had drawn out the first railroads from Augusta, Savannah, Macon, and Atlanta northward, the southern and southwestern parts of the state were ambitious for railways; and if these regions were to be properly developed they felt that they must have transportation facilities. Brunswick, Thomasville, and Albany had ambitions no less than had Savannah, Augusta, and Atlanta. A rivalry between Savannah and Brunswick, which had long been forming, broke out in great virulence when the latter, having failed to make any headway with canals, turned to railroads and induced the legislature to grant a charter for a road to run from Brunswick to Albany. Although the company had a monopoly on a route forty miles wide for a period of twenty-five years, hard times produced by the panic of 1837 prevented the construction of the road. In 1847 the Savannahians executed a flank attack on Brunswick by securing a charter for a road to run from their city to Albany, but difficulties arose which made it desirable for the two rivals to come to an agreement. A new charter was secured in 1856, for the Atlantic and Gulf Railroad, which should begin with the construction of tracks from each city to a point southwest of the Altamaha River, where the roads should join and continue in one line to Thomasville. Aided by a subscription of $500,000 from the state, the road pushed southwestward and reached Thomasville in 1860.

This development still left the regions southwest of Macon unsupplied with railroads. To serve them, the Southwestern Railroad was built southward from Macon to Smithville, where it branched into two lines, one continuing to Albany and the other to Fort Gaines on the Chattahoochee, with another line branching off at Cuthbert on the way to Fort Gaines, and running westward to Eufaula, in Alabama. At Fort Valley, between Macon and Americus, a line was run westward to Columbus, on the Chattahoochee, reaching there in 1853.

By 1860 Georgia had made remarkable railway progress. A network of railroads connected all the principal cities with one another and gave them access to the seaports of Savannah and Charleston. Yet, in all this wealth of railroads there was much confusion. Most of the roads had been built as short lines, generally promoted by some city in its rivalry with another city, and as a result the lines were not integrated or even physically joined to one another. Cities refused rights-of-way across their limits in the pursuit of some grudge against another city or against the railroad, or because they were controlled by their hack-drivers and hotel keepers, who would lose business if through-traffic were established. Macon forced the

Central of Georgia to pay $5,000 annually and perpetually for permission to join its tracks with the road to Atlanta.

Toward the end of ante-bellum times, there had been some consolidation of roads in Georgia, by lease or purchase, or by some special agreement, as was shown in the rise of the Central of Georgia system. Friendliness and co-operation among the railroads of the South were brought about by the organization of a Southern railway association in 1856. It met in various cities and discussed problems common to the railroads, such as rates and management. Rates on the Georgia roads varied with the whims, animosities, or ambitions of the owners, and especially rates on freight might vary with the seasons, the weather, or the stages of water in rivers that might offer competition. Rates for passengers ran generally from three to four cents a mile, while slaves were charged two cents a mile.

With a transportation establishment of railways, rivers, and turnpikes, Georgia was able to serve well the planter and the industrialist.

CHAPTER XX

THE EMPIRE STATE OF THE SOUTH

THOUGH A variety of climate, topography, and soil, and a coast-line with excellent harbors might have seemed to be a perfect assurance to Georgia that she would develop a diversified economic life, the forces drawing her into agriculture were too strong to be deflected. In common with the rest of the South, she accepted a philosophy of life and a civilization based on the soil, and successfully resisted all efforts of reformers to turn her very far toward commerce and manufacturing.

Though cotton became the king of the Georgians, its influence in their political and agricultural thinking went far beyond its actual importance. It had the advantage of being grown on the great plantations, which belonged to the people who largely determined the interests of the state. Yet there was a variety of other crops grown in Georgia, giving a diversity to her agriculture which cotton long eclipsed in the popular fancy. In 1860, a date separating two civilizations, Georgia raised 30,776,000 bushels of corn, 2,544,000 bushels of wheat, 1,231,000 bushels of oats, 52,507,000 pounds of rice, 919,000 pounds of tobacco, and 701,000 bales of cotton (400 pounds each). She also produced more than a million bushels of sweet potatoes, more than a half million gallons of molasses, almost a million pounds of honey, almost a million and a half pounds of butter, as well as various other farm products good for man and beast. Furthermore, she possessed more than a quarter million horses and mules, 74,000 work oxen, more than 600,000 sheep, more than a million cattle, and swine to the number of almost two and a half million. Such wealth might well have attracted Sherman's tired and hungry hordes four years later.

Georgia's agriculture began with the first settlers and reached plantation proportions in late colonial days as the rice plantations spread up the Savannah River and down the coast. After the Revolution, historic Middle Georgia sprang up in the Augusta area and to the northward and westward, and started the development first of tobacco plantations and then cotton fields. At this time cotton began its steady march across the red hills of Piedmont Georgia, and in the late ante-bellum times, it invaded the southwestern part of the state. Fired with the enthusiasm that went with high prices, it spread with a virulence which even Creeks and Cherokees could not withstand. It leaped from a thousand bales in 1791 to 20,000 in 1800; it doubled during the next decade, and reached 90,000 bales in 1821. Five years later Georgia produced 150,000 bales, and thereby became the greatest cotton-producing region in the world.

The plantation with slavery was adapted peculiarly to the raising of cotton in the uplands and rice on the coast, and this agricultural institution captured the imagination of the people as no other economic organization has ever done. Just as cotton was only a part of the agricultural production of the state and yet was crowned king, so was the plantation the possession of only a small minority of Georgians and yet came to dominate agriculture. In 1860 there were more than 31,000 farms of less than 100 acres, while the holdings of more than 100 acres numbered fewer than 23,000; or if only the large plantations of 500 acres or more be considered, then the number was only 3,564. There were 18,823 holdings ranging in area from 100 to 500 acres. Only 2,858 Georgians gave their occupations as planters.[1] Georgia, however, was as definitely a plantation state as existed anywhere, and her 902 plantations of more than 1,000 acres exceeded by 206 Alabama, the state with the next largest number of that size.

[1] Yet if the ownership of 20 slaves or more should be assumed to divide the planter from the farmer, then there were 6,363 plantations.

As slavery was the foundation on which the plantation rested, and as a plantation population, from its very nature, would develop more Negroes than white people, the march of the plantation across the state was readily marked by the growth of the black belt.

Though white cotton and its ally, the contrasting black slaves, dominated the picture of ante-bellum social and economic organization, they represented the minority of the people. In 1860 there were almost 600,000 white people in Georgia, but there were only 41,084 of them who owned slaves. Assuming that every slave owner was the head of a family and therefore drew close to slavery many who did not own slaves, there would still remain about 69,000 families who owned no slaves. Thus it was that for every Georgian who owned slaves, there were almost two who owned no slaves.

As slavery was a powerful force in developing social distinctions, the Georgians tended to separate into three roughly divided groups: the large planters, few in numbers; the yeomanry, the great mass of the people, who owned a few slaves or none; and the dregs of any society, but certainly prevalent in a society dominated by slavery, the so-called poor white trash.

The planter aristocracy was a highly cultured group, who deserved a better fate than to rest on the insecure foundation of slavery. From ancient times nobilities and aristocracies had grown upon landed estates; and when their representatives came to visit America, they found in Georgia and other Southern states a society which made them feel nearest at home. Their culture was genuine, and their manners were easy and unassuming. They took pride in their homes, they were hospitable; they bought many books and read them. Plantation life on the sea islands and the coast early took on a glamour which lasted until the economic organization which made it possible was smashed in the Civil War. Thomas Spalding on Sapelo Island, Thomas Butler King on St. Simons, James Hamilton Couper at Hopeton on the Altamaha, Pierce Butler

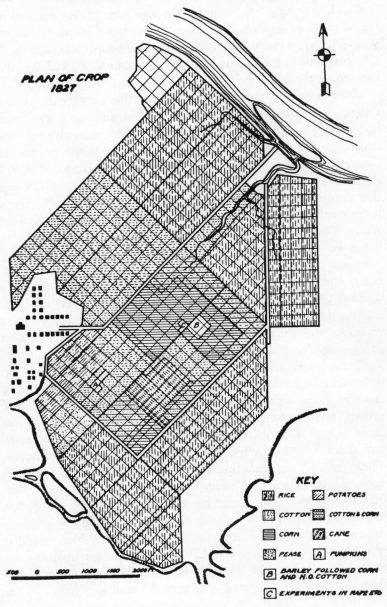

PLAN OF CROP
1827

KEY

▦ RICE   ▨ POTATOES

▦ COTTON   ▦ COTTON & CORN

▦ CORN   ▦ CANE

▦ PEASE   Ⓐ PUMPKINS

Ⓑ BARLEY FOLLOWED CORN
   AND N.O. COTTON

Ⓒ EXPERIMENTS IN RAPE ETO

500   0   500   1000   1500   2000 FT.

PLAN OF HOPETON PLANTATION

at Butler's Island, with Fanny Kemble, his critical and dissatisfied wife, were a few of the coastal planters who lived the life of feudal barons. The upcountry had its planters no less cultured, such as Robert Toombs, Alexander H. Stephens, and Howell Cobb, who added politics to their planting interests, and H. H. Tarver, Richard Peters, and Farish Carter, not so well known because they gave most of their time to their great plantations.

Though most of the planters remained on their estates, except for the hot summer when they went to such watering places as Indian Springs, Madison Springs, or Franklin Springs in Georgia, or White Sulphur Springs, Newport, or Saratoga Springs to the northward, they took a rather keen interest in politics and largely controlled the state. The state legislature in 1830 contained more than twice as many farmers or planters as all other occupations combined.

The mass of Georgians during the ante-bellum times were the yeomanry or middle class. Some of them owned a few slaves, but most of them were the small farmers who did their own labor, the small business men who needed little help, or the skilled laborers and mechanics. Georgia's destiny rested with these people.

They were respectable but not genteel. Some were poor, but with them poverty was more of an inconvenience than a disgrace. Some of them were poor whites, but not the poor white trash, of whom the slaves could say "dey'm long way lower down dan de darkies." As an ante-bellum Southerner said, "Respectability is one thing, and gentility of fashion is quite another. It is respectable to labor—to acquire an honest livelihood by one's own industry—all the world over; but where, we should like to know, is it considered genteel or fashionable?" Most of these middle class Georgians had little money and when spending money was involved they frequently professed greater poverty than was the fact. They lived in rude plenty in respect to food, as Sherman was to find with delight

during his Civil War invasion. Their homes had none of the
pretensions which characterized the planter mansions, yet they
kept away from wind and weather in substantial structures.

The statistics of Georgia school children might tend to
vitiate the statement that the middle class made up the majority
of Georgians; for in 1854 there were 82,467 children on the
Poor School fund, and in 1859, after the law had been changed
to include all children alike, only 47,060 were added. This
would seem to indicate that there were about twice as many
poor children as those able to pay their tuition. But without a
doubt many of these yeoman Georgians during the 'forties and
'fifties forgot pride and took advantage of a loosely worded and
more loosely interpreted law to get their children classed as
"poor" and have them educated at the expense of the state.
These statistics also mean, however, that the majority of Georgians did verge on money poverty or a poverty of pride, irrespective of how much food and land they might possess.

Poverty ground out few paupers in Georgia, even among the
poor white trash. Governor Gilmer in 1830 said, "We have no
such class as the poor. Our lands are so cheap, and the absolute
necessaries of life so easily obtained that the number of dependent *poor* are scarcely sufficient to give exercise to the virtue of
charity in individuals. A beggar is almost as rare with us as a
prince. Children, instead of being an incumbrance to the poor
of our country, are their riches." In 1860 Georgia supported
only 1,451 paupers, as compared with New York's 164,782 and
Massachusetts' 51,880.

The poor white trash were scattered widely, but they lived in
greatest numbers in the mountainous regions[2] and in the pine
barrens of the central and southern parts of the state. Most
plantations were troubled with a few, hovering around in the
waste places. They lived in single-room rude log cabins, with

[2] Those living in the highlands were somewhat different from the poor white
trash living in the pine barrens. In material possessions they were very similar; in
mental attitudes they differed much. They were held down less by social isolation.

a dirty bed or two, a frying-pan, and, perhaps, a skillet. A few
patches of ground nearby were planted in corn, tobacco, and
potatoes. A few razorback hogs, an emaciated horse and rickety
cart, a mangy cur, a rifle, and fishing poles made up the re-

POOR WHITE TRASH

Edward King, *The Southern States of North America*. London:
Blackie & Co., 1875.

maining possessions. They were illiterate, shiftless, and despised. A Southern planter in 1860 characterized them as "the laziest two-legged animals that walk erect on the face of the earth. Even their motions are slow, and their speech is a sickening drawl . . . while their thoughts and ideas seem likewise to creep along at a snail's pace. All they can seem to care for is to live from hand to mouth; to get drunk, . . .; to shoot for beef; to attend gander pullings; to vote at elections; to eat and sleep; to lounge in the sunshine of a bright summer's day, and to bask in the warmth of a roaring wood fire, when summer days are over."

With how many of these beings was Georgia afflicted? As there were only 62,003 farms and plantations in Georgia in 1860, it follows that many Georgians did not possess land or did not cultivate their land. Apart from the planters, the occupations in which there were more than 500 people follows:

Blacksmiths	1,465	Millers	836
Carpenters	3,219	Officers (public)	506
Clerks	3,626	Overseers	4,909
Clergymen	1,015	Painters	529
Factory Hands	2,454	Physicians	2,004
Farmers	67,718	Railroadmen	948
Farm Laborers	19,567	Seamstresses	2,411
Grocers	711	Servants	5,337
Laborers	11,272	Shoemakers	830
Lawyers	1,168	Students	1,621
Machinists	615	Teachers	2,123
Mechanics	1,480	Wheelwrights	592
Merchants	3,195		

Out of these occupations must have come the bulk of the middle class Georgians, prosperous and poor, as well as the poor white trash. From the very definition of the latter, it is evident that most of them must have been farmers, farm laborers, factory hands, laborers, and servants.[3] If they were classed as farmers, their farms must have been small. At this time there were 906 farms in area from 3 to 9 acres, and 2,803 from 10 to 19. Certainly few poor white trash cultivated as much as 19 acres; but assuming that all farmers cultivating less than 20 acres were poor white trash, there could have been in this occupation only 3,709. But since the poor white trash were as much the product of mind as of matter, it follows that they did not fill up these four other occupations. It is impossible to determine the number of poor white trash, but even if they had constituted all the farm laborers, factory hands, laborers, servants, farmers cultivating less than 20 acres, and workers in other minor occupations, they could not have been one-fourth of the white population of ante-bellum Georgia.

Agriculture was the chief interest of Georgia, yet there was little scientific progress made in it. There were reformers who brought about improvements on their own plantations, but they were never able to convince the mass of Georgians that changes could possibly bring improvements. Richard Peters diversified his land by introducing more livestock, improving the breed, and by rotating the crops he raised. In 1854 William Terrell made a gift of $20,000 to the state University, for the purpose of having an agricultural department set up which should try to prevent the red old hills of Georgia from becoming redder. As the price of cotton went down periodically, many Georgians would become more interested in diversification, and then such production as molasses, sugar, indigo, poppies, tobacco, olives, silk, and grasses would be advocated, and methods of restoring the fertility of the soil would be talked. During the later ante-bellum days, Peruvian guano was brought in, and the railways gave cheap rates in order to distribute it widely over the state. Various societies grew up to help agri-

[3] A study of the census figures of 1860 will show that the poor white trash must have been included in the lists as claiming some occupation, regardless of their shiftlessness.

culture, such as the Agricultural Society of Georgia in Savannah, the Wilkes Agricultural Society, and the Agricultural Society of Putnam County. But as long as ignorant slaves, with no incentive to learn, were the source of plantation labor, there could be no great improvement in Georgia agriculture though the worn-out fields which lay in the wake of the plantations must not be attributed wholly to the slave system. In the land of free labor, the wastage was almost as marked. Land was still cheap and plentiful, and the United States, North and South, was prodigal in its use.

The plantation was an economic organization and a business enterprise; it was not set up as a sentiment to afford backgrounds for songs and stories, nor was it contrived by fiends to be a torture chamber in which the noble black man of Africa should be made to suffer. Run by slave labor, it was not an efficient institution; but if there had been no slaves, there would have been no plantations. As a generality, slaves were treated no better or no worse than their economic well-being demanded. With the price of a slave rising from $300 in 1800 to $1,800 in 1860, the plantation could not have lasted so long if inhuman treatment of the slaves had been the rule, for if the retributions of an outraged conscience had not levelled it, economic ruin could not have failed to overtake it. Where the planter was present he generally saw to his economic well-being in the treatment of his slaves, and where he was absent his overseers would likely have a set of rules which served no less the humanitarian instincts of the times than the pocketbook of the planter.

Slavery carried with it many attendant problems: the attitude of Georgians toward the institution, the foreign and domestic slave-trade, free Negroes, and the Pandora's box which the abolitionists flung open.

Although some of the best men in colonial Georgia had induced the Trustees to permit the introduction of slavery, by the time the Revolution had passed, the general opinion of Geor-

gians was that the Negro element in their population was un-
desirable. Yet being practical people, they always based their
actions on slavery as a fact and not a proposition. The Negroes
they had they would keep if they should find no easy way to
get rid of them; but they would be careful not to augment an
existing evil. They forbade the slave trade, both foreign and
domestic, and knowing of no way to absorb free Negroes,
socially or economically, they also forbade setting Negroes free.
As time went on, attitudes and laws changed on all these subjects and on many others, and to accept as the actual rule of
conduct what the law required or forbade would be to assume
that a democracy is a law-abiding society.

A law forbade bringing slaves from other states to be sold,
yet it was often violated, and in 1824 it was repealed. Thereafter, trading in domestic slaves became a lucrative business for
those who cared to engage in it. One of the greatest slaves auc-
tions ever to take place in the state happened in Savannah in
1859, when 460 slaves belonging to Pierce Butler were sold.
Both law and constitution forbade bringing slaves from foreign
countries to Georgia either to keep or sell, and yet this prohibition was disregarded by Georgians as long as slavery lasted.
In attempting to enforce this policy, Georgia passed a law in
1817, requiring all foreign slaves to be brought to Milledgeville
where they should be sold for the benefit of the state, unless
someone would agree to pay their way back to Africa; and the
next year the state offered as a reward to anyone apprehending
illegal importations, one-tenth the price received for the slaves.
For being watchful, the collector of the port of St. Marys received $200 in 1819, and the collector at Brunswick also prof-
ited from his vigilance. Three hundred of these foreign slaves
turned up in Savannah in 1818, which led Governor Rabun to
declare that the law against this "abominable traffic" was being
violated constantly, and that high and low were engaging in
it. Even former governor David B. Mitchell was implicated in
this smuggling business.

The best known case of slave-smuggling took place in 1858, when Charles A. L. Lamar, Savannahian and soldier of fortune, and W. C. Corrie, New Yorker and principal owner of the *Wanderer,* loaded this vessel with 420 Africans, and landed them near Brunswick. The vessel was seized, but the Africans were soon transformed into Georgia slaves.

Though a law of 1801 declared that no slaves should be freed except by the legislature, many Georgians freed their slaves and in one way or another evaded or satisfied the law. The legislature now and then exercised the right. Austin Dabney in the Revolution, not choosing to run away with many of his fellows, joined Elijah Clarke's forces and fought "with a bravery and fortitude which would have honored a freeman." As a reward, the legislature, in 1786, set him free, and in 1821 gave him 112 acres of land in Walton County. Sam, in 1833, saved the state capitol from a dangerous fire; and for the heroism he showed, the legislature set him free.

The free Negro was a pariah in the land; his position in Georgia was no better than in the other slave states, and little worse than in the free states. In 1793 free Negroes were allowed to enter the state, provided they registerd their presence within thirty days, and within six months secured a certificate of honesty and industry from two magistrates. Later they were required to register annually. In 1818 they were prohibited from entering the state under penalty of $100, on the non-payment of which they should be thrown into slavery. In 1852 those in the state were required to pay a poll tax of $5 annually, and seven years later all free Negroes who were vagrants were ordered to be sold into slavery. To prevent abuses, a slave formerly a free Negro was given a chance in court to prove his right to freedom.

Free Negroes were not citizens; they were tried in the same courts where slaves were tried, for the same crimes, and were punished in the same degree. They were not allowed to use or carry firearms, dispense medicine, set type, or be taught to

Top: FRANKLIN COLLEGE IN THE 1850's. THIS WAS THE ONLY PART OF THE UNIVERSITY OF GEORGIA IN EXISTENCE AT THAT TIME. *Bottom:* FORSYTH FEMALE COLLEGIATE INSTITUTE. THIS WAS A TYPICAL SCHOOL FOR GIRLS IN ANTE-BELLUM TIMES. George White, *Historical Collections of Georgia.* New York: Pudney & Russell, 1855.

THE COUNTRYMAN.

BY J. A. TURNER. —"BREVITY IS THE SOUL OF WIT"— $1 A YEAR.

VOL. III. TURNWOLD, PUTNAM COUNTY, GA., MONDAY, OCTOBER 6, 1862. NO. 2.

Anecdote of Rev. Wm. Arnold.

Rev. Wm. Arnold was very much opposed to dancing, but manifested no opposition to a good joke at the right time, and in the right place.

Going home, one evening, with becoming solemnity and without cracking a smile he said to his companion—(it was towards the close of the year)—"Wife, I am going to have a dance here, christmas!"

Mrs. Arnold was dumbfoundered. What in the world could her husband mean? He have a dance at his house? He who of all others always opposed dancing to the death?

But Mr. Arnold still insisted that he would have the dance. There was no use in opposing it. His mind was made up. Have the dance at his house he would, let what might be said, or thought.

Mrs. Arnold was in deep distress. Retiring in sorrow and agony, she sought her daughter, and said, "Mary, I really am afraid your father has lost his mind. He says he is bent on having a dance here, christmas!" And a dance he did have in his own house. But before christmas came, the good old divine's family were rejoiced to be told that the dance would be

ankles and wrists—the chains being constructed of block tin, I believe, though that fact detracts very little from the daring character of his performance—carrying a balancing pole, over twenty feet long, said to weigh forty-eight pounds. He walked a short distance; and, stopping, shook the rope. Going a little farther, he again stopped, and lay down at full length on his back, keeping his pole at right angles across his body. Assuming a sitting posture, he moved along in a strange manner, putting one foot out as far as he could reach, the other hanging down below the rope, then rising on the extended foot, putting the other out in the same manner as the first, allowing the first to hang down, and so on.

Again he started off in a run, and then stopped to stand on his head, striking his heels together, while in that position. He first placed the pole at right angles across the rope, his head either on or very near it, and then raised his body gently into an upright position. While walking or running, he held his arms extended, at nearly full length before him, and the pole well balanced, at right angles with the rope. After getting from his head on his feet, he pro-

French cook, with a sheet-iron stove on his shoulders. He walked firmly and rapidly to the middle of the rope, where he stopped, set down his stove, kindled a fire, broke eggs, cooked an omelette, and let it down in a plate, at the end of a cord, to the passengers on the Maid of the Mist, as she was moving about directly underneath him! This was the crowning and finishing exploit of the most wonderful performance I ever witnessed, and I can testify that it was done fairly, without trick of any sort.

After Blondin reached the shore, I had an opportunity of observing him closely. He was rather small, but looked hard, wiry and muscular. His complexion was somewhat cadaverous, his hair, moustache, and goatee nearly white. This, I suppose, was their original color, and age had nothing to do with it, for he appeared to be about thirty years old.

Blondin was one of the wonders of the age. W. W. T.

Epigram.

"New England's dead, the poet said,
On every field they lie:
In fact a few five doodles do
As much before they die."

THE CHRISTIAN INDEX.

EDITED BY JESSE MERCER AND WILLIAM H. STOKES.

No. 5. Vol. 7. WASHINGTON, Ga., JANUARY 31, 1839. $2 50 cts. in advance. $3. at end of the year.

TERMS—PER ANNUM.

The Christian Index, will be published on Thursday, in each week (except Christmas week) and furnished to a single Subscriber at $2 50 cents, always paid in advance, (unless there be a willingness to pay $3.) Arrearages will always be charged at $3.

Where no Agent is, a five dollar bill (on any specie paying Bank in this, or other States) will be received, of any one Subscriber, for two years—or of two, for one year, which, in either case, may be sent by mail, at our risk and expense.

Post-Masters, where our paper may be received, are requested to act as Agent; and Ministers of the Gospel are particularly solicited to become Agents. Every Agent shall be entitled to a sixth copy (if requested) as a compensation for his trouble and expense.

Remittances by mail, not receipted in due time, must be signified to the Editors, and established by the Post-Master's certificate within three months, to render the claim valid.

Requests for changes or discontinuances, must mention the Post-Offices at which the papers had been previously received, and post-paid, to ensure attention.

All letters on business, or covering remittances, (except as above, or from Agents who act gratuitously) or communications, must be addressed to the Editors, post paid.

☞ Literary Notices and Advertisements, of a general character, may be inserted on the usual terms. Always however, at the discretion of the Editors. January, 1839.

Christ tells his apostles that, as a reward for their fidelity and zeal, they shall receive a superior degree of glory in his heavenly kingdom; which he represents by their sitting "upon twelve thrones, judging the twelve tribes of Israel." (Matt. xix. 28.) He speaks of those who shall "see Abraham, and Isaac, and Jacob, and all the prophets in the kingdom of God; (Luke xiii. 28,) and of others who shall "come from the east and from the west, and shall sit down with Abraham, and Isaac, and Jacob, in the kingdom of heaven;" (Matt. viii. 11,) and to the penitent thief he says —"This day shalt thou be with me in paradise." (Luke xxiii. 43.) As if he had said—"Thy body is perishing; but thy soul shall retain its life, its activity, its consciousness; and being received in the paradise of God, shall see and know its Redeemer, even as it is seen and known of him." These several expressions intimate, if they do not prove, that the saints will recognise not only the Saviour in his glorified human nature, but his twelve apostles also, in their exaltation, whatever it may be; and that they may be able to distinguish "Abraham, Isaac, and Jacob, and all the prophets;"—and if these, then why not all the others of "the general assembly of the church of the first born whose names are written in heaven," and our immediate friends among the number! There are two passages in St. Paul's Epistles, which seem to place this subject beyond all question. They prove "that St. Paul anticipated on the last day a personal knowledge of those on his personal re-union with them, with whom he had been connected in this life by the ties of pastoral af-

---

Top: A NEWSPAPER PUBLISHED ON A PLANTATION. JOEL CHANDLER HARRIS, AS A BOY, BEGAN HIS LITERARY CAREER ON THIS PAPER. *Bottom:* A BAPTIST PAPER WHICH HAS CONTINUED TO THE PRESENT DAY.

read or write. They could not preach without a license from a justice of the peace, they could not traffic with slaves, their testimony was not accepted against whites in courts. In Savannah, a free Negro could not peddle goods unless he wore a badge, costing $10; and in Augusta, he could not carry a cane or stick unless blind, smoke in a public place, or follow a parade, and he must be off the streets by 9:15 in the evening.

Though these laws might seem severe, many of them were never observed. Perhaps no laws ever enacted were so thoroughly ignored where convenience suggested as were those relating to Negroes and slavery. Some free Negroes progressed far in Georgia. Anthony Oddingsells, of Chatham County, owned 200 acres of land and fifteen slaves; Gower, of Lexington, was a physician so skillful and respected that he entered into a partnership with a white physician; and Wilkes Flagg, who lived in Milledgeville, had at the outbreak of the Civil War acquired property worth $25,000. The lot of the great majority of free Negroes was, nevertheless, hard; and many of them found it convenient to attach themselves to a white person as guardian, and a few actually had themselves cast into slavery by law, as did Jane Miller, of Clarke County. The free Negroes in Georgia were about one per cent of the Negro population in 1860.

The Colonization Society, organized in 1816 for the purpose of restoring Negroes to their African homes, found much support in Georgia, but it was soon evident that returning the Negroes to Africa was an undertaking which could never be completed.

The years following the second war with Great Britain were the most prosperous in all Georgia's history. The economic vigor which led the people to sweep out the Creeks and Cherokees and to reduce to farms and plantations within the next two decades almost six times as much land as had been settled during the whole past of the colony and state, found expression in other ways. The towns of Macon and Augusta grew into great cotton markets, with the latter contesting and winning complete supremacy over Hamburg, a town set up across the Savannah by covetous and spiteful South Carolinians. Savannah was supreme as Georgia's exporting city, despite Brunswick's ambitious efforts, and the more distant competition of South Carolina's chief city, Charleston. In 1816 the value of Georgia products exported through Savannah to other states and to foreign countries amounted to over $10,000,000; two years later it had grown to more than $14,000,000. Within five months, October, 1816, through February, 1817, 105 ships arrived in Savannah. Here, in 1812, the Insurance Company of the City of Savannah was set up, and three years later came the Marine and Fire Insurance Company of the City of Savannah. Her population steadily increased from 5,212 in 1810 to 22,292 in 1860.

This was also an era of banks as well as cotton fields and internal improvements. The Planters' Bank of the State of Georgia had been chartered in Savannah in 1807, and the Bank of Augusta had been set up three years later. So great did the opportunities seem to be in the banking business that the state government began to take great blocks of stock in the principal banks. So excited did it get and so completely did it enter into the general banking stampede of the times that in 1817 Governor Mitchell suggested that all the surplus funds of the state ought to be invested in bank stocks, to usher in that golden age when the state could cease all taxation of her citizens and pay the cost of government with dividends from bank stock. Almost as much an expression of the bank fever as a mark of concern for education and internal improvements was the creation in 1817 of an endowment of $250,000 for free schools. In 1821 the educational endowment was increased to $500,000 and a like amount was set up for internal improvements. In every instance the endowment was to be invested in bank or other profitable stock. In 1821 the state had invested more than $1,000,000 in 12,000 shares of bank stock.

The bank panic of 1819 and the pinch of hard times which set in for the next few years awakened Georgians from their dream of perpetual plenty in a land of banks and led Governor Clark to conclude that banks were a menace to the common people and to question the wisdom of the state's investing its money in bank stocks. Bank disasters began to overtake the people, and much of the blame was laid at the doors of the branch of the Bank of the United States, located in Savannah. A committee of the state senate declared that this bank had been "obtruded upon the State of Georgia without her consent, as an interference with her sovereignty as an independent State." Governor Clark was equally hostile to it.

If the state government needed the facilities of banks, then Clark would have it establish its own bank unassociated with private individuals. This idea took root, and in 1828 the state chartered the Central Bank of Georgia, which belonged to the state and which was in effect the state treasury. It was the depository for the state's money, which was subject to loan to citizens giving proper security. The state, by functioning through this bank, was enabled to issue currency and thereby to sidestep the prohibition in the Federal constitution against a state issuing bills of credit. This bank was opened in 1829, and immediately it was besieged by a mass of farmers and planters, estimated from three to five hundred, seeking to borrow money.

Sound business was much bedevilled throughout ante-bellum times by the great variety of paper notes that circulated as money. The strength of Georgia's banks varied, and, as a result, the value of the paper money they emitted varied likewise. In 1833 the state forbade any bank to issue notes for a smaller amount than $5. It hoped thereby to reduce counterfeiting and lead to the circulation of more specie.

The prosperity of the state for the next few years following 1815 was nowhere better attested than in the state treasury. The $1,250,000 promised by the United States in 1802 for the western lands had been coming into the state treasury steadily, but in 1816 there was $936,558 still due. Much money was being received from bank stock; and indeed, so wealthy did the state government feel that it made large appropriations for river improvements and for schools. In 1816 there was a balance in the treasury of $750,863. In 1821 after the great appropriations had been made for education and internal improvements, the treasury had a balance of $145,316, and the next year it had increased to $283,475. It seemed that the state was as much frightened that it would be smothered by its wealth as later it was fearful it would starve for the want of it. In 1823 the surplus had pushed on up over $400,000, with all that Governor Clark could do to spend the state's money. He looked to the day when Georgia would be a land without taxes, if this surplus were properly invested. It was invested, but alas! not wisely. In less than a decade the surplus had sunk to less than $6,000; and although Georgia was given her part of the $28,000,000 which President Jackson found no use for in Washington and which Congress ordered in 1836 to be given to the states, Georgia was destined, for most of the time that has passed since, to be worried with deficits as much as she had been troubled once by her surplus. Likewise, the people suffered in their prosperity, as when the price of cotton reached five cents a pound in the early 'forties, a level never so low before, and when unsound relief laws were defeated only by the greatest efforts of the wisest leaders.

Instead of becoming a people unafflicted by tax-gatherers, Georgians settled down to taxes, which increased and became more strange as time went by. The system of specific taxation of colonial and early state times, which classified and placed rates on grades, gave way, in 1852, to an ad valorem system, where property was given a value and taxed accordingly. The chief sources of revenue for the state in 1860 were: a real and personal property tax, which included slaves; a poll tax of twenty-five cents on all white males between 21 and 60; a tax of $5 on all free Negroes between 18 and 50; a $5 tax on professions, such as those filled by lawyers, doctors and "daguerrean artists"; and certain specific property taxes, as 31.25 cents on each $100 of bank stock, ½% on the net earnings of railroad companies, and other rates on insurance and express companies. Exempted from taxation, in addition to libraries, religious and educational properties, and other customary categories were all plantation and mechanical tools, three hundred dollars worth of household and kitchen furniture, and all poultry, firearms, and wearing apparel.

Even before hard times hit the Georgians, they were looking for sources of income other than agriculture. The expedition ordered by the state in 1819 to explore the Okefenokee Swamps may have had back of it little more than curiosity; but the geological survey set up in 1836, only to be abolished four years later, pointed to a desire of the state to discover its hidden wealth. It required no geological survey to discover the great timber wealth of the state, but it remained for a Portland, Maine, company to begin the greatest lumbering operations of the times, when it purchased, in 1834, 700,000 acres between the Oconee and Ocmulgee rivers, and set four mills with eighteen saws to cutting the great yellow pines into lumber, which vessels carried down the Altamaha to a lumber yard at Darien.

Troubles leading up to the second war with Great Britain first turned conspicuously the attention of Georgians to manufacturing enterprises. In 1810 the state loaned Zachariah Sims $3,000 for three years to aid him in setting up a paper factory in Greene County, and the same year it chartered the Wilkes Manufacturing Company, which proposed to make cotton and woolen goods. But the rise of manufacturing in Georgia to a position of prominence awaited a later time, and strangely enough, a time when Georgians were most bitterly condemning the tariff, which aided such industry. Augustin S. Clayton, a tariff nullifier, set up on the Oconee River, near Athens, in 1829, a cotton factory, which made such large profits that Clayton, with conspicuous honesty, used this fact to prove that a tariff was unnecessary.

During the next three decades many textile mills were built and a large number of them in order to use water power were located on rivers, such as at High Shoals on the Apalachee, Scull Shoals and Long Shoals on the Oconee, Augusta on the Savannah, and Columbus on the Chattahoochee. In Macon there were not only cotton mills but also foundries and machine and boiler works, and in Atlanta by 1853 there were large tanneries, shoe factories, foundries, and machine shops. Henry Stevens, born in Cornwall, England, set up in Baldwin County large saw mills and pottery works; Mark A. Cooper established near Cartersville a rolling mill and nail factory, which came to be well-known throughout the South; and other Georgians turned their attention toward the state's industrial development. In the little intellectual center of Athens, there was such a wide variety of small manufactories as to suggest a New England village. In 1850 there were forty cotton mills in the state and in 1860 the number of all kinds of manufacturing plants, large and small and including home industries, was 1,890 and the value of their output was almost $17,000,000. Though these manufactories represented interests of Georgians in other fields than agriculture, still the heart of Georgia was in the cotton boll and the soil, and the philosophy of the planter ruled the state with few signs that it should ever be given up.

In the 'fifties the prosperity of earlier times returned to Georgia, and out of it burst forth a buoyancy in the economic world and an assurance of leadership in national politics which was summed up in the name "Empire State of the South," a slogan which the state attached to herself and continued to wear long after it ceased to fit. Preparing herself for this position, she made in the decade from 1840 to 1850 more progress in cotton manufacturing than any other state which did a considerable amount, and her absolute increase was greater than any other state excepting Massachusetts and New Hampshire. The value of her exports to foreign countries from 1845 to 1860 she eloquently recorded at $4,557,435 in 1845, $7,551,943 in 1850, and $18,483,030 in 1860.

Prosperity and county-making have always gone together in her history. During the last decade before the Civil War she created thirty-two new counties, for which in her later days she found she had less and less use. But prosperity brought to her many people from the North, who helped to continued good times and who gave her a reputation among her neighbors of being the Yankee State of the South. They came to help set up factories and build railroads, to teach in the schools, and to become outstanding editors of newspapers, especially in Macon, Augusta, and Savannah.

CHAPTER XXI

THE SOUL OF THE PEOPLE

INTELLIGENT GEORGIANS early came to believe that material prosperity alone would be an unsafe foundation on which to base a lasting civilization. They agreed with Abraham Baldwin when he said, "As it is the distinguishing happiness of free government that civil order should be the result of choice and not necessity, and the common wishes of the people become the law of the land, their public prosperity and even existence, very much depends upon suitably forming the minds and morals of their citizens."

Georgians had not yet emerged from the Revolution before they laid down in their fundamental law the duty of the state to support education. They translated the principle into action when they chartered a university in 1785 and endowed academies in every county. They embraced Jefferson's full program of democracy, which was not simply the rule by the people, but by the educated people so that they might rule wisely. They planned an educational structure, beautiful and logical but too elaborate ever to succeed in a state busied as Georgia was in getting physical possession of herself. A Senatus Academicus was set up whose duty it was to have a general supervision of all educational activities of the state, from the University down through the academies to the lowest schools. For more than a half century it struggled with its own indifference to the scheme and with the lack of interest of those who were to work with it, and then passed out of existence in 1859.

Under the impetus of the original enthusiasm, the state immediately set out to educate the people. The University, though not founded until 1801, tried vigorously to make leaders for the state, and well it succeeded, for from its classrooms in ante-bellum times emerged Augustin S. Clayton, Eugenius A. Nisbet, John A. Campbell, George F. Pierce, Francis R. Goulding, Alexander H. Stephens, Howell Cobb, Robert Toombs, Herschel V. Johnson, Crawford W. Long, John G. Shorter, John and Joseph LeConte, Benjamin M. Palmer, Thomas R. R. Cobb, J. L. M. Curry, Benjamin H. Hill, and many others who became famous in state and nation. It received no maintenance appropriations from the state, and in this respect Georgia fell short of the intentions of her original leaders. The University sold its land endowment in 1821 and made a perpetual loan of the proceeds to the state, for which it received annually $8,000 in interest. The presidents under whom it thrived most in ante-bellum times were Josiah Meigs, Moses Waddel, and Alonzo Church.

The lower grades of education the state promoted in what were called poor or free schools and in academies. There was never satisfactory progress made in any of these schools, though the state made honest efforts. The poor school fund of $250,000 set aside in 1817 was supplanted in 1821 by a endowment of $500,000 divided equally between poor schools and academies. There were no regulations the state imposed on the poor schools, for in fact they were schools set up by any wandering pedagogue who could collect pupils, and they were designated poor schools because the state agreed to pay, from the poor school endowment, the tuition of the children of parents who were too poor to meet the expense. A parent whose annual tax was not over fifty cents was by law declared poor and his children might have three years at public expense, if they were between the ages of 8 and 18, and did not go beyond the subjects of reading, writing, and arithmetic. Some Georgians were too proud to be legally adjudged poor and many more were not interested in education. As a result a great many Georgians allowed their children to grow up in illiteracy. By 1850 twenty per cent of the white Georgians had become adults without having penetrated the mysteries of reading and writing. As each county ran its schools to suit itself, some schools were better than others. Glynn, Emanuel, and a few other counties gave school books free to all children, and Baldwin County provided a real free school system by levying a special tax and allowing all children to participate equally in the school fund. Some of the counties consolidated their academy funds with the poor school income and expended it all for the poor children. Savannah in 1818 organized a Free School Society to provide educational, religious, and moral training for all poor children.

This system of elementary education was a failure, a fact

A SOUTHERN SCHOOLHOUSE IN THE ANTE-BELLUM TIMES

B. J. Lossing, *Pictorial Field-Book of the Revolution*, II. New York: Harper & Brothers, 1860.

which the state was forced to admit by 1829 when the legislature through its joint committee on education reported that the system was "miserably defective" and that the money which accrued to it was squandered and dissipated. In 1836 Georgia set aside one-third of the money which she received from President Jackson's distribution among the states of the surplus revenue and ordered that it be devoted to education and be called the "Free School and Education Fund." It amounted to $350,000. By the same act she provided for a commission to study the educational systems of the other American states and of Europe and to "digest a plan of common school education best adapted to the genius, habits, of life and of thought, of the people of Georgia." As a result a common school system formulated largely by Alexander H. Stephens, was adopted by laws passed in 1837 and 1838 to become effective in 1839. By this legislation all school endowments were to be combined into a Common School Fund, and the income distributed among the counties according to the number of white school children between the ages of 5 and 15. At last poor children as a separate class for school purposes were to pass out of existence and Georgia was to admit her obligation to instruct all alike. Counties might supplement their quotas from the state fund by private subscriptions and by a levy of not over 50% on the general tax rate. Districts were to be laid out; school houses, erected; and teachers, hired. But alas! Georgia immediately became frightened at her boldness and at the expense of such an undertaking. She might improve rivers, promote banks, and build railroads, but she had not yet convinced herself that she could bear the cost of developing her citizenship. In 1840 the legislature repealed the laws setting up this new school system before it had had a fair chance of being tried, and the state now dropped back to the old plan of offering to educate the poor children only. All educational endowments were now transferred into a Poor School Fund, and for the next twenty years Georgia's educational labors were largely wasted.

In explaining the state's educational failure a commission to study school plans appointed by Governor Towns in 1849, consisting of George F. Pierce, Samuel K. Talmage, and Leonidas P. Mercer, declared, "In many counties, there are not to be found, either among the people or their juries, a controlling mind—patriotic, enthusiastic—to stimulate and direct. False views of the duties of citizenship—a meagre sense of parental responsibility—a morbid pride (to be enlightened rather than censured)—a depreciated estimate of the benefits of knowledge compared with the products of manual labor—the debasement and stupefaction of a life of crime, extinguishing all noble aspirations—and the relentless demands of poverty upon the toil of parent and child—all these, and yet other causes (and these have been and yet are numerous)."

During the 'fifties a group of educational reformers carried on a campaign to induce the state to return to a free school system, free to all, and adequately supported. Finally in 1858 the state took the greatest educational step in all its history up to that time, when it provided for the appropriation annually of $100,000 from the rentals of the Western and Atlantic Railroad, supplemented by other funds, for the establishing of free schools. The approach of civil war put an end to this fair promise.

Happily, Georgians were not dependent wholly on the state government for their educational opportunities. With the coming of the 'thirties, the religious denominations awaked to a need of educating their ministers and to the opportunity, if not the duty, of enlightening people generally. The Methodists, Baptists, and Presbyterians all became active about the same time. Adiel Sherwood, in 1831, after attempting unsuccessfully to induce the Baptist Convention to promote a manual labor school, set it up, himself, locating it near Greensboro, where later the town of Penfield appeared. He called it Mercer Institute in honor of Jesse Mercer, who had helped him. For the next few years the Baptists vacillated between making this school into a college and establishing a college at Washington, in Wilkes County. In 1837 they agreed on Mercer Institute and the same year they secured a charter for it. Two years later, under the name of Mercer University, it began classes and played thereafter an important part in the educational history of the state. In 1834 the Methodist Conference set up a manual training school near Covington. Two years later it was chartered as Emory College and in 1838 it began a work from which it never desisted until the coming of the Civil War. The Presbyterians secured a charter for a college in 1835 which they erected near Milledgeville and which they called Oglethorpe. Classes started here in 1838 and continued until the Civil War so crippled it as to cause its ultimate death, after heroic efforts had been made to resuscitate it in Atlanta.

All of these denominations set up or gained control of other schools, most of which they called female colleges. The best known of these was Wesleyan College at Macon, founded in 1836 under the name of the Georgia Female College, as an answer to the widespread demand that women be given educational facilities. It began work in 1839, but soon fell into bankruptcy and was sold. In 1843 the Methodists came into control of it and changed its name. It owed its first release from financial anxiety to George I. Seney, of Brooklyn, New York, who, after the Civil War, gave to it and Emory College $250,000.

The Catholics, though never numerous in the state and confined largely to Augusta and Savannah, set up their first academy in 1845 in the latter city. Later they developed institutions at Augusta, Macon, Washington, and Atlanta.

Examples of schools set up without the support of organized religion or the government were Forsyth Female Collegiate Institute in 1849, Bowdon Collegiate Institute in 1857, and Lucy Cobb Institute the next year.

Conforming to the spirit of the times, Georgians proceeded on the general consideration that education was culture and a reward in itself; yet they developed early the feeling that education also might be specialized and made to serve definitely certain professions. In 1804 a group of Savannahians secured a charter for the Georgia Medical Society, to "improve the science of medicine" and to lessen "the fatality induced by climate and incidental causes." Augusta followed in 1822 with the Medical Society of Augusta, but it was evident from the beginning that the greatest need was to produce doctors of medicine in Georgia, rather than to promote the skill of doctors already practicing; and this necessity was heightened by a law passed in 1825, prohibiting anyone from practicing medicine or to engage in the apothecary's business without a license. The first school designed to teach "the several branches of the healing art" was incorporated in 1828 in Augusta and was an outgrowth of the Medical Society there. It was first called the Medical Academy of Georgia; but the next year its name was changed to the Medical Institute of the State of Georgia and it was given the right to grant the degree of doctor of medicine. It received various grants from the state and from Augusta, and under the control of Dr. Paul F. Eve it developed into an excellent institution. It was forced by the Civil War to close, but in 1873 it became a branch of the state University. Ten years after the founding of this school Savannah secured a charter for a medical college, but it did not begin work until 1853. Closed by the war it reopened in a crippled condition and went out of existence in 1880. Dr. Richard D. Arnold was long interested in the promotion of this institution. The Atlanta Medical College was set up in Atlanta in 1854, and after the war the Southern Medical College grew up in the same city.

Steam doctors and herb specialists had their day, but somewhat more orthodox was the output of the Southern Botanico-Medical College, founded in 1839 in Forsyth, which moved its location to Macon and then to Atlanta, and changed its name three times, ending with Georgia College of Eclectic Medicine and Surgery.

Georgia's interest in the advance of medical science was attested not only in the progress she made in her medical schools, but also in a law passed in 1823 requiring the registration of births. With all her progress, however, doctors neither in Georgia nor elsewhere were able to prevent or retard greatly the deadly march of such scourges as yellow fever and cholera, which periodically visited the state. In 1820 yellow fever swept the city of Savannah and carried away 695 people; and in 1834 Savannah and various other places were visited with cholera. More than 600 slaves died on plantations along the Savannah River and the losses in some places were as great as one out of three of the slave population.

Joseph Henry Lumpkin and Thomas R. R. Cobb were the principal founders of the first law school. This institution was set up in 1859 as a unit in the enlarged University scheme adopted that year, but it was not incorporated into the system until 1867. It was only natural to expect that if a school should be established in Georgia for the purpose of training people for the world of trade, it would arise in Atlanta, and so it did in 1858, set up by B. F. Moore and called Moore's Business University.

Perhaps as a conscious expression in Georgia of the feeling that the state might sometime need more trained soldiers than West Point Military Academy would ever send her, was the founding of the Georgia Military Institute at Marietta in 1851. It was organized largely through the efforts of Colonel A. V. Brumby, but it was nurtured from the beginning by the state, which appropriated annually $2,000 for the education of ten cadets there and which a half dozen years later secured possession of the school. Its war record was so prominent that Sherman burned the institution in 1864 and put an end to it.

A civilized society takes care of both its fortunate and unfortunate members. The Union Society, founded in Savannah in colonial times, included in its program orphans, male and female; but in 1801 the sexes were separated, and this decision led to the formation of the Savannah Female Asylum, run by fourteen women trustees and supported by various religious denominations. In 1852 the Augusta Orphan Asylum was chartered, three years later its doors were opened, and in 1859 it received a bequest of property worth $200,000 from George M. Newton, which made it one of the best orphanages in the South.

Having few deaf mutes but desirous of bringing to them what solace there could be in learning, the legislature influenced by John Jacobus Flournoy, himself a deaf mute, in 1834 appropriated $3,000 to be used in educating these unfortunates in Hartford, Connecticut. After three years of diligent searching, sixteen were found, but only three could be induced to go so far from home. Later, the Hearn Manual Labor School, at Cave Springs, accepted deaf mutes as students, and in 1847 the state erected a building there, and thus began the Georgia Institution for the Deaf and Dumb. The Georgia Academy for the Blind began in Macon as a private undertaking in 1851 and the following year the state assumed the responsibility. In 1837 the state began the policy of taking care of its insane in an institution which it finished four years later in Milledgeville. The insane at that time averaged about one in every thousand people.

Another class of unfortunates with whom the state wrestled was those who had broken the law. Many Georgians were beginning to believe that the purpose of punishing criminals was to reform them rather than take vengeance upon them. In carrying out this idea they turned the attention of the lawmakers toward scientific punishment, involving a new penal code and a penitentiary, and the better care of prisoners in jails. By a law of 1818 sheriffs were required to furnish prisoners with medical attention, fire, clothing, and blankets, services which the state had not before provided. Two years later, prisoners in jail for debt were allowed the freedom of an area of ten acres surrounding the prison, and in 1823 the imprisonment of debtors was forbidden, except in cases where fraud and the concealment of property were proved against them.

The harshness of the law stood out in many instances. After relieving horse thieves of the more severe punishment of earlier days, the law against them in 1809 still administered 39 lashes on three separate days, with one hour each day in the pillory and twenty days to a month in jail. For a second offense, the death penalty was meted out. To bring about a thorough revision of the laws preparatory to setting up a penitentiary, and to digest and to ameliorate them as far as possible, the legislature appointed in 1810 a committee, which the following year completed a new code. As proof that Georgians were becoming more civilized and the punishment of criminals more humane, gouging had become so rare that those who still settled their disputes in this barbarous fashion could be made to desist by the penalty of hard labor, from three to seven years for the first offense and from five to twelve years for the second.

Building the penitentiary edifice was started in 1811, but the work proceeded so slowly that before it was ready to receive criminals, the conscience of Georgia had mellowed again and the code of 1816 resulted. It was now held that cruel punishment was suited only to despotic governments, and that moderation characterized republican rule. Yet, to deny the Deity was a "crime against God," and disqualified the guilty from giving testimony in court or holding office. This code abolished the antiquated right known as benefit of clergy as "a ridiculous and unmeaning privelege and form." The penitentiary was finally completed in 1817. The new plan had attracted a great deal of attention and produced some excitement. Its friends seemed to expect a remaking of human nature and regarded it as "the harbinger of order and peace," while its enemies viewed "its approaches with extreme regret" and some of them threatened to remove from the state. Two years of the penitentiary were enough to convince Governor Rabun that few of the benefits expected had arrived. He believed that instead of making crimes fewer and less enormous, it had produced the opposite effect. The penitentiary was long a bone of contention among the people, and once it was abolished for a year. The trades that the convicts engaged in within its walls did not produce enough to pay for the system.

Though the state was long to keep its penitentiary before it sought another method in dealing with prisoners, it made frequent revisions of its code to keep pace with its constantly changing laws. In 1858 the legislature ordered a new code which is called the code of 1861, erroneously, as it did not go into effect until 1862. This code was remarkable in that here for the first time in any state or country appeared the substantive common law reduced to writing. Thomas R. R. Cobb, one of the ablest men in the state's history, carried out this exacting and difficult task.

Just as there was growth in the state's laws there was likewise constitutional progress. Though the state held no constitutional convention for recasting the constitution from 1789 until after the Civil War, there were many amendments. The meeting of the legislature was changed back and forth from annual to biennial, but ended in annual meetings in the late 'fifties. As the number of the counties increased, the size of the legislature became so unwieldly that the reapportionment of representatives among the counties led to long and bitter struggles, between city and country, slaveholders and non-slaveholders, and between sections of the state. The march of democracy was recorded in the removal in 1834 of property qualifications for membership in the legislature and in 1845 for the governorship. In 1801 the legislature declared that James Echols' treatment of his wife, Rebecca, had "for a long time been marked with great cruelty and injustice, exhibiting more the frantic violence of an insane man than the clemency of a rational and humane husband," and pronounced them divorced. The legislature used much of its time in granting divorces although the constitution did not allow it to act except in cases where the superior court had authorized it "upon legal principles" and except by a vote of two-thirds of each house. To make divorces easier and relieve the legislature altogether of this power an amendment was passed in 1833 making divorces final on the concurrence of two special juries.

Georgia long remained unique as the only state in the

American Union which had no supreme court. She feared the tyranny of judges who might be beyond the reach of the people; she had also had bitter experiences with the United States Supreme Court; and undoubtedly the lawyers found it easier to win their cases where no printed decision of the past could be brought up to refute them. In 1815 when John M. Berrien and three other judges, sitting in convention to make uniform various points of law, had declared certain laws of the legislature unconstitutional, they brought upon their heads a reprimand of the house of representatives, which hoped that this mild procedure would prevent a more harsh remedy in the future. In 1835 the necessity of a supreme court for the state was recognized in a constitutional amendment, but the legislature put off the evil day for ten years, before it would pass the needed legislation. The court was finally put into operation in 1846 with Joseph Henry Lumpkin, Hiram Warner, and Eugenius A. Nisbet as judges. It soon established itself in the confidence of the state so completely that in 1858 the legislature declared that a decision of the court should have the same effect as if it were a law of the state.

Literary developments ran along various lines, but they never attracted the support or attained the excellence which characterized statecraft and economic progress. The mass of Georgians spent little time reading anything except their newspapers, and many were unable to read at all. But there were the few who read much and encouraged literary production; and as the sectional struggle with the North 'became more bitter, Georgians, in order to withdraw themselves from Northern literary influence, came to support widely Southern literary magazines and reviews. From early days there were small groups in almost every community who attempted to promote literary progress. The Savannah Library Society arose in 1801 and it re-arose in 1815 with John M. Berrien as president. The Thespian Society and Library Company was organized in Augusta in 1808; the Eatonton Academy Library Society, in 1818, with

Alonzo Church as librarian; and many other groups organized their libraries. The state set up an official library in the capital in 1831, though it was so rudimentary that it had no librarian until 1847. Societies grew up for almost every cultural purpose that could be promoted and among various groups of people. The Petersburg Union Society came in 1802 for the diffusion of knowledge among its members; the Milledgeville Thespian Society in 1820 for "improvement, and for the correction of vice and immorality"; the Milledgeville Mechanic Society in 1816 for benevolent and social purposes; the Savannah House Carpenters in 1802 for "placing their craft upon a more respectable and social footing"; and the Hibernian Society of the City of Savannah in 1812 for the relief of "indigent and exiled Irishmen" and for promoting social friendship and harmony among them. Scarcely a community in the state was too small or too satisfied with itself not to support a wide variety of travelling musicians, lecturers, and entertainers; and in 1818 Savannah showed her fixed literary and dramatic interests by securing the incorporation of the Savannah Theatre and bringing to the city the outstanding productions of the times.

In 1822 the legislature, desirous of promoting the enlightenment of the people, decided to require no license to anyone peddling books, maps, charts, and mathematical instruments.

Though Georgia was the youngest of the colonies, she soon began to feel old enough and sufficiently important to have her history recorded. Her natural history had already received outstanding attention. Mark Catesby had, a decade before the founding of Georgia, visited the region in search of "Birds, Beasts, Fishes, Serpents, Insects and Plants," and had here and in South Carolina and Florida found inspiration and information for his two-volume *Natural History,* with its superb colored drawings, the first volume being originally published in 1731. The next outstanding naturalist to visit Georgia was John Bartram of Philadelphia, whose journal of observations was not published until 1942. In 1765-1766 he crossed Georgia to

Florida and back again northward. In 1773-1774 his son William with like interests, traversed much the same course and lived to see his *Travels* published in 1791. Six years later another *Natural History* relating entirely to butterflies of Georgia ("Lepidopterous Insects") was published, with remarkable colored plates reminiscent of Mark Catesby's work. It was written and arranged by Sir James Edward Smith, largely from notes and drawings by John Abbot, who lived for many years in Georgia. Still another wrote of Georgia's natural history. Stephen Elliott, a South Carolinian, produced *A Sketch of the Botany of South-Carolina and Georgia,* which was published in thirteen parts from 1816 to 1824.

But most people are interested more in their own history than in descriptions of birds, fish, snakes, weeds, and butterflies. So it was then that J. G. W. DeBrahm, surveyor general of the Southern provinces, wrote about Georgia before the Revolution but published nothing,[1] and Alexander Hewat, a Charleston Presbyterian minister who went to England before the Revolution, wrote and published anonymously in 1779 his *Historical Account of the Rise and Progress of the Colonies of South Carolina and Georgia.* These men, however, were not Georgians, and it remained for Edward Langworthy, born in the colony and educated at the Bethesda school, to be the first Georgian to collect material for a history. He moved away, misfortune overtook him, and though begged by James Jackson to set down Georgia's Revolutionary history before the records of it should grow dim or be destroyed, he never wrote his promised history. Hugh M'Call, though only ten years old at the outbreak of the Revolution, heard much about it and later developed an ambition to write a history of the conflict as well as of the colonial times. Though handicapped by ill health, he published the first volume of his *History of Georgia* in 1811 and the second in 1816.

As no person could write an adequate history of the colony

---

[1] First printed in 1849 under the title, *History of the Province of Georgia.*

and state without the use of many records in London, the legislature in 1837 resolved to have all these documents copied, and the next year Charles W. Howard was sent to do the work. He brought back a mass of material, the result of two years of labor, and deposited it in the state capitol. Unappreciative of the importance of preserving these records, the keeper loaned them to people who removed them, and forty-five years later they were destroyed in a fire which burned the home of an Emory College professor at Oxford, to which they had drifted.

In 1833 Georgia took time from the pursuit of her Cherokees to celebrate her hundredth birthday, to look back over a century of growth and to honor her founder. A half dozen years later there grew up in Savnnah an organization which was to continue without ceasing to collect and preserve the records of Georgia's past and to publish it to the people. It collected an invaluable library in its home, Hodgson Hall. This was the Georgia Historical Society, founded largely through the efforts of Israel K. Tefft, Richard D. Arnold, and William B. Stevens. John M. Berrien became its first president. This society, in 1841, asked Stevens, who was soon to become a professor in the University of Georgia, to write a history of the state. Under its patronage he wrote an excellent history, publishing the first volume in 1847 and the second, after he had removed to Pennsylvania, in 1859. He ended his account with the year 1798.

Stevens had used the valuable colonial documents before they went up in smoke. So did another historian of Georgia, who was, however, born a South Carolinian. The Reverend George White, first a communicant of the Methodist Church and then an Episcopal rector, becoming greatly interested in the history of his adopted state, wrote in 1849 his *Statistics of the State of Georgia* and four years later his more valuable *Historical Collections of Georgia*. Somewhat similar to the *Statistics* but briefer was the *Gazetteer of the State of Georgia,* which became a classic work in its day and thereafter. Written in 1827 by Adiel Sherwood, a New Yorker who had come to Georgia in 1818 and who had two years later become a Baptist minister, it passed through four editions by 1860. Pocket-size, it was a handy source of information on the state, counties, towns, villages, "and whatever is usual in statistical works."

Savannah was the outstanding literary and cultural center of the state in ante-bellum times. Here Israel K. Tefft gathered together a collection of autographs, unsurpassed in the country, which after his death was sold at auction in New York City. His friend A. A. Smets became interested in rare books and manuscripts and formed a collection of great value. The exigencies of war prevented the state from buying it after his death in 1862, and so in 1867 the collection was sold in New York City for $10,000. The most famous of the great Savannah collectors was George Wymberley Jones De Renne, great-grandson of Noble Jones, who confined his activities to works and manuscripts dealing with Georgia. Sherman's troops, when they reached Savannah, destroyed this valuable library; but De Renne, not to be discouraged, set about rebuilding his collection, which was later presented to the state. His son, Wymberley Jones De Renne, built up a collection of Georgiana which at his death in 1916 was unsurpassed anywhere.

Georgians in ante-bellum times engaged in other literary activities. There were poets of different degrees of magnitude. Thomas Holly Chivers, a strange and erratic soul, had the spark of genius which flashed in some of his poems so brightly as to attract and influence Edgar Allan Poe and win recognition for him abroad; Richard Henry Wilde, Irish-born, rested his poetic fame largely on one poem, "My Life is Like the Summer Rose"; and Henry Rootes Jackson handed down his name in various poems which some people read and one of which almost all Georgians learned, "The Red Old Hills of Georgia." As novelist, no Georgian ever reached the acclaim won by Francis R. Goulding, who wrote *Young Marooners,* a book which all children read who liked *Robinson Crusoe.*

In some of their literary endeavors Georgians may have

copied as much as they created, but in the field of humor, local color, and of realistic earthy characterizations they developed an originality which made them masters of their art. Augustus Baldwin Longstreet began in the early 'thirties his rollicking sketches of the manners and customs of his Georgians, first publishing them in various newspapers and bringing them out in book form in 1835 under the title of *Georgia Scenes.* William Tappan Thompson, born in Ohio but soon naturalized in Georgia, carried forward the Longstreet literary style in his *Major Jones's Courtship,* which appeared in 1840, *Major Jones's Chronicles of Pineville,* published three years later, and in various other works.

In scientific investigations few Georgians attained fame; but through long thought and study the brothers John and Joseph LeConte established a reputation in natural philosophy and geology which carried them from the University of Georgia to the College of South Carolina and thence to the University of California, which they made into a great institution; and Crawford W. Long, almost through accident, first discovered the anesthetic effects of sulphuric ether and thereby banished pain from the operating table.[2]

Newspapers were much more the handmaid of politics than evidence of any species of literature, though a thousand budding poets were able to induce editors to publish their esthetic longings; and sketches as able as those by Longstreet and Thompson frequently found their way into the press. Literary, moral, religious, agricultural, medical, and humorous publications, difficult at times to classify, sprang up to live a short time and then disappear; but the *Christian Index* of the Baptists, founded in 1821, has lived to become the oldest Baptist paper in the South, and the *Southern Cultivator,* founded in 1842, has outlived all its original contemporaries. Such literary publica-

[2] Failing to appreciate the importance of his discovery, Long did not immediately make it known to the medical profession. As a result he has never gained full credit for it.

tions as the *Southern Literary Gazette*, the *Orion*, the *Mirror*, the *Southern Miscellany*, and the *Counrtyman*, a paper published on a plantation in Putnam County, arose and soon disappeared. The *Horn of Mirth*, published in Athens for a short time in the 'fifties, outstripped in circulation all its neighbors. The *Southern Medical and Surgical Journal* began its existence in 1845 under the editorship of Paul F. Eve and I. P. Garvan. *The Schoolfellow: A Magazine for Girls and Boys*, edited by William C. Richards, ran its course during the 'forties and 'fifties. Up to the end of the Civil War, more than fifty literary magazines had been published in Georgia. The chief publication centers were Athens, Atlanta, Augusta, Eatonton, Griffin, Madison, Newnan, Penfield, and Savannah.

The strongest vitality was shown by the political newspapers, some of which attained a position of great respectability and influence. With the growing bitterness between North and South in the 'fifties, they greatly increased in numbers as well as in circulation. During this decade the number of newspapers and periodicals grew from 51 to 105 and their circulation jumped from 64,155 to 180,972. The circulation of the *Southern Watchman*, at Athens, increased from 700 to 6,700. Indeed, the people were preparing themselves to do more thinking than they had ever done before. Some of the outstanding papers at this time were the Augusta *Chronicle and Sentinel*, the Augusta *Constitutionalist*, the Columbus *Enquirer*, founded in 1828 by Mirabeau Bonaparte Lamar, later president of the Republic of Texas, the Macon *Georgia Telegraph*, the Milledgeville *Southern Recorder*, and the three Savannah papers, the *Daily Georgian*, *Daily Republican*, and *Daily News*.

Although Georgians were Christian by training and tradition, as late as 1831 not one-tenth of them belonged to any organized religious denomination; but during the next thirty years, by hard preaching and hard praying, Methodist, Baptist, and Presbyterian ministers brought about a vast increase in their membership. In 1844 a schism developed in the Methodist Church, caused by a dispute over the ownership of slaves by James O. Andrew, a Georgia bishop, and the Methodist Episcopal Church, South, grew up as a result. The next year Baptist unity was destroyed as the outcome of a refusal of the Foreign Mission Board to appoint slaveholders as missionaries. Instead of injuring the Methodist and Baptist churches in the South, these controversies were undoubtedly partly responsible for doubling within the next fifteen years the membership in each denomination. The camp-meeting had early been developed into a powerful institution, used principally by Methodists, to bring into the church the wayward.

In 1860 Georgia had 2,393 churches of the various denominations. This was a larger number than was to be found in any other Southern state excepting Virginia. At this time Georgia supported eleven religious denominations as follows: Baptists with 1,141 churches; Methodists, 1,035; Presbyterians, 125; Union, 27; Episcopalians, 25; Christians, 15; Lutherans, 9; Catholics, 8; Cumberland Presbyterians, 4; Universalists, 3; and Jews, 1.

As the slaves generally became associated with the religion professed by their owners, most of them were organized into Methodists and Baptists. Some of them had their own churches and preachers, and others attended the churches of their masters.

Some Georgians specialized in religion, some in literature and learning, others cared little about anything beyond taking care of their physical wants, but all could be easily aroused at the prospect of a political battle. The growing excitement produced by sectional hatreds during the last three decades of antebellum times made all Georgians politically-minded.

CHAPTER XXII

CALCULATING THE VALUE OF THE UNION

SLAVERY ALONE was not responsible for the war between the North and the South. Being more particularly the spectacular evidence of a civilization in the South different from what prevailed in the North, and being an institution opposed to the spirit of the times, it afforded an easy object of attack. As slavery was the keystone in the arch of Southern civilization, the South was maneuvered into a movement to set up a new nation, not so much to defend slavery as to protect the social and economic order which slavery made possible. In a final effort, the South was willing to give up slavery to win her independence and seek other means to preserve her own form of civilization. But even so, slavery was no mean part of that very civilization, and it would likely have been an impossibility for the South to save its ante-bellum self without the support of slavery. Without slavery, there would be a race problem; and the realization of this fact tied to this institution both slaveholders and non-slaveholders alike, and explains in part why all fought with equal bravery in the war that came.

Georgia was the heart and soul of the slavery South. With some slaves selling for as much as $2,000 each in 1860, her Negro property was worth more than all her land and cities combined. Though Georgians in their early statehood looked upon slavery as an evil and as late as 1821 one of them could declare it his conviction that not a single editor in the state dared advocate slavery as a principle, yet Georgia from the beginning held to her constitutional right to deal with slavery within her own boundaries. To her it was a matter of her honor and dignity and equality in the Union, and, indeed, the safety of her citizens; and so it was that in 1804 she passed a law declaring that anyone who incited slaves to insurrection should suffer death and that anyone who, by speech or writing, should incite slaves to "sedition, tumult or disorder" should be banished and if he should return he should be executed.

For years little cause for fear arose, until the ominous rumbles of trouble were sounded in the famous Missouri Compromise debates, which to Thomas Jefferson, old and wanting peace, sounded like a fire-bell in the night. It disturbed Georgians and made them look with startled suspicions upon the slightest criticisms of slavery. While the Missouri question was yet unsettled, a devastating fire swept Savannah, burned 463 houses, and produced estimated losses, direct and indirect, amounting to $10,000,000. Sympathy and aid came from all parts of the country, but out of this calamity and the resultant generosity of New York City arose a bitter sectional dispute. The New Yorkers sent more than $10,000 in money and a few thousands more in goods, with the admonition that all indigent people, "without distinction of color," should be aided. The proud Savannahians took this proviso as an insult, gratuitous and insufferable, and refused to accept the contribution, with the threat that the spirit in which New York City made the gift, if persisted in, would ultimately lead to the destruction of the Union. The Pennsylvania legislature, which had given $10,000, maddened by Savannah's attitude, considered for a time withdrawing its gift. That so unfortunate a dispute should arise in such a time of distress over so trivial a matter, showed how deeply the question of slavery had entered the souls of Georgians.

From this time on until the Civil War, it was easier to provoke a dispute with Georgians over slavery than on any other issue; their suspicions increased and their nerves became more and more frayed. That Governor Troup, a master at disputing, should have found time to leave his Creeks for a tilt over slaves was to be expected. He pounced upon William Wirt, the attorney-general of the United States, and accused him of attacking slavery before the Supreme Court, and he was made to desist only when Wirt brought proof, including a statement from Chief Justice Marshall, that no attack had been made. In 1827 a committee of the Georgia senate declared that it could not "avoid reprobating the cold-blooded selfishness, or unthinking zeal which actuates many of our fellow citizens in other States, to an interference with our local concerns and domestic relations, totally unwarranted whether by humanity or constitutional right. . . . The result of such interference, if persevered in, is awful and inevitable."

In the early 'thirties there arose with little warning one of the strangest phenomena in history. For two hundred years slavery had existed in English America and there had been a few voices in North and South raised against it; but beginning in the miraculous 'thirties, the thoughtful emancipation movement suddenly swept into a violent abolition crusade. Now arose William Lloyd Garrison, who advocated instant action without compromise, and who spurned the government which permitted slavery by publicly burning a copy of the constitution of the United States and declaring it was "a covenant with death and an agreement with hell." About this time Nat Turner's bloody insurrection took place in Virginia, and the South, excited and angry, declared Garrison and his abolitionists were responsible for it. Georgia offered a reward of $5,000 for the arrest and conviction of Garrison or anyone connected with his paper, the *Liberator*. Although Garrison was the best-known abolitionist and the most detested, Theodore D. Weld worked back of the scene in a more effective way, among his activities, writing anonymously a rabid attack on the South, called *American Slavery as it is: Testimony of a Thousand Witnesses*.

In 1835 Governor William Schley declared that the abolitionists were "a sect of crazed enthusiasts who are endeavoring to enlist insurrection and rapine, conflagration and massacre,

under the banner of philanthropy." As Northerners and Southerners arrayed themselves against each other, they lost their
reason as their passions carried them forward, and they sought
no longer to understand each other. They became as two alien
peoples, and so deeply did they mistrust each other that they
parted their Christian union and sought God in opposite directions. The sanction which the church in each section gave to
the bitterness had vast weight in arraying the masses against
each other. Expressing the feeling of the plowman no less than
the Congressman, the Sarepta Association of Baptists, meeting
in Elbert County in 1835, declared that it looked upon the
abolitionists "scattering their incendiary publications among
us, as unchristian and wicked," that they were "intermeddlers
with that which does not concern them," and that it dis-
approved of their "nefarious schemes" and viewed them "as
destructive to the cause of religion, and the occasion of a foul
slander upon the friends of benevolence."

It was in the political arena where the contest went on in the
most spectacular manner. Few measures could be proposed in
the national government which escaped the scorching heat of
the slavery issue, and with the passing of time such a fury was
whipped up that people cried Union when there was none; and
secession in time came as a recognition of the melancholy fact
that the country was already divided—in religion, in politics,
and in every kindly regard and feeling of friendship. And then
Robert Toombs could no longer say, "Our greatest danger is
that the Union will survive the Constitution."

In 1835 the war for Texan independence began which in-
tensified a train of events in American politics, leading straight
to a disruption of the Union. The movement into that part of
Mexico called Texas, begininng in the 'twenties, was made up
largely of Southerners, and among them were many Georgians.
Mirabeau Bonaparte Lamar went in time to assume a position
of leadership so important as to make him later the second
president of the Republic of Texas, and James W. Fannin

arrived in time to lead a small army to their death at the Goliad massacre in 1836. Joanna B. Troutman could not join the Georgians who left Macon for Texas in 1835 to fight for Texan independence, but she presented to them a white silken flag with a lone blue star in the center, saw it adopted as the flag of the new republic, and now rests in the "Texas Arlington" in Austin.

Texans were in fact Americans who had set up a republic out of Mexican territory, and what they wanted most was not independence but admission into the American Union. A strong opinion existed in the North and among Whigs generally that Texas ought not to be admitted, some opposing it because they feared it would produce a war with Mexico, and others because it would add more slave territory to the Union. The presidential election of 1844 was fought on the Texas question, with Henry Clay, the Whig candidate, opposing annexation, and James K. Polk, the Democrat, demanding the "Re-annexation of Texas." Though the Whigs had carried Georgia in 1840 for Harrison in the "hard cider log cabin campaign," they lost it in 1844, for too many Georgians were wedded to Texas by ties of kinship and were convinced that Texas would give the South powerful support in the Union.

What Henry Clay had feared and predicted soon happened. The Mexicans had never recognized the independence of Texas, and they had announced that if the United States annexed it, they would declare war. Fighting began in 1846 and lasted for two years. Georgia was enthusiastic; she responded to all calls for troops, and such Georgians as Josiah Tattnall, David E. Twiggs, and W. H. T. Walker rose to positions of prominence. Many people in the North bitterly opposed this war as the act of a mighty land-grabbing nation despoiling an innocent weakling, all for the power and glory of the slaveholders. This attitude was assumed by many Whigs, including a considerable number in Georgia. Alexander H. Stephens, now in the United States House of Representatives, had not been enthusiastic for the annexation of Texas and he now held that the Mexican War had been unconstitutionally begun and that it was Polk's war. John M. Berrien, in the United States Senate, held similar views.

Yet strangely enough, Stephens and his Whigs seized the opportunity in 1848 to capitalize the Mexican War by running for president Zachary Taylor, the old hero of Buena Vista. Georgians, fearing the attitude Lewis Cass, the Democratic candidate, might take on the slavery question, gave their state to Taylor, who was a slaveholder.

In the meantime, a furor had been raised in Congress which spread throughout the country and gravely threatened the disruption of the Union. In 1846, at the beginning of the Mexican War, David Wilmot, a Pennsylvania Democrat, tacked onto a bill in Congress a proviso that no territory secured from Mexico should be open to slavery, and although it did not pass, it was re-introduced time and again during the next few years to enrage and embitter the South. In the treaty of peace with Mexico a vast area, composing today the southwestern part of the United States, was secured, and if the Wilmot Proviso had been adopted, it would have prevented the South from taking her slaves into this region.

Georgia looked upon this threat as a brutal insult and an attempt to deprive her and the rest of the South of their position of equality in the Union. In the excitement which developed, Georgians began to talk of secession; and throughout the country dark clouds arose. The more radical Southerners began to make preparations for a convention to meet in Nashville, Tennessee, to determine the course the South should follow. Georgia elected her delegates in April, 1850, who were led by the fiery Henry L. Benning and Charles J. McDonald. At the convention, which met in June, much talk of secession was indulged in. It adjourned without adopting a program, but as a threat it reassembled in November. Again, it took no impor-

Top left: JOSEPH HENRY LUMPKIN, GRADUATE OF PRINCETON, CHIEF JUSTICE OF THE STATE SUPREME COURT, AND LAW TEACHER. *Top right:* CRAWFORD W. LONG, FIRST TO USE SULPHURIC ETHER AS AN ANAESTHESIA, 1842. *Bottom left:* JOSEPH E. BROWN, FOUR TIMES GOVERNOR, JUSTICE OF THE STATE SUPREME COURT, UNITED STATES SENATOR, AND INDUSTRIALIST. *Bottom right:* JOHN M. BERRIEN, GRADUATE OF PRINCETON, FOUR TIMES UNITED STATES SENATOR, AND ATTORNEY-GENERAL IN ANDREW JACKSON'S CABINET.

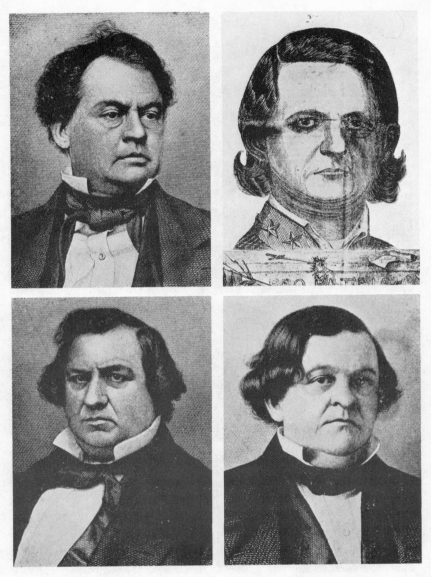

Top left: ROBERT TOOMBS, CHAMPION OF THE ANTE-BELLUM SOUTH, PLANTER-CAPITALIST, AND STATESMAN. *Top right:* THOMAS R. R. COBB, PASSIONATE SECESSIONIST, AUTHOR OF THE CONFEDERATE STATE CONSTITUTION, AND BRIGADIER-GENERAL IN THE CONFEDERACY. *Bottom left:* HERSCHEL V. JOHNSON, GOVERNOR, VICE-PRESIDENTIAL CANDIDATE IN 1860, AND UNITED STATES AND CONFEDERATE SENATOR. *Bottom right:* HOWELL COBB, MEMBER OF THE HOUSE OF REPRESENTATIVES AND SPEAKER, SECRETARY OF THE TREASURY UNDER JAMES BUCHANAN, AND MAJOR-GENERAL IN THE CONFEDERACY.

tant steps, for in the meantime other people had been busy trying to solve the difficulties.

At the very time the Nashville Convention was holding its first session, Henry Clay, Daniel Webster, Alexander H. Stephens, and other national leaders were working out a compromise, which was adopted in five separate measures, and came to be called the Compromise of 1850. California was permitted to come into the Union as a free state and the Wilmot Proviso was dropped. Other issues were settled by prohibiting the slave-trade in the District of Columbia, the passing of a new fugitive slave law, and by satisfying Texas on her boundary claims.

Would this Compromise be acceptable to the South? The position Georgia should take would likely decide the question. She would make her decision in a convention called to meet in the fall; and now a spirited campaign took place for delegates. Party lines began to crumble as the radicals and the conservatives separated. The former early held a meeting in Macon where they heard Robert Barnwell Rhett, of South Carolina, and William L. Yancey, of Alabama, vigorously denounce the Compromise. To defend this last hope of saving the Union, Howell Cobb, the Democratic speaker of the House of Representatives, and Robert Toombs and Alexander H. Stephens, Whig Congressmen, hastened to offer their aid to the conservatives. The conservative or Union element predominated in the convention, which assembled in Milledgeville in December, and they adopted the famous Georgia Platform, written by Charles J. Jenkins. In this platform, they admitted that the South had suffered great provocation, but they held that the Compromise should be accepted as the only alternative to the destruction of the Union. The convention, however, warned the North that Georgia had reached the limit of her patience and that she would not recede further.

The Georgia Platform saved the Union in 1850, as the other Southern states followed Georgia's lead and accepted the Compromise. The issues cut so deeply that they severed party lines and led to the rise in Georgia of the Constitutional Union Party, managed by Cobb, Toombs, and Stephens, and made up of all Union people, whether Whigs or Democrats. The radicals who refused to be satisfied organized the Southern Rights Party. In the campaign for governor in 1851, the Constitutional Union Party, which in fact had the Whigs as its backbone, ran a Democrat, Howell Cobb, and elected him. The Southern Rights Party ran Charles J. McDonald, of Nashville Convention fame. The fact that the Union party elected Cobb by a majority of 18,000 votes showed how weak the radicals had been.

Chaos now reigned among Georgians in their national party affiliations. Northern Whigs and Southern Whigs were finding it increasingly difficult to agree on the questions that were upsetting the country. In preparing for the presidential campaign of 1852 the Constitutional Union Party was confronted with the problem of which national party it belonged to. The Democrats in it wanted to merge it with the national Democrats, but the Whigs who made up the bulk of the party refused. The party now broke up, with the Democrats going their way, and with the Whigs having no refuge, for they were determined not to support General Winfield Scott, the Whig candidate. They formed themselves a special ticket with Daniel Webster for president and their own Charles J. Jenkins as vice-presidential candidate.

The Southern Rights Party, who were in fact mostly Democrats, readily embraced the Democratic national ticket, and the Democrats who had formerly been in the Constitutional Union Party supported the same ticket. Franklin Pierce, the Democratic candidate for president, carried Georgia by a big majority; though the unterrified Whigs gave Daniel Webster more than 5,000 votes despite the fact that he had died before the election.

In the election of the governor in 1853, the political situation was clarified still further. Now most of the Whigs who had not decided to stay in the Democratic Party called themselves the Union Party and ran their former vice-presidential candidate, Charles J. Jenkins, for governor. The Democrats, again united, nominated Herschel V. Johnson and elected him.

In 1854 the Whig Party was given the *coup de grâce* by the passage of the Kansas-Nebraska Bill. Northern and Southern Whigs parted company forever on the question of the repeal of the Missouri Compromise and the organization of the territories of Kansas and Nebraska. The Georgia Whigs, like Stephens and Toombs, who could bring themselves to join the Democrats did so; and the others, like Benjamin H. Hill and Eugenius A. Nisbet, went off after strange gods and joined a political group popularly called the Know-Nothing Party, but officially known as the American Party. Civil war soon broke out in Kansas between those who would make it a slave state and those who would make it free, and the term "Bleeding Kansas" now became a rallying slogan in the North to arouse the people against the South. In line with the other states, Georgia sent her immigrants to Kansas, though not armed with "Beecher's Bibles," another name for Sharpe's rifles, as were those who went out from New England. In 1854 there arose a new party, the Republicans, made up of radical people, who were not afraid to take a decisive stand against the extension of slavery into the territories. In the presidential campaign of 1856 they ran for president John C. Frémont, who had been born in Savannah, and announced their eternal opposition to the extension of slavery one square inch.

Georgia and the rest of the South looked upon the Republican Party as their undisguised enemies who by a perversion of the Constitution would cheat them out of their rightful place in the Union; and many threats were heard that secession would be justified and carried out if Frémont were elected. In 1854 James N. Bethune set up in Columbus the *Corner Stone,* which was the only newspaper in the South at that time advocating immediate secession. The next year Hiram Warner declared that Georgia would soon likely be forced to secede. As the presidential election drew near, in 1856, Herschel V. Johnson, who strongly loved the Union, declared that the success of Frémont would drive the South into secession; and Howell Cobb, who loved the Union no less, announced that he would help withdraw Georgia if the Republicans elected Frémont.

The Democrats nominated James Buchanan for president. The conservatively inclined people, both North and South, united on him and elected him, although Millard Fillmore, the candidate of the Know-Nothings, drew many votes which otherwise would have gone to the Democrats. Georgia gave Buchanan a majority of more than 14,000.

In the election for governor the preceding year, Herschel V. Johnson won for the Democrats by a majority of 10,000 over Garnett Andrews, the Know-Nothing. In this campaign the Temperance Party ran B. H. Overby, a Methodist preacher, and polled 6,000 votes.

Events in state and nation now moved swiftly toward the destruction of the Union. In 1857 the Democrats in their convention at Milledgeville, after a fruitless effort through twenty ballots to nominate a governor, compromised on a candidate, little known to the state but soon to dominate Georgia as completely as Andrew Jackson did the nation a generation previously. This man was Joseph E. Brown, who was born in South Carolina but who early removed to the hills of Georgia. There persevering through poverty, he prepared himself for a career, which must have been as surprising to him as it was to his fellow-citizens. Little suspecting the nomination, he was in the midst of his wheat field, harvesting grain, at the moment he was chosen. The aristocratic element in Georgia looked upon the selection of this North Georgia mountaineer almost with consternation, and Toombs was said to have exclaimed on hearing of the nomination, "Who in the hell is Joe Brown!"

Beginning the campaign under the tutelage of Toombs, who soon became reconciled, Brown early demonstrated his ability to take care of himself, even in a joint campaign with Benjamin H. Hill, whom the Know-Nothings had set up against him. Brown won by a majority of 10,000, and immediately startled Georgia with his boldness in the governor's chair. He effectively stopped the saturnalia of drinking and rowdyism at the inauguration exercises, which heretofore had almost wrecked the mansion every two years, and set up in its place orderly receptions every Friday night. In statecraft and in the state's business he applied himself as assiduously and as minutely as if he were managing his own personal affairs. He appointed John W. Lewis superintendent of the Western and Atlantic Railroad, and so economically did he and Brown manage the property that they were accused of walking the tracks to pick up loose spikes; but in the end, they increased the income of the railroad from $43,000 annually to $450,000 in 1860. The panic of 1857 caused many banks in Georgia to suspend specie payment. Brown, having much the same attitude toward banks which Andrew Jackson had displayed, vetoed the legislation legalizing the suspension, and on being unsuccessful, carried the fight to the people.

Brown's first term made him the inevitable Democratic candidate for another term. In the campaign of 1859, he easily defeated Warren Akin, a Methodist preacher and lawyer in Brown's own part of the state, who was the candidate of the Know-Nothings. Coming from the mountainous part of the state, Brown might well have taken an uncompromising position for the Union; but he soon became as pronounced in his determination to defend Southern rights as Toombs himself. He loved the Union, but when the equality of the states in that Union no longer existed he would stand for independence. There was much searching of hearts in Georgia. Senator Alfred Iverson made a warning speech at Griffin in July, 1859, in which he pictured the inevitable necessity of organizing a

Southern confederacy within the next few years, though Alexander H. Stephens insisted that Georgia's rights were still safe in the Union.

Just before Brown's second inaugural, John Brown made his insane attempt to free the slaves through force, by seizing Harper's Ferry. No more successful act could have been devised to cut the last tie of friendship and understanding which bound the South to the North. Mistaking the fanatical John Brown as representative of Northerners generally, the Georgia legislature passed resolutions declaring that fanaticism had now brought to its aid treason and that murder and rapine had crossed the border and were invading the South. Governor Brown called on Georgia to prepare for the inevitable, by reforming her militia and by setting up powder works and ammunition factories.

CHAPTER XXIII

GEORGIA SECEDES

THE SNAPPING of the last bond of union, the secession of most of the Southern states, four years of bitter war, a decade of blundering reconstruction—such were the events which, beginning in 1860, marched across the national stage for the next fifteen years. During this time Georgia's golden age in the nation's history was to fade away, and with the remainder of the Southern states she was destined to assume long the position of an outer province.

In April, 1860, the Democratic Party held its national convention in Charleston, South Carolina. For the purpose of selecting delegates, the Georgia Democrats held a convention in Milledgeville in December, 1859. Their decision to support Howell Cobb for the presidency produced dissensions over the state which led to a second convention in the following March. Cobb generously removed himself as a disturbing influence, but the Georgia Democrats went to Charleston with upset feelings which augured nothing good.

With the national Democracy no better unified than the Georgia Democrats, the Charleston convention soon broke up over the question of slavery in the territories; and the far South, including most of the Georgia delegates, withdrew. Each wing of the national party now called conventions at separate places, the Northerners at Baltimore and the Southerners at Richmond. Georgia Democrats, genuinely upset by this schism in their party, tried to agree on delegates and a program of united action, but being unable to do so, they sent delegates to both places. Failing to be admitted in Baltimore, the Georgians joined in another hall other Southern delegates who had gained admittance but later had seceded, and nominated John C. Breckinridge for president and Joseph Lane for vice-president. Those who had gone to Richmond ratified there these nominations. The main Democratic convention in Baltimore nominated Stephen A. Douglas of Illinois for president and Herschel V. Johnson of Georgia for vice-president, although Georgia was not represented in the convention. Other Georgians who still could not bring themselves around to become Democrats gave their support to the nomination of a Tennesseean, John Bell, who ran as the champion of a group calling itself the Constitutional Union Party.

In the national election, the confusion in Georgia was almost as great as it was in the nation at large; but the Georgians had one less candidate to vote for than had people in the North, for it was unthinkable that a Georgian would vote for Abraham Lincoln, the Republican nominee. John C. Breckinridge received 51,893 votes, John Bell, 42,855, and Stephen A. Douglas, 11,580. As no candidate received a majority of the votes, the legislature a few weeks later was forced to make a choice. Though Governor Brown was so indignant over the election of Lincoln that he advised the legislature to refuse to go through with a task which could not change the results, this body nevertheless went ahead and chose the Breckinridge electors.

During the presidential campaign, threats had been loud in Georgia and throughout the South that if Lincoln were elected, the Southern states would be forced to secede. There had long been in the South two questions concerning secession: should the Southern states coöperate and secede together, or should each state act for itself when it was ready. Now that Lincoln had been elected and secession was upon the South, quick action was necessary. If coöperation were attempted, there would be delay and the excitement might subside. So it turned out that radical secessionists opposed coöperation, and Unionists supported it. On December 20th, South Carolina seceded and set the style for separate state action.

Many Georgians were no less anxious to take quick and separate action, and if Governor Brown had had his desire fulfilled, Georgia might have seceded even before South Carolina. When the legislature met on November 7th, the day after the election, Brown had reason to believe that the "Black Republicans" had succeeded. He sent two messages to the legislature. One dealt entirely with Federal relations, and in this document Brown bitterly condemned the Northern states and called for quick action. He would make no attempt to have a convention of the Southern states as all of the states would likely not attend. Instead, if it turned out that the "Black Republicans have triumphed over us," he would recommend a state convention to devise means to protect Georgia "against the further aggressions of an enemy, which, when flushed with victory, will be insolent in the hour of triumph." He recommended the immediate appropriation of $1,000,000 for arming the state, and ended his appeal with a call to arms—no more concession, no more compromise, "The argument is exhausted."

Suddenly confronted with the necessity of making a final decision in a quarrel so long drawn out as to become almost a habit of thought, Georgians were awed and stunned; but leaders soon arose on all sides to offer their advice. It was popular to urge action and end forever Northern aggressions and insults, and on this wave of enthusiasm Georgia was ultimately swept out of the Union. As secession would be a step of tremendous consequences and unknown in American history, it should not be taken lightly. The plan adopted by Georgia and nearly all the other Southern states was to have the legislature call a convention of the people, who should thereby have a chance to express their views in the election of delegates. But first the legislators must be induced to act, and in Georgia, with Brown's message ringing in their ears, they set out upon the road. Soon this body was under a barrage of advice. Thomas R. R. Cobb went down to Milledgeville from the red hills of Athens and on November 12th charmed the legislature with his secession oratory; Robert Toombs the next day added his ponderous voice to the chorus; W. L. Harris, a commissioner from Mississippi, brought reassurances from his state; and the fiery Robert Barnwell Rhett from South Carolina and the no-less-determined Edmund Ruffin from Virginia called upon Georgia to act. Amidst this clamor for secession was heard the squeaky voice but sound counsel of sickly Alexander H. Stephens, calling for the legislature not to stampede the state out of a union which the South had made and which was still the South's greatest protection.

Excitement ruled the day; counties all over the state held meetings and most of them passed resolutions calling upon the legislature for action. On November 21st Governor Brown had the pleasure of signing a bill requiring the people to vote for delegates on January 2nd, who should two weeks later assemble in Milledgeville as a sovereign convention, there to determine the future course Georgia would take. The legislature, following the other recommendations of the governor, appropriated $1,000,000 for state defense, authorized the acceptance of 10,000 troops, and provided for fostering the organization of volunteer companies and arming them. It also suggested that if the Southern states should secede they should form a Southern confederacy.

The attention of Georgians was next turned to the election of delegates to their sovereign convention, for the legislature faded out of the picture when it handed over the destiny of the state to a group of delegates yet to be elected. It was popular to talk for secession, and the movement for it grew stronger. Congressmen from the slaveholding states issued an address on December 13th, declaring that there was no Union and that the South could save its honor only by seceding; Howell Cobb resigned the secretaryship of the treasury, which he held in Buchanan's cabinet, returned to Georgia, and called for immediate secession; Robert Toombs, Thomas R. R. Cobb, and many others of lesser note did not relax in their efforts to promote secession; and Wilson Lumpkin, tottering on the brink of the grave, called on the state to vindicate its honor. All recited the insults of the North and its denial of the rights of the South, how Lincoln would rivet the chains of slavery on the South, how secession would be peaceable, and how if the South should want to come back into the Union, it could make better terms on the outside than on the inside. Governor Brown, who represented peculiarly well the non-slaveholding Georgians, sought to scare them into secession by cleverly declaring that if the slaves should be freed, then the United States would be forced to raise $2,000,000,000 by taxation with which to pay for them, that the former slaveholders would receive the money and with it buy up all the land and make tenants of all the small farmers. If the free Negroes should be colonized, it would require a great deal more money, which the taxpayers must raise, and if the Negroes should not be colonized, then they would remain to compete with the laboring white people, and demand social and political equality. Furthermore, secession would not bring war, as Buchanan had already said that the United States had no right to coerce a state.

To combat these arguments of the secessionists Alexander H. Stephens, Benjamin H. Hill, Herschel V. Johnson, and many lesser leaders showed how secession would bring on the bloodiest war in history, how the election of Lincoln was not a sufficient cause for secession, as the Republicans could pass no hostile legislation, since they lacked thirty votes of controlling the House of Representatives and four of controlling the Senate.

In the midst of this campaign, South Carolina seceded, and the excitement it produced throughout the South aided the secession movement. In Atlanta there was a balloon ascension, cannon were fired from noon to nightfall, and when darkness set in a torchlight procession kept up the celebration.

The people voted and those who stood for action won 50,000 to 37,000. The slaveholders and townspeople were the backbone of the secession movement, whereas the mountaineers and pine barrens settlers cast their support for the Union. Yet there were some Georgians, made conservative by their wealth and position, who voted for the Union.

The convention met on January 16th, and never before had the state brought together so completely its leadership. Whether the decision these delegates should make would be wise or not, the people had placed the power in their wisest leaders. Almost every person of note had been included in this convention, excepting Governor Brown, Howell Cobb, and C. J. Jenkins, and these three were invited by the convention to take seats in it. Influences, hidden and open, set to work. The battle against secession seemed lost at the outset, yet Stephens, Hill, and Johnson sought to stay its progress by introducing a proposition calling for a convention of the Southern states to decide on what should be done. This move was voted down 166 to 130. Then a secession ordinance was offered by Eugenius A. Nisbet and it was carried by a vote of 208 to 89. Thus Georgia declared herself a sovereign and independent state on January 19, 1861; and two days later, to show that, since the act was done, all stood as one in maintaining that independence, each member of the convention signed his name to the ordinance.

A momentous step had been taken; Georgia had declared herself an independent republic. As she had no intention of remaining so, long, a few days later the convention appointed delegates to gather with delegates from other seceded states at Montgomery, Alabama, there to organize the Confederate States of America. Her delegates were her most able leaders, such as the Cobb brothers, Benjamin H. Hill, Alexander H. Stephens, and E. A. Nisbet. At the convention, which met in February, they took a leading part in organizing the new government. Howell Cobb became president of the convention; Thomas R. R. Cobb was largely responsible for writing the Confederate constitution; Toombs seems to have missed becoming president of the Confederacy by a strange freak of fate;

and Stephens, by insistent declinations to his friends, escaped becoming the president only to land in the vice-presidency.

Having declared her independence of all past political connections, Georgia was in the meantime under the power of her sovereign convention. It continued its sessions until January 29th, when it adjourned to meet again at the call of its president. On March 7th, it convened in Savannah. This convention acted as a legislature and passed various ordinances and resolutions. It appointed commissioners to go to other Southern states to induce them to secede; it provided further for the raising and equipping of troops; on March 16th, it adopted the Confederate constitution and made Georgia a state in the new Confederacy; it turned over its forts and war equipment to the new government; it offered the Confederacy ten square miles of Georgia territory for a capital; and it appointed a committee to revise the old constitution of 1798 to make it conform to new conditions. Thomas R. R. Cobb, who seemed to be the chief constitution-maker and reviser of his times, dominated the committee and was largely responsible for the new document. It was submitted to the people and adopted in July following.

On January 23rd all of Georgia's representatives in the United States Congress resigned; and the next month when Jefferson Davis, the newly elected president of the Confederacy, passed through Georgia on his way to Montgomery, he was received with great enthusiasm all along the line.

In the meantime, Governor Brown had not been inactive. The principal Federal fortification in Georgia was Fort Pulaski, on the Savannah River, below Savannah, unoccupied but containing a little ammunition and a few old cannon. Now that South Carolina and the Charlestonians were having so much anxiety over Fort Sumter, Georgia and Savannahians were not going to be treated in like manner by one of their forts. The excitement in Savannah was sufficient for a descent upon the fort from that city, had not Governor Brown ordered its occupation on January 3rd. This forward move by Brown had taken place more than two weeks before Georgia seceded, and had the fort been garrisoned by Federal troops, Fort Pulaski instead óf Fort Sumter might have set off the Civil War.

For a few weeks following January 19th, when Georgia seceded, Brown was in theory not simply the governor of the state of Georgia but president of the republic of Georgia. He was not slow to act the part. It was unthinkable that he would peaceably permit a foreign power to hold possession of any portion of his dominions. The United States continued to occupy the arsenal at Augusta; on January 22nd, Brown hastened there and demanded the surrender of this property; and to emphasize his demand 800 Georgia troops made their appearance. Capt. Arnold Elzey, who had no force with which to defend the place, was instructed from Washington to make the best terms possible; and on the 24th, with honor to all he surrendered the arsenal, with its heavy artillery, 22,000 rifles, powder and other ammunition. The United States flag was lowered and the Georgia flag, a white field with a lone red star in the center, was run up while artillery fired a salute. Brown gave a receipt for the material in the arsenal so that a just settlement might be made later. To conclude the exercises Captain Elzey and Colonel W. H. T. Walker, to whom he surrendered, embraced each other and drank toasts. So thoroughly impressed was Elzey with the enemy that he later cast his lot with them and became an officer in the Confederacy.

That Brown considered Georgia's relations with some of the Northern states not very amicable was evident even before Georgia seceded. In 1860 Governor Brown advised the withdrawal of the protection of the Georgia laws from citizens of the offending states; and early in 1861 he had an opportunity to carry out this oft-made threat to protect Georgia property in Northern states, by appropriate actions in Georgia. On January 22nd the New York police seized 200 rifles belonging to a business firm in Macon. Brown's demand on Governor E. D.

Morgan of New York for an immediate surrender went unanswered and unheeded. Establishing the fact that the New York governor had received his demands, Brown seized five vessels in Savannah harbor, belonging to New York citizens, and ordered them either to be held until the guns were released or be sold at auction. Events moved swiftly. News came to Brown that the guns had been released; thereupon, he allowed the ships to sail away. But Brown had been tricked; the guns were still held. He immediately seized two other New York vessels in Savannah and ordered them to be sold at auction; but before the time for the sale had arrived Brown was given unimpeachable evidence that the guns had been released and were on the high seas beyond the reach of New York.

The Confederate government was set up during the gun trouble Brown was having; and though logic might have indicated that Brown should finish the business, yet strict constitutional practice would have demanded that the Confederate government take over the quarrel. The Confederate Congress felt that it was no longer a Georgia matter but a Confederate concern. Brown thought otherwise and continued to the end. In the future, the Confederate government was to learn that Brown was a force to be reckoned with, both for weal and for woe.

CHAPTER XXIV

IN TIME OF WAR

GOVERNOR BROWN took as much interest in managing Georgia as if it had been his farm, and throughout the war he watched over Georgia property and Georgia people with a sharpness often more zealous than wise.

Though the secessionists had predicted that there would be no war, it was still the part of wisdom to be prepared, and so preparations which had been started before Georgia seceded were hastened thereafter. Brown, who had recently had his troubles in securing munitions of war from the North, both for individual Georgians and for the state government, now turned to the Tredegar Iron Works in Richmond and to other munition factories in the Confederacy. He also sent agents to Europe to buy war equipment, and he encouraged the building of armories in Georgia.

The state made considerable progress in manufacturing its own arms. The government offered a bonus of $10,000 to anyone setting up a cannon factory which could make three guns a week and could cast a ten-inch columbiad. The penitentiary was transformed into an armory in 1862 and within a short time it was able to turn out 125 rifles a month. Munition works sprang up in Augusta, Macon, Columbus, and Athens and manufactured large numbers of rifles and sabers. Atlanta came to be one of the greatest munition centers in the Confederacy and was made by the Confederate army its headquarters for the quartermaster and commissary departments. In Augusta the Confederacy set up its largest powder factory, where there was turned out during the course of the war 2,750,000 pounds. To arm the Home Guards, in 1863 Governor Brown had con-

structed an ugly weapon consisting of a dagger on the end of
a pole, to be used in fighting at close quarters and popularly
known as a "Joe Brown pike." In gathering up the metals
necessary for war the munition-makers were presented church
bells by patriotic congregations and were invited to strip the
premises of many Georgia homes.

So successful was Brown in arming the state that the impression was soon abroad over the Confederacy that Georgia
had more arms than she could use and that she was selfishly
withholding them from the other states. Toombs strengthened
this belief when he said, "Joe Brown has more arms than the
whole Confederacy." The fact was that after the first few
months Georgia was in as dire a need of arms as were any of
the other states of the Confederacy.

For the purpose of bringing about a trade connection with
Europe whereby ships would sail directly to and from Savannah, Governor Brown sent Thomas Butler King to England
and Belgium. In pursuance of an arrangement he made with a
Belgian steamship company, the Georgia legislature incorporated in 1860 the Belgian American Company and pledged
$100,000 annually as a guarantee to it of profits of not less
than 5% on its investment. The next year Georgia chartered
the Direct Trade and Navigation Company, capitalized at
$3,000,000, to engage in domestic and foreign commerce. The
blockade which President Lincoln set up against the ports of
the Confederacy gradually put a stop to the activities of these
companies.

Believing with most Southerners that a cotton famine in
England and France would lead those nations to break the
blockade in order to get Confederate cotton, Brown forbade its
exportation. From the very beginning adventuresome Georgians engaged in blockade-running, and despite Brown's embargo, they carried out much cotton. Trading through the
blockade came to be the most lucrative business a person could
take up. Alexander H. Stephens had never believed that a

cotton embargo was wise, but not until 1863 was Brown convinced. Now he induced the legislature to appropriate $750,000 to be used in chartering fast blockade-runners, and within a short time the state government was carrying cotton to Europe and bringing back much valuable war equipment. To relieve the blockade-runners from making the long voyage to Europe, enterprising traders collected vast stores of material at Nassau, on one of the Bahamas, and with this port Georgia did most of her business.

Just as Georgia should organize for war by arming herself, also she should adjust her agriculture to the new conditions. Cotton had long been considered king, and the feeling that this was so had had much to do with leading the Southern states to secede with such confidence in ultimate success. At first Georgia attempted to take care of her cotton planters, whose market was greatly upset by the blockade, by organizing the Cotton Planters' Bank. It was hoped that this bank would stabilize the price of cotton by issuing a medium of exchange based on warehouse receipts. But, it soon became apparent that cotton should be dethroned, and that agriculture should be turned into raising foodstuffs, for the spectre of starvation loomed up before the far-seers as the greatest enemy the Confederate armies would have to confront. A popular movement was aroused against raising cotton; those who planted this crop were looked upon as traitors and those who raised corn and other foodstuffs were considered the greatest patriots. To stay the hand of those who placed the possible profits of cotton-raising over patriotism, laws were passed in the latter part of 1862 limiting each able-bodied workman to three acres of cotton and imposing a fine of $500 for each acre in excess. Thereafter, throughout the war the amount of cotton grown decreased tremendously.

The fall of cotton did not insure a food supply, for the distilleries set feverishly to work to make Georgia grain into whiskey to take the place of the Kentucky supply which had been cut off by the hard exigencies of war. Governor Brown, who had long been a temperance advocate, quickly met the menace by a proclamation in February, 1862. In it he declared that he knew one county in which there were "about seventy stills . . . constantly boiling and consuming more grain than was necessary to feed the whole population of the county." The metal used in the stills over the state would "make many a battery of six-pounders, to be turned against the enemy." Therefore he forbade the further manufacture of corn into whiskey. A militia officer who dared to disobey Brown's proclamation was arrested, courtmartialed, and fined $500. When the legislature met in the following November it translated Brown's proclamation into a law which forbade the distillation of any kind of grain into whiskey except for "medicinal, hospital, chemical or mechanical purposes." The thirst of Georgians outrunning the power and ingenuity of the law-makers soon broke out in the erection of illicit stills which began the distillation of such food products as molasses, sweet potatoes, pumpkins, peas, and dried fruit. The legislature made a counter attack the next year in a law which forbade the distillation of all the articles of food legislative wisdom could enumerate. But even so, Governor Brown with all the power of his government was never able to put down the whiskey-makers.

Brown was so intensely patriotic to Georgia that he never could grasp completely nor understand the problems and purposes of the Confederacy as a whole. He was pervaded too much with the short-sighted view that as long as Georgia remained free from hostile invasion all was well. He wanted Georgia troops left in Georgia; he wanted nothing done which would interfere with his running the state. As a result he was soon to come into inevitable and bitter conflict with the Confederate government when it established a policy of merging the welfare of each state into the common good of the Confederacy, by which all should succeed or fall together.

The length to which the quarrel went threatened at times

to provide a bigger problem for President Davis than meeting the Federal armies. Brown strangely talked about the Confederate president's being as great an enemy to the liberties of Georgia as was Lincoln himself. In this bitter contest, which broke out in 1862 and which continued until the end of the war, Brown was aided by Alexander H. Stephens and his half-brother Linton, by Robert Toombs, and to an extent by Herschel V. Johnson; these were the so-called "anarchists." In support of Davis and the larger view stood out most prominently Howell Cobb and Benjamin H. Hill; these were the so-called "monarchists." Toward the end of the war the political front in Georgia was almost as dangerous to the Confederacy as was the military front around Richmond; and frequently Hill was sent to Georgia to meet the attacks of Brown and the Stephens brothers. President Davis himself was forced to the Georgia front in 1864.

The dispute centered around the military policy of the Confederacy as expressed in conscription and exemptions, the appointment of military officers, the suspension of the writ of *habeas corpus,* and in food impressment laws. Each of the "anarchists" had his specialty to condemn. Toombs, who had refused indignantly to curtail his cotton crop in 1862, seemed to be most interested in property rights; he bitterly condemned the Confederacy's impressment of property at a fixed price. The Stephens brothers, Alexander Hamilton and Linton, who were more doctrinaire in their thinking, found the suspension of the writ of *habeas corpus* to be the most heinous of Davis' crimes. Brown, whose zeal in opposing Davis was all-inclusive, singled out conscription as the monster he would fight hardest.

The original policy of the Confederacy required the governors of the states to provide quotas to make up the national armies, but in May, 1861, the Confederate Congress to speed the organization of its forces adopted the new policy of allowing troops to offer themselves without the interposition of the governor. Brown opposed this method, as it might well break up the excellent state army which he was organizing. He objected further because troops leaving without his knowledge or permission might carry with them state arms. These fears were soon realized. Without giving notice to Brown, Francis S. Bartow in the early summer led to Virginia his Oglethorpe Light Infantry, equipped with Georgia rifles. The governor objected and began a bitter correspondence with Bartow, which led the latter to say, "God forbid that I should ever fall so low as to think it necessary to obtain *your* consent to enter the service of my country." Brown was further displeased at the Confederate policy of refusing to receive from the states military units larger than regiments. This policy prevented governors from appointing officers higher than those who commanded such units, namely, colonels. Brown had favorites whom he wished to see in higher ranks, and he was soon to learn that he could not induce President Davis to appoint them.

The Secession convention, which had carried Georgia out of the Union and had adjourned on January 29th, re-assembled in Savannah on March 7th and on the 23rd passed an ordinance turning over to the Confederacy two regiments of troops. The general understanding was that Georgia should not attempt to maintain a separate army, but Governor Brown thought differently. He immediately began building up his state militia again, but they were taken away by Confederate requisitions as fast as he could organize them. On August 8th Georgia's quota was fixed at 30,000 as her part of the national army of 400,000 which was being organized. After a visit to Savannah the next month, Brown came to the conclusion that the coast was not sufficiently guarded, and fearing that Davis could not be induced to send troops there, he decided to organize again his state militia. He succeeded in recruiting a division of three brigades, consisting of 8,000 men, and he placed them under the command of Henry R. Jackson, who resigned his position in the Confederate army in Virginia. This army worked in conjunction with the Confederate troops in Georgia commanded by A. R. Lawton, and in April, 1862, like all of its predecessors, was swallowed up by the Confederacy. Again Brown was left without an army.

These last troops of Brown's had been a victim of conscription. Less than a year of actual warfare convinced President Davis that a general draft law would be necessary to organize most effectively the man-power of the Confederacy. In answer to this need, the first draft law was passed in April, 1862, and thereafter it was amended at various times in respect to the age of conscripts, exemptions, and other details. Brown immediately began to oppose the law. According to his views it was unnecessary, as Georgia had afforded all the troops asked for; it disorganized any state force the governor might get together; it was unconstitutional. From April to July, 1862, Governor Brown carried on an intemperate correspondence with President Davis; but in the end he obeyed the law.

The question of conscription soon reached the Georgia Supreme Court, where it was upheld unanimously; but this decision did not prevent a joint committee of the legislature, when it met in November, 1862, from declaring in a majority report that the conscription law was void.

Determined to have a state army in spite of the draft, Brown set about enlisting a force from those Georgians who were over 35 years of age, the upper limit set by the Confederate law; but before he could make headway, the Confederate age limit was increased to 45, and again did Brown let loose his wrath against conscription. Believing that there were many good soldiers in Georgia over 45 years of age, Brown issued a proclamation in May, 1863, calling upon every county to raise a force of militia outside the Confederate age limits. The governor had just succeeded in getting a small army together when in the early part of 1864 the Confederacy, using a law which allowed non-conscripts to be called out as Home Guards, asked for 8,000 of these men. Losing his new army, Brown hoped at least to be given the right to appoint its commander; but again he was disappointed. Howell Cobb, who was a political and personal enemy of Brown's, received the command and within a short time these two eminent Georgians had plunged themselves into a quarrel so bitter that it degenerated into charges of personal dishonesty against each other. The quarrel began over Brown's application of the Confederate act of May 1, 1863, allowing governors of the states to designate certain exemptions from the draft. Cobb charged that Brown had exempted 2,000 justices of the peace, 1,000 constables, 3,000 militia officers, and various other people whom the governor claimed were necessary for running the state government. The *Columbus Times* estimated in May, 1864, Brown's exemptions to be more than 25,000; and in the following November President Davis believed the number to be 15,000.

Brown's determination to have a state force was an obsession with him. In December, 1863, Georgia passed a draft law of her own, which provided for the enrolling of all male whites between 16 and 60, for the purpose of raising an army from those people not included in the Confederate age limits; namely, 16 and 17 and from 45 to 60. In February, 1864, the Confederacy raised its age limit to 50, and thus cut off five years of Brown's period at the top. In early July, when Sherman was approaching Atlanta, Brown proclaimed a draft for troops from "the cradle to the grave," and finally obtained soldiers for his exempted militia officers to command. These officers, known as "Joe Brown's Pets," now commanded an army which was popularly known as "Joe Brown's Malish." What happened to these troops will appear hereafter.

Though never reconciled to conscription, Brown ceased his attacks upon it in 1864 long enough to confront another ugly enemy which Davis had sent against him, the suspension of the writ of *habeas corpus*. He called a special session of the legislature which met in March under threatening circumstances. Not only had the suspension of the writ upset many Georgians, but the feeling had by this time grown strong that the war could

be ended with honor and independence to the Confederacy, if
its leaders would only attempt it. Signs of war weariness became evident in the early fall of 1863, soon after the two Confederate defeats of Vicksburg and Gettysburg, and by the early
part of the following year a conviction was growing that Davis
was determined to have peace in his own way or not at all.
So Brown came to the conclusion that a special session of the
legislature should meet to clarify Georgia's views. Before the
meeting, Brown and the Stephens brothers discussed peace
resolutions which should be introduced by Linton Stephens.
These resolutions were passed on March 19th and were vague
to an uncommon degree; but they were definite enough to
show a lack of faith in Davis as a peacemaker. They breathed
the Declaration of Independence and state rights, and called
upon Davis to hold out after every Confederate victory "an
official offer of peace, on the basis of the great principle declared by our common fathers in 1776." Such a course "would
be regretted by nobody on either side, except men whose importance, or whose gains, would be diminished by peace and
men whose ambitious designs would need cover under the
ever-recurring plea of the necessities of war." The resolutions
on the suspension of the writ of *habeas corpus* declared that
this action was unconstitutional and asked Congress to restore
the writ. The fact that the legislature went no further may be
attributed somewhat to the speeches made by Howell Cobb and
L. Q. C. Lamar, of Mississippi, who were allowed to speak
before that body. To influence the state further Brown had
distributed widely over Georgia and among the Georgia troops
in the Confederate armies his message to the legislature and the
address which Alexander H. Stephens made.

Brown also had a quarrel with Davis over space on the
blockade-runners, which the President was trying to appropriate to the Confederacy. The Governor accused the President
of instituting a blockade harder to run than the one Lincoln
had set up.

Yet in all these angry differences Brown never thought of deliberately proving disloyal to the Confederacy as he understood it; and the resolutions which Linton Stephens introduced in the Georgia legislature and which it adopted, though holding that an honorable peace might be obtained, pledged the full power of the state in the war until Confederate independence should be established. Brown was always ready to provide troops and in raising them he claimed the right to force into the Confederate army British subjects residing in Georgia. In trying to carry out this purpose he came into an open conflict with A. Fullarton, the British consul at Savannah. As further evidence of Georgia's patriotic zeal, the legislature passed a law making it grounds for divorce for any Georgia woman's husband to be in the Federal army or to be giving aid or comfort to the Federals.

It was not to be expected that Brown could disrupt Georgia's good relations with the Confederacy and bemean its president without stirring up hostility against himself among his own Georgians; but never a sufficient number became determined enough to dislodge him from the governorship, a position which he occupied throughout the war. He was re-elected twice during the conflict and served, in all, four consecutive terms— a record never equalled before or since in the history of the state. In the election of 1861 he was opposed by Eugenius A. Nisbet, the prince of the secessionists, but he won by 14,000 majority. In 1863 he had the opposition of Joshua Hill, running on a ticket to end the war, and of Timothy Furlow, the candidate of the extreme Confederate element; but he won a substantial victory over both combined.

The lot of the mass of the people during the war was one of great privation and suffering, and toward the end of the war there was danger of actual starvation in the northern and southwestern parts of the state. Georgia was generous in her relief, appropriating amounts which appeared fantastic in the depreciated currency of the times. In 1863 she appropriated

$6,000,000 for the indigent families of soldiers; the next year she appropriated a like amount, and in March, 1865, she appropriated an additional $2,000,000. Strangely enough in all this misery, speculation, largely induced by the depreciating currency, went on to a most outrageous extent, and resulted in many fortunes, which were, however, lost in the crash of defeat. In the midst of these upset conditions, deserters and draft-dodgers congregated in the mountains of the northern part of the state and, encouraged by the disaffection in that region, gave the state a great deal of trouble, until Brown declared them outlaws and sent in an army which arrested more than 2,000 of them. The promising school system inaugurated at the outbreak of the war went to pieces and the school funds were largely used up in aiding the families of soldiers.

Georgia was concerned not only with soldiers' families; she appropriated great amounts of money to feed and clothe the soldiers themselves. In 1862 she spent $1,500,000 for their clothing, and for the following two years $2,500,000 each for the same purpose.

One of the most important needs which the state had the greatest difficulty in meeting was the procuring of salt. As the blockade cut off the accustomed supply, the state was forced quickly to look for a new source. The legislature offered to lend money without interest to anyone who would set up salt works, and Governor Brown offered a reward of $5,000 to anyone who should discover salt springs or wells which would produce as much as 300 bushels of salt daily. The state appropriated in 1862 $500,000 to aid in securing salt in southwestern Virginia and later appropriated much more. Brown proceeded with swift justice against the salt hoarders and speculators. He seized 1,000 bushels from an Atlanta speculator and threatened to use the army to prevent the courts from restoring it.

Though the volume of textile manufacture was larger in 1860 than that of any other Southern state, Georgia was unable to take care of her needs in this respect; and during the upset conditions of war-time there was little chance for her to make appreciable progress. Governor Brown was greatly interested in household manufacturing, and to promote it he had distributed among the people many cards, both for cotton and wool, and in Milledgeville the state set up a factory to make these cards.

In carrying on this expensive war, Georgia soon found it necessary to depart from sound finance. In 1861 Governor Brown seized the Dahlonega mint, which contained at the time only $20,000 in gold coins; but it was not the intention of the Governor to coin money when the printing presses could be run so cheaply. In 1860 the state had an income of $1,453,000. Of this amount $450,000 came from the profits in running the Western and Atlantic Railroad, and most of the remainder was derived from the general property tax, dividends on railroad and bank stock owned by the state, and from special taxes such as those on lotteries, insurance companies, and railroads. As these sources tended to dry up, an income tax, which was based on the sale of goods, was added in 1863, levied on profits of more than 20%, but later changed into a graduated tax on profits above 8%.

These revenues provided only a small part of the money needed by the state in carrying on the war. Though Brown was anxious to have as much of the cost of the war as possible paid for as the expense arose, yet Georgia accumulated a total war indebtedness of $18,035,775. Only $3,308,500 was in the form of bonds, none of which was issued after 1862. Apart from the bonds the debt was made up of treasury notes, treasury certificates of deposit, and change bills. The treasury notes, which did not bear interest, were issued in the form of money and circulated as a currency. These notes in amounts of not less than $5,000 could be exchanged for treasury certificates of deposit, which also did not bear interest. These two forms of indebtedness were redeemable in specie or interest-bearing bonds, six months after peace should be declared. To afford a small medium of exchange, banks, which had suspended specie payment in 1861, were allowed to issue change bills. These were in denominations running from 5c to $1. Also the Western and Atlantic Railroad was allowed to issue change bills, and the state itself soon began issuing them, from 5c up to $4. Shinplasters, as small bills issued by private businesses were called, were prohibited; yet many of these were issued regardless of the law.

Measuring with this depreciating currency, Georgians entered into a financial land of make-believe, where in the midst of misery, poverty, and destruction, they found themselves growing richer than Croesus. In 1860 the total property values were assessed for taxation at $600,000,000; four years later, after the ravages of war had swept the state, they had increased to $1,612,000,000. But at this time money was worth one fiftieth of its value in 1860, and so the person who bought a pair of shoes paid $150 for them instead of $3.

Wars cast afar their withering and destructive effects; Georgia would long have remembered this war, had no hostile soldier ever set foot within her borders. But alas, Sherman came, and then, could she ever forget!

CHAPTER XXV

SHERMAN AND THE END

WHEN THE DAY of argument gave way to bloody warfare, Georgia plunged into the midst of it with as much enthusiasm and determination as any other state in the Confederacy. Following the seizure of Fort Sumter, wild excitement swept over the state, and thousands of Georgians came forward to offer their services to Governor Brown. Even the boys at the University ran away from their classes to join the army, fearful that the war would be over before they could have a part in it. The contagion permeated the mountains and led many people there to form companies, which Brown preferred over others, knowing that the mountaineers might change their minds if they should be put off. The first troops raised were sent into the Confederate armies; but Brown, not proposing to be the commander-in-chief of the Georgia army without having one, as has appeared, soon set about developing state forces, which he was continuously trying to protect against seizure by President Davis.

Georgia's geographic position, in the heart of the Confederacy, made her practically immune from invasion during the early part of the war, with the exception of her vulnerable coast-line; and so for three years the war swayed back and forth through Virginia, swept through Tennessee and Mississippi, and cut the Confederacy into two parts with the fall of Vicksburg, before Georgia was to feel the full ravages of invasion. On almost every battlefield Georgians fought, and before the end came, the state had sent into the armies fighting for Southern independence boys, young men, older men, and old men to a number estimated at 120,000.

War came first to the coast through the prodding of Federal gunboats and landing parties, working their way down the Atlantic seaboard after having seized Port Royal in South Carolina. Before the end of 1861, troops had gained lodgment on the islands of Wassaw and Tybee. Savannah was the prize they had in mind, but in order to seize the city they must first reduce Fort Pulaski. At the first outbreak of war, Governor Brown was apprehensive of invasion along the coast, and to prepare for it he appointed Josiah Tattnall to command a mythical Georgia navy. As before stated, he also collected a few thousand state troops which he sent to the coast under the command of Henry R. Jackson. Commodore Tattnall soon entered the service of the Confederate navy where he commanded a few gunboats which annoyed as much as possible the Federals on the Georgia coast. The Confederate troops were under the command of Gen. A. R. Lawton, and during the latter part of 1861, Robert E. Lee was in the state, building up the coastal defenses.

In the early part of the following year, the Federals, in a determined effort to push on up the Savannah River, laid siege to Fort Pulaski, and on April 10th they forced it to surrender with its 400 defenders. Being unable to approach much nearer Savannah, they contented themselves with raiding the sea island and coastal plantations and seizing supplies. In 1863 they burned Darien and made three determined attacks against Fort McAllister, on the Ogeechee, but were beaten off each time.

Apart from the coastal operations, the only other military excitement to which the state was treated before the grand invasion of 1864 consisted of two efforts of Federal raiders to cut the Western and Atlantic Railroad. The first attempt was made in April, 1862, by James J. Andrews and twenty-one other men who, dressed as civilians, worked their way down into Georgia and at Big Shanty, 25 miles north of Atlanta, seized a train with the intention of running it northward and burning behind them the bridges. An excited race took place when the Georgians discovered what had happened, and so hotly did they pursue the raiders that little damage could be done. The raiders were finally captured and seven were hanged as spies, according to the rules of war. The other attempt to interrupt traffic on the Western and Atlantic Railroad was made by Colonel A. D. Streight in command of 1,500 men, who came into Georgia from Alabama. General N. B. Forrest pursued him, and, aided with information from the heroine Emma Sansom, came upon Streight near Rome and with about 500 men tricked him into surrendering with three times that number on May 3, 1863.

The isolation of Georgia from the area of warfare led to the selection of Andersonville as a site for one of the greatest prison camps in the Confederacy. The first prisoners of war were brought here in February, 1864, and by the middle of the year there were more than 31,000 of these unfortunates concentrated within the stockades. From causes over which the Confederacy had little control, almost 13,000 died.

In the meantime, in other parts of the Confederacy momentous and ominous events had been taking place. After Vicksburg had fallen in July, 1863, the Federals decided to direct their western campaign against the only remaining city of importance in Tennessee, Chattanooga, preparatory to an invasion of Georgia. General W. S. Rosecrans in September maneuvered General Braxton Bragg out of that city and came near suffering a major disaster at Chickamauga Creek across the Tennessee line in Georgia. His troops fled back to Chattanooga where they were almost starved into surrender before General U. S. Grant took charge in the battles of Lookout Mountain and Missionary Ridge and drove the Confederates away. In February, Grant went east to fight General Lee in Virginia and left General William T. Sherman in Chattanooga with an army of 99,000 men. The Confederates wintered at Dalton, Georgia, and in the spring, under their new commander General Joseph E. Johnston, who had succeeded Bragg, they stood ready to oppose Sherman in his march against Atlanta. Being greatly outnumbered, Johnston fought a defensive campaign, fortifying positions and retreating as Sherman outflanked him. The battles of Dalton, Resaca, and New Hope Church followed one another during the late spring and summer, until Sherman foolishly and recklessly attacked Johnston, entrenched on Kennesaw Mountain. He was thrown back with a loss of 3,000 while the Confederates lost only 800—the only military mistake Sherman admitted he ever made. On July 9th, the Federals reached the north bank of the Chattahoochee and made preparations to begin operations against Atlanta.

Unable to see the wisdom in Johnston's strategy of continually retreating, and unable also to find out from the general what his future plans were, President Davis gave way to the clamor for Johnston's removal and on the 18th of July put in his place General John B. Hood, with the distinct purpose of bringing a stop to any further retreating. Sherman's invasion of the state had greatly excited the people and led Governor Brown to the conclusion that President Davis ought to concentrate in Georgia the Confederate forces scattered throughout the country. The governor quickly got together 10,000 troops, known as the "Joe Brown Malish," combing them out of the population which had not been swept up by the Confederate draft. From July 20th, when the battle of Peachtree Creek was fought, throughout August to September 2nd, when Hood evacuated Atlanta, a series of bloody engagements was fought around the city. Thousands of troops on both sides were killed and wounded, and each side suffered the loss of a general— the Federals losing James B. McPherson, and the Confederates, W. H. T. Walker. While these engagements were taking place near Atlanta, General George Stoneman raided the state almost to the gates of Macon; but, for too much rashness at one time and too much timidity at another, he got himself into a position where he was forced to surrender with his 700 men. At

Top left: ALEXANDER H. STEPHENS, LOVER OF THE UNION, MEMBER OF THE UNITED STATES HOUSE OF REPRESENTATIVES AND OF THE SENATE, VICE-PRESIDENT OF THE CONFEDERACY, AND GOVERNOR. *Top right:* BENJAMIN H. HILL, CONFEDERATE AND UNITED STATES SENATOR AND BITTER OPPONENT OF MILITARY RECONSTRUCTION. *Bottom left:* HENRY R. JACKSON, MINISTER TO AUSTRIA, BRIGADIER-GENERAL IN THE CONFEDERACY, AND MINISTER TO MEXICO. *Bottom right:* JOSEPH E. JOHNSTON, SKILLFUL COMMANDER OF THE CONFEDERATE ARMY OPPOSING SHERMAN ON HIS MARCH TO ATLANTA IN 1864.

Top: FEDERALS ATTACKING FORT PULASKI. THIS FORT FELL EXACTLY A YEAR AFTER THE CON-
FEDERATES HAD FIRED ON FORT SUMTER. *Harpers' Pictorial History of the Civil War,* II. New
York: Harper & Brothers. *Bottom:* GEORGIANS FLEEING BEFORE SHERMAN'S GRAND MARCH. SHER-
MAN CLAIMED TO HAVE DESTROYED $100,000,000 WORTH OF PROPERTY ON HIS MARCH TO THE SEA.

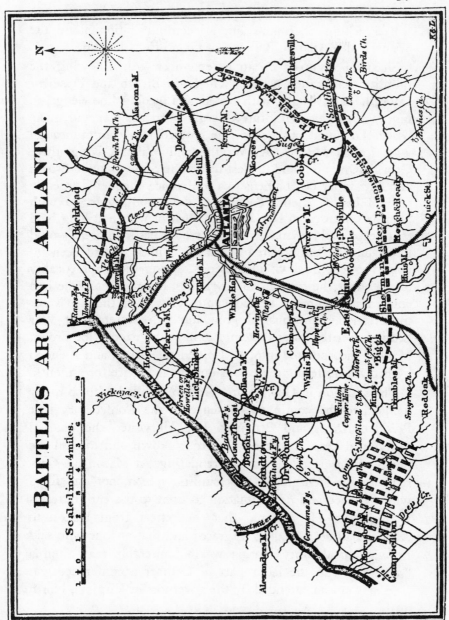

the same time General Joseph Wheeler with his cavalrymen was attacking Sherman's line of communication along the Western and Atlantic Railroad as far north as Dalton.

Sherman occupied Atlanta September 3rd. Knowing the hostility that existed between Governor Brown and President Davis, he now sought, with President Lincoln's knowledge, to induce Brown to withdraw Georgia from the war and make peace. To sound out Brown, he entered into communication with Joshua Hill, R. K. Wright, and William King, three Georgia Unionists, and the last named he chose to invite Brown and Alexander H. Stephens to a conference. Stephens, urgently advised by his friend Toombs to have nothing to do with Sherman, refused to be drawn in. Brown, who had long held that peace could be made if Davis would bestir himself, would likely have accommodated Sherman, if nothing had been involved except his own inclinations. Seeing the impracticality of the move, he rejected the overtures, but not before he had entered into another heated controversy with the Davis administration. This quarrel grew up with Secretary of War Seddon over the latter's attempt to have the 10,000 "Joe Brown Malish" incorporated into the Confederate army, and it ended by Brown mustering the troops out of the service for a month.

The situation in Georgia appeared to be filled with so many dangers to the continued existence of the Confederacy that President Davis and Benjamin H. Hill visited the state in October to keep an eye on Governor Brown and to steel the hearts of the people against surrendering. At Macon the Confederate President made a pessimistic speech, but one filled with defiance and determination to fight to the end, bitter as it might be. He declared that the retreat from Dalton to Atlanta had been a "deep disgrace" and that anyone who said he was abandoning Georgia was a "miserable man" and a "scoundrel." In the latter part of October a conference was held at Augusta, attended by the governors of Virginia, North

Carolina, South Carolina, Georgia, Alabama, and Mississippi; but the outcome was a determination to continue the war.

On entering Atlanta, Sherman resolved to destroy all stores, factories, and public buildings, and preparatory to taking this step he called for the evacuation of the city by the civilian population. A bitter correspondence between Sherman and Hood ensued, in which the latter branded Sherman's purpose as barbarous and inhuman. It was at this time that Sherman said war must be made terrible. He did not say "War is hell," as he later was forced reluctantly to admit after having had a fruitless search made of his war orders and correspondence.[1] He had the torch applied to the city on November 15th, and the great fire which followed was described by one of his men thus: "Our Commissaries have been busily engaged all day in loading rations, and our Quarter Masters in issuing clothing and shoes to the troops. Up to about 3 P. M. this issuing was carried on with something like a show of regularity, but about that time fires began to break out in various portions of the city, and it soon became evident that these fires were but the beginning of a general conflagration which would sweep over the entire city and blot it out of existence; so Quartermasters and Commissaries ceased trying to issue clothing or load rations, they told the soldiers to go in and take what they wanted before it burned up. The soldiers found many barrels of whisky and of course they drank of it until they were drunk; then new fires began to spring up, all sorts of discordant noises rent the air, drunken soldiers on foot and on horseback raced up and down the streets while the buildings on either side were solid sheets of flame, they gathered in crowds before the finest structures and sang 'Rally around the Flag' while the flames enwrapped these costly edifices, and shouted and danced and sang again while pillar and roof and dome sank into one common ruin. The night, for miles around was bright as mid-day;

[1] In a speech made years later at Columbus, Ohio, Sherman referred to war as "hell," but in his later life he had forgotten it and never succeeded in discovering it.

the city of Atlanta was one mass of flame, and the morrow must find it a mass of ruins. Well, the soldiers fought for it, and the soldiers won it, now let the soldiers enjoy it; and so I suppose General Sherman thinks, for he is somewhere near by, now, looking on at all this, and saying not a word to prevent it. All the pictures and verbal descriptions of hell I have ever seen never gave me half so vivid an idea of it, as did this flame wrapped city tonight. Gate City of the South, farewell!"

By this time Sherman had evolved the bold idea of marching to the sea through the heart of the Confederacy, bringing terror and devastation to the people, and putting a stop to the war. At first he thought of marching to Mobile, but he soon determined on Savannah, and after having destroyed Atlanta, he set out with 60,000 picked troops, of whom 5,000 were cavalry needed for foraging. He divided his army into two parts, one going through Decatur, Covington, Eatonton, and Milledgeville, to Sandersville, where they would join the other, which went by Jonesboro and Gordon with a threat at Macon. By cutting loose from all communications and burying himself in the heart of Georgia, Sherman appealed to the imagination of the country and seemed to be engaging in a most dangerous campaign; but in fact it was largely a picnic, for General Hood on the fall of Atlanta had marched up into Tennessee with the hopes of drawing Sherman after him and had left no one to oppose the enemy except General Wheeler, who actually distressed the Georgians almost as much as he annoyed the Federals.

Consternation seized the people as the news of his ravaging march went before him. They buried in the ground their silverware and other valuables, and drove into the hiding places of the swamps and woods as much of their livestock as possible. But little could they prevail against Sherman's hungry troops and "bummers," who plundered and destroyed, almost without stint—so much so that when the march had been completed Sherman could report, with likely some exaggeration, that he had destroyed $100,000,000 worth of food and property, of which $80,000,000 was wanton waste.

On November 17th Brown informed his legislature, then meeting in Milledgeville, that Sherman had burned Atlanta and was on his way to Milledgeville. He asked for quick legislation permitting him to call out the entire population of the state to repel the invaders. The legislators agreed only after exempting themselves and the judges. Even so, Brown on the same day adjourned the legislature "to the front . . . to meet again if we should live, at such a place as the Governor may designate." The most valuable official records were quickly gathered together to be removed to the insane asylum, where it was felt they would be safe; but the plans were changed and they were carried to a place of safety in the southwestern part of the state. Brown hurried to the penitentiary, made the convicts a patriotic speech, and induced them to join the militia and aid in the evacuation of the capital.

The last train had scarcely disappeared before Sherman entered Milledgeville. He burned the penitentiary, but spared the city except for the desecration of the capitol by soldiers who scattered in all directions books and official papers which they did not care to take with them and who in a mock session of the legislature repealed the secession ordinance.

In early December Sherman established contact with the Federal fleet on the coast, made a joint attack on Fort Mc-Allister which fell on the 13th, and soon thereafter entered Savannah and presented the city as a Christmas gift to President Lincoln. This proud city, one of the finest specimens of the culture and refinement of the Old South, was plunged by its conquerors into despair. General W. J. Hardee, with 10,000 troops, who had attempted to hold the city, made his escape into South Carolina, leaving, besides much munitions of war, 31,000 bales of cotton for avaricious speculators to fight over.

Sherman soon passed on across the Savannah River into South Carolina, the home of secession, where his destructions continued unabated, and on into North Carolina where in April General Joseph E. Johnston, who was again confronting him, surrendered. As Lee had previously surrendered to Grant at Appomattox on April 9th, all Confederate resistance was soon to come to an end. Governor Brown had long been fearing such a disaster; and for not making peace, he had accused Davis of being as great an enemy of the Confederacy as was Lincoln. In his message to the legislature in November, 1864, Brown had advocated a convention of all the Confederate states for the purpose of formulating a peace program and forcing it upon Davis, but he had been unable to get the movement started. After Sherman had swept through Georgia it seemed utterly foolish to Brown and to a great many other Georgians for the Confederacy to continue longer the war. He called a special session of the legislature to meet in February, 1865, in Macon, and in his message to that body he boldly came out for a state convention which should propose an amendment to the Confederate constitution, taking away from the president his control over the army. Brown had completely lost faith in Davis. In despair, he said, "The night is dark, the tempest howls, the ship is lashed with turbulent waves, the helmsman is steering to the whirlpool, our remonstrances are unheeded, and we must restrain him, or the crew must sink together submerged in irretrievable ruin."

On May 3rd he called another session of the legislature to meet on the 22nd, and a few days later he surrendered the Georgia troops to Major-General James H. Wilson, who had started an invasion of the state from Columbus. Though protected from molestation by the terms of his surrender, Brown was arrested on May 11th and sent to Washington. There he was imprisoned for nine days before being released by Andrew Johnson, who had become president after Lincoln's assassination. The legislature did not meet, and civil government disappeared until it should be restored in the reconstruction which must follow.

Federal troops spread out over the state and arrested the other principal leaders. Alexander H. Stephens was seized at his home in Crawfordsville, and Benjamin H. Hill, in Lagrange. Robert Toombs made his escape from his home in Washington, Wilkes County, and succeeded in fleeing to Europe. The Confederate government had crashed, and its president and the remnant of his cabinet, in attempting to make their escape, held a last meeting in Washington, Wilkes County. While here it issued its last order and made its last payment to the soldiers of the Confederacy, from a supply of money that was being dragged through the country on wagons. A few days later President Davis was captured near Irwinsville; and the Federals in trying to discredit him declared that he was caught disguised in woman's apparel. To humiliate him further they cast him into prison and weighed down the sick old man with chains—and thereby, in making him a martyr, elevated him into a lasting hero for Southerners.

The great Southern adventure had now ended in disaster; and there awaited Georgia and the other Confederate states rigors which they had pictured in their efforts to hold up the Confederate morale, but which they never had honestly believed could happen.

CHAPTER XXVI

RECONSTRUCTION, SOCIAL AND ECONOMIC

THE WAR MAY have been a political rebellion, but it brought about a social and economic revolution. Ante-bellum became a word to be applied to the times before the Civil War, and to mark another civilization which soon appeared as remote as the Babylonians and as romantic as it seemed old. The South's high hopes of establishing the right to lead an untrammeled life of her own was crushed out in defeat and the memory of that exhilarating dream of early wartime was long to live as the Lost Cause.

Not only was the dream lost and transformed into a poignant memory; but material things went down in the crash, used up forever and best forgotten. Three-fourths of the wealth of Georgia disappeared. Slaves worth $272,000,000 were set free; the money and bonds of the state and the stocks of banks and railroads were made worthless; cities and countryside lay in waste, made so by invasions and wartime neglect; 40,000 of her best citizens were missing, either dead in war or scattered beyond recovery; and the spirit of her people was broken, not beyond repair, but crumbling into movements to desert the land of desolation for Mexico or Brazil.

Out of these fragments of her former self, Georgia set about remaking a new commonwealth; but she was not unassisted by her conquerors whose unwelcomed control plunged her into a turmoil, known as Reconstruction, which was drawn out as long as the war and became as devastating. Throughout this decade of war and Reconstruction the population gained 100,000, which showed that there was still vitality and hope in the state; but this increase was only 12% as compared with

16% during the preceding decade and 30% during the following one. The effects of the war on the population were recorded pathetically in the movement for orphan asylums; the destitution of the people was generously recognized in Kentucky's gift of 100,000 bushels of corn in 1866; and the lack of money was admitted in the state's cancellation of all taxes for 1864 and 1865.

In agriculture, war and Reconstruction recorded a loss. The amount of land under cultivation decreased 3,000,000 acres, and the price receded from an average of $5 an acre to $3. The amount of almost every crop in 1870 was smaller than in 1860, with the exception of cotton, which that year first reached the level of slave days. The break-up of large plantations either through the growth of tenancy or through sale was inevitable with the fall of slavery, and the revolution worked here is shown in the fact that most of the farms in 1870 were in size from 20 to 50 acres, whereas in 1860 they had been from 100 to 500.

The most fundamental revolution worked in Georgia following the war was in the agricultural establishment, where the slave had been as important as the land. The very danger feared by all whites throughout the South had come to pass, and the problems it set up must now be settled. The slave had become a free laborer, and he must be taken care of. The Southerners were not alone interested in the freed Negro, and the fact that the United States government and Northern organizations sought to settle the problem greatly complicated it. This was so especially for the reason that the North appeared to be more interested in the social and political construction of the Negro than in his economic welfare.

The Freedmen's Bureau, a Federal agency set up about the end of the war, took under its charge the Negro in all his relationships to the community and the state. It supervised his contracts with his white employers, set him apart and provided food and raiment for him, and, suspicious of the state courts, it established special tribunals in which he should be tried. The Bureau was a great relief organization for a mass of people who needed help, and as long as it adhered to these principles, it deserved well of the white people and received their respect and support; but when the Bureau forgot its main mission and attempted to establish the Negro's social standing and his political position, then the Georgians turned upon it with bitter opposition. It began in Georgia under General Rufus Saxton, whose unwise management led to his dismissal and the appointment of General David Tillson, who used much tact and common sense throughout his term.

It was difficult to manage the Negroes now suddenly set free, regardless of who should try, whether it be the Freedmen's Bureau, Northern missionary and betterment societies, or the white man of the South. Liberty meant to them license and freedom from all restraint, and to many it meant surcease from all work. They drifted from country to city; and designing labor agents from other states upset them still further and were partly responsible for the migration from Georgia, principally to the northward and westward, of 140,000 within three years following the end of the war. Social and economic conditions became so upset that the penalty for horse-stealing was again made death—the unfailing sign of a primitive situation.

Dissolution stared the planters in the face at the end of the war. Without the labor of their former slaves they were lost. In many instances the good relations that had existed between master and slave led to a freedman's remaining on the plantation and accepting a money wage of from $10 to $15 a month or becoming a tenant of his former master and paying in rent a fifth or a fourth of the crop. For many Negroes nothing less than ownership of the land would fulfill their expectations of freedom, and so the cry of "forty acres and a mule" went up. Sherman had got rid of some of his excess Negro camp-followers when he reached the coast, by colonizing them in the rice fields of the Ogeechee and on the sea islands; and the impossibility of holding ignorant Negroes to labor contracts led to the break-up of the large plantations, which went begging for buyers and permitted the more intelligent and industrious Negroes to become landowners. In 1874 they owned 338,769 acres.

The transportation establishment of the state was little less important than the labor supply. In 1860 Georgia had one mile of railway for every 744 people, while the average for the whole country was one mile for 1,420 people; but four years of war wrecked this superiority. Sherman destroyed about 300 miles of the Central of Georgia and of other roads; Wilson demolished the Atlanta and West Point; and even the Confederates did not hesitate to tear up tracks and burn bridges, stations, and cars. No railroads were built during the war; but the Brunswick and Florida was taken up and moved where it was more needed, and rails from other roads were removed, not only for other locations but for iron-cladding war vessels.

The three main railway interests in the state at the end of the war were the Western and Atlantic, which the state owned and which became a plaything for politicians; the Georgia, under the presidency of John P. King, and the Central of Georgia Railroad, presided over by William M. Wadley. These privately owned railroads were naturally in a bankrupt condition at the end of hostilities, not only because of the destruction carried out against them, but also because of the Confederate debts due them and the Confederate securities held by them. Yet they made a rapid recovery in restoring tracks, water-tanks, stations, and rolling stock, and within a year they were paying dividends as high as 9%. As these two roads had been rivals before the war, they continued their contest for the control of the state, and falling in with the movement of the times, each consolidated smaller roads into its system. Among those secured by the Georgia Railroad was the Atlanta and West Point. The Central of Georgia riveted its control on the Southwestern and the Macon and Western and it established a steamship line to New York served by six vessels.

The enthusiasm for rebuilding and developing the state fully expressed itself in the railroad fever. Within scarcely more than a year following the war ten charters were granted to new railroad companies, and within the next few years the construction of new railroads became mixed up with as much political thievery and dishonesty as ever had beset the Western and Atlantic. Out of the welter of corruption, there ultimately were evolved about a half dozen roads, mostly in the southern half of the state. All told, 840 miles of railroad were constructed before the panic of 1873 and corruption in high places caused the sale of about half the mileage in the state. The Atlantic and Gulf was extended to Bainbridge and a spur was run down to Live Oak, Florida; the Macon and Brunswick was built largely through the efforts of Morris K. Jesup and other Northern capitalists; the Brunswick and Albany was a political product engineered by H. I. Kimball, and seized upon by Henry Clews and other Northerners. In the upper part of the state the greatest railroad accomplishment was the Atlanta and Richmond Air Line, finished to the South Carolina line in 1872.

Financially, the state at the end of the war was in distress. Its debt was about $20,000,000, but being forced by the Federal government to repudiate all indebtedness incurred in aiding the Confederacy, it was relieved of about $18,000,000. But what the state treasury gained by this forced repudiation, the people who held the securities lost, and a Federal government obliging enough to relieve a state treasury of its war debt did not fail to exact the state's quota of the direct tax levied on the states in 1861. Thus a prostrate state was saddled with an additional charge of $600,000 which had been originally demanded for its subjugation, but only $82,000 of this amount was ever collected. During 1866 the state debt was increased by a bond issue of $3,630,000, used to a considerable extent for repairing the Western and Atlantic Railroad and for feeding starving Georgians. Two years later the finances of the state came into the hands of designing and radical politicians who threw upon the people a dishonest debt of such proportions that it was later repudiated. As Confederate money was worthless, the state at first was left without currency, and not until the occupying Federal soldiers began spending money and the market for cotton opened, did United States currency make its reappearance.

Defeat which carried all things down with it demolished the banking establishments. Banks had invested their capital largely in Confederate securities and naturally they had dealt in Confederate currency. The Georgia Railroad and Banking Company and the Central of Georgia Railroad and Banking Company, whose business was not so much in banks as in railroads, were conspicuous examples of the few institutions which came through the crash. Banking in the reconstruction was forced to start from the beginning and it was many years before the banking capital reached its ante-bellum level. In 1872 it was slightly over $2,000,000 as compared with more than $13,000,000 in 1860. Yet progress was steady, and enthusiasm to go forward was evident. In less than a year after the end of the war, twenty banks and loan associations were chartered. During this time two national banks were set up in Atlanta, and the National Bank of Augusta, with a capital of $500,000, was established with W. B. Dinsmore as president.

Though it seemed for a time that the spirit of the people was broken, within less than a year after Lee's surrender the reaction from four years of destruction propelled forward an enthusiasm for rebuilding and developing which lost sight of mundane handicaps. It had the appearance of a situation where everybody had suddenly awakened from a long slumber and was trying to get ahead of some one else. Charters were granted for almost every business a Georgian could imagine. In 1865 and 1866 the state granted more than seventy charters, for railroads, street car lines, banks, insurance companies, steamboat lines, petroleum companies, and various manufacturing companies. The search for gold in the hills was renewed and more than twenty-two charters were issued for mining companies. To take care of the gold that these armies of miners expected to find, the state asked the United States government to restore the assay office in Dahlonega. In 1866 the legislature granted a charter to the United States and West India Telegraph Company, which expected to run cables from the Bahamas and other West Indies to the Georgia coast.

Though Georgians had little capital, these booming business activities were not completely fantastic. Out of the many Georgians who had grown rich during the war, a few had brought a substantial part through the crash; and others of long-standing wealth had been able to save a part. By May, 1866, President Andrew Johnson, who had excepted from amnesty anyone having wealth to the amount of $20,000, had relented and pardoned more than 1,200 Georgians who came within this class.

The enthusiasm which seized the Georgians also permeated the North, and led people from that section to migrate to Georgia to grow rich. Many came to raise cotton at fifty cents a pound and failed because of their inability to manage Negro laborers; others came to take part in the business revival which they expected; and still others sent their dollars to work in Georgia, but they themselves remained in the North. These Northerners were variously received by the Georgians. Their reception depended somewhat on their standing in the North, and somewhat on the part of the state which did the receiving. In Savannah their Northern birth would likely make them unwelcome; in Atlanta their industry and their dollars would much more likely determine the nature of their reception.

People meant wealth, so the Georgians believed in Reconstruction times. Though some feeling might exist against the Northerners, and very naturally so, still they were officially invited to Georgia to help rebuild. In 1868 a hearty welcome was extended "to all good citizens, laborers and capitalists, from all parts of our country and foreign countries" to become Georgians and help make the state "justly deserve the name of the Empire State of the South." A special effort was made to induce respectable foreigners to migrate to Georgia, with a commissioner being appointed for that purpose in 1869; but little success attended, for in 1870 the foreign population was smaller than in 1860. Especially were white laborers wanted, as the Negroes became less dependable and manageable.

The disorganization of agriculture and the rising feeling that the state might best enter the new age by breaking with its agrarian past, led Benjamin H. Hill, Henry Grady, and other Georgians, either new or remade, to call for the industrial age. To the Georgians of the traditional past, this program seemed treason to the Lost Cause; and they had their way, for the factory age was not to make its appearance for a decade or more. Yet there was progress away from agriculture, even though it was not directed into factories. The break-up of the plantation and the rise of tenancy led to the country store at the crossroads, not in such numbers as the filling stations of the gasoline age, but numerous enough to provide work for many drummers to do, and goods-boxes for many sages to whittle.

The growth of cities was a definite trend beginning with the end of the war. It was a concomitant of the rise of the mercantile class, and a distinct product of the destruction of the plantation, which marked the sad decline of gentility in the country. With the Negroes free and the labor supply uncertain, the plantation home could no longer be kept attractive. The best exponents of the ante-bellum civilization moved to the towns and left mansions of beautiful architecture to tenants, white and Negro, and to the ravages of time and fire. The decline of the countryman toward peasantry as the ultimate end marked one of the most melancholy results produced by the new age. To the city also came many wandering and wondering Negroes, there to produce in good time slums for the social workers and crimes for the police. In 1870 Savannah was still the largest city in the state, but Atlanta with its booming spirit was making rapid strides toward the position of first place. Macon, whose prosperity had been bound up more with agriculture, had less reason to respond to the new progress.

During the war the schools had been closed and their endowments had been lost in defeat; but immediately upon the close of the struggle, the people thought of education and began efforts to rehabilitate it. The promising scheme of 1858 had now to be given up; but in 1866 a superintendent of education was provided for to set the schools going in the various counties. Tuition was made free to all white students between six and twenty-one and to all indigent or disabled soldiers not over thirty years of age. This law was to become effective January 1, 1868, but before that time came the state had been handed over to the Federal army, which donated the people's destiny to a semi-alien government of radical politicians. In laudable language these new rulers reaffirmed the free school system in the constitution of 1868, and the following year, with good sense, translated it into a law recommended by the Georgia Teachers' Association. The radical governor appointed J. R. Lewis school commissioner, who, however, did little before he was swept out of power by the political overturn of 1871. The following year Gustavus J. Orr became the commissioner, and he labored in the field until his death in 1887. He it was who became the father of the Georgia free school system, and under him the schools, both for whites and Negroes, were placed on a permanent basis. Even before the state schools had been organized, some of the cities began their own local systems. Savannah was the first, in 1866, and she was followed by Atlanta three years later.

In 1866 the state University reopened after a suspension of three years and, with an attendance soon larger than ever before the war, entered upon a period of increased usefulness. In 1869 it broadened its work by offering new courses and by adopting the elective system. Two years later there began a process of educational development in the state, wise in its inception but unwisely carried out. It first appeared in the organization of a school at Dahlonega, which was made a branch of the University and placed under the control of the University trustees. This school, known as the North Georgia Agricultural College, was an outgrowth of the Morrill land grant act of 1862, whereby Congress allowed the states 30,000 acres of public lands for every Congressman. Being out of the Union at the time, Georgia could lay no claim to this munificence; but in 1866, when she had been forced to return, she accepted the grant and recommended that the land be sold. The state received the right to 300,000 acres and a few years later sold it for $242,202, which was given to the University trustees. The trustees, instead of giving all of this fund to the Dahlonega school, decided to use most of it to set up an agricultural and mechanical school as an integral part of the University, and this they did in 1872.

Though Oglethorpe College dropped out of existence after the war, the other private colleges added strength to their life. Mercer University, which had grown up contemporaneously with the attractive and cultured little country village of Penfield, in 1871 left its rural surroundings and moved to Macon, led there by an endowment of $125,000 and nine acres of land offered by that city. It added a law school in 1873. During this same year, Shorter College was started at Rome, and through the help of the Baptists grew into one of the most excellent schools for young women in the state. Emory College, having suspended in 1862, reopened six years later in its classical surroundings at Oxford, and in 1884 organized a department of technology, which was for a time to give it a special renown.

Directly following the war, the state gave little attention to Negro education, as the Freedmen's Bureau and Northern missionary and betterment societies took up the education of the Negroes and offered them better opportunities than the state for a few years could offer its white population. In 1867 Atlanta University was set up largely through the munificence of Northern friends of the Negroes, and for a time it received an appropriation of $8,000 annually from the state, while the legislature gave the University at Athens nothing. In 1869 an elementary school for Negroes was set up in Atlanta, which in 1877 became Clark University and later won a considerable reputation in its theological and industrial departments. In 1867 the Augusta Institute was set up under Northern support. It languished until 1879 when it was removed to Atlanta and renamed the Atlanta Baptist Seminary. Higher education for the Negroes in Georgia centered in Atlanta.

Newspaper activity and development grew up almost exclusively around the political situation. In 1870 there were five more newspapers in the state than in 1860; but their circulation was 30,000 less. The press was almost wholly Democratic, though the Republicans had two newspapers of some standing, the *Savannah Republican* and the *Atlanta New Era*. The outstanding newspaper, which came to speak for the whole South, was the *Atlanta Constitution,* founded in 1868. In 1876 Evan P. Howell secured control of it and attached to it Henry W. Grady and Joel Chandler Harris, two men on the watchtowers who first spied out the New South and began telling about it.

War and defeat are not typical breeders of men of letters; yet Bill Arp (Charles H. Smith) performed a valuable service in making a sorely beset people laugh amidst their desolation. Among his best known works were *Bill Arp, So-Called, A Side Show of the Southern Side of the War,* published in 1866, *Bill Arp's Letters,* in 1868, and *Bill Arp's Peace Papers,* in 1873. Sidney Lanier, though born in Georgia, spent few of his productive years in the state; yet the state, with laudable pride, laid tenacious claim to him. Richard Malcolm Johnston wrote his *Dukesborough Tales* and other works dealing with educational conditions; and Paul Hamilton Hayne, though born in South Carolina, moved to Georgia following the war and in his little home in the pines near Augusta engaged in editorial work and wrote poetry. It would be difficult to prove that textbooks in arithmetic and algebra could ever be considered literature, but the work done in this field by Shelton P. Sanford, for more than fifty years the head of the mathematics department in Mercer University, helped many Georgians and other Southerners as much as Bill Arp amused them and made his name as famous with those who ciphered as Noah Webster's with those who spelled.

The historian whom Georgians were most delighted to honor was not William B. Stevens, Maine-born, who wrote the first scholarly history of the state, but Charles Colcock Jones, Jr., Georgia-born, who wrote the other classic history of Georgia. Jones wrote not only his two-volume *History of Georgia* (1883), but both previously and thereafter he wrote many other lesser historical works on Georgia. He was Georgia's most prolific historian. Besides, he was a favorite orator for Confederate Veteran meetings. Many of his orations were published in pamphlets.

Just as the principal religious denominations in the state had broken their connections with the North, unable to withstand the strain of the sectional bitterness which led to the Civil War, so after the war they refused in religion a union which in politics they were glad to accept. The Presbyterians and Baptists never reunited, but the Episcopalians, few in numbers, without abating their Confederate patriotic zeal, soon began to include the President of the United States in their prayers, with the secret feeling that he was most in need of them. The Methodists waited until the twentieth century to reunite with their Northern brethren. Religion gained in the troublous times of the Reconstruction, for it afforded a solace and a refuge to people who could see little to look forward to on this earth. The Negroes, who were greatly attracted by clubs and organizations, flocked into churches, Methodist and Baptist principally, with as much the feeling of getting something here as hereafter.

Social and economic reconstruction was longer drawn out and more fundamental in its operation than was political reconstruction, but the latter was more spectacular.

CHAPTER XXVII

RECONSTRUCTION, POLITICAL

GEORGIANS WERE glad the war had ended. Could they have been assured of honorable treatment, a great many of them would have been willing to return to the Union months before Lee's surrender. Now that the war was over, no one of intelligence had a thought of ever again attempting to destroy the Union; but all expected the state would be allowed to resume its old position.

The assassination of Lincoln shortly after the surrender caused some Georgians to fear evil consequences for the state, but by June it had become evident that the new president, Andrew Johnson, would adopt largely the same ideas which Lincoln had had in mind. As civil government had broken down completely, except in local affairs, detachments of troops took charge in the principal towns and cities and proceeded to rule until the president should act to restore the state to its former rights. On June 17th President Johnson took the first step by appointing as provisional governor James Johnson, a native Georgian and a graduate of the state University. Governor Brown, thus ignored, resigned twelve days later.

To the broad-minded leaders of the North, it appeared best to restore the former Confederate states to the Union with as little delay as possible, without vengeance, and under only those conditions which justice to all and the safety of the Union demanded. The president and his conservative followers agreed that only three safeguards were necessary: the states should annul their secession ordinances, they should repudiate their debts contracted in carrying on the war, and they should free their slaves. To assure the acceptance of these conditions, the president would leave the restoration of the state in the hands of the people who had taken no prominent part in the Confederacy. This he hoped to accomplish by refusing immediate pardon to certain classes, who were for the most part the civil, diplomatic, and military leaders.

Governor Johnson, in July, called for an election to be held in October to choose delegates to a constitutional convention which should meet the same month. The qualifications for voting should remain the same as in ante-bellum times except for those people whom the president had not yet pardoned. The effect of this ruling was to cause mostly inexperienced men to be sent to the convention, as almost all of the leaders were still disfranchised. Herschel V. Johnson presided over the body, while Charles J. Jenkins became the most powerful leader in it. It made and adopted a new constitution, not greatly unlike the former one, and agreed to the three conditions which President Johnson had laid down. There was tenacious opposition to the repudiation of the state debt because it was felt that the state's credit would be ruined and also because many Georgians who held state bonds would lose their investment; in abolishing slavery the convention declared it was not disclaiming the right to compensation; and in disposing of the secession ordinance, it merely repealed it instead of nullifying it.

Now with a new constitution complying with the president's conditions, the restoration of the state was quickly completed. Elections were held on November 15th, for all state officials and for members of Congress, and in early December the legislature met. As the United States government felt that slavery could never be completely destroyed until the Federal constituition was amended, the thirteenth amendment had been submitted to the states and its ratification made a condition on which the late Confederate states should be re-admitted. The legislature ratified it on December 9th, and ten days later Governor Johnson handed over his power to Charles J. Jenkins, who had been elected in November. During the latter part of the following January, the legislature completed the official chain binding the state to the nation by electing Alexander H. Stephens and Herschel V. Johnson United States Senators, two men who it felt represented the best leadership in the state.

Feeling secure in the Union again, Georgia set out to make her position conform to the new conditions which surrounded her. The former slaves, now suddenly set free, must have the rights of citizenship. With remarkable liberality, she conferred upon them full civil rights, with one exception. Fearing to trust in court suits the lives and property of her white citizens to the testimony of a people who knew little of the sanctity of an oath, she denied the Negroes the right to testify against white people in certain cases; but Negroes should "not be subjected to any other or different punishment, pain or penalty for the commission of any act or offense, than such as are prescribed for white persons, commiting like acts or offences." Any person with one-eighth Negro blood was declared a Negro, and the intermarriage of the two races was prohibited. Out of the marital turmoil of slavery, where there was more than one wife or husband some order was secured by allowing the wife to choose among her husbands which she would keep or the husband to choose among his wives which he would possess—in each instance with mutual consent. Laws against vagrancy, applying no less to whites than to Negroes, punished the guilty with imprisonment or fine or with disposal to someone for labor.

The state could not forget its Confederate soldiers, living or dead. The former were allowed free wooden legs, $300 a year for educational expenses at the University or other state colleges, and the right to peddle without paying a license fee, provided they should not deal in "ardent spirits." The Confederate dead should be properly buried and their graves kept, and to carry out this work the legislature gave the Memorial Association of Georgia $4,000 in 1866 and $2,000 more two years later.

It was a misfortune that Confederate soldiers had been killed; the state should never let die the memory of the heroic days and of the cause that was lost. The legislature sent a message of sympathy to Jefferson Davis, in his prison cell at Fortress Monroe, and declared that its "warm affections cluster around the fallen chief of a once dear, but now abandoned cause." That the children of Georgians, who had not experienced the thrill of fighting for this "abandoned cause," might learn about it in their schools, the legislature recommended the adoption of the "Southern University Series" of textbooks, written by such men as William Gilmore Simms and Matthew F. Maury, with "sound scholarship and correct sentiment."

To conform further to the new day, the legislature removed the wartime restrictions against the distillation of grain; repealed the law against circulating United States money in the state; excused all soldiers, Confederate and Federal, who had been charged with crimes while acting under military orders; and struck out the word Confederate from the titles of companies and associations.

In thus expressing herself, Georgia felt that she was showing full loyalty to the Union and proper respect for her conquerors, without heaping disgrace upon herself by abandoning the memories of her past heroism. She felt that the sea islands which Sherman had seized and handed over to Negro camp-followers should be restored to their owners, and she also felt that there was no need further to be burdened by an army of occupation, for she had accepted in good faith the issues of the war and had an unalterable purpose to obey and defend the constitution and laws of the land. With equal tenacity she would support and maintain the constituted authority within the state. Anyone attempting to incite combined resistance through violence against the state should suffer death, and if anyone should aid in circulating printed matter tending to incite insurrection, such persons should be subject to imprisonment in the penitentiary from five to twenty years.

For President Johnson, who had dealt with the former Confederate states in a liberal and considerate manner, Georgia had great respect and so expressed herself in resolutions of her legislature. But President Johnson had gone a very short way in his reconstructing of the Union before a vengeful group of Congressmen, led by Thaddeus Stevens and Charles Sumner, fell into bitter abuse of the president and declared that he was a traitor to his country; he had made it too easy for the former Confederate states to get back into the Union. They accused the South of being wholly responsible for the war and began to devise a plan whereby stern punishment should be meted out. They refused to recognize the states which had been reconstructed according to President Johnson's plan, and denied the representatives from these states seats in Congress. The new plan they worked out was embraced in another amendment to the constitution, the fourteenth, which the former Confederate states must ratify before they should be permitted to re-enter the Union; and even then, they might be required to meet other conditions. This new amendment made the Negroes citizens, forced the South to give them the right to vote or suffer a reduction in representation in Congress, disqualified for state and Federal offices many white people, and inflicted other penalties.

Georgia rejected this amendment almost unanimously in November, 1866, as it appeared to her that the acceptance of it would make her a party to her own degradation. President Johnson, himself, had advised the South to reject it. Logic and common reason led the Georgians to declare that they were already in the Union, for if they were not, then the thirteenth amendment had not been legally adopted, for only states could ratify amendments.

The rejection of the fourteenth amendment by all the former Confederate states, with the exception of Tennessee, which was dragged into ratifying it by Governor Brownlow, threw the radical Congressmen into a furor. In March, 1867, they adopted a new plan whereby they converted the rebellious Southern states into military districts, numbered them like convicts, and planted an army upon them. Georgia became a part of the Third Military District over which General John Pope was placed as chief tormentor.

Georgia was now faced with a situation which troubled her soul deeply. The state had been thrown back to the position she had occupied on Lee's surrender in 1865. Would she peaceably submit? Various opinions were held, but there was no one so wild and foolish as to advocate a renewal of the war. Joseph E. Brown, who had early accepted the program of President Johnson, was either one of the wisest men of his time or the best guesser. Seeing far ahead, he concluded that worse would come if the state did not accept this bitter dose. Now the army had been placed upon the necks of the people, and Brown still advised the people to accept it. For joining in with the alien invaders, Brown was loathed with a hatred likely never equalled in the history of the state. Benjamin H. Hill arose with his fiercest denunciations, applied equally to Brown and his radical party and to the military régime. He began in June, 1867, a barrage of newspaper articles, called "Notes on the Situation," and in July from a platform in Atlanta he thundered defiance at the enemy. Robert Toombs returned from exile in Europe about this time, unrepentant for the past except its failures, and defied the Reconstructionists. Governor Jenkins sought to stay the execution of the Reconstruction acts of Congress by going to Washington and bringing suit against the army commanders and the war department. In the case of Georgia *vs.* Stanton, the court, for want of jurisdiction, refused to act.

General Pope was ushered into Georgia on April Fool's Day, 1867; but his coming was no hoax. Trying to live the philosophy of Brown, that it was best to accept the inevitable and thereby escape greater evils, Georgians generally received Pope with good grace, while Brown, himself, welcomed him with a toast at a banquet in Atlanta. However much the general might have wanted to please the Georgians, his position made it doubly difficult. Newspaper editors were soon printing cutting criticisms of his régime, and a University student, by indirection, flayed him in a commencement oration. In retaliation, he removed the legal advertising from the hostile papers and laid hands on the funds of the University. For refusing to obey an order placing Negroes on the jury lists, he removed from office Judge Augustus Reese, of the Ocmulgee circuit.

The purpose of Congress in dividing the South into military districts and setting over them generals was to hasten their reconstruction according to Congressional plans. Though the general had the right to dismiss any officials he pleased, Pope was sparing in the use of this power, as it would have been provocative of further turmoil. One of his first duties was to prepare a registration list of all those people whom Congress had allowed the right to vote. This work began in April with boards of registrars, consisting of one Negro and two whites, scattered throughout the state. Now for the first time, Negroes were given the right to vote in Georgia, and the great mass of them were rounded up and registered. Some, under assumed names, were registered two or three times, and in Augusta many from South Carolina were accepted. To promote a large registration, the boards were allowed twenty-six cents for each name recorded. Though it was difficult for Negroes to escape registration, the white people found that many questions had to be answered acceptably before they would be listed. The conservatives begged the white people to register if possible so that later they might vote down the work of the military Reconstructionists. Although about 10,000 white people were refused registration, the white population was able to secure about 2,000 majority on the registration lists. The total registration was 95,214 white people, and 93,457 Negroes.

The next step was to hold an election, ordered for the five days from October 29th to November 2nd, at which the voters would decide whether a constitutional convention should be held and at the same time elect delegates to the convention. The conservative leaders, such as Herschel V. Johnson, urged the white people to go to the polls and vote against the convention; but most of them were deterred by the weird sight of a mass of ignorant and illiterate Negroes, only recently their slaves, holding sway at the ballot boxes. In Baldwin County, only seven white people voted, and in Jefferson, only one. In McIntosh County, on the dark coast, only three white people voted while 524 Negroes marched forward. Out of a total registration of 192,235, only 106,410 votes were cast, and only slightly more than 4,000 were against the convention.

At the same time 166 delegates were elected to remake the fundamental law of Georgia, and well might the hearts of Georgians have been sickened at the sight of those elected. Thirty-seven were Negroes, the vicious, the innocent, the ignorant, the illiterate: Aaron Alpeoria Bradley, a convict from New York and later to be expelled from the convention; Tunis G. Campbell, a carpet-bagger who had attempted to set up a grandiloquent government on St. Catherines Island directly following the war; H. M. Turner, later to become a bishop in the African Methodist Church; and others, who were clay in the hands of their cunning and designing white friends. Nine were white carpet-baggers, about a dozen were conservative white Georgians, and the remainder were native white Georgians who had turned against the old traditions of their state and who were known under the despicable name of scalawags. The principal leaders in the convention were Ben Conley, Rufus B. Bullock, Foster Blodgett, and A. T. Akerman. Joseph E. Brown, though not a member, addressed the convention, and General Pope and his military staff were invited to occupy seats.

The convention met on December 9, 1867, in Atlanta, and continued until March of the next year. Owing to the good sense of the more conservative white members and to the docility of the more ignorant, the document produced was much more intelligent than what was done in most of the other Southern states. Imprisonment for debt, which had led to the establishment of the colony of Georgia, was finally abolished, lotteries hereafter should not be permitted, and the right to secede from the Union was denied. The road to corruption was made smooth by allowing the state and local divisions to aid with money railways and other public works. The right of a married woman to the complete control of her own property was guaranteed. The privilege of voting was given to the Negroes, but the white people were not disfranchised, as had been done in Tennessee and other states. So much more did these constitution-makers enjoy the bustling city of Atlanta than the sleepy little village of Milledgeville, that they made Atlanta the capital.

To pay for the work of this aggregation of "adventurers from New England, . . . convicts from penitentiaries, and . . . ignorant Negroes from the cornfields," General Pope called upon the state treasury for $40,000. John Jones, the treasurer, refused to pay the money on the ground that it was illegal for him to pay a voucher without the warrant of the governor, and Governor Jenkins refused to sign the warrant on the ground that the constitution and the laws gave him no right to expend money for such a purpose. In the midst of this trouble, Pope was superseded by General George Meade, who made a new demand for the money. On being refused he demolished the state civil government by removing the governor, the treasurer, the secretary of state, and the comptroller-general, and by filling the vacancies with officers from his army. Now for the first time in her history, Georgia had a government of army officers, imposed upon her by force, and alien to her soil. Brigadier-General Thomas H. Ruger became governor, Captain Charles F. Rockwell, treasurer, and Captain Charles Wheaton was given the offices of comptroller-general and secretary of state.

In the meantime Governor Jenkins, having hid the great

seal, left the state, carrying with him $400,000 of the public funds, which he deposited in a New York bank. In Washington he sought the aid of the Supreme Court to prevent the spoliation of Georgia at the hands of Ruger and Rockwell, but this most powerful body had been intimidated by the radical Congressional party to such an extent that it was afraid to act.

General Meade ordered an election for April 20, 1868, to continue four days, for the purpose of adopting the constitution and at the same time selecting all officers under it, including Congressmen. A campaign of great bitterness now developed, for the conservative Georgians were determined to keep the state from falling into the hands of the carpet-baggers, Negroes, and scalawags. They organized clubs throughout the state having previously held in December, 1867, in Macon, the first political convention after the war. In March, the executive committee of the conservatives, who were in fact the Democrats and were coming to call themselves so, nominated for governor Augustus Reese, whom Pope had deposed from a judgeship. As Reese's record did not please the military rulers of the state, he was forced to withdraw, and Judge David Irwin was named. But Irwin pleased General Meade no better, and then the conservatives got the permission of the general to nominate General John B. Gordon.

The radicals, who were in fact the Republicans, nominated Rufus B. Bullock, a New Yorker, who had come to Georgia in 1859 and who had been in the quartermaster's department of the Confederacy. In the election the constitution was adopted by about 18,000 majority and Bullock was chosen governor, but only by about 7,000 majority. However, in the presidential election of 1868 the Democrats were able to carry the state, while all the other former Confederate states, with the exception of Louisiana, cast their electoral votes for the Republicans.

The legislature elected at the same time Bullock was chosen met on July 4th. Although it was somewhat difficult to determine exactly the political classification or complexion of the membership, it was soon evident that the Democrats would control the house and the Republicans, the senate. General Meade, who continued as dictator until Bullock should be inaugurated, accepted the membership of the legislature, though the Democrats were undoubtedly shocked to see twenty-nine Negro members in the house and three in the senate. On the 21st, the legislature ratified the fourteenth amendment; the next day Bullock was inaugurated governor; and on July 30th Georgia was back in the Union and the troops were withdrawn. The legislature elected Joshua Hill and H. V. M. Miller to the United States Senate, much to the discomfiture of Governor Bullock, who had hoped to pay a political debt owed his hench-man Foster Blodgett by having him made Senator, and had promised his powerful ally, Joseph E. Brown, a like reward. Robert Toombs, disfranchised and defiant, watched with vast contempt the political scene. He dismissed Joshua Hill as only "a poor devil" but he took unbounded delight in the defeat of Brown, "the scoundrel."

The presence of the Negro members became increasingly unbearable as the session wore on, and by early September their right to hold office having been taken up and denied, all were expelled from the senate and twenty-five from the house. The other four escaped expulsion as there was some doubt as to their classification as Negroes. The legislature held that the right to vote did not confer the right to hold office, and in support of this view, they cited the debates in the constitutional convention and the opinion of Joseph E. Brown. In the places vacated by the expelled Negroes were seated conservative whites.

Bullock, fearful that his control of the legislature had been completely lost and that the power of his radical Republicans in the state might soon fall, began a campaign to induce the radical Congressmen in Washington to restore Georgia to the Federal army, to be reconstructed again. He used the expulsion of the Negroes with great effect, and re-enforced his arguments with a recital of the outrages that were being daily committed by a secret order known as the Ku Klux Klan.

This organization, founded in Tennessee in 1866, had meant little more than an outlet for the pranks of returned Confederate soldiers, until the supremacy of the white people in the South was threatened by the coming of another organization called the Loyal or Union League and the granting of suffrage to the Negro. Under the control of designing Northern adventurers, chapters of this League made their first appearance in Georgia in 1867, in time to organize the Negro for the first ballot he was to cast. With its regalia and ritual, its military training and guns, it instilled into the Negro dangerous notions of his superiority over his former white master.

For the white people to have tried to combat these dangers with open resistance would have been absurd; instead, they called to their assistance the Invisible Empire of the Ku Klux Klan, and the best elements in the state entered into its secret confines. General Nathan Bedford Forrest was the head of it throughout the South; General John B. Gordon became its head in Georgia. It made its first appearance in Georgia in the spring of 1868, and broke out with greatest violence in the northern part of the state, where it was largely used to regulate the social and economic position of the Negro, and in the upper part of the cotton belt where it sought to deter the Negro from politics. It scarcely ever operated in cities.

With its weird gowns and mysterious movements it struck terror and death to those against whom it rode. G. W. Ashburn, a consorter with Negroes in Columbus, was warned by the Klan and a few days later killed. Severe reprisals were carried out in the name of the law against nine people suspected of the crime. There was considerable violence in the state during this time, but likely little more than the conditions then existing would naturally breed; yet the Klan was charged by its enemies with being guilty of any deed whose perpetrators could not be discovered. At Camilla, in September, 1868, about 300 armed

Negroes were set upon by white people after they had failed to induce the Negroes to disarm, and before the riot was over eight or nine Negroes had been killed and a dozen or more wounded.

The Klan's most spectacular work was done in convincing the Negroes that politics was a game reserved exclusively for the white man. A comparison of the results of the two elections of 1868 is startling. The Negro was almost eliminated in the November voting for president. In April the vote for Bullock in Oglethorpe County was 1,144, in November Grant received 116. In Columbia County the Republicans cast 1,222 in April and in November only one Republican voted.

With exaggerated accounts of Ku Klux outrages Bullock was able to induce Congress to take testimony on Georgia, and in March, 1869, Georgia added another crime to her list by rejecting the fifteenth amendment, which forbade the disfranchisement of any citizen on account of his race, color, or the fact that he had been a slave. Though Bullock wanted Negro suffrage as the surest way of keeping himself in power, yet he wanted the army in Georgia at that time more, so that there can be little doubt that he was responsible for the rejection of the amendment in the hope that it would afford the final argument needed before Congress.

The state was in a curious position in 1869. Was it in the Union or out? The election of Grant was announced with and without Georgia's vote, as in either case the general was still successful. Georgia's representatives had been admitted to the House, but after March, 1869, they were excluded on a technicality; and her Senators were never seated. In the meantime, the legislature, becoming somewhat frightened, sought to settle in the courts the right of the Negroes to the seats they had been made to vacate, but Bullock killed the move, believing that expelled Negroes were better arguments than seated Negroes in inducing Congress to plant the army in Georgia again. In June in the case of White *vs.* Clements, the Georgia Supreme

Top: TAKING THE OATH OF ALLEGIANCE. FOLLOWING THE CIVIL WAR ALL SOUTHERNERS WERE REQUIRED TO TAKE AN OATH TO SUPPORT THE UNITED STATES BEFORE THEY WERE ALLOWED TO PARTICIPATE IN THE NEW STATE GOVERNMENTS. *Bottom:* CONVENTION OF FREEDMEN DISCUSSING THEIR POLITICAL RIGHTS. THE NEGRO WAS GREATLY PUZZLED BY SUCH TERMS AS REGISTRATION AND RATIFICATION.

Top left: CHARLES J. JENKINS, RESOURCEFUL GOVERNOR WHO OPPOSED MILITARY RECONSTRUC-
TION. *Top right:* RUFUS B. BULLOCK, NEW YORKER, RECONSTRUCTION GOVERNOR, AND CAPITAL-
IST. *Bottom left:* JOSHUA HILL, OPPONENT OF SECESSION, A QUIET UNIONIST DURING THE WAR,
AND A UNITED STATES SENATOR, 1871-73. *Bottom right:* JOHN B. GORDON, LIEUTENANT GEN-
ERAL IN THE CONFEDERACY, GOVERNOR, THRICE UNITED STATES SENATOR, AND CAPITALIST.

Court decided that Negroes had the right to hold office. Brown, who had been rewarded by a place on the court, now voted opposite to the contention he had made the preceding year when he said that a Negro could not hold an office.

Bullock and his radical party had their wish granted, when on December 22, 1869, Congress sent the army back to Georgia, with General Alfred H. Terry as the new dictator. Georgia was now out of the Union and under the army again, and the only way she might recover the one and shake off the other was to be duly respectful to Negroes and ratify the fifteenth amendment. In the following January, Bullock called the legislature again—not the one shorn of the Negroes but the one originally elected in 1868. Acting the part of a Cromwell, Terry appointed three of his army officers to purge the legislature of all members who were disagreeable to the Bullock régime. They expelled twenty-one representatives and one senator, and readmitted all the Negroes.

Here was at last a legislature worthy of the radicals, and ready for any corruption or spoils. It promptly ratified the fifteenth amendment, joyously ratified again the fourteenth, and then, disallowing the Senatorial election of the preceding year, chose three men, including Foster Blodgett, to serve out terms and parts of terms. Conservative Republicans and Democrats alike had feared that a raid on the public treasury would result from Terry's purge; and their worst fears were soon justified. Having fewer carpet-baggers than most of the other Southern states, Georgia escaped the worst iniquities meted out in the South. Her greatest corruption and extravagances were in printing and other governmental expenses, and in the endorsement of railroad bonds. The cost of the civil establishment leaped from $20,000 in 1866 to $76,000 in 1870; printing, from $1,000 to $57,000; and advertisements of proclamations, from $5,000 during the years 1855-1860 to $98,300 during the years 1868-1870. The proceeds from the sale of bonds were directed away from the purpose indicated. Henry Clews & Co., in New York, were financial agents of Georgia, and they worked in unison with their master, the Bullock régime. They sold bonds for less than 87 and misapplied the proceeds.

The greatest power in Georgia during the Bullock régime was Hannibal I. Kimball, a Northern adventurer, who became the guide and financial adviser of the governor. He was the president of three Georgia railroads, which secured illegally state bonds; he purchased an unfinished opera house in Atlanta and sold it to the state for a capitol; he sold to the state, for the Western and Atlantic Railroad, cars which were never delivered; he marketed bonds for the state without rendering an account; he built a grand hotel, the Kimball House, and was never able to convince many Georgians that he had not used the state's money in doing it; he was a great manager and plunger, a dispenser of state money lavishly where it would do him the most good, leading the Negroes to concoct a little song:

> "H. I. Kimball's on the floor
> 'Taint gwine ter rain no more."

The legislature promised the endorsement of $30,000,000 of bonds for thirty-seven railroads, but it actually executed its endorsement on only $5,733,000. Yet in this there was great corruption, for bonds were delivered in violation of the law which required a certain amount of mileage to be completed before the state's endorsement should be given. The Cartersville and Van Wert Railroad was later sold for $29,500, though the state had executed bonds for it to the amount of $575,000.

The most flagrant example of the corrupting influence of politics in the railroad business was in the case of the Western and Atlantic Railroad. Being state property, it was peculiarly exposed to the raids of corrupt politicians. At the end of the war it had been seized by the Federal government and held until September, 1865. Thereupon, Georgia recovered it and during the next two years spent $800,000 in re-equipping it and restoring it to a state of efficiency. The Bullock régime took control in 1868, and instead of making a profit for the state out of this rebuilt railroad, within two years piled up a debt of $750,000. A vast system of plunder was worked out under the superintendence of Foster Blodgett. Fictitious jobs were created for members of the legislature and for their select kin, and the railroad paid their salaries. Politicians got themselves made conductors of the trains to fatten on the cash fares paid by passengers. The road was even used to haul Negroes free of charge from Chattanooga to vote in Atlanta elections. A few investigations were ordered under Bullock, but the committees could never find any corruption, blotted out as it was by liquors, cigars, and other entertainment given the committeemen.

Even the plunderers soon came to feel that there must be an end to their plundering, and so in 1870 the legislature passed a law requiring the road to be leased for twenty years for not less than $25,000 a month. Joseph E. Brown, no less astute as a business man than as a politician, quickly organized a company, which, after various negotiations, was forced to admit other groups until the completed company became one of the most unusual conglomerations of people ever assembled in any human endeavor. Besides a United States Senator and other national politicians, railroad presidents, millionaires, Georgia politicians, and business men, there were Alexander H. Stephens and Benjamin H. Hill. Stephens, remembering Brown's excellent business ability, seemed not to notice the malodorous company he was in. The shock his presence gave his friend Toombs blasted Stephens out. There was little surprise anywhere at Hill's association with the company, for he had recently turned from his vigorous crusade against the invaders to surrender to them with the recommendation that others do likewise. The next day after the lease was signed, December 27, 1870, he attended the famous Delano Dinner in Atlanta, and with Brown, Bullock, Secretary of the Interior Columbus Delano, Senator Simon Cameron, and other politicians large and little, drank to the prosperity of the Radicals.

With shame and sorrow, mixed with a bit of humor, the conservative Georgians in adding Benjamin H. Hill to Joseph E. Brown, could remark, "Joseph is not, and now they have taken my son Benjamin."

As another company had offered the state a rental of $35,000 a month, the feeling grew up that fraud and corruption had surrounded Bullock's leasing the road to the Brown group. In 1872, when the Democrats had secured control of the state, a committee to investigate the lease was appointed, and it concluded that the lease "was unfairly obtained."

Satisfied with all the contrition of heart shown by Georgia and perhaps a little amazed at her corruption, Congress admitted her a second time in July, 1870, but refused to seat the new group of senators Bullock's legislature had chosen. In an election of a legislature in December, 1870, the Democrats secured control of both bodies, and to escape the certain impeachment which he knew awaited him, Governor Bullock secretly resigned and left the state in October, 1871, not to return for a half dozen years. In a special election for governor held in the following December, the Democrats chose James M. Smith, whom the radical Republicans did not go to the trouble to oppose.

The Democrats now set to work with great zeal to clean out the Augean stables. They not only exposed the Western and Atlantic Railroad lease, but they also appointed a committee to investigate the official life and conduct of Bullock and another committee to determine the validity of the Bullock bond issues. As a result of these investigations Bullock was declared guilty of indictable offenses and was later tried but acquitted, and the railroad bonds were repudiated by legislative enactment and by the new constitution adopted in 1877.

The return of the Democrats also brought back the great seal of the state; ex-Governor Jenkins in restoring it could proudly say, "I derive great satisfaction from the reflection that it has never been desecrated by the grasp of a military usurper's hand," and to show its appreciation the legislature presented to him a facsimile with the motto "In arduis fidelis."

In the presidential election of 1872, a breach occurred in the Republican Party caused by the unblushing corruption which seemed to have become a fixed party principle. The seceders called themselves Liberal Republicans, nominated Horace Greeley for the presidency, and made a bid for the support of the South. Though the movement was worthy of a better candidate, it appealed sufficiently to the Democratic Party to cause it to forego putting up a candidate of its own and to ratify Greeley's nomination. It set up a hard test to be met in Georgia and the rest of the South. It involved an admission that Reconstruction as carried out by Congress must stand, but it also afforded an opportunity to the South to lead its own life in a new way. It drew the line between the unreconstructed who looked backward to the Lost Cause and those who were willing still to remember but to look forward. The former were led by Alexander H. Stephens and Robert Toombs, who set up the *Atlanta Sun* to better fight their battles, and the latter, by Benjamin H. Hill. There was much bitterness, but the New Departure succeeded in Georgia. It also made it possible for many anti-Bullock Republicans to join the Democrats, and helped many Georgians to understand that Joseph E. Brown and Benjamin H. Hill, in bending their course to the storms of Reconstruction, might have been much wiser than the unreconstructed Democrats who had foolishly opposed the inevitable.

Hill received forgiveness first. Though having been spurned by many of the unreconstructed Georgians continuously since his apostasy, he had early begun to show a repentance which must sometime regain for him the respect of the state. On numerous occasions he had gone out to do battle against the Radicals, asking nothing beyond the good-will of his fellow-citizens. His reward came in 1875, when he was elected a representative in Congress, and in this act his district showed not only that it had forgiven him but also that Georgians were getting away from the war sufficiently to forget their former bitter personal feelings. Brown's return to the fold was to come later and under different circumstances.

Back in the national currents, Hill soon found himself in the midst of a fight, spectacular and bitter, provoked by James G. Blaine for the purpose of getting himself nominated by the Republicans to the presidency of the United States. Early in 1876, Blaine "waved the bloody shirt" in the face of the Southerners by demanding that Jefferson Davis be excepted from a general amnesty bill then before Congress, on the ground that Davis had been responsible for the horrors of Andersonville prison. Hill's pent-up desire to serve Georgia and the South gave way and he engaged in a stormy debate, which may have been unwise for a Southerner to take up at that time; but it gained for him complete forgiveness in Georgia, and made his oratory on that occasion long remembered.

Though this debate might have made it seem that Hill was more fiery and unreconstructed than any other Southerner in Congress, another act of his about this time made it seem otherwise. The year 1876 marked the centennial of the signing of the Declaration of Independence, and Philadelphia decided to be the host to the nation in commemorating the event. A bill providing for the national sanction was introduced in Congress, and every Georgian except Hill voted against it, as they could see no occasion for rejoicing even if America was a hundred years old, for the liberties that Southerners had proudly proclaimed in 1776 were now withheld from them in 1876. Many Georgians agreed with Hill, at least to the extent of journeying to Philadelphia where they saw interesting sights, which they did not forget after their return. And thus, the exposition had its small effect in making Southerners feel more American.

The corruption of Grant's two administrations had become so brazen that many Republicans were sickened even unto a determination to vote for Samuel J. Tilden, the Democratic nominee for the presidency in 1876. Georgia became greatly interested, for it now seemed that the South's delivery from its oppressors was at hand. For the governorship, Alfred H. Colquitt ran against Jonathan Norcross, the Republican candidate. There was little fear of the Republicans in Georgia, for the Bullock régime had greatly discredited them. In the voting, Colquitt defeated Norcross by 111,000 to 33,000; while Tilden defeated Rutherford B. Hayes, the Republican presidential candidate, by 130,000 to 50,000.

A dangerous dispute now arose over the presidential election, and for a time it seemed that civil war might result. It appeared to many people that the Republicans were bent on making Hayes president, though Tilden had received apparently a majority of the electoral votes and without a doubt 252,000 more popular votes than Hayes. The complications in counting the electoral votes ultimately led to the appointment of an electoral commission, which counted Hayes into the presidency. Great excitement prevailed in Georgia, and Joseph E. Brown now recanted so completely his former Radicalism that he advised using force to seat Tilden. But up in Congress, John B. Gordon in the Senate and Hill in the House aided materially in bringing about an understanding with emissaries of Hayes, whereby the president later removed from the South the Federal troops and allowed home rule in those states which had so long been bedeviled by aliens supported by occupying armies.

CHAPTER XXVIII

HOME RULE AGAIN

THE MOTTO, *E Pluribus Unum,* meaning to Americans that out of a multiplicity of peoples and governments there should be one nationality, was for a long time more a hope than a fact. The original thirteen states, though having the common background of language almost completely, and race to a large extent, had grown up as separate colonies under England. When they entered a union they still maintained their individual governments, separate boundaries, and their names, which kept alive their own identity and unconsciously warred against the idea of *E Pluribus Unum.* The first signs of the merging of the people indicated that they were developing into sectional likenesses more than national, a trend which helped to bring on the movement in the South to set up its independence. The North crushed the attempt at independence, but the hard force which it applied thereafter to make the South similar to the North succeeded only in making the South more Southern. By treating all the seceded states to the same hard lot, it created a Solid South, and helped to rub out the lines among the Southern states without obscuring the line which separated them from the North. Not until the twentieth century, with the coming of the motor age, the talking pictures, and all the other levelling forces, did the dreary prospect begin to stare Americans in the face that they were all destined for the same dead level of uniformity and standardization.

Thus, Georgia after the war became less Georgian and more Southern, but finally, less Southern and more American. As this process set in, the state in its own right became less important, and its history merged more into that of the section and of the nation. And so finally, to recount the history of Georgia, apart from the forced artificialities of politics, was to set her in her proper position in the national stream which included all.

To lay the foundations for the new times which should be unhampered by Federal bayonets, Georgia made preparations to throw off the foreign cloak which she had been forced to don and to put on a garment made in Georgia by Georgians. It might turn out that this new garment would be no better than the old, but it would at least seem more becoming because of its workmanship. Scarcely had Bullock fled the state, before a movement was started to hold a constitutional convention, to replace the so-called carpet-bag constitution of 1868. The fear, inherent in a people, of turning over their destiny to a group, even of their own choice, prevented immediate success. After a defeat in the legislature, a motion to submit the question to the people prevailed, and in a popular referendum the calling of a convention was carried by only 9,000 majority. In 1877 the convention met, exactly a hundred years after Georgia had made her first constitution.

A group of able Georgians came together in Atlanta and organized for work under the presidency of Charles J. Jenkins, who had had much to do with making the constitution of 1865. The convention resolved itself into thirteen committees. Robert Toombs, as chairman of the committee on revision, took a preponderant position in the deliberations, and made himself largely responsible for the document which was turned out. Thomas J. Simmons, as chairman of the committee on finance, did a work scarcely less outstanding.

The convention put together more a collection of statutory laws than a body of fundamental principles, so fearful was it of letting any constituted government fully rule over the people. The inevitable result was that when the people developed more confidence in their government, they found it necessary to be almost constantly amending their constitution; and so, as time

went on, it came to be a Joseph's coat of many colors and more
patches, until it could be called "a legal conundrum that no
court can solve." It wisely forbade the formation of more
counties; yet this paragraph of six words, "No new county shall
be created," was to be amended within the next fifty years
twenty-four times to allow twenty-four new counties. By the
process of amendment during the next half century, the meetings of the legislature, fixed here as biennial, oscillated back
and forth between biennial and annual, and the month swung
among November, January, and June. Other parts of the constitution which might well have suffered change remained
adamant against time and reason.

With bitter memories of the Radicals' onset against the
state's revenues in the days of their power, the convention
under the particular guidance of Toombs so restricted the
power of taxation and the incurring of a public debt as to lead
to the common expression that Georgia had locked her treasury and thrown away the key. The legislature could levy a tax
only for the support of the state government, for "instructing
children in the elementary branches of an English education
only," to pay the public debt, "to suppress insurrection, to repel
invasion, and defend the State in time of war," to buy artificial
limbs for the Confederate soldiers, and to pension soldiers
and their widows. All property should bear the same rate,
which should be levied *ad valorem*. The bonded debt should
never be increased "except to repel invasion, suppress insurrection, or defend the State in time of war," and every year the
legislature must reduce the existing debt by at least $100,000.
The Reconstruction bonds already repudiated both by law and
constitutional amendment were here repudiated again; and to
comply with Federal requirements the Confederate debt was
also repudiated. A limit was set upon the debt local divisions
might create, and they, as well as the state, were forbidden to
lend their credit to any individual, corporation, or association.

The governor's term of office was reduced from four years to two, and his salary was fixed at $3,000 a year. To protect the judges from popular passions, they were made elective by the legislature; but later the supreme court justices and then the superior court judges were handed back to the people.

This document, adopted by the convention, was submitted to the people, who accepted it by a considerable majority and in the same election finally selected Atlanta as the state capital, despite the vigorous fight made by Milledgeville to recapture it.

Political parties and politics continued to afford Georgians something with which to be entertained, amused, maddened, and made afraid. When the Federal troops had marched out of the South they carried with them the hope of the Republican Party there. Most of the white people joined themselves into a loose confederation called the Democratic Party, whose inclusiveness bred internal dissensions never to be given up except in the face of a Republican threat. The Negro, though a potential Republican, was made to feel in time that his general prosperity would vary directly with the distance he maintained between himself and the ballot-box; and only when factions within the Democratic Party made of him an article of commerce did he become an arbiter in elections and thereby a threat against white supremacy. His complete elimination was later made a subject of agreement among the Democrats.

The political control of Georgia quickly fell into the hands of an element in the Democratic Party generally referred to as the Bourbons. Their strength lay in the fact that they could look backward and forward at the same time. Their program embraced the philosophy of the prophet Henry W. Grady, who held that the New South should wear the halo and absorb the romance of the olden times, but it should get away from the retarding philosophy of the Old South. It should embrace the new industrialism; it should build towns and cities and develop mines and construct factories; it should do the things which had made the North rich and powerful. A Solid South politically would give it a less powerful position in the councils of the nation, but in no other way could the withering effect of Negro rule be avoided.

These Bourbon Democrats were industrially minded men, who, in their personnel, combined the Confederate tradition and the Henry W. Grady philosophy of the new day: John B. Gordon, the Confederate general who would always typify the Lost Cause, and the big business man who would build and run railroads; Joseph E. Brown, a great deal of everything he had lived through, the fire-eating secessionist, the warrior governor, the peace man, the Reconstructionist and Republican, the philanthropist, and above all else, the successful business man; and Alfred H. Colquitt, the Confederate major-general, and the large planter who raised a thousand bales of cotton a year. This triumvirate ruled Georgia with few intermissions from the restoration of Democratic control until the rise of the small farmers in the early 'nineties. Colquitt and Gordon were governors during most of the period, one of the three was constantly in the United States Senate, and during the last third of the time both Brown and Colquitt were there.

Gordon arose to power in 1873 by defeating for the United States Senate a host of candidates including Hill and Stephens; and Colquitt became governor three years later. Brown did not emerge until 1880 when he entered the United States Senate. Hill and Stephens, prominent Confederates, though not of the Gordon-Colquitt-Brown triumvirate, entered Congress as representatives in 1873 and 1875 respectively. In 1877 Hill entered the Senate.

Though the Confederate tradition permeated this leadership, it was not narrow in its outlook as this article of faith, written by the Democratic convention in 1888 attested: "We seek a manly fraternity among all the states and peoples of the United States, and declare that the only enemies of perpetual American concord are those Republicans who insist upon reviving and maintaining the passions of past conflicts, terminated forever and honorably adjusted." And even when the rise of the small farmers banished the Bourbons, the Confederate tradition continued to live on down through the governorship until 1902. Throughout these thirty years, no person occupied the governor's chair who had not been in either the Confederate army or the civil service of the Confederacy. In 1914 Nathaniel E. Harris arose out of the past to become the last of the Confederate governors, and in his passing to announce the coming of a new day and generation when Confederate service and Confederate votes could no longer be coveted or feared.

This loose confederation of Georgia Democracy had the germs of insurgency and independency in it from the beginning. It had been the vengeful stupidity of the Congressional oligarchy in its reconstruction of the state that had forced the different political elements to coalesce into a solid Democracy; otherwise there would have been a two-party system. In 1874 party rebellion broke out when William H. Felton, of the "bloody seventh" Congressional district, in the northwestern part of the state, opposed the regular candidate as a tool of the "Atlanta ring" and the "developers of resources," who were ruling the state through the "court-house rings." Representing the common man, Felton made this insurgency movement a grave threat against the rule of the rich Bourbons, as he won this election and the next two succeeding ones. Over in the mountains of northeastern Georgia, Emory Speer aided the rising Independent Democracy by securing a seat as a representative in Congress in 1878 and 1880, and he continued to be a threat to the Bourbons until he was silenced by his appointment to a Federal judgeship in the southern part of the state in 1885.

Colquitt's term as governor set off a wave of insurgency and party turmoil scarcely equalled in the history of the state. With a new constitution to go into effect, it seemed that there was no end to the number of Democrats seeking office. Colquitt had about thirty appointments at his disposal; yet three thousand insistent office-seekers laid siege to him. When the spoils had been distributed he had confirmed thirty friendships and made 2,970 enemies. His enemies were soon upon him, some for personal reasons and others because they believed the party leaders were in corrupt alliance with the big business interests. In compliance with the law, Colquitt had endorsed bonds of the North-Eastern Railroad to the amount of $260,000, and thereby brought down upon his head such a fierce denunciation that he called upon the legislature for relief. A special committee investigated and reported the charges to be "vile and malignant slanders." Though Colquitt might be blameless in this particular, the insurgents were convinced that his administration was corrupt, and in pursuance of this belief, the legislature investigated practically every branch of the executive department. It impeached and removed from office W. L. Goldsmith, the comptroller; it impeached and acquitted J. W. Renfroe, the treasurer; and it investigated the school commissioner Gustavus J. Orr and the secretary of state N. C. Barnett, only to find that Orr had traveled over the state at his own expense in the interest of public education, and that Barnett might have been too generous in the use of wax for affixing to documents the great seal of the state.

Though Colquitt had defeated his enemies, there was a deep and widespread discontent with him and with the Democratic leadership which he represented. As he had been elected under the old constitution, his term of office was four years, and so the next campaign for the governorship fell in 1880. In the early part of this year, John B. Gordon, who had been only recently elected to the United States Senate, suddenly decided to resign in order to enter into the railroad business. Colquitt, who was on good terms with Joseph E. Brown, now appointed him to the vacancy, to hold office until the meeting of the legislature. Brown had been long recommending himself for the forgiveness which he was sure his Georgians would give him, if he were patient enough. In 1872 he had drifted back into the Democratic Party and had supported Greeley for president; in

1876 he had fought valiantly for Tilden and the Democrats; now it seemed to him and to many other Georgians that his reward had been justified, and so it appeared to the legislature, which elected him later in the year. Yet there immediately went up from the insurgent Democracy a bitter cry of "bargain and corruption." It was erroneously held that Gordon had resigned on account of favors promised by Brown, who should be placed in the vacancy in return for his support of Colquitt for the governorship.

In the convention which met to nominate a governor, a long and bitter fight took place. The insurgents were determined never to give in to the selection of Colquitt, and as the two-thirds rule, which had lain dormant since ante-bellum days, had been revived, they made good their threat. For six days the scramble went on among five candidates. The convention was brought to adjournment and the contest to an end without a nomination, by the majority recommending Colquitt to the people of the state. Thomas E. Watson, here first breaking into a stormy career, declared that he would never go for Colquitt. After the adjournment the minority remained in the hall, organized a rump convention, and declaring that Colquitt had not been legally nominated, designated Thomas M. Norwood as the Democratic candidate.

Grave dangers lay ahead. Less than a decade after the Radicals and the Negroes had been ousted from control by a united white man's party bearing the name Democratic, there was an opening made for their return through a breach in that party. The Republicans, seeing their opportunity, arose from the lethargy which had gripped them since their downfall, and held a convention. A few white delegates were present, including Jonathan Norcross, who attempted unsuccessfully to have the convention indorse the nomination of Norwood. The delegates adjourned without making a nomination, but their meeting was sufficient notice to the disrupted Democracy that they were a force that could not go unnoticed. Efforts were now made by both factions of the Democracy to secure the votes of the Negroes; the apple of discord had been tossed into the white man's political game and was to go rolling along causing trouble for a generation.

Colquitt was elected by a majority of more than 54,000 votes, a fact which greatly pleased the Bourbon Democracy; but Norwood polled 64,004 votes, and this fact might well have given concern. Two years later, in the next gubernatorial election, the insurgents or Independent Democrats attempted and almost succeeded in working a major strategem on the regulars. Who in all Georgia could give more respectability to any movement than could Alexander H. Stephens? Stephens had been in Congress, but he had never been governor of his state. As he was growing old and feeble, his chances for this honor were fast fading; so, when the Independent Democrats invited him to be their candidate, he did not turn away with a frown. News that Stephens might be the candidate of the Independent Democrats caused great excitement among the regular Democrats, who to prevent such a calamity, hurriedly offered him their nomination, and begged him to accept in the interest of party harmony. Stephens did so, and thereby killed Independency, which was not to be resurrected until 1890.

Just as the Democrats were having their troubles, so, too, were the Republicans. There was always in this organization the danger that Negroes and whites might develop a fight for the control of the party machinery, what little there might be of it. Although the designations "Lilly White" and "Black and Tan" had not yet been coined to describe these two factions, the rift was plainly there. The Republican convention, held in 1882, developed more into a brawl than a deliberation. The white Republicans, under General James Longstreet, who had early turned Republican for all it was worth and for good, tried to secure control of the convention, and before the fight was over, the principal Negro leader was arrested. The Republican factions finally agreed to recommend for governor Gen-

LIBERTY HALL
THE HOME OF ALEXANDER H. STEPHENS

Here, in Crawfordville, surrounded by his dogs and Negroes, little Aleck was hospitable to friend and stranger alike. A. H. Stephens, *Constitutional View of the Late War Between the States,* I. Philadelphia: National Publishing Co., 1868.

Top left: ALFRED H. COLQUITT, GRADUATE OF PRINCETON, MAJOR-GENERAL IN THE CONFEDERACY, TWICE GOVERNOR, AND TWICE UNITED STATES SENATOR. *Top right:* JOEL CHANDLER HARRIS, AUTHOR, JOURNALIST, AND CREATOR OF "UNCLE REMUS." *Bottom left:* THOMAS E. WATSON, "THE SAGE OF MCDUFFIE," FARMER, LAWYER, JOURNALIST, POPULIST LEADER, MEMBER OF THE HOUSE OF REPRESENTATIVES, AND UNITED STATES SENATOR, 1921-1922. *Bottom right:* HOKE SMITH, SECRETARY OF THE INTERIOR UNDER PRESIDENT CLEVELAND, 1893-1896, TWICE GOVERNOR OF THE STATE, AND TWICE UNITED STATES SENATOR.

eral Lucius J. Gartrell, who had previously announced himself
as a candidate of the Independent Democrats.

Stephens was easily elected, but so feeble was he that a trip
to Savannah in 1883, made for the purpose of helping to commemorate the 150th birthday of Georgia, led to his death before his term of office was little more than half finished. He
was succeeded by James S. Boynton, the president of the senate,
who held office until a special election took place. Henry D.
McDaniel was elected almost unanimously. Only 334 votes
were cast for all others, a fact that indicated the death of
Independency in the Democratic Party and the temporary dissolution of the Republicans. The death of Benjamin H. Hill in
1882 left a vacancy which made it possible for Colquitt, the
triumvir, to succeed to the United States Senate, but not before
Pope Barrow had been honored with the election to serve for
the remaining year of Hill's term. John B. Gordon, another of
the triumviri, who had resigned from the Senate in 1880 to
enter the railroad business, either had made his fortune or had
grown tired of private life, for in 1886 he decided that he would
like to be governor. Augustus O. Bacon also desired the position, but his war record was not so well known as was Gordon's and such considerations were important now, for about
this time Jefferson Davis visited Atlanta and revived much
Confederate enthusiasm. Gordon received the nomination and
was elected without opposition. Two years later he was re-
elected, in the last dead political calm before the outburst of
the storms of Alliancemen and Populists.

A disturbance which had long been gathering in Georgia's
political life was destined to break over the state in the early
nineties with such fury as to carry everything before it. Following the Civil War there arose a system of land tenure in
which economic overlords and dictators ruled their tenants to
such an extent as to drive them to the edges of serfdom. The
overlord rented his land to people, white and black, who had
nothing except their labor, and in order to set them going he

paid the expense of their existing until the crops they should raise could be marketed. To do this to his greatest advantage, he set up a store and became a merchant, and to guarantee that he should receive something which he could sell, he required his tenants to raise cotton. Thus, he became a merchant in addition to being a land-owner, and in restricting his tenants to raising cotton made it necessary for them to buy at his store much food which they could have grown on the farm. But since he sold mostly on credit, he charged prices from 20% to 50% higher than those charged at other stores where goods were sold for cash. The tenants were always in debt and could get out only by mortgaging the crop which they had not yet raised. Almost nine-tenths of them were ensnared in this system, which was protected by the laws of the state. Though the lot of the tenants was hard, the land-owners found themselves in scarcely a better position. Added to this dismal outlook was the fact that cotton prices were dropping and taxes were steadily increasing.

Georgians were not alone in their miseries; farmers throughout the United States were in distress. The Patrons of Husbandry, or Grangers as they were familiarly known, sought to help, and in 1872 they began to appear in Georgia. By 1875 they had reached 18,000 in numbers. As Grangers were able to accomplish little, there grew up, first in Kansas and Texas as early as 1876, an organization of farmers called the Alliance. The Alliancemen made their first appearance in Georgia in 1887, when a convention met in Atlanta attended by almost three hundred delegates from various parts of the South. The farmers were in hard circumstances and they had met to seek out the reasons. They were able to discover without much difficulty that they were raising too much cotton and that taxes were too high. They also believed that speculations on Wall Street did them no good, and they were sure that there was a cotton-seed oil trust and that it was bad. From this time on, the Alliance grew fast in Georgia. Within less than three years the number of members had increased to more than 100,000. In 1890 the economically discontented held a Direct Trade Convention in Atlanta, with delegates attending from North Carolina, South Carolina, Georgia, Florida, Alabama, and Tennessee. Its purpose was to organize companies which would deal directly with foreign nations in the sale of cotton and other farm products and thereby eliminate the grasping middleman and the Eastern capitalist.

By this time the Alliancemen had formulated an extensive program, which they hoped would restore prosperity and establish social justice where it had never before existed. The farmers should raise less cotton and more food crops, and they should set up cooperative associations for buying and selling merchandise and farm products. They should enter politics and write their ideas into law: They would regulate the currency by abolishing national bank issues, by coining silver into money free of cost and in unlimited amounts, and by issuing notes based on farm products in warehouses throughout the country; they would regulate more closely the railroads or bring about government ownership; they would abolish the convict leasing system and put the convicts to work making good roads for the state; they would build up better public schools; and they would reduce taxes and the tariff and revise thoroughly the whole system of taxation. Part of this program was for the state, the rest for the nation.

The Alliancemen grew so fast in Georgia that they came to command the profound respect of the political leaders, even though the newspapers might describe them as wild men with wilder doctrines. In 1890 these reformers announced that they intended to see their program adopted into law, and that any candidate for office who refused to subscribe to this platform would be opposed at the polls. The Georgia Democratic organization, greatly fearing the intrusion of a new or third party, took fright immediately and calmly allowed itself to be swallowed up by the Alliance. Democratic candidates everywhere announced their belief in Alliance doctrines, and even John B. Gordon became so good a farmer as to get himself elected to the United States Senate again. W. J. Northen, the president of the State Agricultural Society, fittingly secured the nomination for governor. Thus had the Independency of 1880 finally triumphed in 1890. Even though Northen's farming ability and experience might be sneered at by such men as William H. Felton, yet in his election that followed, the day of the farmer in politics arrived. The Alliance not only captured the governorship, but it also elected 160 out of the 219 members of the legislature, and gained the support of all ten Congressmen elected. In the Congressional delegation was Thomas E. Watson, who now for the first time entered the national arena.

The Alliancemen, liberal in their ideas but many of them inexperienced in office, passed numerous laws guaranteeing greater social justice, but in doing so forgot their plea for economy by appropriating more money than any other legislature in the history of the state, and making it necessary to raise the tax rate $1\frac{1}{2}$ mills. They set up a school for colored youths in Savannah and gave it $8,000 a year, but at the same time passed a Jim Crow law; they prohibited the sale of liquors within three miles of a church or schoolhouse outside of cities; they forbade the blacklisting of laborers and limited the day to thirteen hours for railway trainmen and engineers; they declared Labor Day a legal holiday; and they greatly increased the pensions to Confederate soldiers and to their widows.

Nothing so sobers radically inclined people as the responsibility of power. So it was with the Alliancemen in Georgia. Although their legislation was far in advance of the regular Democratic variety, still it was too conservative to please a considerable element of the Alliancemen. There was the so-called silk stocking faction who held the position of power, and this situation greatly displeased the so-called wool hat element. The latter began to feel that after all, the Democrats had swallowed the Alliancemen rather than the other way around, as they had been led to believe. The desire for a third party, divorced from the Democrats, began to arise in some quarters. Only up in Washington, in Congress, was there a ray of hope for the wool hat Alliancemen. There sat Thomas E. Watson, who was refusing to be bound by any Democratic caucuses or rules of any sort, and he had got himself well known by charging Congressmen with being lobby-ridden and often drunk. He introduced various measures, including his Rural Free Delivery bill, whose passage was long to give him an element of fame.

By 1892 there had arisen in national affairs a party of discontent, made up largely of farmers, which was called the People's Party or the Populists. Here was a hope for those radical Georgia Alliancemen who wanted a third party in which to get away from the Democrats. The bulk of the Alliancemen, or Democrats as they really were, refused to be led into a third party movement for fear that the Negro vote would be made the arbiter in any dispute that might arise. They held their convention and renominated Northen; but Populism made its appearance at this time, held its convention, and nominated W. L. Peek as its candidate for governor. Watson was the logical man, and he was offered the nomination, but as he had learned to like the excitement of Washington, he refused it in order to run again for Congress. Northen was elected, but the Populists with their Republican support secured 58,000 votes for Peek. Though two years before, Watson had carried his district by a ten to one majority with his united Democracy, now with it divided he was defeated. He charged that the most outrageous corruption had been used against him, and it seemed that there was a great deal of truth in his charges.

This election throughout the state was a pathetic example of the venality that too often accompanies the rule by the people. Negro voters were bought and sold like merchandise and herded around the polls like so many cattle. They were fed at barbecues and made drunk and penned up to prevent them from voting, if they could not be otherwise controlled. Most of them who voted were in the hands of the regular Democrats.

In the national election Grover Cleveland was given a second term, succeeding Benjamin Harrison. This victory was indicated as early as 1890, when the Democrats secured a large majority in the House of Representatives. When this Congress met in 1891 it elected Charles F. Crisp, an able Georgian, its speaker, and when Cleveland assumed office in 1893 he made Hoke Smith, another outstanding Georgian, his secretary of the interior. The Republicans might well have rejoiced at the success of the Democrats, for they turned over to them a country on the verge of a disastrous panic. To stay its devastating effects Cleveland called a special session of Congress and forced through legislation which contracted the currency. This action appeared to many Georgians as extremely unwise, and Governor Northen wrote President Cleveland a pessimistic letter in which he predicted that the Populists were certain to capture Georgia at the next election unless speedy measures were taken to prevent it.

Economic conditions continued to grow steadily worse, until cotton was selling for less than five cents a pound; and though wheat was selling in the Middle West for fifteen cents a bushel, wheat bread in many Georgia homes was a delicacy tasted only on the rarest occasions. Property values dropped from $421,000,000 in 1892 to $338,000,000 the following year, and did not fully recover until 1900. This situation turned many Georgians into Populists and made Watson their leader.

In the election for governor in 1894, the Alliancemen, or Democrats, nominated W. Y. Atkinson and adopted a platform which contained many Populist doctrines. By so doing they hoped to prevent party defections to the Populists, who had nominated J. K. Hines. The Republicans made no nominations as most of their votes were, as usual, for sale to the highest bidder. A campaign followed in which Watson travelled widely over the state to tell the people in bitter and sarcastic language how villainous were the Democrats. Watson, himself, was running again for Congress in the "terrible tenth" district, and William H. Felton was making another attempt in the "bloody seventh." The Populists succeeded in electing five senators and 47 representatives to the legislature; but they lost all Congressional contests and the governorship. Their threat was serious, for they polled 44½% of all the votes cast. In this election the Negro vote was so corrupted as to make an unbearable stench to all honest men in both parties. The Democrats succeeded in buying the greater number and the price in this election was $1 apiece.

The hopes for prosperity began to be pinned by many people on making silver into money again and making it worth one-sixteenth as much as gold. They believed that there was not enough money and that this plan would help relieve the shortage. The Populists held that the supply should be increased sufficiently for every person in the United States to have $50 apiece. Georgians became greatly excited about abstruse financial nostrums as they read their *Coin's Financial School,* or looked at the convincing cartoons in it if they could not read. Five thousand people from 104 of the 137 counties met at Griffin in 1895 to discuss free silver and to organize a Bimetallic League. About the only prominent Georgian who disagreed with the free silver doctrines was Hoke Smith, who as a Cleveland supporter could not do otherwise. Other doctrines which the Populists claimed as their own but which were held by many other Georgians, were government ownership of telegraphs and railroads, the direct election of Senators, and the income tax.

Democrats, Populists, and Republicans, in varying numbers, believed in the free coinage of silver; but the Democrats and Populists believed in it with more telling force. In 1896 the Democrats selected for president William J. Bryan, who stampeded the convention into nominating him by his "crown of

thorns and cross of gold" speech. The Populists, seeing that the
doctrines held by the Democrats were much like their own,
decided to accept Bryan as their candidate for president; but
to please the Southerners they nominated a candidate of their
own for vice-president in the person of Thomas E. Watson.
Even though Watson was a Georgian, the Georgia Democrats
refused to swap for him their own vice-presidential candidate,
Arthur Sewall. The Republicans had no hope of carrying
Georgia, but Mark Hanna, a wealthy Ohioan, came to Georgia
in 1895 and rented a house in Thomasville to which William
McKinley soon retired "for his health." The purpose of Hanna
and McKinley was to round up the Southern delegates to the
Republican convention, and in this move they were successful.
McKinley received the nomination of the Republicans.

In the state election the Democrats ran for governor W. Y.
Atkinson, who at that time occupied the chair; and the Populists nominated Seaborn Wright. As usual the Republicans felt
that they should not nominate candidates on which to waste
their votes, as long as the Democrats and Populists were willing
to pay $1 apiece for them. The Georgia Democrats carried both
the state and national tickets, though McKinley won the largest vote ever cast by the state for a Republican since the days
of the carpet-baggers. Bryan received 94,000 to 60,000 for Mc-
Kinley, while Atkinson received 123,000 to Wright's 84,000.

The election of 1896 marked the height of both Populist and
Republican strength in Georgia, the former gradually dying
out completely and the latter continuing only through the
sustenance it received from the national organization, bobbing
up high enough to be observed only every four years as the
presidential elections came along. Though McKinley and his
gold standard had won, Georgia did not immediately give up
the idea that she needed more money. For years the state had
been toying with the belief that it could issue small bonds as
low as $5, which could be used as a medium of exchange; but
the inevitable 10% Federal tax always stood in the way. In

1899 there was a considerable movement to issue state notes which, it was hoped, would be able to escape the tax, but before anything definite could be done, returning prosperity put a stop to the state's financial troubles. It was the discovery of gold in South Africa and in the Klondike and a cheap process of extracting the metal from ores that won the day against silver; but the Republican Party claimed the credit and established in the nation a position as the party of prosperity and morality.

In 1898 the Democrats nominated Allen D. Candler for governor and elected him over J. R. Hogan, the Populist nominee, by a vote of 117,000 to 50,000. The Populists attempted to honor Watson with the nomination, but he refused to be drawn from the certainty of his law practice to the certainty of being defeated for governor. What little strength the Republicans could exert in the election they gave to Hogan. In 1900 Candler was re-elected with slight opposition from the Populists; in 1902 Joseph M. Terrell was elected with only 4,747 votes cast for J. K. Hines, his Populist opponent. Two years later Terrell was re-elected without opposition, for by this time the Populists had passed almost completely out of existence in state affairs, killed by prosperity. The national Populist organization nominated Watson for president, and he accepted as he considered the fame coming from being defeated for the presidency would be worth the cost.

As one of the chief zests in politics came from the fight that accompanied office-seeking, it was to be expected that when once the opposition party should disappear, the loss must be made up in some way. The Georgia Democrats, now without Populist or Republican opposition, set to fighting within their own organization and as time went on, gave no signs of desisting as long as no opponent on the outside appeared. In 1906, in the primary which had recently been set up by law, a bitter fight took place between Hoke Smith and Clark Howell for the governorship. These two Georgians had long been on oppo-

site sides of the principal questions of the day, including bimet-
allism. In this struggle Smith had declared his determination
to regulate the railroads further and free the state from their
clutches; he also had stated that the time had arrived to put the
Negro out of politics and end the disgraceful spectacle of the
wholesale buying and selling of Negro votes and of having the
Negroes the umpire in every dispute between white factions.
The latter principle greatly appealed to Watson, who himself
had felt the effect of Negro votes, and caused him to cast his
full support to Smith. Smith received the nomination and con-
sequently the election, though a Populist named J. B. Ozburn
succeeded in finding for himself 148 votes.

During the next two years Smith treated the state to a great
deal of important legislation, which reminded some Georgians
too much of Populist principles. The railroads were restricted
more severely, state-wide prohibition was adopted, and the convict lease system was abolished. By far the most important act
passed in 1908 and made a part of the constitution was the
elimination of the Negro from politics. Qualifications were set
up which were difficult but not impossible for the Negro to
meet; and any hardships which resulted were felt as much by
the white politicians who had been using the Negro vote as by
the Negroes, who had long ago learned that the suffrage was
of little value to themselves beyond the few dollars they collected for the sale of their votes. In addition to complying with
the residence requirements, anyone seeking to vote must fall
within one of the following classes: a war veteran or a descendant, a person of good character who understood the duties and
obligations of citizenship, a person who could read and write
any paragraph of the constitution of Georgia or of the United
States, an owner of forty acres of land in the state on which he
resided, or the owner of property in the state worth $500. The
effect of this legislation was largely to eliminate Negro suffrage
in the country and small towns; in the cities the Negroes con-

tinued to vote in numbers sufficient to make them an important element in politics on certain occasions.

The chief significance of the year 1908 in the political annals of Georgia was the beginning of the feud between Smith and Joseph M. Brown, and the election of William Howard Taft to the presidency. Shortly after his election Taft came to Augusta to rest ostensibly, but also to strengthen a movement which he had already begun in the campaign, to break the Solid South. He early succeeded in getting himself thoroughly liked by the Georgians, many of whom he convinced of the desirability of developing a respectable Republican Party in the South. He travelled extensively over the state, and visited in January, 1909, the University.

In his attempt to succeed himself in 1908 Smith was defeated by Brown, whom he had removed from the railroad commission. Brown marshalled all the forces of discontent at hand and by skillful campaigning was able to win. The panic of 1907 had made itself felt not only on Wall Street; in Georgia there was distress, and the battle cry "Hoke and hunger, Brown and bread" emphasized it. Smith also lost the support of Watson, who disagreed with him in his attempt to reform the undemocratic county unit system of elections whereby some of the country dwellers were given representation fifty times greater than that held by people living in the larger cities. The feud between Smith and Brown did not stop here. In 1910 Smith defeated Brown for the governorship, but before the end of his term he was elevated to the United States Senate, to remain until 1920, when Watson dislodged him.

In 1912 John M. Slaton was elected governor; but the greatest interest this year was in the presidential contest. Georgia was divided in her sentiments on the outstanding Democrats, who were seeking the nomination. Oscar Underwood had the advantage of an early start in the Georgia contest for delegates and of the sentimental attachment that went with the fact that he was both a native and a resident of the South; whereas Woodrow Wilson, though a native of the South, was a resident of the North. Though William J. Harris worked with great zeal to secure the Georgia delegates for Wilson, Underwood was successful. After Wilson's election he rewarded Harris by making him the director of the Census and later made him a member of the Federal Trade Commission. Pleasant A. Stovall, of Savannah, he made minister to Switzerland.

Slaton's two-year administration of Georgia was destined to be remembered not so much for his efforts to establish economy in state government as for his having commuted to life imprisonment the death sentence passed on Leo M. Frank, a Jew convicted of a heinous crime. Aroused by attacks on Frank in Thomas E. *Watson's Magazine* and his *Weekly Jeffersonian,* a mob broke into the penitentiary in August, 1915, seized Frank, and hanged him on a tree 175 miles away. Slaton had been followed in the governor's chair in June by Nathaniel E. Harris, the last of the Confederates, during whose administration the United States entered the First World War. Though Harris desired another term, he was defeated for the nomination by Hugh M. Dorsey, who had gained a widespread reputation in prosecuting Frank. For the next few years politics was adjourned in Georgia.

CHAPTER XXIX

FINANCIAL AND ECONOMIC PROGRESS

THE PROFLIGATE use made of the state's credit constituted one of the major crimes of Reconstruction. Georgia did not fare as ill as did South Carolina or Louisiana; but the financial record of the Bullock régime might well have left the state in utter bewilderment. The work of re-establishing its credit, begun immediately on the assumption of power by the native whites in 1872, was relentlessly continued until 1877, when in the constitution of that year the state was led out of the miasma of Reconstruction and placed on the high grounds of financial stability. Georgia's quick financial recovery marked one of the outstanding accomplishments in all her history and set up a monument to the honesty and sagacity of her leaders. Accomplishments like this led even to Radical praise, voiced here by a correspondent of the *Cincinnati Commercial*: "The old southern fire-eating Democrats, we are taught, were wicked men; and wicked they were, about some things, but they did not use their offices to fill their pockets. They did not form rings to make money, or establish gift enterprises. This old-fashioned honesty, this abhorrence of anything that looks like prostituting public office to private gain, is as abhorrent to the southern people now as it ever was, and probably more, for they have been called upon since the war to have considerable experience with that sort of thing, and to know it is not to love it, especially when it is done at their expense."

The fact that the state's repudiation of $6,500,000 Bullock Reconstruction bonds did not hurt its credit was rather convincing proof that they had been fraudulent. The almost impregnable defenses set up in the constitution against financial extravagances and manipulations were a convincing warning in the state and a wholesome announcement to the nation. The sound policy of its rulers had been well shown even before the adoption of the new constitution, for Governor James M. Smith in his parting words to the legislature in 1877 could well say with pride that the securities of the state were selling above par, when only a few years previously they had been at a discount as high as 30%. The state was not only living within its income, but at the end of the year 1877 it had in its treasury a balance of more than a half million dollars. Georgia had in the course of a half dozen years established a financial stability as strong as that of any state in the Union.

The bonded debt, which amounted in 1877 to $10,645,897, must by the constitution be reduced $100,000 a year, and as the Georgians joyously pursued this task they celebrated each reduction and came to visualize the debt as a monster which they were gradually strangling. So deep was their antipathy toward a bonded debt, that for the next sixty-eight years they could not be induced to amend their constitution to allow an increase, though they were easily made to change the document more than three hundred times in other particulars. The high standing of the state's credit was reflected in the refunding operations which provided 4½% bonds in 1888 that sold at 104½. Two years later a 3½% issue was sold at par. Never before had the state attained such financial strength. With balances in the treasury, the state tax rate was reduced during the six years preceding 1882 from 6 mills to 2½ mills.

In 1892 the Federal government further strengthened Georgia's treasury by returning to it $83,031.03, which represented the amount it had been able to collect from Georgia following the war, on the direct levy made upon the states in 1861. Having been surprised by this gift, Georgia did not hesitate to investigate the possibilities of securing further monies from the same source. The intricacies of the agreement and its execution, made in 1802, by which Georgia sold her western lands to the United States, were resurrected in 1893; and the state was able to convince itself though not the United States that it had not been fully paid all of the $1,250,000 promised.

On the fullness of its treasury the state in 1883 imposed the obligation of $1,000,000 to be used in constructing a capitol building in Atlanta. There were to be no hated bonds; a special tax should do it. The capitol was completed in 1890, to serve not alone as a home for the state government, but also as a monument to be pointed to as one of the few edifices of its character in America ever to be completed within the cost

THE STATE CAPITOL, ATLANTA

Harper's Encyclopaedia of United States History. New York: Harper & Brothers.

originally set. When it was finished, there still remained in the fund appropriated for its construction $118.43! Until this project was begun, there existed some uncertainty over the state, and much fear in Atlanta, that a fickle populace might change its mind and locate the capital elsewhere. Milledgeville, small and sleepy but dignified, with memories of the old capitol and a feeling of resignation, seemed to be contented with the penitentiary and the insane asylum; but Macon, ambitious and growing, began an unseemly contest in the legislature which she carried on year after year. With the argument that she occupied the geographic center of the state, she sought to convince that body that she should be made the capital; but the main results seem to have been, if anything, to quicken the hospitality of Atlanta toward the visiting law-makers. As late as 1916, Macon was still disturbing the peace of mind in Atlanta.

In the ante-bellum South the philosophy of living had little place for industries and trade; the planters, who gave content to this philosophy, believed there was a direct antagonism between plantations and factories. In the war that followed, the industrial North won; and many people in the South who groped for a reason, gradually converged on the inevitable conclusion that it was so because the North was industrial. Benjamin H. Hill was among the first to sense this fact and to proclaim it loudest. In a remarkable address before the University of Georgia Alumni Society in 1871, he called upon Georgia to cast off the strangulations of a past age: "Our coal and iron will not always sleep in the shallow earth because we think it unbecoming the social position of an educated gentleman to wake them up and lift them out. Our magnificent trees will not always grow and fall and decay because our young men think the style of a gentleman is a soft hand in a kid glove. Nor will the educated laborers of other States and countries always, or even much longer, send here and freight away, at great expense and labor, our raw material, to foreign shops for manufacture." The South had been bound down by the Negro as much as the Negro had been enslaved by the South. The North had freed the Negro, now the South should free herself. Fifteen years later Henry Grady, in his "New South" speech before the New England Society, in New York City, announced that the new day had arrived and that Georgia was fast transforming herself: "We have let economy take root and spread among us as rank as the crab-grass which sprang from Sherman's cavalry camps, until we are ready to lay odds on the Georgia Yankee as he manufactures relics of the battlefield in a one-story shanty and squeezes pure olive oil out of his cotton seed, against any down-easter that ever swapped wooden nutmegs for flannel sausages in the valleys of Vermont." Joel Chandler Harris turned aside from conversing with bre'r rabbit long enough to add the approval of a voice which was fast coming to speak with authority not only in Georgia but throughout the South.

It was only natural to expect that there should be those who would be unreconstructed economically as well as politically. They declared that people who would change the heart of the Old South were traitors and they fell upon Hill as one of the chief offenders. But in the end they were forced to adjust their conception of the Lost Cause, abandon that part which was dead, and agree with Hill, "We shall live! We shall rise!! We shall command!!! . . . We have given up the dusky Helen!"

Georgia abandoned the philosophy implied in the couplet,

> When Adam delved and Eve span,
> Who was then the gentleman?

and began to delve and spin in a much more extensive fashion than had ever characterized her ante-bellum days. Indeed, it had never been beyond the right of a gentleman in Georgia to dig for gold, and from the days of the Spaniards down to the outbreak of the Civil War there had been delvings of this kind going on. After the war it was only natural to continue it. In 1880 the state produced $1,000,000 in gold bullion. As had been true in all times when gold fever was in the air, there was about as much promotion activity as actual digging. This was particularly true of Georgia during the decades of the eighties and nineties. In the latter decade one of the best known mining schemes was the British-Georgia Gold Mining Company with a capital of $5,000,000; it, however, succeeded in raising more hopes than gold. But there could be no doubt about the gold in the Cherokee hills of Georgia, nor was there reason to believe that as long as gold glittered it would cease to attract people there to dig.

In the extreme northwestern part of the state there was coal to mine; and Joseph E. Brown added to his many other activities the business of coal-mining. In 1881 one hundred thousand tons were taken from the ground. There was, however, wealth under the Georgia soil much more valuable and more extensive than the coal deposits. In many parts of the state were large areas of various kinds of clays, which could be made into anything from bricks to the finest vases. In 1888 the state made 95,600,000 bricks and it continued to make them in great numbers; but it also sold its raw clay for little more than the price of earth, to be sent to the North and to Europe to be returned in expensive pottery. By 1907 the clay products of Georgia's own make were selling for as much as $2,000,000 annually. Vast marble deposits in Pickens County, discovered before the Civil War and worked slightly, were later developed into one of the greatest businesses of the state, relentlessly sawing away on a mass estimated to be worth $165,000,000,000. Georgia marble became famous throughout the world. The state also had much granite and limestone. In 1928 the total mineral products were sold for $14,740,000.

Following the war Georgia developed an economic position which made her in fact the Empire State of the South, and in no field did she merit this name more than in manufacturing. Before the end of the century she had attained superiority over every other Southern state, a superiority which she lost, however, during the next quarter century.

Georgia ushered in her manufacturing era with a great "world's fair" or International Cotton Exposition, as she called it. For a century she had been raising much cotton, but she had never given much attention to its manufacture. Now, to popularize the processes of cotton production from the opening boll to the finished cloth, she held her exposition in Atlanta in 1881, from October 5th to December 31st. Joseph E. Brown became its president and Samuel G. Inman, its treasurer. The director-general was H. I. Kimball, who had successfully outlived the malodorous reputation he had won during Reconstruction. Preparations were made on a scale gigantic for a state lately impoverished by war. Not only were all the Southern states to be represented, but even foreign countries were invited, if for no other reason than to warrant the use of *International* in the title. The building was in the shape of a great cross, and so extensive was it that there were eleven miles of aisles within, and it was necessary to have three steam engines to afford power for the great display of machinery, which included every sort of mechanical contrivance from a Corliss engine to a potato peeler. There were also collected under this roof a great variety of minerals and woods, textile manufactures of various kinds, agricultural products, livestock, and even an art gallery. On the outside were grouped cotton stalks in every stage of growth.

The exposition was opened with a prayer by Bishop Robert W. B. Elliott and closed with a poem by Paul H. Hayne, who paid tribute in it to Atlanta's greatness. During the three months this exposition continued, it was visited by 286,000 people. Here was proof that the South no longer labored under a defeatest complex; the bold ambitions of the olden times had returned to hold sway. The South had vast latent wealth and she had the courage to develop it. Here was proof even more important that the South was freeing herself from the strangling clutches of politics. This exposition was a friendly challenge to the nation by Georgia to show that the Philadelphia Centennial could be equalled or surpassed. The rhymester made Uncle Sam say of the Centennial,

> I gev a show in '76,
> In Filadelfy town,

> And you can bet I did it slick;
> I allus do things brown.

but the Georgia cracker said of the International Cotton Exposition,

> I come from Georgia's hills, sar!
> To see this whoopin show,
> And I'll be dogged ef thar ever war
> Such another hyar below.

Not only did the Georgians attend; there were governors from many states, and the legislatures from Kentucky, Tennessee, and South Carolina came in bodies. In 1876 the South could consider herself politically a part of the Union, in 1881 she could announce that she was a part economically. Governor Colquitt in adjourning the exposition declared that not since the signing of the Declaration of Independence had "fraternal sympathy so abounded, so diffused itself among our people." As final proof of the financial ability of Georgians, this exposition made a profit of $20,000.

The purpose of the exposition was not merely to show what Georgia and the South had done, but especially to fire the soul of the people with the desire to go forward in manufacturing. And to what better use could the exposition building be put than to make it the home of a cotton factory, and thus arose the Exposition Cotton Mills. For years thereafter Georgia led all the Southern States in the manufacture of cotton goods. The greatest centers were Columbus and Augusta. Manufacturing activities were soon spreading into other fields, such as cotton oil, sulphuric acid, fertilizer, and farm machinery.

During the two decades from 1870 to 1890 Georgia went through an economic regeneration. She quadrupled her capital engaged in manufacturing, she trebled her railroad mileage, and she increased her property values from $215,000,000 to $820,000,000.

Having succeeded so well with her exposition in 1881,

Georgia decided to attempt a much bigger one in 1895, held in Atlanta and called the Cotton States and International Exposition. No city the size of Atlanta had ever been selected as the seat of such a large undertaking. Charles A. Collier became president of the exposition, and just as H. I. Kimball had demonstrated his return to the good graces of Georgians by his selection as director-general of the exposition in 1881, now Rufus Bullock showed that he had been forgiven by his appointment as chairman of the committee on arrangements. The Federal government showed its approval of the undertaking by appropriating $200,000 for the erection of a building. The little daughter of President Cleveland pressed an electric button in Massachusetts which swung wide the gates in Atlanta. A million and a quarter people attended this exposition and received ocular proof of the remarkable progress Georgia and the rest of the South had been making.

An outstanding feature of this exposition was the demonstration it gave of the progress the Negroes had made since slavery and the promise it held out for a more perfect harmony between the races. The Negroes erected and maintained a building in which they exhibited their own handiwork, but more remarkable was the fact that Booker T. Washington was invited to make a principal address, and most remarkable was the address he delivered. Never before on an important occasion in the South had a Negro made a speech before an audience of white men and women. He praised the progress the Negroes had made since starting out thirty years before "with the ownership here and there of a few quilts, pumpkins and chickens (gathered from miscellaneous sources)." He warned his race away from politics and ideas of social equality and directed its attention to honest toil. He declared, "No race can prosper until it learns that there is as much dignity in tilling a field as in writing a poem" and "The opportunity to earn a dollar in a factory just now is worth infinitely more than the opportunity to spend a dollar in an opera house."

The promise of better race relations so eloquently held out by this exposition was long to remain unfulfilled. For years lynchings had disgraced the state and had led Georgians to condemn the practice as bitterly as any reformer in Boston or Chicago had cried out against it. In 1893 the state had passed a law against lynching, which made it a crime to participate in a mob and which made every member of a mob equally guilty of any crime committed by it. Two years later Governor Atkinson condemned in vigorous words lynch law, declaring that it was a great injury to the reputation of the state, that it was a denial of the rights of man and a disgrace to civilization, and that mobs were unjustifiable, shocking, and horrifying. Laws and expressions of indignation seem to have had little effect on the lower element of the state, for within the next few years there was a wave of mob outbreaks. A particular reason for the increasing activity of mobs seems to have been the unwise practice of President McKinley in making Negro appointments which peculiarly exasperated the white people. His selection of a Negro to be the postmaster at Hogansville led to an outbreak there, and his appointment of a Negro to be the collector of internal revenues caused widespread opposition. The legislature passed resolutions against the practice of making appointments which would give offense to white people.

The very economic opportunity which Booker T. Washington had plead for at the Cotton States and International Exposition was denied in Atlanta two years later when 1,400 workmen in a cotton factory struck because twenty Negroes had been hired and placed near them; and in 1909 a strike of the trainmen on the Central of Georgia Railroad was called because Negro firemen were being employed. In the first strike the Negroes were removed; but the latter was settled by a board of arbitration which decided that the Negroes should have the same pay and chances of employment as the white workmen.

In 1906 a race riot broke out in Atlanta which was quelled

by troops only after seventeen people had been killed. A backward step in good race relations was evident here; but outbreaks of this character directed the attention of many thoughtful people to the necessity of building up a better understanding between the races. Later there was organized an inter-racial commission, which began to accomplish much of what had been promised by the expositon in 1895.

This exposition was more successful immediately in directing the attention and energies of Georgians into the lines of manufacturing. In 1900 thirty-six new cotton factories were constructed, and the total number of fertilizer plants by the next year had reached 112. At this time Georgia used more fertilizer than any other state.

One of the outstanding facts in the economic growth of the state was the rise of Atlanta out of the ashes left by Sherman. The spirit of progress which seized the inhabitants led to the development of this metropolis of southeastern United States. Strategically located at the southern spur of the Appalachian Mountains, it became the center of a great railway system which made it the basing point for rates from almost all directions. It therefore became the distributing point for all the Southeast, sending out the products not only of the Northern manufacturers but of her own varied industries. So great a manufacturing center had Atlanta become by 1910 that its productions were greater than those of the whole state combined in 1870. The industrial growth of the city as well as of the whole state was greatly aided by the liberal attitude of the *Atlanta Constitution,* whose preachments of progress, especially by Henry W. Grady and Joel Chandler Harris, became well-known.

At the beginning of the twentieth century Georgia stood third in the production of raw cotton. This position she did not necessarily relish, not because it was not first but because it was not last. Too much cotton raising had long been a complaint not only in Georgia but throughout the cotton South. In 1897 a meeting composed of delegates from six Southern states took place in Atlanta, where the advantages of limiting cotton acreage and diversifying farm activities were recommended. Georgia became genuinely interested in diversification, and in her determination to act upon it, she developed new interests that became permanent and brought fame and money to the state. During the nineties peaches made their entry as an important article of commerce and not only laid hold on the regions south of Macon but also northward into the upper Piedmont, from Jackson County to Floyd. In 1895 Macon held a peach carnival in which she celebrated the gathering of the ripened fruit; but later it was discovered that a more beautiful spectacle could be made out of the blooming trees, so the peach festivals were made to come earlier in the spring. Samuel Rumph, Sr., developed the Elberta peach as an outstanding Georgia contribution to the fruit world. With the coming of peaches, a movement to commercialize apples began and resulted in the conversion of much of the upper Piedmont region into apple orchards. By the beginning of the twentieth century, pecan orchards began to make their appearance, and so productive were they that Georgia became as famous for its pecans as for its peaches. In 1919 there were more than 12,000,000 peach trees in the state, more than 1,300,000 apple trees, and more than 1,000,000 pecan trees.

The diversification of agricultural activities led the state further away from cotton, into fields other than fruits and nuts. About the turn of the century a great deal of enthusiasm was developed for raising corn, and within the first seven years of the new century, the acreage devoted to this grain was increased by a third. Agriculture made great inroads into the pine barrens and wire grass regions of the southern part of the state. Here the production of tobacco was started, which was later to grow into a major interest, and here also began the cultivation of cane which was to make famous the Georgia cane syrup.

South Georgians also gave much attention to the growth of watermelons.

The pine forests of the central and southern parts of the state had since colonial times afforded naval stores, and though uncontrolled forest fires had frequently caused great damage, yet the naval stores industry continued into the twentieth century, bringing to the state in 1919 $10,874,000. The Okefenokee and other great swamps yielded up much cypress for lumber, and the forest areas throughout the state added to the total supply, which in 1919 was worth $26,836,000.

Early in the twentieth century a movement for draining the wide swampy areas along many of the streams became well established, and resulted in the reclamation of more than 65,000 acres by 1920; but later it dawned upon Georgians that they already possessed a great surplus of arable land, and soon the movement was reversed. Now they began to cover with water great stretches of river lands, for the era of hydroelectric power had arrived. But as most of the power projects were in the upper Piedmont, the land lost bore little relation in value to the advantages gained in the wealth of power developed, and only when such scenic beauty as existed at Tallulah Falls was destroyed, could the power project be considered as costing the state more than it was worth.

Though Georgia might appear in song and story as simply "the land of cotton," in reality it was becoming less and less so.

CHAPTER XXX

SOCIAL ADVANCEMENT

Soon AFTER the Civil War two problems of wide social effects arose prominently before the people of Georgia, which were long to be discussed and wrestled with. The one related to the disposal of convicts and the other involved the control of the drinking of whiskey. The former came up for attention first.

In ante-bellum times the convicts had been put into a penitentiary; but following the war, with the Negroes unadapted to their new freedom, the number became so large that the penitentiary would not hold them. So a policy was adopted first in 1866 of leasing the convicts to contractors on public works, and eight years later the law was changed to permit for five years their leasing to private individuals. In 1876 a new policy was adopted, going into effect in 1879, which provided for leasing the convicts, with a few exceptions, to three companies for a period of twenty years. These three companies were organized by some of the principal political leaders and business men of the state, including Joseph E. Brown, John B. Gordon, and W. D. Grant. In return for the use of the convicts they promised the state $500,000 to be paid in twenty annual instalments. An interesting peculiarity in the working of this lease system was the fact that the more lawless the state became and therefore the more criminals there were, the more money the companies stood to make out of their contracts; and from another standpoint, the more exact and even-handed justice was in the state and the more enforcement there was behind the laws, likewise the more the companies would prosper. And there even existed the temptation to convict innocent persons to provide a larger labor supply.

These convicts were put to work mining coal and cutting wood, farming on great tracts of land, making bricks, and constructing railroads. Most of them were Negroes, there being in 1877 eleven hundred convicts of whom 994 were Negroes. Eleven years later there were 1,388 Negroes and 149 whites.

The state threw certain safeguards around the convicts, such as requiring medical attention and forbidding work on Sunday. The convict must be properly fed and clothed, and on the expiration of his sentence he must be given a new suit of clothes worth not less than $6 and a railroad ticket to the county from which he had been received. It was made the duty of the grand juries of the counties in which the convicts were located to investigate periodically the camps. The chief arguments for the system in addition to the humane treatment required by law were the inability of the state to construct a large penitentiary and the fact that the lease system produced an income for the state, whereas the penitentiary system had regularly produced a deficit.

With all these safeguards there were grave dangers of cruelty and abuse. The use of the lash was not prohibited, and the state had no representatives in the various camps. Rumors of atrocities soon arose and multiplied; in 1880 the legislature appointed a special penitentiary committee to investigate conditions. They visited all the camps, found a few cases of cruel whipping, and discovered certain other weaknesses of the law which they thought should be eliminated. They came to the conclusion that there was nothing in the system that tended "to the reformation of the criminal." They declared further: "It impinges with a crushing force upon the great work of the moral regeneration of the prisoners. The old felon, who has led a life of sin and degeneracy, continues in the practice of his immoralities. The youthful convict is chained by his side day by day, and night after night, and is compelled to serve out his sentence under the pale of this evil influence. He naturally contracts the habits and vices of his companions, and, at the end of his time, instead of being a reformed man, he is turned loose on the country and society trained in habits and practices that are destructive to everything which may be called good."

Certain reforms followed, but the subject of the convicts rested heavily on the consciences of many Georgians. William H. Felton and his wife Rebecca fought the system fiercely, and long kept the agitation going. The Alliancemen and Populists made the reform of the convict system an article of their political principles. Now and then a governor held investigations, as was the case in 1887 when Governor Gordon had fines of $2,500 imposed on two companies for cruelty to their convicts, and in 1896 when Governor Atkinson levied a fine on the Dade County coal mining company.

Finally in 1897 the agitation, which had been going on for a decade and a half bore fruit. A law was passed this year amending the convict leasing system when the contracts with the companies should expire two years later. A prison commission was set up and instructed to secure a prison farm where the old, the young, and the ailing should be placed to help make their keep, isolated from the hardened criminals. Of the other convicts, those sentenced for five years or less were apportioned out to the counties to be worked on chain-gangs making roads, while those whose sentences ran for more than five years were leased first for $100 a year for each convict, and later to the highest bidder.

Through this system the state received revenue from $200,000 to $300,000 a year; but the old evils of the lease system speedily returned. The convicts scattered over the state in farming, mining, and lumbering enterprises could not be easily protected against cruel treatment. A clamor arose which in 1908 resulted in the abolition of the system and the announcement of the policy for the future that the control and management of the state's convicts should "never pass from it and its public officials into the control and management of any private corporation or person." C. Murphey Candler led the fight for this new principle. Thereafter the convicts who were not sent to the prison farm should be turned over to the counties to be used in road work. Long experience with county chain-gangs proved to many Georgians that some county officials had little more conscience and feeling of responsibility in connection with convicts than had private lessees, and so an agitation sprang up to have all the convicts placed directly under the control of the state. This problem was to wait for more than a quarter of a century for a solution.

The outcry against strong liquors had spread widely over the land in ante-bellum times; but the leaders had been mostly preachers and impractical reformers, who had sought through personal conversion to aid the cause of temperance. Legislating morality into people was not thought of in those days as being a practical process, except for areas surrounding certain churches and educational institutions. After the war the movement against whiskey was pushed by new methods and for purposes other than for purifying the soul of the individual. The Negro in slavery had been prevented from becoming a drunken menace by the same power which held him in subjection, but when he became free, he had the same right to make himself drunk which the white man possessed. But a drunken Negro was looked upon as a greater menace than a drunken white man, and both were considered objectionable for reasons economic as well as moral. The onset against strong liquors had now fallen into the hands of more practical preachers, politicians, and industrialists, and the conversion of the individual was not considered necessary if enough votes could be secured to pass a law making it impossible for the individual to get whiskey.

The temperance leaders made their entry into the legislative field by first securing laws for further banishing liquor from the vicinity of churches and school houses. With the growth of these centers of religion and education and with their strategic location, dry areas were peppered all over the state. Then the legislature began drying up areas as large as counties. By 1881 there were 48 dry counties. The success of the movement emboldened the temperance workers to hold a convention in Atlanta this year, in July, at which they organized for a more determined campaign throughout the state. At this time the temperance movement was strongest in the northern, southeastern, and southwestern parts of the state. It was also generally true that the country favored prohibition and the cities opposed it. Now the local option movement, which required a separate law to give each county or militia district the right to vote on the prohibition of whiskey, was considered too slow and cumbersome. Why should there not be a state-wide local option law?

By 1884 the prohibition question was one of the chief issues before the state. At that time there were ninety counties which were either totally dry or partly so, and to speed the movement a bill was introduced in the legislature this year providing for state-wide local option. The opposing forces defeated it, but the next year it was introduced again and was passed. It allowed any county, without further action of the legislature, to hold an election on prohibition if one-tenth of the voters in the county asked for it. Emboldened by their success, the prohibition forces made an attack this year on the greatest stronghold of the liquor interests in the state, Atlanta and Fulton County. The fight was bitter and hotly contested. Strange things were seen and done. Republicans and Democrats joined hands against liquor and called in the Negroes to help them. On the same platform all three groups could be seen sitting together and urging dry arguments. Catching Atlanta off her guard, they voted Fulton County dry by a majority of 225 in a total vote of 7,000. The distilleries, the wholesale liquor stores, and the saloons now for the first time thoroughly recognizing the menace to their continued existence, made preparations for a counter-assault not only on Fulton County but in various other dry areas throughout the state. In 1887 another election was secured in Fulton County which resulted in the routing of the temperance forces by a majority of 1,112 in a total vote of 9,244. Thereupon the liquor forces made a general assault all along the line and succeeded within a year in capturing 26 dry counties.

In 1899 the prohibition forces made a determined effort to clear the state of distilleries as well as saloons. They succeeded in passing a bill to that effect in the house, but after three days of bitter opposition in the senate it failed. The main argument in favor of the continued manufacture and sale of whiskey was the $150,000 it added yearly to the school fund. It had been a stroke of good luck for the liquor forces when soon after the Civil War the legislature had allotted the saloon fees to education and had thereby tied up the liquor interests with such a force for righteousness and progress as the schools. This fact afforded an argument which brought conviction to many people who could have been reached in no other way. The fact, too, that in 1900 there were 135 distilleries operating in the state had weight both in the contributions they were able to make to fight prohibition and in the taxes they paid to the local governments.

Throughout the whole period of the temperance struggle down to the turn of the century, the issue had been kept for the most part out of party politics. In their platform in 1902 the Democrats opposed making prohibition a party issue. They held that the cause could be best promoted by allowing it to remain the moral issue which it was and by allowing all, irrespective of parties, to support or condemn it. As there was in reality only one political party in Georgia, prohibition might well be left out of the Democratic Party officially; but it was certain to be tossed into the campaign for nomination by some candidate. And along this road it entered the party and ultimately attained success.

In 1907 prohibition became a party measure under Governor Hoke Smith, and its passage through the legislature this year assured the signature of the governor. But it was largely a failure from the beginning. Governor Joseph M. Brown, who succeeded Smith in 1909, had shown no friendship for the law, and he was opposed to further legislation to strengthen it unless the people were given a chance to vote on the subject. Some of the political leaders favored the repeal of the law and a return to local option. Under the benign influence of this political uncertainty if not opposition to the prohibition law, near-beer saloons sprang up in great numbers and soon became bold enough to sell liquors generally without let or hindrance; and when their owners were prosecuted, the juries often failed to convict. Another obstacle to the complete enforcement of the law was the right individuals were given to buy whiskies in wet states and have them shipped into Georgia. An immense business was done by the express companies in bringing into the state these shipments, as was shown by the stacks of small boxes unloaded at almost every railway station. The Webb-Kenyon Act passed by Congress in 1913, forbidding railways to transport liquors into dry territory, contrary to state law, made it possible for Georgia to exclude outside shipments; but as long as the near-beer saloons dispensed their beverages to the public, and private clubs kept their lockers full for their members, there was little chance of Georgia's actually becoming dry.

Nathaniel E. Harris, who became governor in 1915, was a strong friend of prohibition. After deadlocking his legislature in his attempt to force through a law which would dry up the state, he called a special session, which passed it in 1915. It closed the near-beer saloons and the locker clubs, and adopted the benefits of the Webb-Kenyon law for the state; but it left open a great spigot through which every person might legally draw each month for his own use two quarts of whiskey, one gallon of wine, and forty-eight quarts of beer. By the coming of national prohibition in 1919, the state had enacted such stringent laws on the subject that it was not only a crime to manufacture and sell intoxicating liquors but even to possess them.

So watchful were the constitution-makers of 1877 over the expenditure of money that they forbade the state making appropriations for any other educational activity than the elementary schools and the state University. There was still considerable doubt that the state had an obligation to afford education to its citizens, especially if private schools could fulfill the need. Hence it was that no provision was made for aid to high schools, which should bridge the gap between the elementary school and the University. That gap must be crossed, if crossed at all, by the privately controlled academies. The elementary schools were to receive all their support from the state, and to provide a fund for this purpose Georgia set aside by constitutional provision the poll tax, a special tax on shows and exhibitions, the liquor tax, and a dog tax. Additional funds were added later, such as one-half the rental on the Western and Atlantic Railroad, dividends from certain stocks of the Georgia Railroad owned by the state, and the hire received from the convicts. The income in 1871 amounted to $174,000 and by 1893 it had reached $1,000,000. In 1904 the constitution was amended to permit local divisions smaller than counties to levy a tax for the elementary schools. In 1910 a constitutional amendment was adopted permitting taxes to be levied likewise for high schools, and two years later these schools were made a part of the state educational system. In 1931 the public schools received from all sources more than $21,000,000, of which almost $7,000,000 was appropriated by the state. This onset against illiteracy wore much of it away. In 1870 twenty-seven per cent of the white were illiterate, in 1940 the percentage had been reduced to about 2 per cent. The law passed in 1916 compelling children to attend school became a valuable re-enforcement.

As money to be used for higher education could be appropriated only to the state University and to one college "for the education of persons of color," the constitution-makers of 1877 had evidently determined to prevent the dissipation of the state's revenues among many weak institutions. It did not follow, however, that they intended to make the University strong, for they declared that the legislature might "from time to time, make such donations thereto as the condition of the treasury will authorize." There was no obligation to support higher education.

The need to expand higher educational activities was soon recognized. The people should be afforded more technical training, women should be given opportunities for education at the state institutions, and prospective teachers should be taught how to teach. According to the constitution all these activities must be carried on by the state University, if the state was to promote them; but localism and log-rolling were destined to prevent making the University into a strong institution. A restricted point of view at the University prevented it from embracing these new activities, and so they came to be provided for elsewhere. The constitution could have been amended to set up other institutions to participate in the bounty of the state, as was done in other particulars frequently. Instead, a clever legal fiction was invented which made it possible to set up new institutions to be called branches of the University though they might be located hundreds of miles away.

Before the adoption of the constitution of 1877 the North Georgia Agricultural College at Dahlonega had been made a branch of the University in order to satisfy the provisions of the Federal land-grant act of 1862; but the first institution to be made a branch to escape the provisions of the new constitution was the Georgia School of Technology. Nathaniel E. Harris began the fight for this institution in 1882, but he failed to secure a charter until 1885. Fearing the disintegrating process which would begin with the developing of separate institutions, the University strongly opposed the movement. The legislature appropriated $65,000 to be used in setting up a technological school to be located in the place offering the greatest inducements, and to be modelled after the Institute of Industrial Science at Worcester, Mass. Atlanta was selected as the location, and three years later an institution costing $100,000 opened its doors to usher into the state that industrial age which the exposition in 1881 had sought to promote. This institution quickly developed strength and a standing which made it the best known technical school in the South.

Practical training, the need for which Georgians had recognized in the eighties and which had been provided for the men in the Georgia School of Technology, was now offered to the women, who for the first time in the history of the state were be become the object of legislative solicitude. W. Y. Atkinson, later elected governor, became the champion for the education of women. In 1889 the legislature declared that all branches of the University should be thereafter opened to women students, and the same year it provided for a special college to serve their needs, and to be located in the old state capital of Milledgeville. To this school it gave the name Georgia Normal and Industrial College, $35,000 in money, and property consisting of the old executive mansion and twenty acres of land known as the penitentiary square. It should have a normal department "for the thorough training of teachers" and an industrial department which should teach "telegraphy, stenography, typewriting, photography, book-keeping, domestic economy, cutting and making dresses, printing, industrial and decorative art in its practical application, and such other practical industries as may tend to fit and prepare girls for occupations which are consistent with feminine refinement and modesty." Thus dawned the era of the business girl in Georgia and the direction she should take was pointed out. Indeed a vast change had come since ante-bellum times in the conception of what women should do. The corner-stone of the first building was laid in 1890, and later the name of the institution was changed to the Georgia State College for Women.

Now that such an elaborate program had been organized for the women, to instruct them in the mysteries of teaching as well as in many other arts and sciences, the legislature felt that it should do nothing less for the men. In 1891 it set up in Athens the State Normal School for men only, but two years later it admitted women, who within the next few years overran the place and drove the men out almost completely. The name was later changed to the Georgia State Teachers College. In 1933 it was incorporated into the University. There had long been a feeling that although the University had in Athens an agricultural and mechanical college, it was attempting to teach farming without going near a plowed field. In 1897 the legislature established this fact to its own satisfaction in an investigation which it made; but nothing was done to remedy the situation until 1906, when it set up in Athens the Georgia State College of Agriculture. At the same time it scattered throughout the state small agricultural and mechanical schools, apportioning them among the Congressional districts. The confusion was more confounded by making these schools branches of the College of Agriculture. Thereafter the multiplication of branches of the University continued so fast that it was not halted until there was fastened upon the state an educational monstrosity with twenty-four branches bearing the misnomer, University of Georgia.

During this time, what was happening to the University at Athens, or Franklin College as it was more strictly called? With the legislature seeing no need to make donations "from time to time," the old institution was left to its own devices and those of its friends to secure its sustenance. An old professor, Charles McCay, made it a unique donation in 1879. It consisted of $7,000, to be held and the interest compounded until twenty-one years after twenty-five persons whom he named should have died. Calculations based upon the probabilities of human life and the rules of interest showed that the fund should become available about 1979 and amount to almost

$2,000,000. The interest on this fund was to be used in paying the salaries of professors.

It was natural for professors to provide for professors; but Joseph E. Brown, who had never been a professor, had experienced the hardships of a student struggling in poverty to secure an education, and therefore he was interested in helping students. In 1882 he offered to the state, in memory of his son Charles McDonald Brown, who had died the preceding year, $50,000 for the benefit of students in the University; but his stipulations as to the method of its investment caused the state to reject it. Brown thereupon offered it directly to the University, which accepted it, invested it, and used only the interest each year to be loaned to needy students. In 1945 this fund amounted to $458,769.24.

The University continued to be ignored by the legislature unless to be assaulted by its enemies or to be made the stem on which to graft more branches, until Walter B. Hill, the greatest educational genius the state had produced since the Civil War, was made chancellor in 1899. He took the institution, the first to be chartered by any American state, then doddering with age, and instilled life into it and developed for it a vision so remarkable as to attract the attention of the educationl leaders of the nation and cause them to predict that it would develop into the first great Southern university. He secured for it the first annual appropriation ever made for its maintenance, he enlisted the interest and philanthropy of George Foster Peabody, and he gave other Georgians his vision of a great university by taking them on a tour to visit some of the outstanding educational institutions of the nation. To the great misfortune of the state he died in 1905, and with him died his vision. The conscience of the University was not quickened again until almost two decades had gone by.

Higher education for the Negroes went forward mostly through the gift of wealthy friends in the North; but just as the state provided separate elementary schools for the Negroes, it was felt that an institution of higher learning should be set up for them or aid should be given to some Negro institution already in existence. Even with the feeling that Negroes should not receive higher education, it would have been wise to help them, for otherwise the state would stand to lose the income from the land grant fund. In 1874 an agreement was made with Atlanta University whereby it should receive annually an appropriation from the state of $8,000, and this arrangement was carried out until 1887, when the state denied the Negro University further aid, on the ground that it was admitting white students to its classes. A great deal of excitement prevailed, especially in the legislature where a bill was introduced but not passed which provided heavy punishment for anyone instructing classes made up of students from both races. The fund denied Atlanta University was given to another Negro school, Morris-Brown. To prevent future misunderstandings which might be brought about by the lack of control the state had over private institutions, the legislature in 1890 set up the Georgia State Industrial College for Colored Youths, made it a branch of the University, and located it near Savannah.

A school for Negroes largely promoted by Southern white people was founded in 1883 in Augusta, and named Paine Institute to honor Moses U. Paine of Iowa, who made the initial gift of $25,000. In 1933 it celebrated its semi-centennial with a pageant showing the progress the race had made. In Fort Valley was founded in 1898 an industrial school for Negroes, patterned after the Tuskegee school, in Alabama. Agreeing with Booker T. Washington that an industrial school was of the most value to Negroes, the state made a small annual appropriation for this school. One of the greatest centers of Negro education in the world grew up in Atlanta where were founded the Spelman Seminary in 1881 particularly for Negro girls, Morris-Brown in 1885 to train Negroes for the ministry, and the Gammon School of Theology with its $1,000,000 given by Elijah H. Gammon of Illinois. By the end of the century so rich were the Negro colleges of Georgia that Governor A. D. Candler admitted that all the colleges and universities of the white Georgians could not equal them in wealth.

The literary developments following Reconstruction were exemplified at their best in the work of Joel Chandler Harris, who felt that controversial writing flowing out of sectionalism would wither the soul of the people and kill a true literature. He believed that Georgia and the South afforded a wealth of subjects for interpretative writing, and in this belief he worked for a better understanding between the North and the South. The only Negro problem which he saw was that created by the Northern politicians who "insisted that the property and the intelligence of the South should be placed in charge of those who had no property and intelligence." In books, in the *Atlanta Constitution,* and in periodicals of his own, he exerted his influence.

In journalism the *Atlanta Constitution* was outstanding in Georgia, and came to be one of the best known papers in the South, speaking the point of view to a great extent of the whole region. The *Atlanta Journal,* founded in 1883, in time came to exercise great political influence in the state. William Randolph Hearst entered the field of Georgia journalism in 1906 by establishing his *Atlanta Georgian.* The most fearless journals of reform were the Columbus *Enquirer-Sun,* which for a brief day in the twentieth century under the editorship of Julian Harris impressed itself upon the nation, and the *Macon Telegraph,* which celebrated its hundredth anniversary in 1926 and entered its second century of existence with unabated vigor. The oldest journal in the state was the *Augusta Chronicle,* with its line going back to 1785.

Public libraries supported by public funds began to make their appearance by 1898, when the state set up a library commission to give advice on establishing and maintaining libraries and in selecting books.[1] The next year the beginning of the Carnegie Library in Atlanta was made possible by the gift of $100,000 by Andrew Carnegie.

Georgians were never loath to express the opinion that their state had made a great deal of history; but they seldom seemed to realize the importance of preserving their records. In 1900 Governor A. D. Candler in his annual message to the legislature called for the collection and publication of the most important documents. In 1902 the legislature provided for the copying again of the colonial records in London, and at the end of his term as governor, Candler was appointed to edit them. He not only secured copies of the colonial records, but he also gathered many others, relating to the Revolutionary War and to the Civil War and the years of Reconstruction following. The result of his labors was published in 37 volumes. The necessity for a permanent department to preserve the state's records was recognized in 1918, when the Department of Archives and History was created.

Sentiment in Georgia never ceased to be stirred by Confederate veterans as long as one of them should live. Here it was an expensive sentiment, for unlike the states of the victorious North, Georgia could not depend on the bounty of the treasury of the reunited country for pensions. Education and artificial limbs for the veterans had been provided soon after the war. Beginning in 1886 out of respect for Confederate soldiers, tinged with a fear of their votes, the state began a pension system which was soon to become the most liberal of any state in the Union, which came to include both veterans and widows of veterans, and which in 1931 provided $1,685,000 for distribution. In 1896 a commissioner of pensions was set up, and two years later a home for Confederate soldiers was accepted by the state, open to all who had been honorably discharged from the army. In 1945 there were only eleven vet-

---

[1] Indeed, various libraries and literary associations maintained by a membership had been growing up since colonial times, notably in Savannah, Augusta, and Atlanta.

erans left, three of whom were living in the Soldiers' Home. There were 1,043 widows of veterans still living. The state was at this time expending on these eleven honored remnants of the Lost Cause and on these thousand and forty-three reminders almost a half million dollars for the year.

The provincialism brought on by defeat and isolation began to crumble before the twentieth century had appeared. In 1895 the Chickamauga Park, donated by Georgia to the nation, was dedicated with Vice-President Adlai E. Stevenson and many other prominent people present. The fraternization of the soldiers who had fought on opposite sides in the great battle there, amazed people everywhere; and the invitation to the soldiers in blue to come to Atlanta to see the Cotton States and International Exposition then being held and peaceably to fight over again the battles around Atlanta made the sectional line fade farther away.

In the Spanish-American War the Georgians almost forgot the Civil War, as the flag took on a glow which it had not shed for them since 1861; and when Joe Wheeler appeared at the Confederate reunion in Atlanta in 1898, recently back from the war and dressed in his blue uniform, he received as much applause as if the color had been gray. The part the state played in the war was enthusiastic and spontaneous. Three thousand Georgians sought service in Cuba, but most of them for the brief period of the war impatiently paced back and forth on drill fields in Chickamauga Park, Griffin, Macon, or Athens.

In December, 1898, Georgians held a Peace Jubilee in Atlanta, to celebrate a national victory with as much fervor as they had ever shown in earlier times on receiving news of the battles of First Manassas or Fredericksburg. President McKinley added further forgetfulness to Civil War animosities by visiting the state at this time and attending the Jubilee. In an address to the legislature he deeply touched the hearts of all Georgians when he declared that Confederate graves were graves of honor and that it was the duty of the United States government to help keep them green. When he visited Macon, Confederate veterans welcomed him and presented him with a Confederate badge, which he wore.

As proof of Georgia's rising importance in the Union, the next year the state was awarded a Federal penitentiary to be constructed in Atlanta and to cost $2,000,000.

In the First World War Georgia was merged with the nation in her efforts and in her contributions. Thomas E. Watson attempted to arouse opposition to drafting soldiers, and other Georgians were slow in supporting President Wilson because cotton dropped in price from fifteen to six cents a pound; but war enthusiasm soon silenced all who expressed doubts as to the wisdom of having entered the conflict. In unison with the nation, Georgia had her hopes and fears, she passed her work or fight laws, and when the war had been won, she celebrated the signing of the armistice as noisily as the rest of the country.

The First World War came and went, and the world thereafter was never to be quite the same again. Though it had been the mightiest war in all history up to that time, it had affected Georgia much less than had the Civil War, and powerful though the conflict was, it could never change the meaning of *ante-bellum* in Georgia. Yet Georgia was now living in a new world and she could not escape it.

CHAPTER XXXI

BETWEEN TWO WARS

FOLLOWING THE First World War there was a short period of unexcelled prosperity, which came with such suddenness that few people could learn how to use it before it disappeared as quickly as a dream, leaving memories more bitter than sweet and a feeling that never again would such Elysian fields be entered. Banks failed throughout the state, mortgages on farms and homes were foreclosed, and many people were forced to start life anew.

Then came the little insect called a boll weevil, which had long been working its way northward and eastward from the Rio Grande. It entered the state in 1915 and during the next few years completely infested the cotton regions. It recorded its devastating march in such startling statistics as these: in 1919 Georgia produced 1,660,000 bales of cotton; in 1920, 1,415,000; in 1921, 787,000; in 1922, 715,000; in 1923, 588,000. War against the weevil raised the number to 1,002,000 bales the next year, which thereafter continued at more than a million bales annually, until Federal crop limitations reduced it to 852,000 in 1938. During the following years it gradually settled down by 1959 to an average of less than a half million bales annually.

In 1929 a panic broke upon the nation, never equalled in intensity throughout its history; but Georgians, who had long been living in a state of deflation, felt its force much less keenly than those parts of the country which had been living in castles built upon the sands. Though money became extremely scarce in Georgia, there was no need for anyone to become gnawingly hungry, for there were few great cities to set their unemployed to tramping the streets. There was farm land awaiting all who should become hungry enough to start delving in the ground for a living. The march back to the farm became perceptible enough to be seen, as city-dwellers began to occupy the country places evacuated by toilers who had sought to escape the boll weevil. The average cash income for farmers during this decade was $678, which was less than forty-three other states.

More mobile than white Georgians had ever thought, the Negroes, taking full advantage of the prosperity in Northern industrial centers, fled in great numbers from the weevil-infested fields of Georgia and hurried away to Chicago, Detroit, and Pittsburgh. It was the glitter of gold more than the glare of racial inequalities and the fear of the modern Ku Klux Klan that led them to go northward; and when the gold ceased to glitter for Negroes in the North, many of them looked longingly toward the South and made their way back.

The decade of the nineteen-hundred-twenties added no cubits to the height of Georgia. She was far surpassed in population and industrial growth by her neighbor, North Carolina, and was forced by Tennessee into third place in the values of her manufactures; and thus only Georgians without a sense of humor could still apply to their state the proud title, once true but now out-of-date, "The Empire State of the South." In the booming nineties Georgia had kept most of the people she had produced, and she had through a conscious effort attracted many to cast their lots with her. The state was holding out again some of the Utopian promises which had engaged the attention of people in the days of Oglethorpe. The Grand Army of the Republic promoted a colony at Fitzgerald; Germans settled south of Macon; Shakers, Dunkards, Mennonites, Congregationalists, and Lutherans, from various parts of the North, came in; and the interesting Ruskin Colony moved down from Tennessee. The most interesting movement was a group from widely scattered areas of the North, who congregated on an old plantation near Columbus, here as a Christian Commonwealth to try out Christian communism. They began coming in 1896, but within a few years they had scattered to the winds in failure. But people in the twenties were not coming to Georgia; they were leaving. During the ten years from 1920 to 1930, the actual increase was slightly more than 13,000.

There was a widespread feeling during this decade that one important reason why the state did not prosper was her nearly impassable highways; and this fact was spread throughout the country by the great number of people attempting to cross the state on their way to participate in the Florida boom. The hardships they endured in their efforts to cross Georgia became the modern counterpart of the early trek across the plains by the covered wagons on their way to California. All attempts to have the state issue highway bonds were smothered out by an instinct implanted in the days of Bullock when bonds had been issued on the slightest provocation.

One of the most far-reaching movements in modern America was the coming of the motor age with the paved roads it brought. Georgia entered the movement in 1916, when she gave the prison board the additional duty of looking after the highways. To provide money, she placed a tax of one cent on each gallon of gasoline sold, which she later increased to six and one-half cents. Also she created a new highway board, which soon came to be an object of bitter contention in politics. Here was the largest business organization in the state; it spent more money yearly than any other enterprise, private or governmental. As it received most of the revenues from the gasoline tax and the automobile license fees, it spent more than half of all the money which came into the state treasury. Indeed, the state had now become the victim of road enthusiasm, for it was placing on the construction of highways a value greater than all the other activities organized humanity in the state could devise. Materialism had at last seemed to conquer things of the spirit in Georgia. Holding in 1930 the position last in rank among the forty-eight states in public education, she would seek a first place in paved roads. Thus would she make amends to those mud-bound nomads on their way to spend the winter in Florida.

In statecraft, Georgia was like all the other states and the nation; she had allowed her government to sprout out many tentacles which sapped her financial strength. One governor after another sharpened his sabre to cut off these parasitic growths, but none seemed to be as successful as Perseus of old in cutting the snaky locks from the Gorgon's head.

A drama if not intended to be a tragedy should not end in futility and defeat. If in the nineteen-hundred-twenties the curtain had fallen on the drama of Georgia it would have made the play appear to be a tragedy. But there was still life in the land and during the next fifteen years, though there were depths to be penetrated yet there were heights to be scaled; and on the latest watchtowers, Georgia was not only to be seen in a more resplendent light than had surrounded her for generations, but she herself could see into a future which looked bright and promising.

A decade of futility was not without its value, and those governors who sought to bring their state out of debt and disstress were making the road smoother for their successors. Thus it was that Thomas W. Hardwick, long in national prominence in Congress but in 1918 defeated for re-election to the Senate, in 1920 sought nomination for the governorship of Georgia in the "Race of Three Toms"—Tom Hardwick, Tom Watson, and Tom Jefferson. Watson, a changed man from his Populist days, was running for the United States Senate, and Thomas Jefferson was in theory in the keeping of the other two Toms. The first two Toms won, but whether Tom Jefferson established his ancient principles was for Georgians to argue about thereafter. Governor Hardwick had an intelligent program of economy and of simplification of the state government, as well as a reorganization of the many state supported higher educational institutions into a system controlled by a board of regents. His legislature would not listen to his recommendations, and after he had served one two-year term the people of Georgia unwisely refused to heed him further.

Instead of giving Hardwick a second term, which was generally awarded to governors, the people chose Clifford M. Walker to be their governor in 1922 and then re-elected him. After four years of talk about taxes and deficits and of failure of all efforts to remedy the situation, the governor returned to the people through the door he had entered.

Vanity of vanity, all was vanity. Lawyers came as governors and lawyers went; many laws were passed but few seemed fundamental enough to help the state. In 1926 a man who had been running on the edges of the gubernatorial race for some years finally by his perseverance won out. He was not a lawyer; he was Dr. Lamartine G. Hardman, not only a doctor of medicine but a successful businessman—a farmer with many acres, a cotton manufacturer, a banker, a merchant. The state needed a business administration; surely he could give it. He hired an expert to analyze the difficulties of the governmental organization and make recommendations for simplification; he tried to make Georgia land produce revenues for the empty state treasury even as he had made his farms grow grain for his bins. His program was wise; his legislature was foolish. Georgia seemed to be even past the help of a businessman.

Finally in 1930 there was a ray of hope. A young man and a lawyer, a member of a numerous family whose eldest member had long served on the bench of the state Supreme Court, Richard B. Russell, Jr., became governor of the state. The field was growing ripe for the harvest. A legislature now appeared on the scene willing to do the governor's bidding; the depression which began in 1929 was making people serious-minded. One way to settle debts, deficits, and extravagance was to reduce the cost of government. This could be done by an economical administration of a less complex government. This had been "Little Dick's" program which he had let no one forget from his first entry into the gubernatorial race. One hundred and two boards, bureaus, and commissions were now combined, eliminated, and reduced to eighteen. Twenty-six boards of trustees ruling over twenty-six educational institutions were made into one board of regents of about a dozen members to rule over one educational system. This board soon laid the axe to this wilderness of ne'er-do-well schools and left standing only a few more than half. The University System of Georgia was by 1959 made to include one university, seven senior and eight junior colleges, and three senior colleges for Negroes.

Governor Russell was doing well by his state, but near the end of his first term that will-o'-the-wisp, the United States senatorship, which most governors set their hearts on and blindly follow after, made its appearance by the death of Senator William J. Harris. Russell entered the race against Charles R. Crisp, long a member of Congress, who had been first elected in 1896 to succeed his father, and won. Russell's swapping his second term for a senatorship opened the floodgates of gubernatorial oratory earlier than had been expected. Out of the eight contestants for the honor emerged Eugene Talmadge, a former commissioner of agriculture. Throughout his generation no one was destined to fire the feelings of Georgians with either such loyalty or enmity as did this "Man from Sugar Creek."

Like Abraham Lincoln and Tom Watson, he knew there were more common people than any other kind of creature and that each man, and woman too, had a vote. He also knew something which most politicians never succeed in learning: how to hold an irreducible backlog of common people's votes and at the same time command the substantial support of rich men and corporations. His constantly reiterated philosophy of economy in government, reduction in governmental services, decrease in taxes, and non-interference by government with the individual by gift, dole, or regulation—this together with home-spun talk on the platform and in the "Eugene Talmadge Says—" column of his political newspaper *The Statesman,* suiting his college vocabulary to the most illiterate hearers, the lock of unruly hair streaking down his forehead, red suspenders, a campaign water-gourd drinking cup, hillbilly fiddlers, trained strong men to carry him away from the campaign platform, simplification of his name to the one syllable "Gene," the appeal for white supremacy—all this and more made Governor Talmadge.

Having gained his nomination through a county-unit primary system peculiar to Georgia, whereby a majority only of the unit votes and not of the popular votes was necessary, Talmadge had, in this campaign and in subsequent ones, by defending this system cleverly tied to himself the country people as opposed to city dwellers. He also gained the support of many of those 159 local machines which ran Georgia's 159 counties. For purposes of nominations counties had so-called unit votes ranging in number from six for the most populous county to two for the least populous, though, if based on population, this proportion of three to one, would have been one hundred to one. The result was to give the small rural counties control of the state. Naturally to protect this system the number of counties must not be reduced, irrespective of how weak and poor many of the small ones might be. As an example of how it was possible through the county unit system to nominate a candidate by a rural county minority of the total number of voters in the state, Eugene Talmadge in the gubernatorial primary of 1932 received 118 more county unit votes than his seven opponents combined; but his opponents received over 43,000 more popular votes. As there was only one party in Georgia, there was only one candidate to be voted for in an election. Thus, nomination really meant election; for the only time there could be a contest was in the primary, generally held in September, and not in the election in November.

Adding to his political strength by pitting rural people against city dwellers and championing small counties, Governor Talmadge reduced in 1933 by executive order all automobile license tags to $3. This saved the mass of Georgians from

$5 to $10 each, but it saved large corporations as much as $1,112 on some of their large trucks; yet nothing that Talmadge ever did as governor appealed to the masses so completely as this tag reduction. It helped to make him governor two additional times; and so happy an inspiration was his $3 tag that in 1936 when he sought the United States senatorship he made one of his planks call for a reduction of postage from three cents to two.

Talmadge's fundamental philosophy of life and government was in complete opposition to the whole program of Roosevelt's New Deal. It was not long before the inevitable clash with the Federal government took place, even as Edward Telfair, George M. Troup, Joseph E. Brown, and other Georgia governors in the historic past had engaged in heated combat with the central government. It was this feud with Roosevelt that cost Governor Talmadge the United States senatorship. The trouble began in the Governor's attempt to bring economy in the Highway Department, which resulted in his dismissal of the chairman and other members of the board, in his declaration of martial law in a restricted area, in a terribly tangled highway board situation, and finally in the refusal of the United States to distribute to Georgia further money for roads. Issues with the Federal government now multiplied thick and fast. Governor Talmadge disagreed with the National Recovery Administration (NRA) and the forty cents an hour wages it set up; and when one of his road contractors was enjoined for refusal to pay this scale of wages, the Governor set the state itself to building roads at its lower wages. Harold L. Ickes, Harry Hopkins, and other distributors and controllers of Federal favors soon found it impossible to deal with Governor Talmadge, and the Governor retaliated by refusing to co-operate in old-age pensions, health work, and other New Deal activities. Postmaster General James Farley threatened to take the second-class mailing privileges away from the *Market Bulletin* because of its political activities and heated attacks on the New

Deal. This publication was run by Tom Linder, Commissioner of Agriculture and a strong supporter of Eugene Talmadge.

Governor Talmadge's attacks on the New Deal and on President Roosevelt himself, his dismissal of members of the highway board and also of the Public Service Commission because it did not reduce utility rates, his declaration of martial law and the use of state troops—all gained the Governor and the state much notoriety over the nation. And yet it appealed to many Georgians, who even if they might not agree with the Governor still loved a fight. Thus it was that Talmadge was reelected in 1934.

His second term eclipsed his first in the turmoil that the state found itself in. In 1935 the legislature failed to agree on an appropriation bill and adjourned without passing one. Governor Talmadge, who had always found a way out of his difficulties heretofore, seemed unperturbed. He merely declared that the old appropriation act would remain in force, but the Treasurer and Comptroller General refused to pay out funds under the old act. The Governor thereupon dismissed both from office and appointed other men who agreed to obey him. The state funds being in various bank depositories, the bank officials feared to release the money until the Governor was able through a re-made Supreme Court to get his own acts declared constitutional. This was excitement for Georgians and for the nation too; but there was yet more. In 1934 the worst textile strike in Georgia's history swept across the state as flying squadrons of striking emissaries in trucks raced from one cotton mill town to another to force workers to quit their jobs. Governor Talmadge called out the state troops, armed them with tear gas bombs and machine guns, and arrested many of the strike agitators and lodged them in concentration camps. La Grange and Manchester were storm centers.

Having been governor two terms and being forbidden by the constitution to serve again in immediate succession, Talmadge decided to appoint his own candidate for governor and run for the United States Senate against Senator Russell—though, since this was a presidential election year, he might accept the nomination for the presidency if it were offered by the "true" Democrats divorced from the "bogus" New Dealers. In furtherance of this idea he promoted a grass roots convention in Macon. A strange performance it was in this dyed-in-the-wool Democratic state of Georgia, which after much oratory endorsed Talmadge for president. As there did not seem to be much substance to this nomination, the Governor decided to push his campaign for the United States Senate against Russell. He was disastrously defeated in the primary for the nomination, carrying only 16 of the 159 counties. In the gubernatorial primary Eurith D. Rivers, a South Georgian born in Arkansas, received the nomination, running on a New Deal platform which promised everything that Talmadge had rejected.

Now for the first time Georgia entered the empire of the New Dealers. Service and spending, not economy and simplicity, were emblazoned on her banners. Governor Rivers with his smooth oratory and legislative skill hurriedly pushed through pensions for the old, health service for the ailing and the well, homestead exemption from taxation of $2,000 for home and $300 for household and kitchen furniture and tools, seven months school and increased salaries for teachers, and free textbooks. President Roosevelt could now visit his "other home" at Warm Springs without the fear that the Georgia chief executive within his heart might not have a welcome for him. Georgia also sought to prevent any future governor from giving the state a one-man rulership as Talmadge had done. A constitutional amendment was passed to allow the legislature to call itself into extra session, a law was enacted to guard the Supreme Court against the governor's manipulating its membership in certain contingencies, and other holes were plugged.

Governor Rivers' first term was his honeymoon of spending and preparing to spend; his second term, to which he was elected in 1938, was to usher in the bills for payment. Mindful earlier of the inevitable day, the Rivers administration had induced the legislature to provide for the classification of property for taxation and to pass a law taxing intangibles, a species of property which had heretofore evaded taxation because of excessively high rates. The Governor had failed, however, to secure the enactment of a sales tax and a tax on chain stores, which he had especially advocated. There was a vast quantity of alcoholic liquors being consumed in Georgia on which no tax was being paid, for some people foolishly felt that it was much better to be hypocritical, violate the law, and lose millions of dollars of income than to compromise with the devil by legalizing the traffic and collecting a handsome revenue. It was a strange turn of fate that lined up the bootleggers with some of the best people in the state in their determination not to legalize liquor. Twice the legislature, in 1935 and 1937, unwilling to assume the responsibility of legalizing liquor, had passed the question to the people in referendum, and twice by slight majorities the people had voted it down. In 1938 strictly as a revenue measure the legislature passed a law allowing counties to vote on legalizing the sale of liquors, and soon various counties began acting and going wet. Previously beer and wines had been legalized and they were bringing in considerable revenues. As a further source of money the legislature sold the rentals of the Western and Atlantic Railroad for four years ahead, getting a little more than two and a quarter million dollars. This method of getting revenue had been resorted to previously by Governor Russell.

Yet with all these efforts at money-getting the state was forced to scale down its payments to 74 per cent of the appropriations, except for a few services that were to be paid in full. Among the latter were the salaries of school teachers. Dogged by deficits mounting higher and higher, Governor Rivers decided to levy on the highway fund, which was generally swollen by the allocation of most of the gasoline taxes to it. The chairman of the highway board refused to divert the money and

Governor Rivers dismissed him. Refusing to accept this dismissal, the chairman took the matter to the courts, and now Governor Rivers, to get around court decisions, taking a leaf from the book of Talmadge, whom Rivers had so bitterly denounced for his high-handed and dictatorial ways, declared martial law in a restricted area and put the state troops in charge. The trouble spread to the Federal courts and a judge found Governor Rivers in contempt of court and had him arrested. The Governor ultimately got out of his troubles with the court and he got the highway money, but he was unable to get rid of the chairman of the highway board. As Governor Rivers' second term was drawing to a close, the deficit had reached about $22,000,000.

Governor Rivers had given Georgia a taste of the richer life promised by the New Deal, but the people, inured to a frugal life for a century past and innately fearful of large debts, felt that the fling they had taken with Rivers must be sinful. It was easy, therefore, for Talmadge, now constitutionally able to run for governor again, to charm the people afresh with his homespun sayings and philosophies, with his rustic prejudices and his bucolic occupation. In 1940 he became governor a third time, after the people had got assurances in some way that Talmadge was a changed man—that never again would he use dictatorial methods in ruling the state. During his third term the constitution was amended to allow the governor to serve for four years but be ineligible immediately thereafter for the office.

As the governor's office had an especial charm for Talmadge, it was soon evident that he would be in the race in 1942 for the four-year term—he had never been defeated for governor. Though he would prefer a United States senatorship, he seemed unable to secure that position. After having been defeated by Russell in 1936, he had tried, unsuccessfully, two years later to dislodge Senator Walter F. George. If he should fail in this campaign, his official life might well come to a close. As Talmadge had heretofore thrived on turmoil and the exciting of the multitude, he may or may not have planned as campaign strategy an agitation that got completely out of hand. Appearing to believe that the University and other units of the University system were flirting dangerously with the idea of allowing Negro students to enroll, he demanded that the Regents dismiss a few members of the various faculties, whom he had designated as the conspirators. When the Regents remained unconvinced of the truth of the charges, the Governor, who was a member of the board, by unusual procedures remade the board and had it dismiss the so-designated culprits. To add a remarkable performance to the procedure, an open hearing or trial was held in the chamber of the House of Representatives in Atlanta, which before it was finished partook much of the nature of an athletic event with a noisy crowd on the sidelines.

Undoubtedly the Governor had not planned all this excitement, for it not only spread over the state and into almost every home but it attracted attention throughout the nation. It appeared to be an attack not only on academic freedom and the integrity of the teaching profession but also a most dangerous interference of politicians in educational matters. People who had the best opportunities to know the facts denied absolutely that there had ever been the remotest contemplation of mingling of whites and Negroes in the same educational institutions. Among those so testifying were Steadman V. Sanford, Chancellor of the University system, and Harmon W. Caldwell, President of the University. The various accrediting agencies and educational associations throughout the nation held investigations and came to the conclusion that there had been a most dangerous and insidious interference with the educational institutions of Georgia and that all should be dismissed from membership until proper safeguards for the future should be adopted. This would mean that Georgia students could not transfer their credits to other institutions.

Amidst the emotions of this controversy the gubernatorial campaign took its course. Even before this storm had broken, a youngster whom Governor Talmadge never mentioned by name during the whole campaign—who bore the name Ellis Gibbs Arnall—had entered the race for the nomination. Now to his aid from all over the state came the embattled students who could not vote, and many of their parents and kin who could vote, determined to put into the governor's chair a man who had promised to rescue the state's educational institutions from political domination. To the surprise of many Georgians and to the utter amazement of Governor Talmadge, Arnall won. The Governor came to realize as never before the power of the state press, which had been almost unanimously against him, and the danger of even the appearance of political interference with the cherished schools of the Georgians, which they might not support very well but which they nevertheless loved.

Georgians enjoyed their politics (within the prevailing Democratic party there was factionalism as sharp as ever separated any two political parties), but they found time to be interested in as many other kinds of happenings as were the people in any other American state. They could dispute with Tennessee over the boundary line, as they had been doing for more than a century, and they could threaten to run the correct line which would put Chattanooga in Georgia. Their latest grumblings on this subject took place in 1942. Without a great deal of prodding they could continue to be interested in their history, as when the legislature in 1918 set up the Department of Archives and History to safeguard the state's records, official and otherwise, putting Lucian Lamar Knight in charge. In 1933 they could celebrate their two hundredth birthday with much historical pageantry in Savannah and with speeches and banquets over the state. They could develop and appreciate a heroic memorial to the Confederacy to be carved on the side of Stone Mountain, a vast outcropping of granite near Atlanta; and they could employ, in 1916, Gutzon Borglum, the great

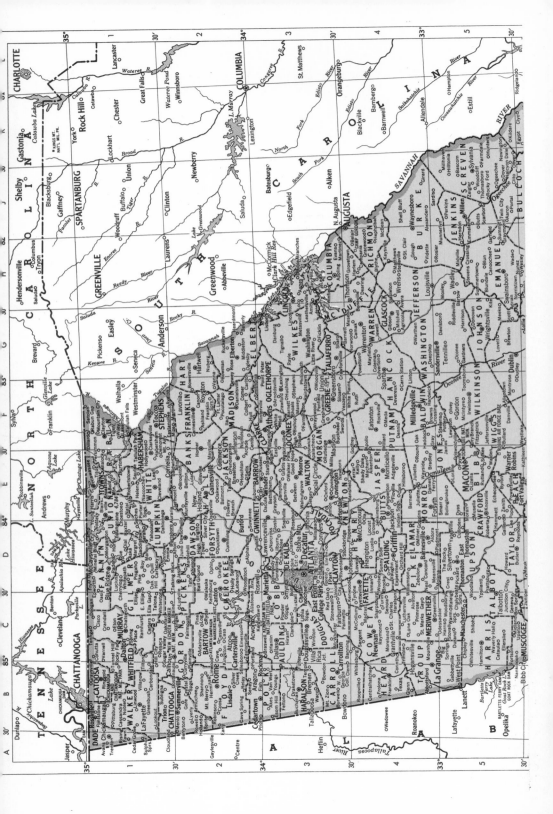

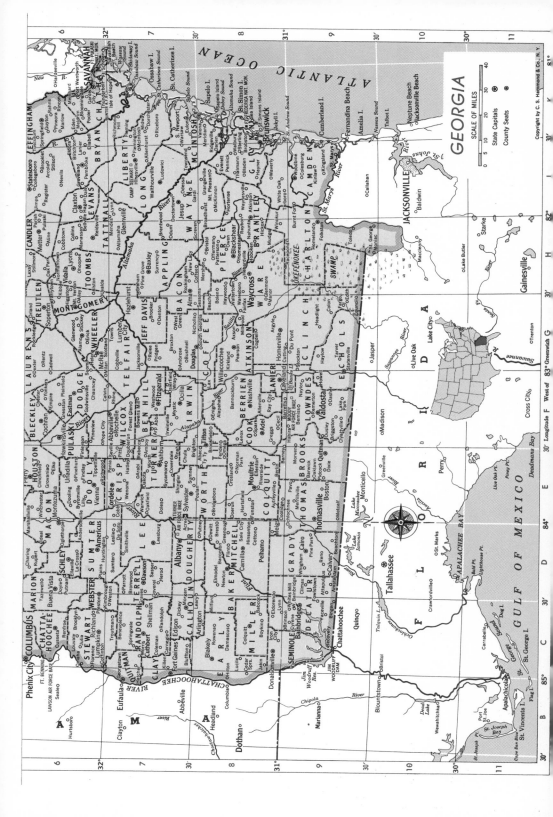

GEORGIA

SCALE OF MILES

0 5 10   20   30   40

⊛ State Capitals

⊙ County Seats

Copyright by C. S. Hammond & Co., N.Y.

sculptor, to carve Lee, Davis, Stonewall Jackson, and other Confederate heroes in the rock; they could induce in 1925 the United States government, in aid of this project, to strike a half-dollar coin as a "Memorial to the Valor of the Soldier of the South"; but they were unable to deal with the artistic temperament of Borglum in a sufficiently practical way as to lead to the completion of the memorial. Quarrels ensued, Borglum was dismissed, another artist was employed who died before much work had been done; the memorial remained unfinished, a sort of finger of scorn pointing at unworthy descendants of illustrious forebears.

Though Georgia might not be able to erect a memorial to the Confederacy on Stone Mountain, one of her daughters, Margaret Mitchell (Mrs. John R. Marsh), instituted a mighty vogue for the Confederate war and the Reconstruction in her historical novel *Gone with the Wind*. Read by millions, it was then made into a motion picture and seen by many more. Miss Mitchell was one of a distinguished group of Georgia writers, some of whom were passing off the stage while others were just making their appearance. Frank L. Stanton was becoming a tradition a little less nostalgic than Joel Chandler Harris. His "Mighty Lak a Rose" was sung by people irrespective of race, nationality, and creed, and his column "Just from Georgia," in the *Atlanta Constitution,* was widely read. Harry Stillwell Edwards was much of the same tradition, writing in 1920 when he was sixty-six years old his immortal and inimitable *Eneas Africanus*. Of this older generation was Corra Harris, born on a plantation and married to a Methodist preacher, whose best-known work was *A Circuit Rider's Wife*. For sheer love of the romantic past and loyalty to Georgia traditions, Lucian Lamar Knight had no peer. He spent a long life writing *Georgia and Georgians* and many other works, and at the end chose to be buried in the old church-yard near historic Frederica. Of the newer generation, in addition to Miss Mitchell, was Caroline Miller, who in 1934 won the Pulitzer Prize for her book *Lamb in His Bosom,* a local color novel of South Georgia. The two *enfants terrible* were Erskine Caldwell, who made the unthinking beyond the Southern borders believe that his *Tobacco Road* depicted conditions typical of Georgia, and Lillian Smith, whose *Strange Fruit* was even stranger to Georgians and was in the eyes of the Supreme Court of Massachusetts "obscene, indecent and impure."

Dealing with race relations in a different fashion were the insidious, dishonest, and traitorous American Communists, who to enlist a few gullible Negroes were planning a Negro soviet to embrace the black belt of the whole South which would, of course, cut across Georgia. Angelo Herndon, a Negro emissary from the North, was caught in Atlanta with this incriminating evidence. The state quickly prosecuted him under an old statute passed in 1866 which provided punishment as high as twenty years' imprisonment for anyone circulating printed matter which might incite an insurrection. After long court battles, liberally financed by New York Communists, the case reached the United States Supreme Court, which declared the Georgia law unconstitutional and freed Herndon.

In her political allegiance Georgia showed increasing signs of clinging closer to the Democratic party. The greatest excitement in a recent national election occurred in 1928, when strange forces were made to play upon the voters, but Georgians resisted them all successfully and gave to Alfred E. Smith 129,000 votes and 99,000 to Herbert Hoover. And thereby she maintained the unique record in American political history of being the only state never to cast her electoral votes for a straight-out Republican. In 1932 she gave almost twice as many votes to Franklin D. Roosevelt as she had ever cast for any presidential candidate throughout her history. Roosevelt's Democracy was sufficient for Georgians, but his frequent visits to Warm Springs were irresistible. As Republicanism never thrived in Georgia, that human frailty which called for heated political campaigns found its outlet in intemperate contests within the Democratic party among the candidates seeking the offices.

Though President Roosevelt did not please Governor Talmadge and a considerable number of other Georgians, his New Deal program, with its many aids for farmers and other people, was too powerful for the mass of Georgians to resist. The New Deal could not stop tornadoes, yet it could act swiftly to alleviate damages wrought by them. In the presidential year of 1936 a tornado struck Gainesville, killed about 200 people and destroyed $5,000,000 worth of property. The New Deal quickly came to the rescue, though Governor Talmadge was still ruler over the state; and it was possible that through this timely aid the tornado helped to blow many Georgia votes to Roosevelt, for the state voted seven to one for him over Alfred M. Landon. In 1940 the Second World War was raging throughout much of the world, and though it had not yet reached America the feeling was widespread that President Roosevelt must be given a third term in the interest of American safety. So again, Georgia cast her vote for him. In 1944 the United States was in the midst of this dreadful maelstrom, and it now seemed more than ever desirable to keep the steady hand of Roosevelt at the national helm; so Georgia now cast her vote a fourth time for Roosevelt.

In 1932 and for years thereafter Georgia's two United States Senators were Richard B. Russell, Jr., and Walter F. George, who had begun his service in the Senate ten years previously. Eugene Talmadge had tried unsuccessfully to unseat both Russell and George, and in 1938 President Roosevelt had unwisely protruded himself into state politics in his unsuccessful attempt to purge Georgia of George. George was an outstanding member of the Senate, reputed to be its greatest authority on constitutional law, and a conservative leader too dangerous for New Dealers to tolerate.

Among the reforms which Arnall had promised the state in his campaign for governor, there stood out boldest schools and prisons, for in dealing with each Governor Talmadge had been held to be a great sinner. The schools making up the University system had been discredited and dismissed from membership by various associations and agencies throughout the nation, but the date set for the dismissal to become effective was fixed far enough ahead so that a new administration would have an opportunity to institute the needed reforms before much inconvenience would be suffered. To make it impossible hereafter for a governor to lay violent hands on the Board of Regents, the legislature passed a law removing the governor from the board, increasing the terms of members (who should number one from each Congressional district and five from the state at large) to seven years, and allowing the Board itself to fill temporarily all vacancies which should develop during a recess of the legislature. The governor should continue to appoint the members with the approval of the senate, but as the constitution forbade a governor to serve two terms in succession, it was made almost impossible for a governor to appoint a majority of the board. This law was later made a part of the constitution. As a result of this legislation, no educational institution of Georgia lost its accredited standing for long.

The other outstanding reform related to Georgia's penal institutions. Almost constantly charges had been made against Governor Talmadge, as, indeed, frequently against governors before him, that pardons were being bought and sold. Too often the evidence did seem to point to a pardon racket from the governor's door on down a line of lesser officials. To abate this evil the constitution was amended to set up a Board of Pardons and Paroles which was given the sole power to pardon and parole prisoners, thus removing from the governor that ancient but dishonored power.

Oftentimes the evil which Georgians came to deplore even more than criminals being set free was the sad lot of those who remained in custody. Barbaric conditions grew up in spots in Georgia's prisons and chain gangs, despite the efforts of humane officials. Manacles, leg irons, neck irons, sweat boxes, cages on wheels, stripes, too often characterized the chain gangs, whose members might chant:

> One star in de east,
> One star in de west,
> An' 'twixt de two dey ain' neber no rest.

The sharp attention of the whole nation was drawn to these dark spots by a book, *I Am a Fugitive from a Georgia Chain Gang,* written in 1932 by Robert E. Burns, who had escaped to the North. It was later made into a moving picture. Another book written the same year, *Georgia Nigger,* by John L. Spivak, presented a powerful argument for prison reform. That Georgia might never again be reproached by such conditions among her prisoners, Governor Arnall saw to it that a Board of Corrections with a Director of Corrections at its head should watch over the welfare of the state's prisoners. While Talmadge was still governor a modern prison had been constructed with Federal funds near Reidsville, known as Tattnall Prison. To this place the prisoners were removed from the antiquated structure at Milledgeville and from other points. Governor Arnall now instituted a new regime. For them as well as those who still remained in the custody of county authorities, all shackles, chains, and other impediments must be removed. Whipping was outlawed, and no prisoner should thereafter wear stripes except in punishment for the infraction of prison rules. So enticing had Georgia's penal institutions and their administration now become that fugitive Burns decided to return to see what would happen to him; his sentence was immediately commuted and he was speeded back to his New Jersey home rejoicing.

Arnall was the most dynamically constructive governor Georgia had had within the memory of its oldest inhabitants. Too often previously the attention of the nation had been directed toward Georgia for her sins and the sins of her leaders, and feature writers in their articles for national magazines had

brought Georgia into shame and disrepute. Now the picture
was completely reversed. It seemed none came to Georgia but
to praise—to praise the state and its governor.

This new attitude toward Georgia was not the result only of
school and prison reforms; it sprang from a rich program of
progress and reform which Arnall had been promoting. He
became governor in the midst of the Second World War, but
so thoroughly had the national organization for making war
been developed that it left little for the states as such to do.
There was plenty for Georgia boys and girls and men and
women to do, and long before the Selective Service Act had
been passed Georgians had set an enviable record for volun-
teering in the United States Army and Navy. But when the
national law required boys of eighteen to enter the armed
services, then it was that Governor Arnall, who already felt a
special debt to the youth of Georgia for the part they had
played in his election, decided that if the age of eighteen made
a fighter it ought also to make a voter. He pushed this law
through the legislature, which made Georgia the first state in
the Union to reduce the voting age to eighteen.

With a few other Southern states Georgia had for years been
the object of intemperate and insincere attacks by forces in the
North, mostly radical, because she exacted a poll tax from her
voters. Despite the reiterated charges to the contrary, this tax
kept no Georgian from voting, white or black, who had annually a dollar's worth of interest in his government. In reality
the poll tax was more of a nuisance than a revenue producer
or a deterrent to voting. Recognizing this fact and desiring to
escape the application of a law to repeal the poll tax then being
agitated in Congress, which many doubted would be constitutional, Georgia repealed the tax but continued in her constitution the statement that no poll tax should ever be more than
one dollar—this without reference to whether such a tax should
or should not be made a qualification for voting. In line with
the ideas of the state's obligation to guarantee social security

to its citizens, Georgia passed a law establishing a system of teacher retirement whereby compensation should be granted to all, based on length of service and previous salary. In 1945 the legislature appropriated $1,000,000 to put this law into effect.

Georgia had long been pushing against the frontiers of illiteracy, inertia, and educational neglect. During the nineteen-hundred-twenties she had been giving to her highways a great deal more money than to all her social and educational services combined. By the nineteen-hundred-forties the pendulum had swung far to the right; now she was spending on education almost twice the amount for highways: in 1944 the former got $20,153,000; the latter, $10,962,000. Out of the money expended for education the state's colleges received $2,158,000. It was now no mean honor for Georgia to be able truthfully to say that she spent for education more out of each dollar's revenue than any other state in the Union—that was, of course, the real test of educational effort, more eloquent than $100,000,000 that a richer state might have spent.

Georgia was also making commendable progress agriculturally and industrially. In 1943 she stood first in the nation in the production of velvet beans, peanuts, pimiento peppers, sweet potatoes, watermelons, and pecans. Though often referred to as the "Peach State," she rarely ranked first in that fruit; and although she was certainly "The Land of Cotton," she only ranked fifth in that staple, though it was her most valuable farm crop, selling in 1943 for $107,258,000. The crops in which Georgia stood first indicated how diversified her agriculture was, and this was what her wisest agricultural leaders had long worked for. A specialized method for agricultural betterment called the Callaway Plan was agitated widely in the nineteen-hundred-forties by Cason J. Callaway and his supporters, but it later faded out. Economic diversity had certainly reached Georgia by this time, for in the year 1943 her manufactured products—amounting to about $700,000,000—were worth about twice all her agricultural crops, and the output of her mines was $21,000,000.

The population of the state had by 1940 passed the three million mark, reaching in this year 3,123,723; but because of wartime migrations Georgia, in line with thirty-five other states, lost population for a few years thereafter. In 1943 it was estimated at 3,015,336.

When Arnall became governor in January, 1943, he inherited a debt of $36,000,000. He had promised in his campaign to levy no new taxes during his administration. With this large debt and with a disquieting decrease in gasoline revenues on account of rationing that fuel, the outlook for affording the people during the next four years adequate governmental services looked dismal. Yet in 1944 the state revenues amounted to $61,772,000 and by a judicious expenditure of this fund there was no breakdown in providing for the general welfare, despite the fact that the governor seemed to be making good his promise that the state should be paid out of debt by the end of his term. Georgia had by this time come near exhausting the various kinds of taxes devised by American states. There were the general property tax, intangible property tax, various alcoholic and soft drink taxes, gasoline tax, automobile tag tax, income tax and various other taxes and fees. Conspicuously absent was the sales tax.

Few years passed from the days of Reconstruction down to 1945 without the cry being heard that the railroads had fixed a set of freight rates, if not designed to cripple and retard Southern economic development, at least having that effect, for these rates were much higher than for equal distances in the North. Governor followed governor in Georgia and elsewhere, and effort after effort was futilely made to induce the Interstate Commerce Commission to right this wrong. Finally in 1945 Governor Arnall determined to by-pass the Interstate Commerce Commission and go directly to the United States Supreme Court and ask leave from that body to bring a suit against twenty railroad companies on the ground that they had violated the Sherman Anti-Trust Law in that they had conspired to fix rates to the detriment of the South. Amazing as it was true, the Court allowed such a suit to be instituted. This movement resulted in the South getting its plight prominently before the country, and some good resulted.

The subjects of government which Georgians had talked most about during the first forty-five years of the twentieth century were tax reform, mismanagement of pardons and paroles, prison reforms, county consolidation, county unit system of nominations, deficits, and constitutional revision. All of these subjects had been dealt with by 1945 in some fashion, except the county unit system of nominations, and county consolidation beyond the addition of Milton and Campbell counties to Fulton.

The last of these subjects taken up was constitutional revision. The procedure adopted was unique in Georgia, for instead of calling a constitutional convention, a move which probably would have been doomed to failure because of the popular basis for representation in that body, the legislature in March, 1943, provided for a commission of twenty-three whose duty it was to amend the old constitution or make a new one. On this commission were the governor, the president of the senate and the speaker of the house, other members of these two bodies, certain other state officials including judges, three practicing lawyers, and three laymen. After laboring on the document and holding public hearings for more than a year and a half, they submitted their work to the legislature in January, 1945. This body adopted it and submitted it to the people in an election in August. It was adopted by a substantial majority in a light vote. The people had shown considerable interest in the work of the committee and engaged in much discussion concerning it, and some of the older politicians expressed the fear that the ancient rights of the people might be jeopardized. Yet this new constitution was in reality mostly the old one written in new words. It was more a revision of language than of powers and organization of government. Could Robert Toombs, who had much to do with the old one, have awakened from the dead and read this one, he would have found the meaning little changed. He would have rubbed his hands in glee as he read: "The bonded debt of the State shall never be increased, except to repel invasion, suppress insurrection or defend the State in time of war." Such in different words was in the old constitution and was put there by Toombs. Equally pleased would he have been in reading the clause repudiating the old Reconstruction bonds. Many other clauses in their meaning would have sounded familiar. He would have concluded that times had not changed much after all.

Yet there were changes sufficient in number and in significance to allow Georgians to shout their approval of this new document or view it with alarm. It raised the salary of legislators to $15.00 a day and of the governor to $12,000 a year, though not without legislative power to reduce it; it included the previously passed law fixing the voting age at eighteen years; it provided for a lieutenant-governor; it forbade the old evil of allocating a certain tax to certain services or departments; it continued the Board of Regents in this fundamental law and added boards; it omitted all reference to primary elections in the hope of avoiding the heavy hand of the United States Supreme Court against the denial of Negroes voting in those elections; it authorized a board to administer a merit system "under which state personnel shall be selected on a basis of merit, fitness, and efficiency"; and it made possible under certain restrictions home rule to counties and cities. In denying that the power of the state to tax could be abrogated by "any gift, grant or contract, whatsoever," and re-enforcing it with the statement that all "exemptions from taxation heretofore granted in corporate charters are declared to be henceforth null and void," the constitution opened the road for the state to move to collect taxes on certain railways which had been given originally in their charters exemption from taxation and which for a century and more had been enjoying that freedom.

During Governor Arnall's administration the state climbed upward in the estimation of critics and observers throughout the nation; but so accustomed had some Georgians become to the slings and arrows from the North that they suspected anyone who received praise from that direction. For bringing this about they blamed Arnall rather than praised him.

CHAPTER XXXII

UP TO NOW

LIVING IN GEORGIA during the nineteen-hundred-fifties differed little from living in the neighboring states, but Georgians had a heritage and a name which set them apart. They elected rulers who might be wiser or more foolish than those in other states, and they had their own peculiar problems to solve. Nevertheless the people could live little unto themselves. Any force powerful enough greatly to affect their lives would touch the life of all of the South equally, and would most likely be widespread enough to become national. Georgians would be a part of any war in which South Carolinians might fight; any agricultural pests that might devastate Alabama would equally disturb Georgia; and any financial disaster which might overtake New York would also make itself felt in Georgia. With all the wisdom of her rulers Georgia would not be able to escape these forces.

Like many Americans throughout the nation, Georgians feared that inflation, if unchecked, might prove as great an enemy as the rulers behind the Iron Curtain with their imperialism disguised under the name of communism. For if the value of the dollar continued to fall, it would ultimately wipe out all accumulations of savings and the American economic system with it, followed by convulsions leading to dictatorship—the first fruits of communism.

For the decade and a half following 1945, the state, the nation, and the whole world were irresistibly being drawn closer together. Georgia as part of the nation had her problems to tussle with because of this relationship; but also as part of the nation she helped to formulate and support American policies both for home and in dealing with foreign countries. And also she had her own local problems related less directly to the nation and the world outside. Most of her problems, and the most serious ones, were produced by the fact that the world was growing smaller and smaller, through inventions and developments which greatly minimized distance.

Yet Georgians had not been sentenced by some terrible fate to a life over which they could have no control. The latest decades of their existence gave much evidence that they still had problems which they alone could solve, and that there still might be some virtue in the old slogan now going out of vogue, "It's great to be a Georgian."

True to the American tradition, Georgians could never get far away from their politics, state and national. Every two years they voted for a new legislature, both house and senate, and every four years for governor and president (as well as for lieutenant governor and vice president). Also every two years they voted for United States Representatives, and for Senators in a two-year and four-year sequence, as in 1948-1950, 1954-1956, and 1960-1962. Then there were various city and county elections, but apart from some of these local elections, the state and national elections were always held on the same day. In Georgia as in most of the South, the state elections were of little interest, for in a one-party state whoever won the nomination in the primary voting was assured of victory in the election following, for there would be only one candidate to be voted for.

Georgia continued to cast her votes for Democrats in state and national elections, never having voted for an official Republican nominee, though she did vote in 1872 for Horace Greeley, who ran as the nominee of the Liberal Republicans but who also was nominated by the Democrats that year. Before the Civil War, Georgia voted several times for Whig candidates both in state and national elections. And during the Reconstruction Era, when the will of the people was curbed by the national government, Georgia elected a Republican governor. But since that time the Republicans had little importance in Georgia, their strength lying mostly in some of the mountain counties and in the Atlanta metropolitan area. Even in the conservative break-away from the National Democratic party in the presidential election of 1948, when the States Rights Democrats (popularly known as Dixiecrats) nominated J. Strom Thurmond of South Carolina, Georgia held fast to her old Democratic moorings. In addition to the fact that Democracy was ingrained in Georgians, there was a desire to conserve the advantage the state held in the leadership her Senators and Representatives enjoyed in Congress, which if she should desert the Democratic Party, she could no longer expect.

Three of the most powerful committees in Congress were presided over by Georgians. Senator Richard B. Russell, Jr. was chairman of the Armed Services Committee and Senator Walter F. George, of the Finance Committee and later of the Foreign Relations Committee. Representative Carl Vinson was for sixteen years chairman of the Naval Affairs Committee and later the chairman of the Armed Services Committee of the House.

Russell first went to the Senate in 1932 and continued thereafter; George was first elected in 1922 and was re-elected without interruption until 1956, when on account of failing health he declined to make the race again. This decision was forced upon him as much by political conditions in Georgia as by considerations for his health. Herman E. Talmadge, the son of Eugene, who had inherited much of his father's political flair and had succeeded to his political partisans, was anxious to go to the Senate. He was confronted with the decision to run against George now or wait four years and then probably have to oppose the powerful Russell following. Herman Talmadge did not publicly announce his intentions, but it was made plain to George that he would have to oppose Talmadge. Rather than risk a strenuous campaign, George chose to retire. Out of recognition of his long patriotic services, including his deep knowledge of the United States Constitution and of foreign affairs, President Eisenhower appointed him special ambassador to the North Atlantic Treaty Organization (NATO); but soon thereafter on August 4, 1957, George died in his home town of Vienna, Georgia. In the senatorial primary of 1956, Herman Talmadge was nominated, and, of course, elected later in the year, for as usual the Republicans put up no candidate.

Herman Talmadge's election to the United States Senate was the culmination of a rapid political advancement. Exactly ten years previously, his father, Eugene, who had already been governor for three terms, had decided to run again. His chief opponent was James V. Carmichael, a Marietta lawyer and former member of the legislature. Former Governor Rivers also entered the race, though for no known reasons beyond adding confusion to the campaign. With his ever-ready county unit system working for him, Talmadge received a majority of the county unit votes; but Carmichael won more popular votes. This was the second time Eugene Talmadge had had his political life saved by the county unit brand of democracy. Here was further proof of the value of this system, for the Negroes had almost solidly voted against him, now that they were for the first time allowed to participate in a Georgia primary, taking advantage of a recent United States Supreme Court decision.

It was well known during the campaign that Eugene Talmadge was a sick man. In December, 1946, he died, a month before his scheduled January inauguration. Immediately there arose a puzzling political situation, but not at all puzzling to the Talmadge organization, which sensing the danger of Eugene Talmadge not living to be inaugurated, saw to it that 675 write-in votes were cast for Herman Talmadge. The die-hard supporters of Carmichael cast 669 write-in votes for him. There were scattered write-in votes for twenty-eight other persons, mostly ludicrous, such as the one for "Mortimer Snerd."

The constitution of 1945 had for the first time in the history of the state provided for a lieutenant governor. To this position

Melvin E. Thompson, whose public services heretofore had largely been in the educational field, was elected. The constitution also stated that the governor should serve four years, "and until his successor shall be chosen and qualified." The normal constitutional procedure in declaring the election of a governor following the popular voting was for the General Assembly to meet as one body and in its presence the speaker of the house and the president of the senate should count the votes and publish the returns. If no one should receive a majority of the votes (a situation which could never develop under the one-party-one-candidate system), then the General Assembly should choose the governor from the two candidates having the highest number of votes.

The well-laid plans of the Talmadge organization were now to bring the desired results. The General Assembly being made up largely of Talmadge supporters declared that Herman Talmadge was the next governor. Now a dangerous situation was fast developing, which had some of the characteristics of a coup d'état and which in a less stable society would inevitably have produced civil war. Governor Ellis Arnall refused to recognize Talmadge as governor, but soon the latter forcibly took possession of the gubernatorial offices in the capitol and also the gubernatorial mansion. A suit immediately reached the Georgia Supreme Court, designed to clarify the succession to the governorship. The decision of the court, though not unanimous, was that the General Assembly in this instance had exceeded its powers in electing a governor, and that therefore Herman Talmadge was not governor but that Ellis Arnall should continue as governor until his successor had qualified. Soon after the General Assembly had presumed to elect Herman Talmadge, it certified Thompson as lieutenant governor. Immediately thereupon, Arnall resigned and Thompson was sworn in; and so it turned out that for two months Georgia had two persons claiming to be governor; but in the light of the court decision Herman Talmadge had never at all been governor.

According to the constitution, when the lieutenant governor should succeed to the office of governor, he should serve only until the next election for members of the General Assembly. Since the next election for legislators was in 1948, there was now included an election for governor, to fill Eugene Talmadge's unexpired term. Herman Talmadge ran against Thompson in the primary and defeated him by 357,865 to 312,035. The act of the Thompson administration that had created the most public comment became a political football. It was his purchase of Jekyl Island from a group of Northern millionaires, whose fathers and grandfathers had enjoyed this "Golden Isle." Their descendants lured further southward by the charms of Florida, lost interest in Jekyl and sold it to the state for $650,000, though its value a dozen years later was reckoned at more than $20,000,000. The Talmadge forces decried ·his expenditure of the state's money and built up propaganda which helped Herman Talmadge defeat Thompson; though later when a bridge was built from the mainland to this island recreational center, the marker commemorating its completion conspicuously bore the name of Herman Talmadge.

Having had only a fragment of a four-year administration, Herman Talmadge in 1950, when the term for which Eugene Talmadge had been elected ran out, announced for the full four-year term. Thompson having had even a smaller slice of the Eugene Talmadge term was also anxious to serve a four-year-term. Three others, "smaller fry," entered the contest, but the race was between Herman Talmadge and Thompson. Talmadge won, both by the popular vote as well as by the county unit vote; but it emphasized to Herman Talmadge, who like his father had always supported this species of democracy, the vital personal importance of the unit system. For his popular vote over Thompson was a mere 8,000; but he had the impressive unit victory by a vote of 295 to 115.

During his four-year term, both by the spoken and written word, Herman Talmadge sang the praises of the county unit system, and tried twice unsuccessfully to get an amendment to the constitution extending the system to the general elections. (It must be kept in mind that the county unit system was used only in primary nomination elections.) Although he had the popular argument that this election device would greatly dilute the Negro vote now concentrated in cities, since the boll weevil and other developments had driven many Negroes from the rural counties, he was unable to convince the people of its wisdom.

Since a governor was ineligible to succeed himself for a second four-year term, Herman Talmadge was now left without a political roof over his head, but as has been previously noted, he trod the sands of Sahara for only two years, for then he came to the Washington oasis and pitched his tent there. In Georgia, in the year 1954, nine contestants sought the governorship, including the ever-hopeful Thompson; but just as Thompson as lieutenant governor had succeeded Arnall, so now, Marvin Griffin, the lieutenant governor elected in 1950 with Herman Talmadge, was to succeed to the governorship. He won by a big county-unit majority but received only 236,690 popular votes out of a total of more than 647,000. Great was the County Unit System! Griffin had been a secretary to a governor, a member of the legislature, a soldier in the wars, and an adjutant general of the state.

Governor Griffin deserved well of those interested in higher educational developments, especially scientific education following the Russians placing earth satellites in the skies. He reached into a surplus of state funds and drew out almost $8,000,000 to hasten completion of a Science Center being constructed at the University of Georgia in Athens. He deserved not well at all in the eyes of the *Atlanta Constitution* and the *Atlanta Journal* and a few other large city newspapers when he forbade them to carry advertisements of spirituous liquors, leaving the smaller newspapers to carry such advertisements, if they should so choose. This may have given an impetus to the *Atlanta Con-*

stitution to pry into the Griffin administration and turn up a surprising amount of carelessness and worse in the management of state funds, pointing the finger especially at the Revenue Department and the Highway board. The defensive answer that such had been going on for years did not entirely satisfy the people of the state.

Four years later, in 1958, there was another governor to be elected. The campaign was listless and all on one side. Ernest Vandiver swept the state, and by his election seemed to confirm a precedent that had been building up for some time, that the lieutenant governorship was a stepping stone to the governorship; for every lieutenant governor up to this time had become governor. Governor Vandiver, who was inaugurated in January, 1959, had succeeded to many problems, but none as fundamentally shocking and soul-searching for a solution as the segregation-integration issue.

Back with the birth of English civilization in America there began to develop an attitude toward a distinctly different race of people when most regrettably Negroes were brought from Africa as slaves. For the next century and a half slavery spread throughout the English colonies. With the close of the Revolution this institution was soon given up in the North, but the racial attitude persisted. Another war brought freedom to slaves everywhere in America, leaving in the South most of the Negro population and with it the problem of racial adjustments. The solution was for whites and colored to maintain their racial integrity, with the goal of separate but equal treatment in all public services and before the law. In 1896 this program received the sanction of the United States Supreme Court as meeting the requirements of the United States Constitution, and more particularly the Fourteenth Amendment to that document. Georgia and the rest of the South having long put more emphasis on the separate than the equal facilities, in more recent times, spurred by their own consciences and of that of the world, were fast closing the gap of difference. In fact in some few places the educational facilities for Negroes had passed the equal stage and had become superior, and now the whites could petition for facilities equal to what had been given to the Negroes. This situation was more markedly so in South Carolina than in Georgia. Thus did Southerners hope to ward off criticism that they were not living up to the "separate but equal" decision of the United States Supreme Court in 1896.

The National Association for the Advancement of Colored People (NAACP) was now on the move, inviting and aiding Negroes to seek entrance into state colleges and universities, especially into law schools and graduate schools, on the grounds that the states not only did not provide equal facilities in these respects but in fact provided none at all. Since 1943, Georgia had been taking care of this problem by granting scholarships for attendance in Northern universities to Negro students who sought graduate and professional work not offered in the Negro institutions of the University System of Georgia. From the beginning of this program down to 1957, almost $1,500,000 had been expended on scholarships. During the year 1956-1957 more than 2,100 Negro students received almost $272,000.

This arrangement was not a satisfactory solution for these Negroes and other reformers and agitators who believed that *separate* but *equal* were contradictory words, that equal educational opportunities for Southern Negroes could be had only in Southern schools in associating with Southern white people, irrespective of how good Northern schools might be and how genteel Northern students might be. Southerners, however, did not take this as a compliment. Nevertheless this point of view received the sanction of the United States Supreme Court.

In 1952 a Negro sought to enter the University of Georgia Law School, and after long delays brought about principally by his service in the United States army, the case finally in 1956 reached the United States District Court for the Northern District of Georgia. Judge Frank A. Hutchins in his decision held that the evidence showed that the Negro had not been denied admission on account of his race but that he had not complied with the entrance requirements. To protect the state schools against racial integration the Georgia legislature in 1951 had passed a law cutting off all appropriations to any school which should enroll a Negro student.

It had been the hope of liberal Southerners that if the races must be mixed in schools, it should be gradual and should begin with higher institutions of learning. Several Southern states were admitting Negroes to such institutions. Even with this mental preparation, Georgians were little less than shocked at the decision of the United States Supreme Court in 1954 when it declared that the separate but equal doctrine was no longer constitutional and that Negroes must be admitted to all public schools everywhere. The next year the Court ordered it to be done "on a socially non-discriminating basis with all deliberate speed." To many, integration of the races was less shocking and portentious than the method whereby it had been ordered. On May 16, 1954, the segregation of the races was constitutional and had been so from the beginning of the nation and sanctioned by usage for a century and a half previously; on May 17 it was unconstitutional. The constitution had not been amended to bring this about; Congress had passed no law requiring it; nor had the President, by following the precedent of Lincoln's Emancipation Proclamation in 1863, decreed it. This method of amending the constitution was very perplexing to many Southerners, for if the Supreme Court had the power to do it in this instance, where might its power stop? Could it declare that according to the true meaning of democracy as understood in 1959, it was preposterous for Nevada to have two Senators and New York with many times more people have only two? If any decision of the United States Supreme Court must be accepted as the law of the land, what might it not do? Furthermore, many Georgians were puzzled by the fact that the United States Supreme Court had based its decision, in addition to the acceptance of sociological writings, on the Fourteenth Amendment, which it was thereby enforcing, when that Amendment clearly stated in its last section: "The Congress shall have power to enforce, by appropriate legislation, the provisions of this article." On the other hand, there were Georgians who held that the appointment of a person to the United States Supreme Court made him infallible and that the Court could not make an unconstitutional decision. The *Atlanta Constitution* asserted that it was "an impossibility" for the court to violate the Constitution, which led others to assume that according to this doctrine if the Court should award one Senator to Nevada and one hundred to New York in the name of more perfectly comporting with the spirit of a new and better day, then also this act would be constitutional.

"Deliberate speed" was now clicking and time was fast running out. Though there was no popular panic in Georgia, the people in 1954 amended the state constitution to allow the General Assembly to "provide for grants of State, county or municipal funds to citizens of the State for educational purposes, in discharge of all obligation of the State to provide adequate education for its citizens." The next year the legislature passed a law to set up private schools when a direct attempt to force integration should be made by the national authority; and to clear the deck further, permission was given to the governor to suspend the compulsory school law.

Re-enforced by the United States Supreme Court's decision in 1954, three Negro women sought to enroll in the Georgia State College of Business Administration in Atlanta. Being refused admission on the grounds that they had not complied with the entrance requirements, they brought suit in the United States District Court. The case was heard by Judge Boyd Sloan in December, 1958, and in January following, he handed down his decision holding that the entrance requirement calling on applicants to an institution "to furnish certificates as to their personal qualities which may be certified to only by alumni" of that institution, in effect excluded Negroes. Therefore this requirement was null and void; but all other requirements not based on race or color must be met. The effect of this decision was to open all of the units of the University System to Negroes qualified scholastically and morally. In the hearing the Attorney General of Georgia charged that the National Association for the Advancement of Colored People had promoted the litigation through prospective students neither morally nor scholastically qualified and that the Association had violated a Georgia law against barratry.

So far Georgia had warded off the force of the Supreme Court Decision of 1954, but she saw the day of reckoning not far away when an attack would be made on the elementary and secondary schools; for Little Rock, Arkansas had felt the heel of Federal troops and the jab of their bayonets and had in 1958 closed their high schools rather than integrate. In Virginia massive resistance was in full sway in Prince Edward County and other places. Georgia was now greatly disturbed by the prospects of having to close her public schools. Some Georgians argued that the state would soon be confronted with having to decide between mixed schools or no schools at all. Both United States Senators, Russell and Talmadge, were adamant against mixed schools and insisted that private schools would solve the problem, at least for a time. Marietta was already making plans to organize a private school system. Governor Vandiver and his General Assembly had as their most pressing problem for 1959, the public school system. Indeed, many Georgians had never been so upset since the days of the Civil War and the Reconstruction, and what was being attempted reminded them of a continuation of the Reconstruction into the twentieth century.

Georgia's public schools had long been one of her most cherished possessions. For a decade she had been spending more than half of her total revenues on her schools. In 1949 Georgia's educational soul and conscience were brought into the practical realities of life in a fundamental charter on which her educational structure was to be built. This charter, which became law on February 25, was known as the Minimum Foundation Program for Education, and was largely the inspiration of Dr. O. C. Aderhold, then Dean of the College of Education of the University of Georgia, and later President of the University. Serving as Secretary of a Special Committee on Education appointed by the General Assembly and aided by a professional staff of educational experts, Dr. Aderhold made a searching investigation of Georgia's educational needs, and on January 1, 1947 he transmitted to the legislature a book of 420 pages entitled *A Survey of Public Education of Less than College Grade in Georgia*. A bill was submitted to the General Assembly, embracing the recommendations of the Committee, and with no substantial changes was enacted into law, almost unanimously— only two adverse votes in the House. The broad purpose of the Foundation, as expressed in the law, was to equalize educational opportunities for *all* citizens of Georgia, to fix a minimum school term (not less than nine months) and a minimum for teachers' salaries, to provide teacher scholarships and a multitude of other educational services. The minimum total budget was set at $96,067,178, of which the state was to provide $69,251,720, the remainder coming from local governments and from Federal grants.

Practical considerations made it necessary to insert this proviso in the law, that it should become effective only "when sufficient funds have been realized from taxes." Since this budget was far beyond what the state had previously set up, the Minimum Foundation dream could not come true until some means could be found for raising more revenues. Almost every source had already been tapped, and the tax rates then were about as high as it seemed the people would tolerate. There was, of course, the much-talked-about sales tax, which other states were using successfully; but the Georgia politicians were afraid of it, since it could be easily argued that it was a tax on the common people—and candidates for office always remembered that it was the votes of the common people that brought victory. Herman Talmadge in his campaign for governor in 1950 had promised that there would be no more taxes, sales tax or other kinds, if he were elected. Now he was in a dilemma. A 3-percent sales tax would undoubtedly more than finance the Minimum Foundation, which was fondly looked to by the people, but Talmadge had promised no new taxes. When it was made evident to the Governor that he would lose more public support by opposing a sales tax and thereby effectively kill the implementation of the Minimum Foundation than he would by supporting a sales tax, thereby violating a promise but setting up the Foundation, he agreed not to veto the bill if it were passed, but refused to work for its passage. The law was passed and signed by the Governor in 1951; the Minimum Foundation came to life; and in 1957 the state expended for education not just $96,000,000 but $156,000,000.

Of course, this whole amount did not go for common schools (elementary and secondary) alone, but also a part went to higher institutions of learning as well—that is to the University System of Georgia, which under the leadership of Chancellor Harmon W. Caldwell and the Board of Regents had been brought by 1957 to include the University of Georgia (Athens), the Georgia Institute of Technology (Atlanta), the Georgia State College of Business Administration (Atlanta), the Medical College of Georgia (Augusta), the North Georgia College (Dahlonega), the Georgia State College for Women (Milledgeville), Georgia Teachers College (Statesboro), and Valdosta State College—all senior institutions; Albany State College, Fort Valley State College, and Savannah State College—all senior institutions for Negroes; and Georgia Southwestern College (Americus), West Georgia College (Carrollton), Middle Georgia College (Cochran), South Georgia College (Douglas), and Abraham Baldwin Agricultural College (Tifton)—all junior institutions. In 1957 the state appropriated for these institutions $27,753,081. Income from other sources brought their total income to $61,782,811. There were 29,175 students in residence in these institutions, exclusive of correspondence students in off-campus centers. To take care of an ever-increasing number of students the Board of Regents in 1958 and 1959 set up additional junior colleges in Columbus, Augusta, and Savannah.

The principal private and denominational colleges and universities were Emory University (with its new president Dr. S. Walter Martin, who was inaugurated in 1957), Mercer University, Oglethorpe University, and the three colleges for young women, Agnes Scott, Tift, and Shorter. An outstanding grouping of higher educational institutions for Negroes was in Atlanta with Atlanta University allied with several colleges on other campuses in the city.

The greatest center for medical education and research was one of the divisions of Emory University, with additional facilities for services provided by the immense new $26,000,000 Henry Grady Hospital, whose fruition was greatly aided by Hughes Spalding and John A. Sibley. The state-supported Medical College in Augusta with its new hospital, named for Eugene Talmadge, was also providing new doctors of medicine for Georgia's increasing number of hospitals. The basic law for new hospitals was passed in 1946, and during the next dozen years fifty-eight hospitals were constructed. When the law should have gone fully into effect, it was estimated that no Georgian would be more than thirty miles from a hospital.

To nurture things of the spirit there were, in 1958, almost 6,000 churches with a membership of 1,319,460. Communicants of the churches composing the Southern Baptist Convention in Georgia numbered more than the membership of all the other churches combined—760,698. The next three in the order of the number of their members were Methodists (338,148), Presbyterian Church in the United States (56,442), and Roman Catholic Church (30,900). There were thirty-nine different religious denominations in Georgia in 1959.

Love of country and love for God spring from the same generous source of good things with which the human heart and mind are endowed. Thus Georgia continued to wrestle with that hard monolith, the greatest piece of granite on the face of the earth exposed to the human eye, known as Stone Mountain. Almost a generation ago there was a great fervor to carve on its face heroic figures to commemorate the Southern Confederacy. Gutzon Borglum and then another chiseled away, but left only an almost unrecognizable ruin, the former giving up through a quarrel and the latter carried away by death. Instead of being a monument to the Confederates it was an ever present reminder of the ineptitudes of their descendants. Finally in 1958 the State of Georgia purchased the huge rock for the purpose of completing the memorial and making it an outstanding recreational area, catering to all who would come to enjoy it.

Other parks, including Jekyl Island, already mentioned, were scattered all over the state, numbering at least two dozen. And the National Park Service established in 1945 the Fort Frederica National Monument, to commemorate the great British military outpost in colonial Georgia. Another National park had been established in 1937 consisting of 329,000 acres of the Okefenokee Swamp, the land of "Trembling Earth," popularly known as the Okefenokee Swamp Park, but officially designated Okefenokee National Wildlife Refuge. Though for recreation, this park was primarily designed to preserve a wealth of rare plants, and animal life including bears, deer, raccoons, bobcats, o'possums, foxes, alligators, otters, ducks, herons, egrets, cranes, owls, and other denizens of the water, land, and air commonly found in sub-tropical regions.

During the three centuries of her existence Georgia had made much history; but she had been slow in exploiting it or even making it mildly known to visitors or even to her own citizens. To remedy the situation the state created a division of the office of the Secretary of State, called the Georgia Historical Commis-

sion, which immediately set about erecting markers all over the
state to indicate important historical events which happened on
the spot or in the vicinity. The military advance of General
Sherman to Atlanta, during the Civil War, was especially well
marked—probably this and other less significant historical
events were overmarked, which tended to reduce the important
events to the common-place and inclined people to disregard all
of them. And in fact, people in automobiles as they sped along
the highways at the legal limit of sixty miles an hour (and
sometimes faster) found it impossible to read these markers,
and it was so even if they had gone much slower, since the
markers were not announced ahead of time, and when reached
unexpectedly there was no drive-out whereby people might
park and read.

Fortunately the Commission interested itself in other means
of promoting the people's understanding of the history of their
state, by rehabilitating and preserving historical buildings.
Two of great interest were the Vann House in Spring Place,
Murray County, the old home of the Cherokee Indian Chief
James Vann; and the building in Jefferson, Jackson County,
where Dr. Crawford W. Long performed the first major operation with an anesthetic in the history of the world, using sulphuric ether as an anesthesia. Another house, an ancient tavern,
built sometime before 1800, known as the Jarrett Manor, out
in the country near Toccoa, was also rescued from disintegration.

The cultural value of preserving and making known historical spots was not the only purpose of the Historical Commission; exploitation by slowing down the Florida-bound
vacation-seekers was thought to be some defense for the
spending of considerable amounts of money on these activities. As Governor Griffin said in reference to the Stone Mountain development: picking tourists was easier and more profitable than picking cotton. But without any beckoning by tourist-
exploitation bodies, prominent men living beyond Georgia's

borders had long ago discovered the state. Northern million-aires had found the charm of Jekyl Island, others such as Mark Hanna had developed estates around Thomasville, and three presidents of the United States had made Georgia a vaca-tion-land. President-elect Taft had come to Augusta to play golf and get away from politics long enough to plan his cabi-net membership; President Franklin D. Roosevelt had made many trips to the healing waters of Warm Springs and to the Little White House there; and President Eisenhower could never for long resist the allure of the Augusta golf links and the balmy Georgia climate, to find leisure and dispense hospi-tality in Mamie's Cabin.

Chief Vann's Cherokee Indians had many moons ago been taken from Georgia's hills to the plains beyond the Mississippi; and the Creeks, who had inhabited and owned the rest of Georgia, had also been removed. The Cherokees had given up their lands through voluntary treaties and had been paid for it; but in 1814 after Andrew Jackson's victory over an army of hostile Creeks, he seized most of Georgia south of a line from Fort Gaines to Jesup, comprising an area of 7,612,800 acres, despite the fact that the Creeks owning this land were the friendly Creeks, who had helped him defeat the other Creeks. Manifestly this treatment was unjust, as were, indeed, many other acts of the United States against many tribes of Indians. In 1946 Congress passed a law setting up the Indian Claims Commission, inviting suits before this body for recovery of any damages that could be proved. The Creeks brought suit before the Commission, about 700 living in Georgia and being de-scendants of the original friendly Creeks. The hearing was held in 1957 and the next year the Commission handed down its decision, awarding $3,573,810, which included payment for 1,373,853 acres in southern Alabama. Some thousands of Creeks would share in the distribution of this fund after certain credits and off-sets were deducted.

As the nineteen-hundred-fifties were coming to a close, Georgia was more prosperous than she had ever been before; also the state government was spending more money. In 1957 the state revenues amounted to $315,590,081; for the fiscal year ending in 1958 the state appropriations amounted to $362,000,000, indicating that if the revenues for this year were not greater than during the previous year, there would inevitably be a deficit.

The basis for the state's prosperity and for its increased income and expenditures was one that had been advocated and dreamed of for a century and more. That was a diversified economy. Though the picture was not yet perfect, it was far along. The country population and the city population were now about even, and in this decade for the first time the value of Georgia's manufactures was greater than her agricultural production.

To attract industries there was set up the Georgia Department of Commerce, which advertised throughout the nation in its *Newsletter* the coming of new industries and the opportunities the state afforded. The smaller towns were attracting many; over 40 per cent of the new plants were located in towns of 5,000 population or less. The annual value of the textile manufactures was over a billion dollars, placing Georgia fourth in the whole country. From her 25,000,000 acres of timber land, the state was receiving an annual income approaching a billion dollars, being about $700,000,000 in 1955, ranking third in the nation in timber products. In 1959 the state stood first in the production of gum naval stores, contributing about 80 per cent of the nation's output. In the paper-making industry, Georgia supplied and processed immense amounts of pulpwood, leading all the states in this raw product. Savannah was the greatest center of the paper-making industry. There was a variety of other products from Georgia's manufacturing establishments, all running in value into the hundreds of millions of dollars annually, such as chemicals, clothing, transportation equipment (including assembling of automobiles), and food products. An important part of the last-named item was poultry production. Originally putting emphasis on eggs, the poultry industry soon gravitated into processing broilers, in which Georgia soon became easily first in the nation.

In the field of minerals, Georgia had never been a producer of such basic items as coal and iron, unlike the neighboring states of Alabama and Tennessee; but in the variety of her marketable minerals the state could hardly be surpassed. Georgia produced and sold twenty-five different kinds of minerals, amounting to more than $75,000,000 annually. She stood first in the production of ochre and marble, second in fuller's earth, barites, bauxite, and granite; and she mined three-fourths of the nation's supply of kaolin.

Georgia first became famous agriculturally as the land of cotton and peaches; but in both products she gave way to other states, though she still carried on her automobile tag "Peach State." Somewhat reticent about letting South Carolina surpass the state in the production of peaches, Georgians were willing to brag about dethroning "King Cotton." In fact in 1958 Georgia planted fewer acres of cotton than at any time during the preceding forty years, and the number of bales dropped to 355,000. Here was finally the fruition of the great campaign during the Civil War to dethrone King Cotton and enthrone King Corn. In 1958 corn stood at the top of the list in value of all agricultural products. Out of Georgia's cornfields came 86,752,000 bushels, with an estimated value of $108,440,000; whereas the estimated value of the cotton crop was only $69,367,000. Crowding toward the front were peanuts, which reached third place in the value of Georgia crops ($64,-962,000 in 1958) and remained in first place in the nation; also tobacco, in 1958 worth $54,464,000. Although not of outstanding monetary value, Georgia's watermelons, velvet beans, blue lupine seed, pecans, and pimiento peppers stood first in the whole country. The total value of Georgia's agricultural crops in 1958 was estimated at $365,586,000.

Ante-bellum Georgians sought faithfully but never found a winter grass which would beautify their red fields when the summer greenery had faded, and which would feed their imaginary herds on a thousand hills. By the nineteen-hundred-fifties Georgia's fields were green with new-found grasses, on which grazed great herds of white-faced Herefords, Black Angus, and other improved breeds of cattle. Wilkes County adopted the slogan "The County that has gone to Grass." Although the cattle business had some uncertainties in price fluctuations, it gained a substantial foothold and came to stay and grow greater. Herds of swine, especially in the southern part of the state, became an important adjunct for the farmers and led to the establishment of several packing houses.

Almost equally for the country and the town, and especially for the manufacturing industries, power in the form of electricity was basic both for making wheels go round and producing light. Few rivers in Georgia were allowed to flow unvexed to the sea; instead they were stopped by great dams and made to feed dynamoes. There were no fewer than ten great dams thrown across the Savannah River and its tributaries, Clark's Hill producing 280,000 kilowatts being the greatest and Hartwell with 180,000 coming next. The flow of the Chattahoochee was impeded by an equal number of dams, with Buford as the largest. There was an immense dam built across the Etowah at Allatoona. The Flint, the Oconee, and other Georgia rivers had their power dams, and on all the rivers of the state more were in the offing. Some of these power plants were owned by the national government, some by private companies (especially the Georgia Power Company), and at least one was owned by a city (Cordele). These dams not only produced power and provided flood control (probably, however, covering up as much rich bottom land as they saved from occasional overflows), but they also provided thousands of miles of shoreline where fishing camps and summer homes sprang up to afford recreation for tens of thousands of people.

Another source of power in Georgia which had become of major importance was natural gas piped from Mississippi, Louisiana, and Texas. A network of gas lines began threading its way across the state, serving the principal towns and cities of the Piedmont and northern Georgia, with prospects of extending throughout the state. Where natural gas had not yet made its appearance, manufactured gas was likely to be found, but principally for heating.

Transportation, by whatever means it might be arranged, was basic for all social and economic life. No more railroads were being built, and to take advantage of every device to reduce costs and stave off bankruptcy, the old coal-burning locomotives had been retired everywhere except on the Gainesville Midland (from Gainesville to Athens), and diesel engines were being used.

To take care of the ever-increasing movement of people from place to place, which characterized this new age of transportation, in 1958 there were 1,055,895 passenger vehicles and 255,506 trucks, running over a state system of roads extending in every direction for 15,207 miles. Each gallon of gas burned bore a state tax of 6½ cents. But when automobiles stopped in a region of population concentration greater than that around a country cross-roads store, parking the vehicle became a major problem. Very soon there spread from the big cities to almost every country town the vexatious parking meters, where five or ten cents would gain for one hour protection against being fined one dollar for over-parking. The argument for parking meters generally given out by the authorities setting them up was that they would allow more people to park on the streets and would especially aid merchants in serving more customers; but many people held that this was a disguised way of getting more revenue out of the owners of automobiles. Air travel was becoming more popular, and by the end of the nineteen-hundred-fifties, all the larger cities had airports, and many of the smaller ones were also developing them.

As for people, Georgia was not one of the fast-growing states like Florida, California, or Texas, but she was not losing population like Arkansas. In 1950 there were 3,444,578 people in the state, of whom about 31 per cent were Negroes. The United States Census Bureau estimated the total population in 1958 to be 3,818,000. There was probably at this time a smaller percentage of Negroes, and in the future an even smaller percentage might be predicted, and even reduced further if a bill which Senator Russell promised to introduce in Congress in 1959 should by some miracle be passed into law. This bill would "assist those Negroes who wanted to move North and also white people who wanted to move South," and thereby make the population more even according to color. This the Senator believed would give the Northern politicians and "civil righters" a better understanding of the racial problem in the South, and somewhat solve the problem by relieving the Negro concentration there.

As the nineteen-hundred-sixties drew near, the future of Georgia seemed more than ever before bound up with that of the United States and even that of the whole world itself. With the discovery of atomic power man seemed to have come into possession of more than he yet knew how best to use or to restrict. Indeed, all human existence was becoming problematical; no Biblican tower of Babel could now save mankind from having learned too much; man's Frankenstein monster might be upon him before he knew it. From now on, what Georgians did about Georgia might matter much less than what Georgians contributed to make the world at large come to terms with itself.

SELECT BIBLIOGRAPHY

NOTE ON SOURCES

The greatest bibliography on Georgia is the *Catalogue of the Wymberley Jones De Renne Georgia Library at Wormsloe, Isle of Hope near Savannah, Georgia* (3 vols. Wormsloe [Savannah], 1931). This Library has recently been removed to the University of Georgia. Another bibliography, useful though restricted in scope, is Robert Preston Brooks, *A Preliminary Bibliography of Georgia History* (Bulletin of the University of Georgia. Athens, 1910). Valuable especially for listing pamphlets as well as other works is Ella May Thornton, *Finding-List of Books and Pamphlets Relating to Georgia and Georgians* (Atlanta, 1928). Ulrich Bonnell Phillips, "The Public Archives of Georgia" (*Annual Report of the American Historical Association for the Year 1903* [Washington, 1904], I, 439-474) is a brief but suggestive listing of the official state archives in Atlanta and of the local archives of Milledgeville and of Baldwin County. Unfortunately, some of the records noted in this work can no longer be found.

The official manuscript archives of the state are in the Department of Archives and History and in the state capitol in Atlanta, while the collections of local manuscript archives of varying importance and value are to be found in the county courthouses. Especially rich in collections of unofficial manuscripts relating to Georgia are the libraries of the University of Georgia, of Emory University, and of the Georgia Historical Society in Savannah. Noteworthy collections outside the state are in the libraries of the University of North Carolina, and of Duke University, and in the Library of Congress. Of course, the official manuscript archives of colonial Georgia are in the British Public Record Office in London.

As for printed official records, many of Georgia's colonial archives were copied in London and later published in Georgia by Allen D. Candler, ed., *The Colonial Records of the State of Georgia* (26 vols., Atlanta, 1904-1916). Not all these copies brought back from London were published. The unpublished material is in the Department of Archives and History. Other archives published by the state are Allen D. Candler, ed., *The Revolutionary Records of the State of Georgia* (3 vols., Atlanta, 1908); and Allen D. Candler, ed., *The Confederate Records of the State of Georgia* (5 vols., I-VI, Vol. V never having been published. Atlanta, 1909-1911). The laws passed by the legislature as well as the journals of the house and of the senate, with few exceptions in the years following the Revolution, were published contemporaneously as *Acts [and Resolutions] of the General Assembly* and as *Journals of the House of Representatives* and *Journals of the Senate*. In the ante-bellum times there were occasionally published the governors' messages together with various accompanying documents. In later times the amount of published official material emanating from the various departments and bureaus became tremendous. The early compilations and codes of laws are: Robert and George Watkins, *Digest of the Laws of the State of Georgia* from the beginning through 1800 (Savannah, 1802); Augustin S. Clayton, *A Compilation of the Laws of the State of Georgia* from 1800 through 1810 (Augusta, 1812); Lucius Q. C. Lamar, *A Compilation of the Laws of the State of Georgia* from 1810 through 1819 (Augusta, 1821); Oliver H. Prince, *A Digest of the Laws of the State of Georgia* to 1820 (Milledgeville, 1822); Arthur Foster, *A Digest of the Laws of the State of Georgia* from 1820 through 1829 (Philadelphia, 1831); William C. Dawson, *A Compilation of the Laws of the State of Georgia* from 1819 through 1829 (Milledgeville, 1831); Oliver H. Prince, *A Digest of the Laws of the State of Georgia* to 1837 (Athens, 1837); Thomas R. R. Cobb, *A Digest of the Statute Laws of the State of Georgia* to 1851 (Athens, 1851); and R. H. Clark, T. R. R. Cobb, and D. Irwin, *The Code of the State of Georgia* (Atlanta, 1861). Thereafter various other codes were published.

The judicial decisions of the Superior Courts were published now and then, as for instance Thomas U. P. Charlton, *Reports of Cases* for the Eastern District (New York, 1824). In 1841 the legislature required the publication of the decisions of the Superior Courts. The first publication under this law was *Decisions of the Superior Courts of the State of Georgia* for 1842 (2 vols., Augusta, 1843). The decisions of the Supreme Court, which was first organized in 1845, were published as *Reports of Cases*, beginning in 1847 and continued thereafter.

An unrivalled source of information for Georgia history is her newspapers, beginning with the *Georgia Gazette* in 1763 and developing into such modern papers as the *Atlanta Constitution*, the *Atlanta Journal*, the *Augusta Chronicle*, the *Augusta Herald*, the *Columbus Enquirer*, the *Macon Telegraph*, the *Macon News*, the *Savannah Morning News*, and the *Savannah Evening Press*. Apart from these papers, some of which go back for a century and more, there were many other newspapers which played a prominent part in their day and then disappeared. Some of these historic papers were the *Athenian*, the *Southern Banner*, and the *Southern Whig*, in Athens; the *Columbian Sentinel*, the *Constitutionalist*, and the *Chronicle and Sentinel*, in Augusta; the *Intelligencer* and the *New Era*, in Atlanta; the *Columbus Times;* the *Georgia Journal*, the *Southern Recorder*, and the *Federal Union*, in Milledgeville; the *Georgia Messenger*, the *Journal and Messenger* and the *Telegraph and Messenger*, in Macon; and the *Georgia Gazette*, the *Columbian Museum*, the *Savannah Republican*, and the *Georgian*, in Savannah.

The *Christian Index*, the oldest religious paper in the state, is outstanding as a source of information on the Baptist Church. Other denominations have their papers. The greatest repository of agricultural information from 1843 on for many years was the *Southern Cultivator*. The only historical magazine of state-wide scope ever published in the state is the *Georgia Historical Quarterly*, which began in 1917. In each issue appear historical articles and one or more documents. The handiest guides to periodical material are Gertrude C. Gilmer, *Checklist of Southern Periodicals to 1861* (Boston, 1934); and Bertram H. Flanders, *Early Georgia Magazines. Literary Periodicals to 1865* (Athens, 1944).

For the thousands of items on Georgia, primary and secondary, book and pamphlet, no better guide can be found than the De Renne Catalogue, mentioned already.

The following list of readings is composed largely of the most available secondary works. Few references are made to the sources, as the general reader would have little opportunity to consult them. *G. H. Q.* stands for *Georgia Historical Quarterly*.

482　　SELECT BIBLIOGRAPHY

I. In the Beginning

Andrews, Evangeline W., and C. M. Andrews, eds., *Jonathan Dickinson's Journal or, God's Protecting Providence. Being a Narrative of a Journey from Port Royal in Jamaica to Philadelphia between August 23, 1696 and April 1, 1697* (Reprint. New Haven, 1945), 1-100.

Bolton, Herbert E., *Arredondo's Historical Proof of Spain's Title to Georgia* (Berkeley, Calif., 1925), 115-219.

Bolton, Herbert E., *The Spanish Borderlands* (New Haven, 1921), 46-78, 120-164.

Bolton, Herbert E., and Mary Ross, *The Debatable Land* (Berkeley, Calif., 1925), 1-44.

Johnson, Amanda, *Georgia as Colony and State* (Atlanta, 1938), 1-50.

Jones, Charles C., Jr., *The History of Georgia* (Boston, 1883), I, 1-33, 34-66, 67-81.

Lanning, John T., *The Diplomatic History of Georgia. A Study of the War of Jenkins' Ear* (Chapel Hill, 1936), 1-33.

Lanning, John T., *The Spanish Missions of Georgia* (Chapel Hill, 1935), 235 pp.

Lovell, Caroline C., *The Golden Isles of Georgia* (Boston, 1932), 3-17.

Lowery, Woodbury, *The Spanish Settlements within the Present Limits of the United States. Florida, 1562-1584* (New York, 1911), 244-263, 275-292, 339-358, 394-398.

Pickett, Albert J., *History of Alabama, and Incidentally of Georgia and Mississippi, from the Earliest Period* (2 Vols. 3rd edition. Charleston, 1851), I, 1-53.

Stevens, William Bacon, *A History of Georgia* (New York, 1847), I, 1-55.

Swanton, John R., *Early History of the Creek Indians and their Neighbors* (Smithsonian Institution Bureau of American Ethnology, Bulletin 73. Washington, 1922), 456 pp.

II. The Genesis of Georgia

Anderson, Mary Savage, Elfrida De Renne Barrow, Elizabeth Mackay Screven, and Martha Gallaudet Waring, *Georgia, a Pageant of Years* (Richmond, 1933), 11-30.

Barrow, Elfrida De Renne and Laura Bell, *Anchored Yesterdays* (Savannah, 1923), 19-36.

Bruce, Henry, *Life of General Oglethorpe* (New York, 1890), 1-92.

Clark-Kennedy, Archibald E., *Stephen Hales, D.D., F.R.S.* (Cambridge, Eng., 1929), 131-150.

Corse, Clarita D., *The Key to the Golden Islands* (Chapel Hill, 1931), 69-108.

Crane, Verner W., *The Southern Frontier, 1670-1732* (Durham, N. C., 1928), 235-325.

Ettinger, Amos A., *James Edward Oglethorpe. Imperial Idealist* (Oxford, Eng., 1936), 1-128.

Jones, C. C., Jr., *History of Georgia*, I, 82-105.

Knight, Lucian L., *A Standard History of Georgia and Georgians* (Chicago, 1917), I, 41-63.

Lanning, J. T., *Diplomatic History of Georgia*, 34-54.

McCain, James R., *Georgia as a Proprietary Province* (Boston, 1917), 17-136.

M'Call, Hugh, *The History of Georgia* (Reprint. Atlanta, 1909), I, 1-20.

Saye, Albert B., *Georgia's Charter of 1732* (Athens, 1942), 63 pp.

Saye, Albert B., *New Viewpoints in Georgia History* (Athens, 1943), 3-50.

Stevens, W. B., *History of Georgia*, I, 57-84.

III. SAVANNAH

Bruce, H., *Life of General Oglethorpe*, 93-131.

Ettinger, A. A., *James Edward Oglethorpe*, 129-206.

Fries, Adelaide L., *The Moravians in Georgia* (Raleigh, N. C., 1905), 235 pp.

Jones, C. C., Jr., *History of Georgia*, I, 112-131, 187-201.

Knight, L. L., *Standard History of Georgia and Georgians*, I, 64-77.

Lewis, Bessie Mary, "Darien, a Symbol of Defiance and Achievement," in *G. H. Q.*, XX, 3 (Sept., 1936), 185-198.

Lovell, C. C., *Golden Isles of Georgia*, 18-31.

McCain, J. R., *Georgia as a Proprietary Province*, 137-172.

M'Call, H., *History of Georgia*, I, 21-70.

Stevens, W. B., *History of Georgia*, I, 85-116.

IV. Building a Buffer against the Spaniards

Bolton, H. E., and M. Ross, *The Debatable Land,* 45-76.

Bruce, H., *Life of General Oglethorpe,* 154-166, 188-201.

Collections of the Georgia Historical Society (Letters of Oglethorpe to the Trustees) (Savannah, 1873), III, 1-156.

Jones, C. C., Jr., *History of Georgia,* I, 163-186, 215-274, 314-325.

Knight, L. L., *Standard History of Georgia and Georgians,* I, 93-108.

Lanning, J. T., *Diplomatic History of Georgia,* 55-84.

M'Call, H., *History of Georgia,* I, 71-105.

Stevens, W. B., *History of Georgia,* I, 140-179

V. The War of Jenkins' Ear

Bolton, H. E., and M. Ross, *The Debatable Land,* 77-97.

Bruce, H., *Life of General Oglethorpe,* 202-232.

Collections of the Georgia Historical Society (Spanish Accounts of the War) (Savannah, 1909), VII, Pt. I, 70 pp.; (Savannah, 1913), VII, Pt. III, 108 pp.

Ettinger, A. A., *James Edward Oglethorpe,* 207-254.

Jones, C. C., Jr., *History of Georgia,* I, 326-369.

Kimber, Edward, *A Relation or Journal of a Late Expedition to the Gates of St. Augustine on Florida. Conducted by the Hon. General James Oglethorpe with a Detachment of his Regiment, etc. from Georgia* (Reprint. Boston, 1935), 36 pp.

Knight, L. L., *Standard History of Georgia and Georgians,* I, 143-163.

Lanning, J. T., *Diplomatic History of Georgia,* 85-235.

Lovell, C. C., *Golden Isles of Georgia,* 32-52.

M'Call, H., *History of Georgia,* I, 106-140.

Stevens, W. B., *History of Georgia,* I, 180-199.

VI. A Peculiar Colony

Clarke-Kennedy, A. E., *Stephen Hales. D.D., F.R.S.,* 170-188.

Corry, John P., *Indian Affairs in Georgia, 1732-1756* (Philadelphia, 1936), 22-82.

Johnson, A., *Georgia as Colony and State,* 70-89.

Jones, C. C., Jr., *History of Georgia,* I, 106-112, 132-162.

McCain, J. R., *Georgia as a Proprietary Province,* 226-279.

Saye, A. B., *New Viewpoints in Georgia History,* 51-105.

Stevens, W. B., *History of Georgia,* I, 216-284.

VII. The Utopia Fails

Corry, J. P., *Indian Affairs in Georgia, 1732-1756*, pp. 95-132.

Coulter, E. Merton, "Mary Musgrove, 'Queen of the Creeks'; A Chapter of Early Georgia Troubles," in *G. H. Q.*, XI, 1 (March, 1927), 1-30.

Coulter, E. Merton, "When John Wesley Preached in Georgia," in *G. H. Q.*, IX, 4 (Dec., 1925), 317-351.

Grice, Warren, *The Georgia Bench and Bar* (Macon, 1931), I, 17-37.

Jones, C. C., Jr., *History of Georgia*, I, 202-214, 275-313, 370-449.

Jones, Charles E., *Education in Georgia* (Washington, 1889), 11-16.

Journal of the Rev. John Wesley (New York, 1921), I, 15-77.

McCain, J. R., *Georgia as a Proprietary Province*, 280-342.

M'Call, H., *History of Georgia*, I, 141-177.

Stevens, W. B., *History of Georgia*, I, 285-370.

Strickland, Reba C., *Religion and the State in Georgia in the Eighteenth Century* (New York, 1939), 11-99.

Wade, John D., *John Wesley* (New York, 1930), 61-81.

VIII. Georgia Becomes a Royal Province

Anderson, M. S., *et al.*, *Georgia, A Pageant of Years*, 31-42.

Barrow, Elfrida De Renne, and Laura Bell, *Anchored Yesterdays*, 49-60.

Bolton, H. E., and M. Ross, *The Debatable Land*, 98-112.

Corry, J. P., *Indian Affairs in Georgia, 1732-1756*, pp. 133-152.

Grice, W., *Georgia Bench and Bar*, I, 39-57.

Johnson, A., *Georgia as Colony and State*, 101-125.

Jones, C. C., Jr., *History of Georgia*, I, 450-467, 502-544; II, 1-17.

Knight, L. L., *Standard History of Georgia and Georgians*, I, 171-180.

M'Call, H., *History of Georgia*, I, 178-200.

Saye, A. B., *New Viewpoints in Georgia History*, 106-133.

Stevens, W. B., *History of Georgia*, I, 385-459.

IX. Growth under the King

Alden, John R., *John Stuart and the Southern Colonial Frontier* (Ann Arbor, Mich., 1944), 101-136, 176-191, 294-313.

Cate, Margaret D., *Our Todays and Yesterdays. A Story of Brunswick and the Coastal Islands* (Revised edition. Brunswick, 1930), 38-83.

Collections of the Georgia Historical Society (Letters of James Habersham) (Savannah, 1904), 245 pp.

Jones, C. C., Jr., *History of Georgia*, I, 491-501; II, 18-55.

Knight, L. L., *Standard History of Georgia and Georgians*, I, 221-257.

M'Call, H., *History of Georgia*, I, 201-221.

McMurtrie, D. C., "Pioneer Printing in Georgia," in *G. H. Q.*, XVI, 2 (June, 1932), 77-113.

Smith, George G., *The Story of Georgia and the Georgia People, 1732 to 1860* (Macon, 1900), 38-72.

Stevens, W. B., *History of Georgia*, I, 371-384; II, 17-34.

Strickland, R. C., *Religion and the State in Georgia in the Eighteenth Century*, 100-139.

X. The Rise of Discontent

Johnson, A., *Georgia as Colony and State*, 126-140.

Jones, C. C., Jr., *History of Georgia*, II, 56-146.

Knight, L. L., *Standard History of Georgia and Georgians*, I, 261-278.

M'Call, H., *History of Georgia*, II, 257-275.

Saye, A. B., *New Viewpoints in Georgia History*, 134-156.

Stevens, W. B., *History of Georgia*, II, 35-74.

XI. The Georgians Revolt

Barrow, Elfrida De Renne, and Laura Bell, *Anchored Yesterdays*, 63-74.

Collections of the Georgia Historical Society (Letters from Governor Wright), III, 157-378.

Jones, C. C., Jr., *History of Georgia*, II, 147-251.

Knight, L. L., *Standard History of Georgia and Georgians*, I, 279-283.

M'Call, H., *History of Georgia*, II, 276-309.

Stevens, W. B., *History of Georgia*, II, 75-99.

XII. The War of the Revolution

Anderson, M. S., *et al.*, *Georgia, A Pageant of Years*, 43-54.

Collections of the Georgia Historical Society (Siege of Savannah) (Savannah, 1901), V, Pt. I, pp. 129-139.

Johnson, A., *Georgia as Colony and State*, 141-161.

Jones, C. C., Jr., *History of Georgia*, II, 288-363, 375-416, 442-514.

Knight, L. L., *Standard History of Georgia and Georgians*, I, 284-318.

Lovell, C. C., *Golden Isles of Georgia*, 53-71.

M'Call, H., *History of Georgia*, II, 309-554.

Shipp, John E. D., *Giant Days or the Life and Times of William H. Crawford* (Americus, Ga., 1909), 12-21.

Smith, G. G., *Story of Georgia and the Georgia People*, 73-110.

Stevens, W. B., *History of Georgia*, II, 100-289.

XIII. CIVIL GOVERNMENT DURING THE REVOLUTION

Anderson, M. S., *et al.*, *Georgia, A Pageant of Years*, 55-69.

Collections of the Georgia Historical Society (Letters of Governor Wright), III, 157-378.

Grice, W., *Georgia Bench and Bar*, I, 59-77.

Jenkins, Charles F., *Button Gwinnett, Signer of the Declaration of Independence* (New York, 1926), 69-172.

Johnson, Elizabeth L., *Recollections of a Georgia Loyalist* (New York, 1901), 224 pp.

Jones, Charles C., Jr., *Biographical Sketches of the Delegates from Georgia to the Continental Congress* (Boston, 1891), 211 pp.

Jones, C. C., Jr., *History of Georgia*, II, 252-287, 364-374, 417-441.

Knight, L. L., *Standard History of Georgia and Georgians*, I, 325-328.

Saye, A. B., *New Viewpoints in Georgia History*, 157-195.

Stevens, W. B., *History of Georgia*, II, 290-383.

XIV. CONSOLIDATING THE STATE

Caughey, John W., *McGillivray of the Creeks* (Norman, Okla., 1938), 3-57.

Coulter, E. Merton, *College Life in the Old South* (New York, 1928), 1-17.

Davidson, Victor, *History of Wilkinson County* (Macon, 1930), 35-71.

Hartridge, Walter C., ed., *The Letters of Don Juan McQueen to his Family* (Columbia, S. C., 1943), 79 pp.

Jones, C. C., Jr., *History of Georgia*, II, 515-528.

Jones, C. E., *Education in Georgia*, 17-29, 40-48.

Phillips, Ulrich B., *Georgia and State Rights* (Washington, 1902), 15-38.

Saye, A. B., *New Viewpoints in Georgia History*, 196-236.

Stevens, W. B., *History of Georgia*, II, 384-456, 497-505.

Strickland, R. C., *Religion and the State in Georgia in the Eighteenth Century*, 139-186.

XV. LAND SPECULATIONS AND SETTLEMENTS

Barrow, Elfrida De Renne, and Laura Bell, *Anchored Yesterdays*, 91-97.

Davidson, V., *History of Wilkinson County*, 72-96.

Gilmer, George R., *Sketches of Some of the First Settlers of Upper Georgia, of the Cherokees, and the Author* (Reprint. Americus, Ga., 1926), 7-179.

Knight, L. L., *Standard History of Georgia and Georgians*, I, 329-342.

McLendon, Samuel G., *History of the Public Domain of Georgia* (Atlanta, 1924), 200 pp.

Phillips, U. B., *Georgia and State Rights*, 39-65.

Pickett, A. J., *History of Alabama, and Incidentally of Georgia and Mississippi*, II, 158-177.

Stevens, W. B., *History of Georgia*, II, 457-496.

XVI. DEVELOPING NATIONALISM

Barrow, Elfrida De Renne, and Laura Bell, *Anchored Yesterdays*, 111-120.

Corse, C. D., *Key to the Golden Islands*, 109-139.

Couter, E. Merton, *Thomas Spalding of Sapelo* (University, La., 1940), 190-211.

Halbert, Henry S., and T. H. Ball, *The Creek War of 1813 and 1814* (Chicago, 1895), 294 pp.

Harden, Edward J., *Life of George M. Troup* (Savannah, 1859), 85-158.

Knight, L. L., *Standard History of Georgia and Georgians*, I, 460-470.

Pickett, A. J., *History of Alabama, and Incidentally of Georgia and Mississippi*, II, 240-370.

Shipp, J. E. D., *Giant Days or the Life of William H. Crawford*, 98-100.

XVII. Pushing against the Frontier: Creeks and Cherokees

Anderson, M. S., *et al., Georgia, A Pageant of Years,* 70-106.

Bass, Althea, *Cherokee Messenger* (Norman, Okla., 1936), 345 pp.

Battey, George M., Jr., *A History of Rome and Floyd County* (Atlanta, 1922), I, 33-90.

Foreman, Grant, *Indian Removal. The Emigration of the Five Civilized Tribes of Indians* (Norman, Okla., 1932), 107-190, 229-312.

Foreman, Grant, *Sequoyah* (Norman, Okla., 1938), 83.

Gabriel, Ralph H., *Elias Boudinot. Cherokee and his America* (Norman, Okla., 1941), 178 pp.

Gilmer, G. R., *Sketches of Some of the First Settlers of Upper Georgia, of the Cherokees, and the Author,* 249-344.

Harden, E. J., *Life of George M. Troup,* 194-493.

Knight, L. L., *Standard History of Georgia and Georgians,* I, 527-541, 548-560, 565-572.

Lumpkin, Wilson, *The Removal of the Cherokee Indians from Georgia* (New York, 1907), I, 369 pp.; II, 319 pp.

Phillips, U. B., *Georgia and State Rights,* 66-86.

Pope-Hennessy, Una, ed., *The Aristocratic Journey. Being the Outspoken Letters of Mrs. Basil Hall Written during a Fourteen Months' Sojourn in America, 1827-1828* (New York, 1931), 216-248.

Starr, Emmet, *History of the Cherokee Indians and Their Legends and Folk Lore* (Oklahoma City, 1921), 55-119.

Walker, Robert S., *Torchlights to the Cherokees* (New York, 1931), 332 pp.

XVIII. Party Politics

Coulter, E. Merton, "The Nullification Movement in Georgia," in *G. H. Q.,* V, 1 (March, 1921), 3-39.

Gamble, Thomas, *Savannah Duels and Duellists, 1733-1877* (Savannah, 1923), 37-221.

Gilmer, G. R., *Sketches of Some of the First Settlers of Upper Georgia, of the Cherokees, and the Author,* 216-249.

Grice, W., *Georgia Bench and Bar,* I, 237-251, 253-266.

Johnson, A., *Georgia as Colony and State,* 192-229, 249-283

Knight, L. L., *Standard History of Georgia and Georgians*, I, 496-526.

Lawrence, Alexander A., *James Moore Wayne. Southern Unionist* (Chapel Hill, 1943), 3-77.

Phillips, U. B., *Georgia and State Rights*, 87-142.

Shipp, J. E. D., *Giant Days or the Life of William H. Crawford*, 44-76.

Shryock, Richard H., *Georgia and the Union in 1850* (Durham, N. C., 1926), 90-125.

XIX. TURNPIKES, RIVERS, CANALS, AND RAILROADS

Coulter, E. Merton, *Thomas Spalding of Sapelo*, 212-234.

Felton, Rebecca L., *Country Life in Georgia in the Days of my Youth* (Atlanta, 1919), 57-76.

Johnson, A., *Georgia as a Colony and State*, 385-410.

Johnston, James H., *Western and Atlantic Railroad of the State of Georgia* (Atlanta, 1931), 5-52.

Jones, C. C., Jr., *Dead Towns of Georgia*, 255 pp.

Knight, L. L., *Standard History of Georgia and Georgians*, II, 647-655.

Phillips, Ulrich B., *History of Transportation in the Eastern Cotton Belt to 1860* (New York, 1908), 46-131, 221-334.

XX. THE EMPIRE STATE OF THE SOUTH

Armstrong, Margaret, *Fanny Kemble. A Passionate Victorian* (New York, 1938), 207-252.

Bancroft, Frederic, *Slave-Trading in the Old South* (Baltimore, 1931), 222-236.

Beeson, Leola S., *The One Hundred Years of the Old Governor's Mansion Milledgeville, Georgia, 1838-1938* (Macon, 1938), 67 pp.

Cate, M. D., *Our Todays and Yesterdays*, 93-160.

Coulter, E. Merton, ed., *Georgia's Disputed Ruins* (Chapel Hill, 1937), 263 pp.

Coulter, E. Merton, *John Jacobus Flournoy. Champion of the Common Man in the Antebellum South* (Savannah, 1942), 1-54.

Coulter, E. Merton, *Thomas Spalding of Sapelo*, 36-190.

Kemble, Frances A., *Journal of a Residence on a Georgia Plantation in 1838-1839* (New York, 1863), 337 pp.

Lovell, C. C., *Golden Isles of Georgia*, pp. 72-155, 183-254.

Owens, Hubert B., *Georgia's Planting Prelate* (Stephen Elliott, Jr.) (Athens, 1945), 51 pp.

Phillips, Ulrich B., *Life and Labor in the Old South* (Boston, 1929), 259-273.

Phillips, Ulrich B., *The Life of Robert Toombs* (New York, 1913), 155-166.

Shryock, R. H., *Georgia and the Union in 1850*, pp. 9-89.

XXI. THE SOUL OF THE PEOPLE

Alderman, Edwin A., and A. C. Gordon, *J. L. M. Curry* (New York, 1911), 45-60.

Beeson, Leola S., *Sidney Lanier at Oglethorpe University* (Macon, 1936), 52 pp.

Bullock, Henry M., *A History of Emory University* (Nashville, 1936), 17-71.

Coulter, E. Merton, "The Ante-Bellum Academy Movement in Georgia," in *G. H. Q.*, V, 4 (Dec., 1921), 11-42.

Coulter, E. Merton, *College Life in the Old South*, 18-300.

Coulter, E. Merton, "A Georgia Educational Movement during the Eighteen Hundred Fifties," in *G. H. Q*, IX, 1 (March, 1925), 1-33.

Coulter, E. Merton, *John Jacobus Flournoy. Champion of the Common Man in the Antebellum South*, 55-82.

Damon, S. Foster, *Thomas Holley Chivers, Friend of Poe* (New York, 1930), 282 pp.

Flanders, Bertram H., *Early Georgia Magazines. Literary Periodicals to 1865* (Athens, 1944), 208 pp.

Jones, C. E., *Education in Georgia*, 60-121.

Ragsdale, B. D., *Story of Georgia Baptists* (Atlanta, 1932), I, 1-117.

Smith, G. G., *Story of Georgia and the Georgia People*, 492-513.

Taylor, Frances L., *Crawford W. Long and the Discovery of Ether Anesthesia* (New York, 1928), 41-109.

Wade, John D., *Augustus Baldwin Longstreet* (New York, 1924), 241-288.

White, Henry C., *Abraham Baldwin. One of the Founders of the Republic, and Father of the University of Georgia, the First of American State Universities* (Athens, 1926), 196 pp.

XXII. Calculating the Value of the Union

Avery, Isaac W., *The History of the State of Georgia, 1850-1881* (New York, 1881), 31-113.

Coulter, E. Merton, *Thomas Spalding of Sapelo*, 235-306.

Fielder, Herbert, *A Sketch of the Life and Times and Speeches of Joseph E. Brown* (Springfield, Mass., 1883), 25-90.

Flippin, Percy S., *Herschel V. Johnson of Georgia* (Richmond, 1931), 54-83.

Hill, Louise B., *Joseph E. Brown and the Confederacy* (Chapel Hill, 1939), 1-19.

Johnson, Zachary T., *The Political Policies of Howell Cobb* (George Peabody College for Teachers Contributions to Education. Nashville, 1929), 75-136.

Knight, L. L., *Standard History of Georgia and Georgians*, II, 688-703, 707-715.

Pearce, Haywood J., Jr., *Benjamin H. Hill* (Chicago, 1928), 22-31.

Phillips, U. B., *Georgia and State Rights*, 143-192.

Phillips, U. B., *Life of Robert Toombs*, 49-115.

Shryock, R. H., *Georgia and the Union in 1850*, pp. 126-364.

XXIII. Georgia Secedes

Anderson, M. S., *et al.*, *Georgia, A Pageant of Years*, 127-143.

Avery, I. W., *History of the State of Georgia*. 114-157.

Battey, G. M., Jr., *History of Rome and Floyd County*, I, 125-136.

Fielder, H., *Sketch of the Life and Times and Speeches of Joseph E. Brown*, 170-201.

Flippin, P. S., *Herschel V. Johnson of Georgia*, 161-206.

Hill, L. B., *Joseph E. Brown and the Confederacy*, 20-47.

Johnson, A., *Georgia as Colony and State*, 443-465.

Knight, L. L., *Standard History of Georgia and Georgians*, II, 161-206.

Pearce, H. J., Jr., *Benjamin H. Hill*, 32-54.

Phillips, U. B., *Georgia and State Rights*, 193-210.

Phillips, U. B., *Life of Robert Toombs*, 167-231.

Richardson, E. Ramsay, *Little Aleck, A Life of Alexander H. Stephens* (Indianapolis, 1932), 182-218.

XXIV. In Time of War

Avery, I. W., *History of the State of Georgia*, 161-280.

Brantly, Rabun L., *Georgia Journalism of the Civil War Period* (Nashville, 1929), 55-127.

Coulter, E. Merton, "Planters' Wants in the Days of the Confederacy," in *G. H. Q.*, XII, No. I (March, 1928), 38-52.

Fielder, H., *Sketch of the Life and Times and Speeches of Joseph E. Brown*, 256-317.

Grice, W., *Georgia Bench and Bar*, I, 307-323.

Hill, L. B., *Joseph E. Brown and the Confederacy*, 48-265.

Hornaday, John R., *Atlanta Yesterday, Today and Tomorrow* (Atlanta, 1922), 16-30.

Johnson, A., *Georgia as Colony and State*, 490-523.

Pearce, H. J., Jr., *Benjamin H. Hill*, 55-85.

Richardson, E. R., *Little Aleck, A Life of Alexander H. Stephens*, 241-272.

Robinson, William M., Jr., *Justice in Grey. A History of the Judicial System of the Confederate States of America* (Cambridge, Mass., 1941), 223-264.

Thompson, C. Mildred, *Reconstruction in Georgia, Economic, Social, Political, 1865-1872* (New York, 1915), 13-41.

XXV. Sherman and the End

Avery, I. W., *History of the State of Georgia*, 281-332.

Battey, G. M., Jr., *History of Rome and Floyd County*, I, 147-208.

Coulter, E. Merton, "Sherman and the South," in *G. H. Q.*, XV, 1 (March, 1931), 28-45.

Fielder, H., *Sketch of the Life and Times and Speeches of Joseph E. Brown*, 202-242.

Harden, William, *Recollections of a Long and Satisfactory Life* (Savannah, 1934), 150 pp.

Hesseltine, William B., *Civil War Prisons* (Columbus, O., 1930), 133-158.

Hitchcock, Henry, *Marching with Sherman* (New Haven, 1927), 13-210.

Hornaday, J. R., *Atlanta Yesterday, Today and Tomorrow*, 31-67.

Johnson, A., *Georgia as Colony and State*, 466-489.

Knight, L. L., *Standard History of Georgia and Georgians,* II, 751-798.

LeConte, Joseph, *'Ware Sherman. A Journal of Three Months Personal Experience in the Last Days of the Confederacy* (Berkeley, Calif., 1937), 144 pp.

Lunt, Dolly S., *A Woman's Wartime Journal* (Macon, 1927), 65 pp.

Richardson, E. R., *Little Aleck, A Life of Alexander H. Stephens,* 17-42.

Winther, Oscar O., ed., *With Sherman to the Sea. The Civil War Letters, Diaries & Reminiscences of Theodore F. Upson* (Baton Rouge, 1943), 106-145.

XXVI. Reconstruction, Social and Economic

Anderson, M. S., *et al., Georgia, A Pageant of Years,* 144-153.

Brooks, Robert P., *The Agrarian Revolution in Georgia, 1865-1912* (Madison, Wis., 1914), 114 pp.

Bullock, H. M., *History of Emory University,* 149-215.

Coulter, E. Merton, *College Life in the Old South,* 301-360.

Edwards, Harry Stillwell, *Eneas Africanus* (Macon, 1920), 44 pp.

Johnston, J. H., *Western and Atlantic Railroad of the State of Georgia,* 52-70.

Leigh, Frances B., *Ten Years on a Georgia Plantation since the War* (London, 1883), 240 pp.

McKeithan, Daniel M., *A Collection of Hayne Letters* (Austin, Texas, 1944), 499 pp.

Nixon, Raymond B., *Henry W. Grady. Spokesman of the New South* (New York, 1943), 350 pp.

Thompson, C. M., *Reconstruction in Georgia, Economic, Social, Political, 1865-1872,* pp. 42-135, 279-401.

XXVII. Reconstruction, Political

Avery, I. W., *History of the State of Georgia,* 335-514.

Felton, Mrs. William H. (Rebecca L.), *My Memoirs of Georgia Politics* (Atlanta, 1911), 47-78.

Fielder, H., *Sketch of the Life and Times and Speeches of Joseph E. Brown,* 410-486.

Hill, Benjamin H., Jr., *Senator Benjamin H. Hill of Georgia, His Life, Speeches and Writings* (Atlanta, 1893), 42-67.

Hill, L. B., *Joseph E. Brown and the Confederacy,* 266-290.

Johnson, A., *Georgia as Colony and State*, 524-549.

Knight, L. L., *Standard History of Georgia and Georgians,* II, 799-852.

Pearce, H. J., Jr., *Benjamin H. Hill*, 86-264.

Thompson, C. M., *Reconstruction in Georgia, Economic, Social, Political, 1865-1872*, 136-167, 171-275.

Wooley, Edwin C., *The Reconstruction of Georgia* (New York, 1901), 110 pp.

XXVIII. Home Rule Again

Anderson, M. S., *et al.*, *Georgia, A Pageant of Years*, 154-171.

Arnett, Alex M., *The Populist Movement in Georgia* (New York, 1922), 228 pp.

Avery, I. W., *History of the State of Georgia*, 515-608.

Banks, Enoch M., *The Economics of Land Tenure in Georgia* (New York, 1905), 116 pp.

Bonner, James C., and Lucien E. Roberts, eds., *Studies in Georgia History and Government* (Athens, 1940), 155-171.

Felton, Rebecca L. (Mrs. W. H.), *Country Life in Georgia in the Days of My Youth*, 193-213.

Felton, Mrs. W. H., *My Memoirs of Georgia Politics*, 159-182, 258-311, 641-678.

Fielder, H., *Sketch of the Life and Times and Speeches of Joseph E. Brown*, 487-495.

Harris, Nathaniel E., *Autobiography* (Macon, 1925), 268-522.

Hill, B. H., Jr., *Senator Benjamin H. Hill of Georgia*, 55-68.

Hill, L. B., *Joseph E. Brown and the Confederacy*, 291-327.

Johnson, A., *Georgia as Colony and State*, 572-601.

Johnston, J. H., *Western and Atlantic Railroad of the State of Georgia*, 71-81.

Lamar, Clarinda P., *The Life of Joseph Rucker Lamar, 1857-1916* (New York, 1926), 284 pp.

Woodward, C. Vann, *Tom Watson. Agrarian Rebel* (New York, 1938), 1-415.

XXIX. Financial and Economic Progress

Anderson, M. S., *et al.*, *Georgia, A Pageant of Years*, 172-198.

Avery, I. W., *History of the State of Georgia*, 631-655.

Felton, Mrs. W. H., *My Memoirs of Georgia Politics*, 202-250.

Harris, Julia C., *Joel Chandler Harris, Editor and Essayist* (Chapel Hill, 1931), 3-92.

Harris, N. E., *Autobiography*, 247-268.

Hill, B. H., Jr., *Senator Benjamin H. Hill of Georgia*, 332-350.

Johnson, A., *Georgia as Colony and State*, 631-657.

XXX. Social Advancement

Avery, I. W., *History of the State of Georgia*. 609-630.

Byers, Tracy, *Martha Berry, the Sunday Lady of Possum Trot* (New York, 1932), 268 pp.

Felton, Rebecca L. (Mrs. W. H.), *Country Life in Georgia in the Days of My Youth*, 270-279.

Felton, Mrs. W. H., *My Memoirs of Georgia Politics*, 581-624.

Harris, Julia C., *Joel Chandler Harris, Editor and Essayist*, 93-176.

Harris, N. E., *Autobiography*, 139-247.

Johnson, A., *Georgia as Colony and State*, 658-683.

Jones, C. E., *Education in Georgia*, 121-152.

Mell, Patrick H., Jr., *Life of Patrick Hues Mell* (Louisville, 1895), 187-243.

Mitchell, Frances L., *Georgia Land and People* (Atlanta, 1893), 436-495.

Powell, Arthur G., *I Can Go Home Again* (Chapel Hill, 1943), 301 pp.

Reed, Thomas W., *David Crenshaw Barrow* (Athens, 1935), 295 pp.

Tuck, Henry C., *Four Years at the University of Georgia, 1877-1881* (Athens, 1938), 251 pp.

XXXI. Up to Now

Anderson, M. S., *et al.*, *Georgia, A Pageant of Years*, 199-230.

Atlanta. A City of the Modern South (New York, 1942), 237 pp.

Bullock, H. M., *History of Emory University*, 283-376.

Burns, Robert E., *I Am a Fugitive from a Georgia Chain Gang* (New York, 1932), 257 pp.

Georgia. A Guide to its Towns and Countryside (American Guide Series) (Athens, 1940), 517 pp.

Gosnell, Cullen B., *Government and Politics of Georgia* (New York, 1936), 244 pp.

Johnson, A., *Georgia as Colony and State*, 684-1021.

Pound, Merritt B., and Melvin E. Thompson, *Georgia Citizenship* (Richmond, 1940), 278 pp.

Raper, Arthur F., *Tenants of the Almighty* (New York, 1943), 99-364.

Savannah (American Guide Series) (Savannah, 1937), 194 pp.

Spivak, John L., *Georgia Nigger* (New York, 1932), 241.

Steed, Hal, *Georgia: Unfinished State* (New York, 1942), 336 pp.

Woodward, C. Vann, *Tom Watson Agrarian Rebel,* 416-486.

XXXII. Up to Now

The period of history discussed in this chapter is too recent to be included in secondary works. For sources of this information it is necessary to consult year books, census reports, state documents, magazines, and newspapers.

The following works, recently published, may be read with profit on various topics in the present book:

Abbot, W. W., *The Royal Governors of Georgia, 1754-1775* (Chapel Hill, N. C., 1959).

Bryan, T. Conn, *Confederate Georgia* (Athens, Ga., 1953).

Coleman, Kenneth, *The American Revolution in Georgia, 1763-1789* (Athens, Ga., 1958).

Coulter, E. Merton, *Auraria. The Story of a Georgia Gold-Mining Town* (Athens, Ga., 1956).

Coulter, E. Merton, ed., *The Journal of William Stephens, 1741-1743* (Athens, Ga., 1958).

Coulter, E. Merton, ed., *The Journal of William Stephens, 1743-1745* (Athens, Ga., 1959).

Coulter, E. Merton, *Wormsloe, Two Centuries of a Georgia Family* (Athens, Ga., 1955).

Fleming, Berry, *Autobiography of a Colony* (Athens, Ga., 1957).

Grantham, Dewey W., *Hoke Smith and the Politics of the New South* (Baton Rouge, La., 1958).

Green, Constance McL., *Eli Whitney and the Birth of American Technology* (Boston, 1956).

Griffith, Louis T., and John E. Talmadge, *Georgia Journalism 1763-1950* (Athens, Ga., 1951).

Heath, Milton S., *Constructive Liberalism, The Role of the State in Economic Development in Georgia to 1860* (Cambridge, Mass., 1954).

Johnston, Edith D., *The Houstouns of Georgia* (Athens, Ga., 1950).

King, Spencer B., Jr., *Ebb Tide, As Seen through the Diary of Josephine Clay Habersham, 1863* (Athens, Ga., 1958).

Lawrence, Alexander A., *James Johnston, Georgia's First Printer* (Savannah, Ga., 1956).

Lawrence, Alexander A., *Storm over Savannah* (Athens, Ga., 1951).

Malone, Henry T., *Cherokees of the Old South. A People in Transition* (Athens, Ga., 1956).

Montgomery, Horace, *Cracker Parties* (Baton Rouge, La., 1950).

Montgomery, Horace, ed., *Georgians in Profile* (Athens, Ga., 1958).

Nichols, Frederick D., and Frances B. Johnston, *The Early Architecture of Georgia* (Chapel Hill, N. C., 1957).

Nixon, Raymond B., *Henry W. Grady, Spokesman of the New South* (New York, 1943).

Pound, Merrit B., *Benjamin Hawkins—Indian Agent* (Athens, Ga., 1951).

Range, Willard, *A Century of Georgia Agriculture, 1850-1950* (Athens, Ga., 1954).

Range, Willard, *The Rise and Progress of Negro Colleges in Georgia 1865-1949* (Athens, Ga., 1951).

Stokes, Thomas L., *The Savannah* (New York, 1951).

Vanstory, Burnette, *Georgia's Land of the Golden Isles* (Athens, Ga., 1956).

Ware, Louise, *George Foster Peabody, Banker, Philanthropist, Publicist* (Athens, Ga., 1951).

Wightman, Orrin S. and Margaret Davis Cate, *Early Days of Coastal Georgia* (St. Simons Island, Ga., 1955).

CHIEF EXECUTIVES OF GEORGIA

COLONIAL

James Edward Oglethorpe, Resident Trustee.. 1733-1743
William Stephens, President...................... ...1740
Henry Parker, Vice President........... 1750
Henry Parker, President........ : 1751
Patrick Graham, President...................... 1752
John Reynolds, Captain General and Governor in Chief
    and Vice Admiral................. 1754
Henry Ellis, Lieutenant Governor...................... 1756
Henry Ellis, Captain General and Governor in Chief........ 1759
James Wright, Lieutenant Governor..................... 1760
James Wright, Captain General and Governor in Chief
    and Vice Admiral.................. 1762
James Habersham, President and Commander in Chief....... 1771
James Wright, Captain General and Governor in Chief
    and Vice Admiral.................. 1773

REVOLUTIONARY

George Walton, President of the Council of Safety........... 1776
William Ewen, President of the Council of Safety............ 1776
Archibald Bulloch, President and Commander in Chief....... 1776
Button Gwinnett, President and Commander in Chief. 1777
John Adam Treutlen, Governor..................... 1777
John Houstoun, Governor................... 1778
John Wereat, President of Supreme Executive Council....... 1779
George Walton, Governor (of Whig faction opposing Wereat) . 1779
Richard Howley, Governor[1]..................... 1780
Stephen Heard, President of Executive Council............. 1780
Nathan Brownson, Governor..................... 1781
John Martin, Governor..................... 1782
James Wright (Restored Royal Governor) 1779-1782

[1] Governor Howley having been elected to the Continental Congress, January 11, 1780, left the state in the summer and was present in Philadelphia, July 6. He was out of Georgia for the remainder of his term.

STATE

From this time the chief executive bore the title of governor
unless otherwise indicated

Lyman Hall..1783
John Houstoun...1784
Samuel Elbert...1785
Edward Telfair..1786
George Mathews..1787
George Handly...1788
George Walton...1789
Edward Telfair..1790
George Mathews..1793
Jared Irwin...1796
James Jackson...1798
David Emanuel...1801
Josiah Tattnall, Jr.......................................1801
John Milledge...1802
Jared Irwin...1806
David B. Mitchell...1809
Peter Early...1813
David B. Mitchell...1815
William Rabun...1817
Matthew Talbot..1819
John Clark..1819
George M. Troup...1823
John Forsyth..1827
George R. Gilmer..1829
Wilson Lumpkin..1831
William Schley..1835
George R. Gilmer..1837
Charles J. McDonald.......................................1839
George W. Crawford..1843
George W. Towns...1847
Howell Cobb...1851
Herschel V. Johnson.......................................1853
Joseph E. Brown...1857
James Johnson, Provisional Governor.......................1865

Charles J. Jenkins..................................1865
Brig. Gen. Thomas H. Ruger, Provisional Governor..........1868
Rufus E. Bullock, Provisional Governor....................1868
Rufus E. Bullock...................................1868
Rufus E. Bullock, Provisional Governor....................1869
Rufus E. Bullock...................................1870
Benjamin Conley....................................1871
James M. Smith.....................................1872
Alfred H. Colquitt.................................1877
Alexander H. Stephens..............................1882
James S. Boynton...................................1883
Henry D. McDaniel..................................1883
John B. Gordon.....................................1886
William J. Northen.................................1890
William Y. Atkinson................................1894
Allen D. Candler...................................1898
Joseph M. Terrell..................................1902
Hoke Smith...1907
Joseph M. Brown....................................1909
Hoke Smith...1911
John M. Slaton.....................................1911
Joseph M. Brown....................................1912
John M. Slaton.....................................1913
Nathaniel E. Harris................................1915
Hugh M. Dorsey.....................................1917
Thomas W. Hardwick.................................1921
Clifford Walker....................................1923
Lamartine G. Hardman...............................1927
Richard B. Russell, Jr.............................1931
Eugene Talmadge 1933
Eurith D. Rivers...................................1937
Eugene Talmadge....................................1941
Ellis Arnall 1943
Melvin E. Thompson.................................1947
Herman E. Talmadge.................................1948
Marvin Griffin.....................................1955
Ernest Vandiver....................................1959

INDEX

treaty in 1773, 99; trouble with during Revolution, 179; make treaty of 1804, 223; removal of from Georgia, 230-237; refuse further cessions, 230-231; progress of in civilization, 231-232

Chesapeake, mentioned, 208

Chickamauga Creek, 253; Cherokee town on, 179

Chickamauga Park, dedication of, 429

Chickasaws, 5; make treaty with Oglethorpe in 1739, 42; at Indian conference at Augusta in 1763, 91

Chief Justice, in Revolution, 150, 176, 177

Chisholm *vs.* Georgia, United States Supreme Court case, 172-173

Chivers, Thomas Holley, 299

Choctaws, 5; make treaty with Oglethorpe in 1739, 42; at Indian conference at Augusta in 1763, 91

Cholera, 290

Christ Church, colonial parish, 106

Christian Commonwealth, 432-433

Christian Index, 300

Christian Monitor and Companion, book sent to colony, 22

Christians, religious denomination, 302

Church, Alonzo, president of University of Georgia, 285; literary interests of, 295-296

Church of England, established, 106; disestablished, 150

Churches, incorporated, 188-189; number of in 1860, 302; number and membership in twentieth century, 470

Cincinnati, 259

Cincinnati Commercial, quoted, 401

Circuit Rider's Wife, A, 445

Cities, growth following Civil War, 355-356

Civil War legislation, repealed, 363

Clark, John, Revolutionary hero, 142; rejoices at Florida purchase, 216; observations of on land policy, 219; leader of Clark party, 240, 241; fights duels, 242; elected governor, 243; moves to Florida, 244; attitude of toward banks, 280

Clark party, opposes nullification, 245;

becomes Union party and then Democrats, 246-247

Clark's Hill, power dam, 476

Clark University, Negro school, 358

Clarke, Elijah, at Kettle Creek, 139; Revolutionary hero, 142; leads women and children into Tennessee, 144; unsuccessful attack of on Augusta, 144-145; aids in capture of Augusta, 145; receives confiscated lands, 162; visits Florida, 166; fights Cherokees, 179; on Indian Board, 180-181; lands granted to, 195; trans-Oconee River land speculation, 198-199; expedition to Florida, 199

Clarke County, mentioned, 221

Clay, Henry, 307, 309

Clays, mining of, 406

Clayton, Augustin S., in Cherokee troubles, 234; nullification leader, 245; cotton manufacturer, 281; alumnus of University of Georgia, 285

Clergy, colonial, 106-107

Clermont, steamboat, 254

Cleveland, Grover, 394, 395

Clews, Henry, railroad capitalist, 352

Clifton, William, colonial attorney-general, 83

Clinch, Duncan L., destroys Negro fort, 215

Coal, mining of, 406

Coastal Plain, 3, 4

Cobb, Howell, planter, 269; alumnus of University of Georgia, 285; aids cause of Union in 1850, 309; elected governor, 310; threatens secession in 1860, 312; suggested for president in 1860, 315; advocates secession, 318; invited to secession convention, 320; president of Montgomery convention, 320; a "monarchist," 328; quarrels with Brown, 330-331; speaks to legislature, 332

Cobb, Thomas R. R., alumnus of University of Georgia, 285; founder of law school, 291; codifier of laws, 294; secessionist, 317-318; in Montgomery convention, 320; makes constitution of 1861, 321